D1042386

E. B. WHITE *A BIOGRAPHY*

E.B. WHITE

A BIOGRAPHY

SCOTT ELLEDGE

W · W · NORTON & COMPANY

NEW YORK   LONDON

The text of this book is composed in 12/13 Bembo by computer (CRT),
with display type set in Bembo. Composition and
manufacturing by The Haddon Craftsmen, Inc.
Book design by Margaret M. Wagner
Title page illustration by E. B. White

Library of Congress Cataloging in Publication Data
Elledge, Scott.
E. B. White: A Biography
Bibliography: p.
Includes index.
1. White, E. B. (Elwyn Brooks), 1899–   —Biography.
2. Authors, American—20th century—Biography.
I. Title.
PS3545.H5187Z64   1984   818'.5209 [B]   83–4032

ISBN 0-393-01771-0

W. W. Norton & Company, Inc., 500 Fifth Avenue, New York, N.Y. 10110
W. W. Norton & Company Ltd., 37 Great Russell Street, London WC1B 3NU

FOR
LIANE

CONTENTS

ILLUSTRATIONS

Following page 38

William Hart, White's grandfather. (Courtesy of E. B. White)
101 Summit Avenue, Mount Vernon, New York. (E. B. White Collection; Department of Rare Books, Cornell University Library)
Family portrait, 1899.(E. B. White Collection)
Elwyn White at nine months. (E. B. White Collection)
Elwyn playing the mandolin. (E. B. White Collection)
Lillian and Elwyn, about 1904. (E. B. White Collection)
Elwyn and Stanley in Old Town canoe. (E. B. White Collection)
Elwyn and Lillian on Flexible Flyer. (E. B. White Collection)
Elwyn and his mother. (E. B. White Collection)
Elwyn and his father. (E. B. White Collection)
Cover and page 2 of "Belgrade Lake and Snug Harbor Camps." (E. B. White Collection)
Pages 3 and 4 of "Belgrade Lake" pamphlet. (E. B. White Collection)
Pages 5 and 6. (E. B. White Collection)
Cornell and Lake Cayuga. (Department of Manuscripts and University Archives, Cornell University)
Professor Bristow Adams. (Department of Manuscripts and University Archives, Cornell University)
Kappa Nu Chapter of Phi Gamma Delta, 1921. (Department of Manuscripts and University Archives, Cornell University)
Professor William Strunk, Jr. (Department of Manuscripts and University Archives, Cornell University)
Gustave S. Lobrano. (E. B. White Collection)
Alice Burchfield. (E. B. White Collection)
Counselor Andy White, Camp Otter, 1921. (E. B. White Collection)
Howard Cushman in Hotspur, 1922. (E. B. White Collection)
White in Seattle, 1923. (E. B. White Collection)

Following page 136

Harold Ross, about 1925.
Ralph McAllister Ingersoll.
Harold Ross, in the thirties.
Katharine Sergeant (Mrs. Ernest) Angell, about 1928. (E. B. White Collection)
Katharine Angell and James Thurber, 1929. (E. B. White Collection)
A drawing of White by Thurber. (E. B. White Collection)
An example of advertisements parodied by White, 1927.

An advertisement designed and written by White, 1927. (Courtesy of *The New Yorker*)

One of White's editorials on Lindbergh's flight, 1927. (Courtesy of *The New Yorker*)

Dust jacket for *Is Sex Necessary?*, 1929. (E. B. White Collection)

White and Thurber, 1929. (Courtesy of Milton Greenstein)

A Thurber Drawing, 1929. (E. B. White Collection)

White and son, Joel, 1931. (Courtesy of E. B. White)

"Talk of the Town," in *The New Yorker* for 7 August 1937. (Courtesy of *The New Yorker*)

Wolcott Gibbs.

John McNulty. (Courtesy of Faith McNulty)

Following page 278

The farm in Maine. (E. B. White Collection)

The farmhouse. (E. B. White Collection)

Katharine White on board *Astrid,* about 1935. (Courtesy of E. B. White)

White in Maine in the forties. (Courtesy of E. B. White)

Joe White at Exeter, about 1945. (Courtesy of E. B. White)

Katharine White at *The New Yorker,* about 1941. (E. B. White Collection)

E.B. White in *Vogue,* 1948. (Courtesy of Milton Greenstein)

White's drawing of Zuckerman's barn.(E. B. White Collection)

The boathouse on Allen Cove. (E. B. White Collection)

An early version of the opening chapter of *Charlotte's Web.* (E. B. White Collection)

A later version. (E. B. White Collection)

A late draft of the final version. (E. B. White Collection)

White at 62. (E. B. White Collection)

A rondeau for Valentine's Day, 1970, from EBW to KSW. (E. B. White Collection)

Joel White, 1976. (E. B. White Collection)

White in the seventies. (Courtesy of E. B. White)

Corona Machemer, 1980. (Courtesy of E. B. White)

White en route to Sarasota, 1982. (Courtesy of E. B. White)

White with geese, 1973.

F O R E W O R D

IN THE SUMMER OF 1968, while I was in Georgetown, Maine, I mailed a letter to E. B. White, in North Brooklin, Maine, informing him of my wish to write a biography of him and requesting his permission to examine the collection of private papers he had recently given to the Cornell University Library. He opened his reply as follows:

Dear Mr. Elledge:
    As a man who has frittered away the best years of his life writing about E. B. White, sometimes with affection, sometimes with distaste, always with charity aforethought, I can sympathize with your project without envying your labors. But whether I sympathize or not, the Constitution empowers you to write about anything that comes along, and although being written about is not my favorite diversion (I prefer sailing) I deem it my civic duty to meet you half way—which in this case would be somewhere around Damariscotta [Maine]. Or you could come here and view Fred's thorny grave, if you want to begin at the bottom of the barrel. . . .

(Fred was a "large and dissolute" dachshund to whom White was "quite attached . . . in a half regretful way" for thirteen years.) During the years following that characteristic reply, Mr. White has always met me half way.
    I accepted Mr. White's invitation to visit him and his wife, and in the course of a memorable day I saw not only Fred's grave near the private

dump "with its useless junk of all kinds including a wrong-size crank for a broken ice-cream freezer," but the boathouse on Allen Cove where *Charlotte's Web* was written, the barn in whose cellar Wilbur met Charlotte, and the large, comfortable, and handsome late-eighteenth-century farmhouse where White has lived, off and on, for fifty years. Since then I have visited Mr. White in North Brooklin several times, I have written him scores of letters asking for information, and during the past year I have occasionally spoken with him on the phone. He has never failed to be friendly and prompt in his responses to my requests for facts that only he could supply. Beyond that, however, he has left me completely on my own. Early on, he answered one of my questions by saying in effect that he couldn't remember the answer, that I could look it up, and that after all *I* was the biographer. From the start he viewed my activities with mild interest, slight skepticism, and some amusement, but he gave no sign of wishing to get in the game or to coach from the sideline.

He granted me permission to "poke about" in his papers in The E. B. White Collection at Cornell provided I understood that he would retain "strict and absolute censorship as to the use of anything" I found in them. He made this provision, he explained, to protect not himself but others from "indecent exposure." I would be perfectly free "to pull off [*his*] clothes" if I wished. I took him at his word and wrote down the facts as I saw them, undisturbed by the knowledge that the subject of this biography would one day be one of its readers. Following the advice he gives in *The Elements of Style,* I wrote to "please and satisfy" myself.

When the manuscript was finished and had been accepted for publication, I asked Mr. White how he would like to exercise his right to censor the use I had made of the material contained in his papers: I could simply send him the particular parts of the manuscript based on that material, or I could send him the complete manuscript. I am glad that he elected to read the entire work, for he helped me make it, not an authorized biography, but a better one than it might otherwise have been.

White made no comment on the book as a whole except to say that he found it too long (but, then, he has never, by his own admission, "had a very lively literary curiosity": it took him fourteen months to read *Anna Karenina*). He did, however, offer a dozen pages of editorial notes, most of them made in the interest of accuracy of fact and clarity of expression; none concerned the substance of what I had said about him. In one he asked me to delete my quotation of a remark made by one of his friends because he thought it might embarrass another friend and might, moreover, mislead my readers. In another he said he thought I had not furnished my readers with the background they would need to understand the behavior of an acquaintance. At one point he said he disagreed with inferences I had drawn from two of his published pieces, though he would not, of course, expect me to change my mind (which I didn't). In two instances his memory of events did not correspond with the facts as I knew them from records at hand. Several of his notes, on the other hand, saved me from inaccuracies ("Mary Osborn's home town was Birmingham, Alabama," not, as I had said, Buena Vista, Virginia, where she went to school; "No, the piano was a Steinway baby grand," not a Waters, as I had said). Quite a few notes corrected misspellings. (White unreasonably holds that no one in possession of a good dictionary need ever misspell, and shares Stuart Little's notion that a misspelled word is "an abomination in the sight of everyone.") A few times he recommended stylistic revisions: "The White of Strunk and White thinks that you should reword this sentence to read . . . ." "You got yourself into one of life's incredible rhetorical snarls when you followed the phrase ' . . . ' with ' . . . . ' I guess the easiest way out of this snarl is to say, ' . . . . ' In writing. so much depends on luck." He concluded his notes by saying that he considered these latter suggestions "cheeky," in as much as they overstepped the bounds of mere correction of fact and got into the writing itself; but, he said, he could not resist the temptation when he saw an "easy fix" for a passage that had stopped him when he read it. In short, he helped me like "a true friend and a good writer," but he neither approved nor disapproved of the biography itself. True to his word, he met me half way, and now that the book is finished I allow myself to think of him as a friend and to believe that he feels friendly toward me.

NOW IN HIS EIGHTIES, E. B. White looks and acts considerably younger than his age. In his mind's eye he has always seen himself as a young man ("a lad of about nineteen"), and this vision may have done as much as his genes to keep him young. He carries himself straight—a habit that makes him appear taller then he is (five feet, seven); his face is tanned; and his hair, though now white, has not markedly thinned. In the years I have know him, the quickness, precision, and grace of his mind have remained unchanged, as has his love of perfection in whatever he does.

Several years ago White gave up sailing his twenty-foot sloop in the costal waters off Brooklin, Maine, but as I finish this Foreword he is planning to celebrate his eighty-fourth birthday by canoeing with a friend on a lake in the interior of Maine.

1 July 1983   SCOTT ELLEDGE

E. B. WHITE *A BIOGRAPHY*

ALL that a man has to say or do that can possibly concern mankind, is in some shape or other to tell the story of his love—to sing; and, if he is fortunate and keeps alive, he will be forever in love.

HENRY DAVID THOREAU

CHAPTER I

Summit Avenue

1 8 9 9 — 1 9 0 5

"I don't know whether a passionate love of the natural world can be transmitted or not, but like the love of beauty it is a thing one likes to associate with the scheme of inheritance."

E. B. WHITE'S BIRTHDAY IS JULY II, CLEARLY A lucky day, he once said, because seven and eleven are lucky numbers. He was born in 1899, the third year of the presidency of William McKinley, in a period of prosperity that seemed to warrant general optimism. He was born in the fashionable section of Mount Vernon, New York, in Westchester County, from which commuters could reach Grand Central Station, in New York City, in about twenty-five minutes. His parents' house stood at the top of Chester Hill, on the corner of Summit and Sidney avenues, across the street from the house of his late maternal grandparents. It was a large, elaborate frame house, painted gray and trimmed in white, set in a small yard containing a large black cast-iron urn, and surrounded by a privet hedge. In a neighborhood of substantial, expensive houses, it bespoke the owners' concern for style as well as substance, and its octagonal tower on the corner and its large porch on the two sides facing the streets helped make it a good example of American domestic architecture at the turn of the century. The screened-in corner of the porch, following the contour of the tower, vaguely resembled the bridge of a ship, and Elwyn's father liked to call it "the Togo" after the admiral who led the Japanese navy to victory at Port Arthur in 1904. Samuel and Jessie White had had the house built for them and their large family in 1891. Handsome, solid, and comfortable, it was a source of pride for Samuel, and a haven of security for Jessie. E. B. White once said, "My parents came from Brooklyn; I suppose they moved because Mount Vernon sounded tonier and would be better for the children."[1]

When he was born, Elwyn's mother, Jessie Hart White, was forty-one; his father, Samuel Tilly White, was forty-five; his sisters were eighteen, fifteen, and five; his brothers, eleven and eight. He was the last child born to Jessie and Samuel. He was named Elwyn because shortly before his birth his mother had met a woman whose pretty little boy bore that Welsh name. His brothers and sisters had more familiar names: Marion, Clara, Albert, Stanley, and Lillian. According to one of his sisters, his middle name, Brooks, was that of the minister of the Mount Vernon Congregational Church, of which his father was president of the board of trustees. White himself thinks he was named for Phillips Brooks, a well-known Episcopal minister of Boston.[2]

Unlucky as he may have been in his name, Elwyn Brooks White was lucky to be the youngest in a large family and the last child of parents who loved children. He was also lucky to have been born at the beginning of the period of his father's greatest prosperity, when his father could afford to make some of Elwyn's most extravagent dreams come true. Elwyn owned the first small-sized bicycle on the block, and when he was only eleven he was given a sixteen-foot, dark green Old Town canoe that, as his father might have said, was "the best money could buy." It was safer than other canoes because cork sponsons, running along the outside top edges of its hull, made it more stable and gave it more flotation. With it came an extra-short paddle. It was to be paddled (with an older brother) on Great Pond, North Belgrade, Maine, where the Whites had been spending the month of August ever since Elwyn was six years old. But the love of this fifty-six-year-old father for his youngest child expressed itself in more lasting forms than expensive gifts.

On Elwyn's twelfth birthday, in a letter written in a firm, flowing hand, on stationery of the "absolutely fire-proof" Park Avenue Hotel, about fifteen blocks uptown from his office at 134 Fifth Avenue, Samuel White undertook to describe what he hoped his son would understand to be his most valuable inheritance:

Elwyn, my dear boy,

All hail! with joy and gladness we salute you on your natal day. May each recurring anniversary bring you earth's best gifts and heaven's choicest blessings. Think today on your mercies. You have been born in the greatest and best land on the face of the globe under the best government known to men. Be thankful then that you are an American. Moreover you are the youngest child of a large family and have profited by the companionship of older brothers and sisters—this is no small matter for you are wiser by reason of their experiences. You haven't had to learn wisdom you have absorbed it. You are the object of the affectionate solicitude of your mother and father. Then you have been born a Christian. When you reflect that the great majority of men are born in heathen lands in dense ignorance and superstition it is something to be thankful for that you have the light that giveth life. These and many other things I might mention and if the time comes, as come it will, when you are fretted by the small things of life remember that on this your birthday you heard a voice telling you to look up and out on the great things of life and beholding them say—surely they all are mine. In conclusion, I congratulate you again and with my warmest felicitation I wish you great joy, I wish you all happiness and I wish it for you with all my heart.

Father.[3]

The author of this remarkable letter, Samuel Tilly White, was born in Brooklyn in 1854, one of five children of Andrew and Mary Ann Elizabeth Tilly White. His grandfather was a successful building contractor, but his father, a carpenter, was a hard-drinking man who died in a drunkards' home. Samuel left school at thirteen to work in Manhattan as an errand boy for Horace Waters, who manufactured pianos. As a bundle-boy he learned how to wrap packages ("give yourself enough string"), an art he later taught Elwyn. He was otherwise not much good with his hands. His wife said he couldn't put a nail in the wall; and he never learned to drive, though he liked automobiles and bought several, which his sons drove. But he got on well with people; he liked hard work and efficiency; he was orderly, conscientious, and passionate about details. He was a planner and manager. He instinctively took charge. He was bound to succeed.[4]

When he was thirty-two, he was made one of the four stockholders and trustees of the newly incorporated Horace Waters & Co. Five years later, in 1891, he was able to move his family from Brooklyn to the large new house in Mount Vernon.

Upon the death of Horace Waters in 1893, six years before Elwyn was born, Samuel White, at the age of thirty-nine, became vice-president and secretary of the company. He was already its general manager and owned about twenty-five percent of its stock. The new president was Horace Waters' son Leeds, who had inherited fifty-one percent of the stock. Though White did not trust Leeds Waters' judgment ("a good parlor magician," White once called him, "but no businessman"), the two men apparently got on well together, and under White's direction the company prospered. By 1899 Samuel Tilly White was clearly a success. A few months after Elwyn's birth, however, he made an error that for several years soured the taste of that success.

In what he considered to be the best interests of all the stockholders, White advised Leeds Waters to agree to the issuing of three shares of stock to the cashier of the company, an old employee who already owned a few shares and who could be trusted in stockholders' or board meetings to vote as White advised him to. White told Waters that in issuing the stock the company would repay part of a debt it owed the cashier and at the same time increase his loyalty to the company. Apparently White did not point out that when the three new shares were issued, Waters would no longer own a majority of the stock. Waters signed the agreement, and from that time on White could run the company with the support of the other stockholders, all of whom respected his judgement. Whether Waters objected to the disingenuousness of White's advice when he finally discovered the consequences of following it we do not know, but in 1905 Leeds Waters' wife, Fanny, on behalf of herself and her husband, sued White and others for fraud.

Because the decision of the first court before which the case was tried was twice appealed, the litigation lasted six years, from the time Elwyn was six until a few months before the birthday that occasioned that optimistic and loving birthday letter beginning "All hail!" During those years Samuel White carried a burden of fear and shame. The older children knew what troubled their father. One daughter remembered hearing her father say, "Leeds Waters doesn't know it, but I have one more share than he does so that when trouble comes, I can have the say." The younger children knew only that he was often sick during this period.[5]

Fanny Waters charged that the board of directors had defrauded the company by failing to consult all the stockholders before issuing the stock to the cashier, and that the issue of the stock "was done at the instigation of the defendant White and to his nominee, and the issue of such stock was a part of a scheme and plan on the part of White to obtain control of the corporation, and was a fraud." In his defense, White testified that he had

> talked with Mr. Waters about [the issue of the three shares] in a general way, and Mr. Waters was agreeable to it, or was favorable to it, and [the cashier] wanted [the stock]. . . . We desired to sell Mr. Hamilton stock in order to fasten him or identify him with the business very much. He was very useful to us. He was a man of good judgment, and his services were very valuable. Mr. Waters felt in that regard even more than I did. . . .

The court proceedings reveal the curious fact that when the cashier died shortly after being given the shares, Samuel White bought them from his

widow at par value with money he borrowed from the company and
which he promptly paid back to it when Fanny brought suit.

In 1905 the court of the first instance judged that the gift of stock to
the cashier was "illegal and a fraud" and ordered the shares cancelled; but
four years later, in March 1909, the appellate court unanimously reversed
the decision of the lower court on the ground that the plaintiff had erred
in bringing action in the name of the company, since all the stockholders
except her had agreed to the sale of the stock. That decision was sustained
by the state supreme court in an appeal argued late in 1910 and decided
March 14, 1911. The court found that the issuing of the shares had not
"affected the control of the corporation in any manner injurious to its
business interests or prosperity or was otherwise harmful *to the corporation*
in any legal sense." "Unauthorized acts," it said, "are not necessarily
fraudulent. Illegal acts are not per se fraudulent."[6]

Samuel White must have been gratified by the court's distinction between illegal acts and fraudulent acts, but he may not have felt completely
vindicated. His youngest son has described him as "a man of great probity,
scrupulously honest and fair," and for such a man the pain of a guilty
conscience would have been especially poignant.[7]

Although he does not remember ever hearing of the accusation of fraud
brought against his father, having been too young at the time it happened,
E. B. White wrote a children's story when he was seventy in which a
character very much like his father commits a well-intentioned but illegal
act. The story is *The Trumpet of the Swan,* and its most lifelike, distinctive,
and attractive character is the father swan, who steals an object needed by
his handicapped son. White has not left a better portrait of his father than
his comic but kindly characterization of the old cob, who resembles Samuel
White most in his style, in his sense of himself, and especially in his
rhetoric. Just before he steals a trumpet from a music store he says to
himself:

> "Now is my time to act! . . . Now is my moment for risking everything on
> one bold move, however shocking it may be to my sensibilities, however
> offensive it may be to the laws that govern the lives of men."

As he heads home, "In his beak was the trumpet. In his heart was the
pain of having committed a crime."

> "I have robbed a store," he said to himself. "I have become a thief. What a
> miserable fate for a bird of my excellent character and high ideals! Why did
> I do this? What led me to commit this awful crime? My past life has been

blameless—a model of good behavior and correct conduct. I am by nature law-abiding. Why, oh, why did I do this?"

Then the answer came to him, as he flew steadily on through the evening sky. "I did it to help my son. I did it for love of my son Louis."[8]

Samuel White did not commit a crime. Nor were any of his sons in need of help that called for desperate measures. Apparently his intentions, like those of the old cob, were generous and pragmatic. What was good for the Waters Piano Company was good for White's family.

The old cob was proud of his style, and when he addressed his cygnets before their first swim, he sounded much like Samuel White exhorting Elwyn on his "natal day":

"Welcome to the pond and the swamp adjacent!" he said. "Welcome to the world that contains this lonely pond, this splendid marsh, unspoiled and wild! Welcome to sunlight and shadow, wind and weather; welcome to water! The water is a swan's particular element, as you will soon discover. Swimming is no problem for a swan. Welcome to danger, which you must guard against —the vile fox with his stealthy tread and sharp teeth, the offensive otter who swims up under you and tries to grab you by the leg, the stinking skunk who hunts by night and blends with the shadows, the coyote who hunts and howls and is bigger than a fox. . . . Be vigilant, be strong, be brave, be graceful, and *always* follow me! I will go first, then you will come along in single file, and your devoted mother will bring up the rear. Enter the water quietly and confidently!"[9]

Samuel White resembled the old swan in other ways: in his love for his wife, in his male pride, in his pleasure in fatherhood, in his vanity, his competence, his decisiveness, his courage. Samuel White's children were amused by the comic aspects of their father's pride, but they loved and respected this benevolent master and disciplined leader whose family was his chief concern and greatest joy. All his life, but especially during the years preceding Elwyn's twelfth birthday, Samuel White's business competed with his family for his attention, but it was virtually the only competitor. He and his wife had few friends and almost no social life. He had an eye for good-looking women, but something other than religion or law made him a faithful husband—something more perhaps than his deep affection for his pretty wife. His first loyalty was to his family, and he was, as his son says, "a good man."[10]

By 1911 Samuel White had sold two of his three carriage horses and had bought a Pope-Tribune one-cylinder automobile, which he kept until he bought a Maxwell roadster, in which Elwyn later learned to drive. Two years before the conclusion of the lawsuit he had become president of Horace Waters & Co., and by 1922 he was chief executive of a corporation that, in its factory in Harlem, produced excellent pianos of various kinds, including the best of all player-pianos, and that sold its products in its four retail stores in Manhattan. By 1925, however, when White was seventy, the company had ceased to prosper, and in 1929, when the whole piano industry collapsed, Horace Waters & Co. was forced to liquidate to avoid going into bankruptcy. Sixty-two years after he ran his first errand for Horace Waters, Samuel White supervised the liquidation, which was completed in 1933. He used part of the proceeds that fell to him to set up a business for his son Albert.[11] In 1917, just before Elwyn entered Cornell, his father sold the big house on Summit Avenue and moved to a modest house on Mersereau Avenue, where, in 1935, at the age of 82, he died a melancholy man.

But in 1911 Samuel White's birthday letter to his son expressed the sanguine temper of pre–First World War America. Elwyn's first blessing was, he said, that he was an American. Samuel was convinced of the superiority of American democracy and the freedom it made possible. He took his duties as a citizen seriously, and he was fascinated by politics, local, national, and international. Although, according to the older children, he bought "good books," and read them to the children, his own reading, his self-education, consisted mainly of reading the newspapers, the *Times* in the morning and the *Globe* in the evening.

Politically Samuel White was a "moderate Democrat," according to his son Stanley, who remembered hearing his father say with pride that he had voted for Samuel J. Tilden for president in 1876 because as governor of New York he had helped overthrow Tammany Hall's corrupt Tweed Ring, and that he had voted against William Jennings Bryan because of his extreme populism. He thought Teddy Roosevelt was dishonest—as he later thought FDR was a "trimmer."[12]

The second of Elwyn's blessings, according to the birthday letter, was his family. Samuel White succeeded in giving his children what he had lacked himself as a boy. His hard-drinking father, according to the family lore, was rough on his children. Samuel was a teetotaler most of his life, and he was firm but gentle with his children. Every child had a bicycle, but every bicycle was to be in its slot in the shed by dark. Every child was free to roam in the afternoon, but everyone had to be home on time for dinner. He did not drive them in their schoolwork, but he encouraged them all to learn. When he had to chastise one of the children, he did not raise his voice; he simply looked right through the little culprit. When children quarreled, he did not adjudicate the dispute but only reminded them that quarreling spoiled the pleasant family atmosphere. He was not moralistic. He had no religious sense of sin. His word for sin was *mistake*. He disapproved of idleness and disorder, and he loved to get things right and to help make things go right. He brought to the rearing of his family an abundance of paternal love, the liberal optimism that characterized his feelings about America, and the flair for management that had made the piano company prosper.

His observations about Elwyn's third blessing are revealing. Being born a Christian meant being born in an enlightened country free of "dense ignorance and superstition"; and the "light that giveth light" seems to have meant for him not so much the Holy Light of Christ by which believers are saved as the enlightenment that freed people from superstition. He loved learning, he was fascinated by language, and he tried to share with his children his interest in words. He encouraged his children to study what interested them. His two older daughters married soon after graduation from high school, but Lillian went to boarding school and graduated from Vassar. All three sons graduated from Cornell.

The style of the birthday letter is interesting because it is so unlike that of E. B. White, who once said that his father was "quite a talker and didn't hesitate to say in twenty words what could be said in six."[13] Its rhetoric is that of a self-educated man of the late gilded age who, liking politics and sermons, learned his style from politicians and preachers. The strongest influence on the style of Samuel Tilly White was Henry Ward Beecher, minister of the Plymouth Church in Brooklyn, which White attended regularly until he moved to Mount Vernon. Like thousands of Beecher's followers, he admired the dramatic oratory of a man who believed that a sermon should "effect a moral change in the hearer." By the time Samuel White was born, Beecher was drawing congregations of twenty-five hundred. His doctrine was liberal Protestant, and American. He favored women's suffrage, he believed in evolution, and he welcomed scientific biblical criticism. White's loyalty was not shaken when Beecher was sued for adultery in the seventies. He owned a set of Beecher's *Sermons,* one of the few literary works E. B. White can recall his father reading. Stanley remembered that his father knew how to pray well out loud.

During Elwyn's boyhood, Samuel White's faith, or his formal religious life, underwent a crisis from which it never recovered. Fifteen years after Samuel's death, E. B. White wrote:

When I was a child, I could feel heaven slipping. My father was a God fearing man, but he never missed a copy of the New York *Times* either. At sixty he began changing back and forth between the Congregational and the Baptist church, grumbling and growling. At seventy he let go altogether, and for the next ten years lived in a miasma of melancholy doubt and died outside the church, groping and forlorn.[14]

Samuel White "had a sentimental turn of mind, which led him into song-writing,"[15] and when he was twenty-one, "Sweet Dreams of Childhood, Song and Chorus, Words and Music by S. T. White" was published by Oliver Ditson & Co., in Boston, and his "Debut, Waltz for Piano," dedicated "To Bessie," appeared in New York. He was also an amateur photographer; he was interested in "natural history" and astronomy; and he loved the outdoors.

Samuel spent more time with Elwyn than he had been able to spend with the older children. When Elwyn was ten, Samuel wrote to his oldest son, Albert, then in college, "Oh, the joy, the joy of my little boy; we have lots of good times together."[16] After dinner the two often had long conversations, so long that Lillian never understood how her little brother endured them. As time passed, father and son found it hard to exchange confidences, but in his most impressionable years Elwyn was much influenced by his father's love and by his character. On the occasion of the hundredth anniversary of his father's birth, E. B. White wrote his brother Stanley a letter in which he speculated about that influence:

Pop was a golden man living in a golden age, doing it well, and barely realizing that he was dumping six kids into an age of terror and destruction. I think at the end he worried a bit about this, and he did not underestimate either the meaning or the damage of the First War; but I'm glad he died before the real carnage began—not because he wouldn't have had the character to stand up to it but because it would have destroyed the pattern that you and I like to remember, and that he fitted so beautifully.

It is hard to know, precisely, what a parent transmits to a child, and I have often wondered—not only about what I received from Father but about what I handed along to [my son]. Pop was not only conservative (in a rather sensible and large-spirited way) but he was tidy in large and small ways, and I think those are the traits that found their way into the second generation. I can see it in my work. I don't always like it, but I can usually see it. I don't know whether a passionate love of the natural world can be transmitted or not, but like the love of beauty it is a thing one likes to associate with the scheme of inheritance.[17]

E. B. White also learned from the old cob to respect the responsibilities of the head of a family as well as the rights of all its members to privacy, independence, and self-realization. Samuel may have been a Victorian father and husband, but he respected his wife as a partner, and his children did not learn from him to look on the relations between men and women as a Thurberesque war between the sexes.

From his father came his love of trains, of vacation trips, of cars and boats, and even perhaps of New York, because his father provided the opportunities to learn to love them. But much more important, during his most impressionable years he learned from his father to be an optimist, and to believe in his luck. In the birthday letter, his father advised Elwyn "when fretted by the small things of life . . . to look up and out on the great things of life and beholding them say—surely they all are mine." This E. B. White has done.

I N T H E "scheme of inheritance" that White spoke of in his letter to Stanley, his mother, Jessie Hart White, naturally made her own genetic contribution to Elwyn's character; but the evidence of her personal influence on him is slight, or hard to identify. After his birth she was not very strong; she had never been a robust person. She lived on in relatively good health till shortly before she died of cancer at the age of seventy-eight, in 1936. She was, as one of her daughters put it, a "Victorian mother" in a patriarchal family.[18] Her children were her consuming interest; her letters consisted mainly of news about them and about her grandchildren. In an early letter to Elwyn she spoke with pleasure of her flowers in the yard and of a new brood of baby chicks. Her strong motherly love must have helped implant in her son his lifelong fascination with the miracle of birth and his reverence for life's cycles. When he was twenty-one his mother wrote him about going to Washington to help her daughter Clara at the time of the birth of "Dear wee 'Janet' ": "I am perfectly well [she was sixty-two] with it all and feel gratified that I have been able to serve Clara who is doing wonderful work in bearing and bringing up a family of children" (Janet was the sixth of Clara's nine children).

Like her husband, Jessie had not gone beyond grammar school. She admired Samuel's way with words, but her own style was plain and unpretentious. Her letters right up until her death were clear and strong, and reflected her joy in life as well as her love for her children. She was rather shy and, like her husband, not much interested in people outside her family, and she may have been the chief reason why there were seldom guests in the house. White has several times remarked on the isolation and self-sufficiency of his family:

For the first eighteen years of my life I never even knew there *was* such a thing as a dinner party. Nobody got into our fashionable house unless he was kinfolks, and even then he had to beat his way in. I might as well have been living in the Rain Forest.[19]

Samuel and Jessie were happiest when they were with one another, and though Jessie was apprehensive about train travel, they took many trips together, including one to the West Coast and one to Europe. On their fortieth anniversary Jessie wrote her son from Atlantic City:

We saw any number of Brides and Grooms on the board walk today—but as you know none of them were any happier than Father and I. Of course with them the morning of the day is just breaking. While with us the sun is setting but all sunsets are beautiful.[20]

Lillian, Elwyn's youngest and favorite sister, was amused by her parents and shared with her little brother a youthful toleration of the quaintness of an older generation. At Vassar she learned to think of women's careers in different terms from those of her mother, who in a letter to Elwyn confided that she hoped someday to see Lillian settled "in a nice little home of her own with a good husband and some children to crown her happiness." When Elwyn was elected editor of the *Cornell Daily Sun* his mother wrote:

Father has written you of our great joy because of the honor bestowed on you last Tuesday. It's great! I never saw Father so thrilled, his eyes fairly glistened. But only a mother can enjoy to the full the honor bestowed on her children as, I wonder if you know this, no one loves or is capable of loving like a mother.[21]

By the time Elwyn was twelve, this pretty, maternal, religious, white-haired lady, who tended to tire easily and to be disorganized in her management of the household (she had a maid and a cook), may have seemed to Elwyn more like his friends' grandmothers than their mothers; but his memory of the love that nurtured him in infancy and supported him in boyhood may nonetheless have subtly influenced the character of a man who never ceased to love the role of nurturer. When he was thirty and she was seventy-one, E. B. White dedicated his first book of poems to "Janet Hart White," thinking that "Jessie" was a nickname for "Janet." In the first of White's children's books, *Stuart Little,* when the young hero leaves home to seek his beloved and at the same time to see the world—somewhat as White left home in 1922—he carries with him a lock of his mother's hair.

Through his mother he inherited the genes of the Harts, a strong and interesting family. Her grandfather, a weaver in Paisley, Scotland, driven from his trade by the Industrial Revolution, brought his wife and ten children to America in 1830. Having survived a shipwreck, they settled in Albany, New York. A year later William Hart, Jessie's father, was apprenticed at the age of eight to a coachmaker, from whom he learned to decorate door-panels with little landscapes, seascapes, and figures, six or eight inches wide. The boy's miniatures adorned the doors of the stage-coaches on Broadway, in New York City, and a New Yorker who admired them encouraged young Hart to become a painter. By the time he was eighteen he was in business for himself as a portrait painter. Using his father's woodshed as a studio, he painted "likenesses" for a dollar a head and was so successful that he opened a studio near Troy. During this time he continued to teach himself landscape painting. It was said that he had an unusually good visual memory and could paint in his studio with great accuracy a scene he had visited some time before. A few years later he moved to Michigan, where for three years he painted portraits for twenty-five dollars a head. After a three-year visit to Scotland he settled in a green, residential area in Brooklyn, opened a studio in Manhattan, and from then on painted only landscapes. His skill became widely recognized, his work sold well, and in the 1870's some of his paintings fetched as much as five thousand dollars. His first exhibition was at the National Academy of Design in 1848. He was elected an associate of the National Academy in 1855 and at the age of thirty-five was made an "Academician." He helped organize the American Society of Water-Colorists and was the first president of the Brooklyn Academy, where in a lecture on landscape painting William Hart gave advice that his grandson would have endorsed:

> There should always be an idea, either preceding or succeeding the subject, and that idea should be [the artist's] own—an idea or sentiment which should be wrought with his pencil in such a manner as to interpret his own thought and not an imitation of another man's.[22]

E. B. White remembered his mother's pride in her father's gift, achievement, and fame:

> My mother, although a shy and simple person, liked being the daughter of an illustrious father, and she often referred to him as "an Academician." The word gave her a lift. She worshiped my father, but I think in a subtle way she pulled rank on him, now and then, by pulling William Hart on him. After all, Father was just a businessman, son of a carpenter. Her father was an artist. Mother herself had no knowledge of art beyond the limits of her father's studio. She

had no artistic pretensions or gifts. But it meant something to her to have an artist for a parent—an artist was special.[23]

When Jessie and Samuel were married, William Hart wrote a memorandum dated at his studio in the YMCA, April 27, 1880:

> This day I give to my daughter Jessie W. Hart $5,000 = Five Thousand Dollars in seven per Cent Bonds = at present in the Brooklyn Safe Deposit Co. The Principal to be held by and for *her own* Benefit or children as a Wedding Present from her Father. William Hart.[24]

He died in his house on Sidney Avenue, in Mount Vernon, in 1894, at the age of seventy-two, five years before Elwyn was born. He was in good health until the death of his wife, "which affected him greatly." He survived her only a year (Jessie survived Samuel only eight months).

One of the several long obituary notices published in New York papers concluded with a patriotic paragraph that his grandson would not be embarrassed by:

> He was true to his adopted country. He chose the materials for his pictures here, and found that there was an inexhaustible fund of subjects among our hills and beside our streams. . . . He refused to be an imitator and his pictures, therefore, have a value that certain ostentatious and clever works by disciples of French and German schools can never obtain.[25]

Like his grandson, William Hart was devoted to his art, was not noticeably influenced by other artists, found his subject matter close to home, and was well paid for his work. His paintings were distinguished not by a grandeur of conception but by the "poetic strain in his imagination" by which he expressed his joy in the life he observed and recorded.

T H E   A T T I C of the house White was born in was large and memorable. There he first experienced the beauty of birds' eggs when he found a cabinet containing a large collection of them arranged according to size —from an ostrich egg to a hummingbird's. He remembers a winter day when the snow arrived in blizzard force: "At eight o'clock the fire siren, muffled by the blast, wailed the 'No School Today' signal, and [I] retired in ecstasy to a warm attic room and to Meccano" (a popular construction set for children, containing parts with which to build bridges, cranes, machines, and other works of engineering). And what he remembered most clearly was "the coziness, the child's sense of a protective screen having been quickly drawn between him and his rather frightening world."[26]

By the time he was five, his sisters Marion and Clara had married, and on the second floor the remaining children had rooms of their own. In Albert's room was *Webster's Unabridged Dictionary* (mounted on a cast-iron tripod stand), to which Samuel White sent his children to discover the meanings of words they did not know. In Stanley's room was the Oliver typewriter of which White later said: "It was the noisy excitement connected with borrowing and using this machine that encouraged me to be a writer." Elwyn's room, according to his brother Stanley, was always shipshape—quite unlike George's room as rendered by Garth Williams in *Stuart Little.* By the time he was twelve his brothers and sisters had all left home, and for the next five years Elwyn and his mother and father (and a cook) were alone in the big house.[27]

Some of his most vivid memories of the time he spent indoors are of being alone in his room, listening to noises outdoors: the chirping of starlings outside his bedroom window who "sit up all night . . . swapping stories"; the sounds of early morning, such as the tinkle of milk bottles in the milkman's carrier, and "the creak of wagon wheels, the lazy scupping of horse's hoofs . . . mysterious matins celebrating the break of day, the beginning of life"; and on winter nights after his bedtime, the cries of lucky, "late revellers with their Flexible Flyers and their bobs," about to take off at the corner for the long coast down Sidney Avenue. When the wind was right he could hear the "solemn and ominous bellow of the foghorn on Execution Rock at the western end of Long Island Sound— the body of water where he would later learn to sail. Once when he was sick in bed, he made a pet of a mouse (the original Stuart Little), for whom he made a home, complete with a gymnasium and to whom he taught "many fine tricks."[28]

On the first floor of the house, to the left as you entered the "massive front door" and passed the oak hat-rack and the umbrella stand, was the parlor. It was the family living room while the children still lived at home. It was, as White remembers,

well supplied with musical instruments: a Waters grand piano, a reed organ with phony pipes, and, at one period, a Waters player piano called an "Autola." There were six of us children, and we were practically a ready-made band. All we lacked was talent. We had violins, cellos, mandolins, guitars, banjos, and drums, and there was always a lot of music filling the air in our home, none of it good. We sang, composed, harmonized, drummed, and some of us took lessons for brief spells in an attempt to raise the general tone of the commotion. My brother Stanley was a fiddler. I played piano, picked at the mandolin, and at one point acquired a three-quarter-size cello and took lessons. But I failed to develop musical curiosity, learned nothing about the works of the great, and was content to make a noise, whether ragtime or schmalz or Czerny. Like my father, I liked the *sound* of music but was too lazy to follow it to its source.

Of the reception room, the rather dark room on the other side of the hall "where no one was ever received," White's earliest recorded memory is of finding his mother one day stretched out on the settee, recovering from an accident with a runaway horse. He thought she was dead.[29] But the reception room had also a happy association, for it was there that the Christmas tree stood each year. White's earliest published piece of reminiscence is of Christmas at 101 Summit Avenue in 1908:

A German band playing "Heilige Nacht"—playing with a wobbly sincerity, in the snow of a street in a suburban town. The gas lamp at the corner, as though approving of the holy music, throws a yellow radiance on the serenaders, and the snow sifts softly down into their faces and into the bell of the bass horn. Ever since morning the parlor of the house has been shut off behind two heavy oak doors that are never closed at any other time of year, and the mere fact that one room in the house has been dedicated to mystery is about as much excitement as the heart can stand.

Across the hall from the parlor—in what was called the reception room, for a reason that was neither understood nor questioned—is the prickly smell of holly, the green smell of fir, the red promise of a paper bell. The front doorbell rings: one of the musicians appears, his horn under an arm. As he stands there, grinning and cold, a little parcel of snow comes whispering in through the door. The stranger is rewarded from the left-hand trouser pocket of the Good Provider. "Merry Christmas!" he says, and leaves. From the window he can be dimly seen joining the others in front of Billy Denman's house.

It is time to go to bed and leave the prickly smell, the green smell, and the mystery. The stair landing affords the last perfect view of the hatrack in the hall, on which are ten paper parcels of known content. They contain ten varieties of hard and soft candy, which are to be mixed into a kind of candy punch and introduced with the provision that they must last until New Year's Day. They will have entirely disappeared, as is well known throughout the household, by the afternoon of the twenty-seventh: the small round chocolate ones with the white trimmings will be gone by the morning of the twenty-sixth.[30]

The decorations for the Christmas tree always included at its base a miniature farm, "Mother's beautiful 'dream farm' with the duck pond etc., etc. and the lovely blue sky and the moon and the stars shining so brightly."[31]

Below the reception room and the parlor, and the dining room and kitchen, with all their assurances of security and love, was the cellar, which White remembers for "its darkness and dampness, its set wash-tubs, its Early American water closet for the help, its coal furnace that often tried to asphyxiate us all, and the early sound of the Italian furnace man who crept in at dawn and shook the thing down." "As a very small boy," he writes, "I used to repair to the cellar, where I would pee in the coal bin —for variety." White once referred to a part of his troubled, middle-aged psyche as "the 'notself,' " which, he said, "lives in the dark sub-basement of the psyche [and] helps the janitor." But the cellar had other associations:

> [It] was the only place [I was] allowed to put [my dog Mac] (the barn was too cold, the house was too clean), yet [I] never felt right about it, and [my] childhood was suffused with a kind of gloomy guilt. There must be millions of adults in the world who are the way they are because of once having kept a dog in the cellar, opening the door and always finding him sitting there on the landing at the top of the stairs. [I] even remember the special smell that a cellar puppy has—a blend of ashes and vigor-kept-under.

The following winter Mac moved to sheepskin-lined quarters that Elwyn built for him in the barn. Mac was memorable:

> I can still see my first dog in all the moods and situations that memory has filed him away in, but I think of him oftenest as he used to be right after breakfast on the back porch, listlessly eating up a dish of petrified oatmeal rather than hurt my feelings. For six years he met me at the same place after school and convoyed me home—a service he thought up himself. A boy doesn't forget that sort of association.[32]

Such was the house, the fortress, the home—lovingly built, maintained, managed by Samuel and Jessie. As White has said, he was not deprived or unloved, and his home was a haven. But, as with most children, it was also a place to sally forth from, not always "to do battle" but more often to escape boredom and loneliness, and to explore larger worlds: his own backyard, the precincts of 101 Summit Avenue, school, and (in August) his family's camp on the shore of a lake in Maine.

White remembers his young consciousness finding in these excursions "a sense of living somewhat freely in a natural world." His "first and greatest love affair," he once wrote, "was with . . . freedom, this lady of infinite allure, this dangerous and beautiful and sublime being who restores and supplies us all." The affair began, he said,

> with the haunting intimation (which I presume every child receives) of his mystical inner life; of God in man; of nature publishing herself through the

"I." This elusive sensation is moving and memorable. It comes early in life: a boy, we'll say, sitting on the front steps on a summer night, thinking of nothing in particular, suddenly hearing as with a new perception and as though for the first time the pulsing sound of crickets, overwhelmed with the novel sense of identification with the natural company of insects and grass and night, conscious of a faint answering cry to the universal perplexing question: "What is 'I'?"[33]

Outdoors, in his own yard, there was a garden, and there were animals. One spring his father bought the children an incubator and fifty eggs. The day the chicks began to hatch, Jimmy Bridges, the coachman, called the children to come and look. Elwyn, so small he could hardly see over the table into the egg tray, was the most excited of all as he watched the chicks slowly pip their shells and emerge. At last there were only three unpipped eggs left. Declaring them infertile and therefore containing no chicks, Jimmy took them out of the tray and put them on the manure pile outside the stable. There, in the warmth of what the heroine of *Charlotte's Web* was to celebrate as the "dung and the dark," the eggs hatched, and Elwyn, hearing the peeping, in great excitement ran out and found the chicks. He never forgot his initiation into the mystery of incubation or his first sight of the "bacchanalia of a chick's first drink of water at the fountain."[34]

The barn was another world, where at various times lived pigeons, ducks, geese, and a turkey. It was not the farmer's barn of *Charlotte's Web*, of course; it was only a stable, but it was nonetheless an exciting place, with its

two straight stalls, a box stall, a carriage room, a carriage washstand with drain in floor, a harness closet, a toilet for the coachman, a manure pit, and, up above, a loft for baled hay and an oatbin equipped with a chute to carry the grain to the ground floor. There was also the coachman's room upstairs, to which boys were seldom admitted. Everything smelled wonderfully ripe: the horses, the hay, the harness dressing, the axle grease, the liniment, the coachman— everything.[35]

Under the stable lived rats and, occasionally, a wild cat. Like Wilbur in *Charlotte's Web*, Elwyn was lucky to be surrounded by such various and sensuous manifestations of life—by "everything."

As Elwyn moved into the world beyond the privet hedge surrounding the fortress in which all people were family, he found other boys, who became friends. There was Billy Denman next door, and Freddie Schuler, son of a German piano-maker, across the street. And there was Barrett Brady, son of a writer for the *Saturday Evening Post*. One of his neighbors owned a pony and a cart (at one point Elwyn tried to sell subscriptions to the *Saturday Evening Post* in the hope of winning a pony of his own).

Not far away was the home of Kenny Mendel, whose father owned a restaurant in Grand Central Station and was the richest man on the block. About half the houses in this part of town had stables, and the coachmen, usually Irish, were friendly to the boys. White remembers that he knew well the stables and coachmen of quite a few neighbors whose houses he never entered. When he was a little older, he and other boys gathered in Stratton's barn, where the coachman allowed the boys to swing down from the loft on a rope.

Though Mount Vernon was a suburban town and many of its residents were essentially New Yorkers, it was properly called "the village," and the life of children as lucky as Elwyn and his pals was a happy rural one. At the bottom of the Sidney Avenue hill was a "slick place" called the Dell, where, when he was old enough, Elwyn played hockey:

> There was a stream in the Dell, and a small pond on which we skated in the beautiful winter twilight. There was a big willow tree, and a house that was sort of out of key with other houses—a little mysterious to me. . . . I played goalie, wearing my strap-on rockers. The wind would drop down with the sun, the sky would turn red. . . .[36]

Within a few hundred yards of the Whites' house was a slope where the children learned to ski, and beyond the Dell, quite a way east, was Wilson's Woods, memorable for its jack-in-the-pulpits, anemones, and dogwood in spring. In it was Snake Pond, where Elwyn went looking for "salamanders, frogs, or trouble," or for "garter snakes [that could] be surprised under last year's wet oak leaves." Beyond Wilson's Woods and Snake Pond was the reservoir, around which Samuel White liked to ride early on summer mornings before going to the office. In the village were good streets for bicycling, and sidewalks for roller skating. Once asked what dime novels he remembered reading as a boy, White replied in two sentences: "I do not remember ever having read a dime novel. Spent my youth on a bicycle, and in trees."[37]

On Saturday afternoons Father occasionally took some of the children to matinees in New York City—to the Hippodrome, to the circus in Madison Square Garden, and to plays and musicals which he selected with some care, often according to his opinion of one or more members of the cast. In the declining years of the Hippodrome, White described an early memory of that once exciting place, using the editorial "we" of *The New Yorker*'s anonymous editorial-writer:

> We happen to belong to the generation to whom the Hippodrome means only one thing—the place where, in the long ago, marvellously beautiful maidens

used to walk down a flight of stairs into the water, remain for several minutes, and later appear dripping and nymphlike from the unthinkable depths. Incidentally, it is the mansion where we lost, forever, our childlike faith in our father's all-embracing knowledge; for when we asked him point-blank what happened to the ladies while they were under the water, his answer was so vague, so evasive, so palpably out of accord with even the simplest laws of physics, that even our child mind sensed its imbecility, and we went our way thereafter alone in the world, seeking for truth.[38]

Until he was twelve, Elwyn (or En, as he was nicknamed) went to Sunday school and church with his family, and Sunday afternoon meant a ride in the surrey (later in the Pope Tribune), or a bicycle ride to the house of his sister Marion in a nearby suburb, or a visit to the zoo:

My father sometimes broke the awful spell of Sunday afternoon by a trolley trip to the Bronx [Zoo]—always after a heavy dinner, and with many difficult [streetcar] transfer arrangements.[39]

For Sunday night supper there was always cocoa, a drink that in later life always made him a bit sick.

Most of White's published remarks about school concern what happened outside the classroom. He made good grades, but from kindergarten on he wanted out. Once, in *The New Yorker,* commenting on a prospectus for a private school, White wrote:

We were interested in one paragraph of the prospectus, which said "We gauge our educational success by the richness of the children's experiences rather than by the amount of factual information acquired." . . . Our rich experiences, as a child, were secret, unexpected, and unreported. Sometimes they were vaguely obscene and calamitous; sometimes they were truancies of the mind during periods of extreme academic drowse. We are fairly sure that nothing in our face or in our manner ever gave us away during the onslaught of a rich experience. Adults can often tell when a child is gay, or troubled, or frightened, or amused; but a teacher who thinks she knows when a pupil is having a rich experience is just kidding herself.[40]

Elwyn's first-grade teacher remembered, fifty years later, the day his mother brought him to Lincoln School (P.S. 2) to enroll him: he wore a "spick and span white linen suit," was "interested in everything," and had a "pleasant smile." One of his classmates remembered him, a little older, wearing tweedy knickers. "Grammar school days were the days of our greatest valor," White later wrote. "Life was red and real, and some boy was always 'after' us." Elwyn was a little short for his age but not cowardly, and after Christmas of 1908 he had his own small bike, which increased his confidence and independence.[41]

He remembers the names of all his teachers at P.S. 2, but the one who "lit the fuse" for him was Mrs. Schuyler, who "was rather pretty . . . and enjoyed the gift of life. He was delighted when she entered a room, felt let down when she left." He needed such moments of delight to compensate for periods of anxiety as well as boredom. One of his strongest fears was the fear of public speaking:

> It was in P.S. 2 that I contracted the fear of platforms that has dogged me all my life and caused me to decline every invitation to speak in public. For the assembly performances, pupils were picked in alphabetical order, and since there were a great many pupils and my name began with W, I spent the entire term dreading the ordeal of making a public appearance. I suffered from a severe anticipatory sickness. Usually the term ended before my name came up, and then the new term started again at the top of the alphabet. I mounted the platform only once in my whole career, but I suffered tortures every day of the school year, thinking about the awesome—if improbable—event.[42]

School was not fun for Elwyn White; the three months of vacation were what made the other nine months endurable.

CHAPTER II

Belgrade Lake and Siwanoy Pond

1905 — 1917

"To him a miracle was essentially egg-shaped."

HITE WAS BORN LUCKY, AS HE HAS OFTEN said, but he was also born scared, and of his early anxieties he once gave a fairly specific account:

As a child, I was frightened but not unhappy. I lacked for nothing except confidence. I suffered nothing except the routine terrors of childhood: fear of the dark, fear of the future, fear of the return to school after a summer on a lake in Maine, fear of making an appearance on a platform, fear of the lavatory in the school basement where the slate urinals cascaded, fear that I was unknowing about things I should know about."[1]

As he grew older the objects of his fears changed, and to the discomforts of specific fears he added the chronic distress of unspecific anxiety, of what he called a "panic or amorphous" fear.

Much of the story of the life of E. B. White is the story of how he has come to terms with his fears; and that story begins early. Elwyn was not a weakling or a sickly child, but he was not robust, and as early as the summer of 1905 his hay fever was so severe that his father took him (with the rest of the family) to Maine for the month of August in the hope of escaping the pollen that made him miserable. He seems not to have been babied or spoiled by his family, but as the last of their children he must have seemed especially precious to Jessie and Samuel, and he may have learned to be anxious by observing the anxieties of his parents. In any case, at a fairly early age he was forced to find ways to deal with fears—and, at times, with melancholy, as he once recalled in an autobiographical sketch entitled "A Boy I Knew":

> I remember this boy with affection, and feel no embarrassment in idealizing him. He himself was an idealist of shocking proportions. He had a fine capacity for melancholy and the gift of sadness. I never knew anybody on whose spirit the weather had such a devastating effect. A shift of wind, or of mood, could wither him. There would be times when a dismal sky conspired with a forlorn side street to create a moment of such profound bitterness that the world's accumulated sorrow seemed to gather in a solid lump in his heart. The appearance of a coasting hill softening in a thaw, the look of backyards along the railroad tracks on hot afternoons, the faces of people in trolley cars on Sunday—these could and did engulf him in a vast wave of depression. He dreaded Sunday afternoon because it had been deliberately written in a minor key.
>
> He dreaded Sunday also because it was the day he spent worrying about going back to school on Monday. School was consistently frightening, not so much in realization as in anticipation. . . .
>
> The fear he had of making a public appearance on a platform seemed to find a perverse compensation, for he made frequent voluntary appearances in natural amphitheaters before hostile audiences, addressing himself to squalls and thunderstorms, rain and darkness, alone in rented canoes. His survival is something of a mystery, as he was neither very expert nor very strong. Fighting natural disturbances was the only sort of fighting he enjoyed. He would run five blocks to escape a boy who was after him, but he would stand up to any amount of punishment from the elements. He swam from the rocks of Hunter's Island, often at night, making his way there alone and afraid along the rough, dark trail from the end of the bridge (where the house was where they sold pie) up the hill and through the silent woods and across the marsh to the rocks.

What encouraged this boy in the face of "an unusual number of worries" was "a faith nourished by the natural world rather than by the supernatural or the spiritual." In the church of nature his pew was "a granite rock upholstered with lichen" at the edge of a lake, and his worship was an act of intense, enchanted observation. The natural world that nourished the boy's faith was largely an animal world:

> This boy felt for animals a kinship he never felt for people. Against considerable opposition and with woefully inadequate equipment, he managed to provide himself with animals, so that he would never be without something to tend. He kept pigeons, dogs, snakes, polliwogs, turtles, rabbits, lizards, singing birds, chameleons, caterpillars and mice. The total number of hours he

spent just standing watching animals, or refilling their water pans, would be impossible to estimate; and it would be hard to say what he got out of it. In spring he felt a sympathetic vibration with earth's renascence, and set a hen. He always seemed to be under some strange compulsion to assist the processes of incubation and germination, as though without him they might fail and the earth grow old and die. To him a miracle was essentially egg-shaped.[2]

His equipment for keeping his little menagerie seemed "woefully inadequate" in comparison with that of Kenny Mendel down the street, whose father had built cages alongside the stable. Kenny owned rabbits, turtles, a monkey, a raccoon, squirrels, and a pheasant. It wasn't to be compared with the Bronx Zoo, but it certainly was superior to Elwyn's small collection.

In the fields near his house, in the Dell, by Siwanoy Pond, by Great Pond in Maine, in his own backyard, and at both Kenny Mendel's and the Bronx Zoo—at all these places Elwyn "lived a life of enchantment; virtually everything he saw and heard was being seen and heard by him for the first time, so he gave it his whole attention." He was intensely curious about the behavior of animals and naturally became curious about reproduction. In notes he once made for an autobiographical poem called "Zoo Revisited," White recalled a "backyard zoo he used to pass on his way home from school at the end of morning":

[The hero of the projected poem, Olie] gets his cap from the cloak-room when class is dismissed and hurries away up the street. The yards of the town are dry and warm and sad—hydrangeas and ripening grapes. He is thinking how good it will be to get to a water closet at last, thinking about lunch; but when he gets to Kenny Whipple's [i.e., Mendel's] house he thinks about animals. . . . Kenny has a theory that turtles lay eggs. Olie doesn't believe this, but it occupies his mind and he wonders what turtles do do. All animals have to do something. Olie wishes to stop and examine the squirrels to try and see where baby squirrels come out of the female but he can't stop because he needs to go to the bathroom too badly. He passes the Belknaps, the Gants, the Immelmans, the Riches—only five more houses, five more hedges, then he will be home. He sees the Belknaps' coachman John cleaning harnesses in the stable door. He reaches his bathroom at last. Lunch is ready. During lunch he plans to stop in the Whipples' yard on the way back to school to examine squirrels, rabbits, turtles, for clues to reproduction.[3]

In its final version the poem makes clear that his curiosity about reproduction is mixed with his fear that what the "buck does with the doe" is "sad and terrible to know."[4]

Elwyn's parents, and even his older brothers and sisters, were not likely to have been helpful in these matters, and the books he might have found on "sexology" were confusing and misleading. But whatever his education in these matters, it left intact his happy devotion to nature and animals. Initiation, though terrible and sad, was also natural, and in retrospect sometimes funny.

In a satiric essay called "What Should Children Tell Parents," E. B. White warns children to be careful when they undertake to instruct adults about the facts of life: "It is best to explain things in a matter-of-fact way, rather than resort to such cloudy analogies as birds and flowers." Watching bees, he points out, may lead to the grossest misconceptions and most aberrant behavior.[5]

White's humor in *Is Sex Necessary?*, written with James Thurber in 1929, is rooted not in anxieties or repressions, but in a disposition to celebrate a natural phenomenon that only a human being finds threatening —or comic. Ever since his youthful discoveries about reproduction, White's reverence for the power of nature to perpetuate herself has helped to reassure him in periods of anxiety and melancholy. His faith has been "nourished by the natural world," and the egg has been the symbol of that faith. Biology—not philosophy or religion—has given him reason for optimism. Recording his observations helped teach him how to write. Anyone interested in the art of writing can see in the following paragraph from the high school biology notebook of Elwyn White how his respect for the phenomenon he was describing is reflected in the clarity and grace of his style:

GERMINATION OF BEAN

I saw the testa of the bean splitting and a little primary root grew out of the hypocotyl and grew downward. Soon the testa loosened more and the primary root grew longer. Then the primary root sent out secondary roots and a hypocotyl stem formed from the hypocotyl and grew upward. Next the hypocotyl stem arched and pulled the cotyledons up out of the ground. The cotyledons separated, turned green, then brown and finally dropped off the hypocotyl stem which by this time had straightened up. The little plumule grew into two large green leafs and a new bud formed between them. The epicotyl stem was between the cotyledons and the two leaves.[6]

THE SUMMER WORLD of the Belgrade Lakes in Maine was Elwyn's favorite biology laboratory. Summertime was glorious in itself, but it was particularly so at the lake in Maine, because there he had greater freedom to roam and observe nature than in Mount Vernon. After school was out in late June, "July was a waiting time at 101 Summit Avenue." Elwyn spent its sultry nights, as he remembered long afterwards, swinging in a hammock on the screened-in porch "with the mosquitoes buzzing outside, and school all over with for the year, and the smell of honeysuckle." He felt content. "Life is always a rich and steady time when you are waiting for something to happen or to hatch," he observed in *Charlotte's Web.* [7]

In the summer of 1905, while Fanny Waters was preparing her lawsuit against Samuel White et al., the White family first went to Great Pond, one of the Belgrade Lakes. The choice of this vacation spot had come about by chance. The two older White boys, Stanley and Albert, then fourteen and seventeen, had gone in July to visit friends in that region, and their father, either curious or worried, had followed them a week later, had fallen in love with the place and, moreover, seems to have thought that there Elwyn might find relief from hay fever. He instantly rented two cottages, returned to Mount Vernon, and organized a move that took all the Whites to Great Pond for August.

The move presented problems in logistics that Samuel White liked. It involved the transport of his oldest daughter, Marion, with her two-year-old son; of his other five children; of a servant named Walter; of Beppo, the Irish setter; and, of course, of his wife and himself. E. B. White remembers "the great importance of the trunks and . . . father's enormous authority in such matters." Mr. White reserved a drawing room and a sufficient number of Pullman-car berths on the fashionable Bar Harbor Express, which left Grand Central Station at "eight o'clock in the evening and arrived at Belgrade next morning at half past nine—a thirteen-and-a-half-hour run, a distance of four hundred and fifteen miles, a speed of thirty-one miles an hour." When the trip became an annual event, certain pleasures became part of the memorable routine. The family would get to Grand Central well before departure time and go "in a swarm to Mendel's restaurant for dinner, and Mr. Mendel himself . . . would come to our table to greet us and we would all jump to our feet, including Mother, at the excitement of being recognized and singled out in a great public dining hall by the proprietor himself." When the Bar Harbor Express roared under the overpass in Mount Vernon, Elwyn would look up from the observation platform to wave goodbye to Billy Denman and Freddie Schuler, who were waving from the railing of the overpass.[8]

From the station in Belgrade the family and the trunks rode ten miles in a farm wagon to the two camps, named "Happy Days" and (for the two older boys) "Alstan." As the years passed and the children married, the undertaking became somewhat less elaborate and the Whites rented only one cottage, called "Rocky Shore Camp." One summer Freddie Schuler came to Belgrade, after Elwyn had prepared for him a brochure describing "Belgrade Lake and Snug Harbor Camps," complete with pasted-in snapshots for illustrations and a dedication reading: "This pamphlet was compiled by Elwyn B. White—It is respectfully dedicated to Mr. Frederick Schuler for his personal use."[9]

An important part of vacation on the lake was boating. All his life, boats have fascinated E. B. White and have been exciting symbols of freedom. He remembers vividly the building of the first boat that interested him. One winter, when he was still very young, Albert persuaded their father to let him and Stanley build a motorboat that could be taken to Maine the following summer. Mr. White bought the blueprints for a sixteen-foot launch, together with precut frame and hardware, and when the job proved too much for the boys, he called in a boat-builder from Long Island Sound to show them how to trim the deck, fit the combing, and caulk the seams. When the hull was finished, a serviceman installed a one-cylinder, three-horsepower Palmer motor, and set the propeller shaft and stuffing-box. The boys name her Jessie, "after Mother, who couldn't swim, and who hated and feared the water." In August the boat went to Belgrade on a flatcar, and from Belgrade to Great Pond on a hayrack. White never forgot his early voyages in that boat:

Only through the indulgence of Providence did my family survive those crossings, for the *Jessie* was almost always in a seriously overloaded condition, gamely dragging her ensign in the wake and right on course for disaster. Father would be in his round white flannel hat, Mother shading herself with a parasol, Lillian in ribbons and bows, Albert and Stanley nursing the brave little engine. Leaving the Gleason shore, we would steer straight for Horse Point a mile away, give the Point a berth of only twelve feet to take advantage of the deep water, then veer in a westerly direction for the long two-mile hitch to Allen Point, passing between Wentworth Shoal and the Ledges, then on to the well-concealed mouth of Belgrade Stream, which led to the Mills. At Bean's store, Father would treat us to a round of Moxie or birch beer, and we could feed the big bass that hung around the wharf and then head back across the lake, sometimes adding to the boat's already intolerable burden a case of Moxie —Father's favorite drink.[10]

Memories of summer on the lake recur in White's writing. They are charged with remembered love and are full of detail. Shortly after his parents died White made a lonely pilgrimage to Great Pond. From there he wrote Stanley a letter with the motif "things don't change much":

On rainy days swallows come and dip water, and the camps are cold. When the wind swings into the north, the blow comes. It comes suddenly, and you know a change has come over things, instinctively. Next day you will see a little maple, flaming red, all alone in a bog. It's cold and fearsome by the lake. The wind still holds strong into the second morning, and white caps are as thick as whiskers.

When you get back on the road, away from the lake, the road lies warm and yellow, and you hear the wind fussing in the treetops behind you and you don't care. The rocks in the stream behind the Salmon Lake House are colored red and colored green, where the boats have scraped them under water. The clothesline behind Walter Gleason's house is flapping with white wash. . . . There's a house on a hill where a lady lived that used to keep cats. Along the road the apples are little and yellow and sweet. Puddles dry in the sun, and the mud cakes, and yellow butterflies diddle in the new mud. Cow trails lead up slopes through juniper beds and thistles and grey rocks, and below you the lake hangs blue and clear, and you see the islands plain. Sometimes a farm dog barks. . . . Things don't change much. I thought somebody ought to know.[11]

Stanley was the right, perhaps the only, person to address this report to. No one else would have understood all its allusions or responded to all its images. What's more, now that their father was dead, White would remember how much as a kid he had learned from his brother. It was Stanley who had first taught him to see the fauna and flora of Maine, as well as other things that his father had been too old or too preoccupied to teach him. Stanley loved to learn and loved to teach and eventually became a voluble, enthusiastic, and distinguished professor of landscape architecture. Sixty years after Elwyn had been his pupil, his by then famous brother paid him this tribute:

Stan taught me to read when I was in kindergarten and I could read fairly fluently when I entered the first grade—an accomplishment my classmates found annoying. I'm not sure my teacher, Miss Hackett, thought much of it, either. Stan's method of teaching me was to hand me a copy of the *New York Times* and show me how to sound the syllables. He assured me there was nothing to learning to read—a simple matter. He imparted information as casually as a tree drops its leaves in the fall. He taught me the harmonic circle on the pianoforte. He gave me haphazard lessons in the laws of physics: centrifugal force, momentum, inertia, gravity, surface tension, and illustrated everything in a clowning way. He taught me to paddle a canoe so that it would proceed on a straight course instead of a series of zigzags. He showed me how to hold the scissors for trimming the fingernails of my right hand. He showed me how to handle a jackknife without cutting myself. Hardly a day passes in my life without my performing some act that reminds me of something I learned from Bunny. He was called Bunny because he wiggled his nose like a rabbit.[12]

In the early years of their Augusts in Maine, Bunny and En were much together, and among other branches of biology that Bunny introduced "the kid" to was what he liked to call "testudology," or the knowledge of turtles and tortoises. Stanley reinforced his brother's passion for observing animal behavior. By the time Elwyn was twelve, however, Stanley had graduated from college and had left home; for the rest of his life Stanley saw little of the brother he loved and greatly admired.

Observing the natural world and learning interesting facts about it were not the only means of escape Elwyn White found from loneliness, boredom, and fear; writing, from a very early age, fascinated him and reassured him. He soon discovered that by stringing words together in the right way he could express clearly and interestingly what he saw, heard, felt, and thought, and end up with a joyful feeling of achievement. He remembers, "really quite distinctly, looking a sheet of paper square in the eyes when [he] was seven or eight years old and thinking 'This is where I belong, this is it.' "13

In the earliest extant sample of White's prose, a letter to his brother written at the age of nine, Elwyn not only expressed his pleasure in writing, but touched on some of the same topics that were to preoccupy him for the rest of his life:

Dear Albert,
. . . Yesterday I received a letter from Kezzie [Elwyn's English nursemaid, now married, who had named her first child Elwyn]. She says Elwyn her little boy don't like Sunday school. One day Kezzie asked him why he didn't and he answered that he s'posed he'd never been brought up that way.

To-day the big Albany day-boat "New York" was into the pier being repaired when it caught on fire and burned up. The paper does not say whether or not anyone was killed.

I wrote a poem about a little mouse Sunday. It is on the next page.

I am sorry I wrote that poem because I am trying to catch a mouse and that won't encourage them, will it? It isn't a very nice day and I've got a cold so I didn't go to school. Mama bought me a tennis ball and if I be very careful can I use your racket? Lil just heard now while I'm writing this letter that Philis Goodwin died. They wouldn't have a doctor and so you see. Pa bought me a new book of music. I am also composing pieces too. There isn't much more to say except we are all well,

Lovingly
Elwyn

P. S. Write soon if you can.14

White's long and interesting literary association with mice began early. In the spring of 1909 he won a prize from the *Woman's Home Companion* for a poem about a mouse. Throughout his life he has also had a good deal to do with medicine, which Phillis Goodwin's Christian Scientist family so imprudently shunned. And he has played the piano as a skillful amateur all his life and "composed" other "pieces."

Elwyn won his second literary prize (a silver badge) when he was eleven and his third (a gold badge) when he was fourteen. They were awarded by *St. Nicholas Magazine,* a popular monthly for young readers. His contributions, both prose, were published in the department of the magazine devoted to the work of members of the "St. Nicholas League," a band of aspiring artists under nineteen years old, whom White remembered years later as "an industrious and fiendishly competitive band of tots; and if some of us, in the intervening years of careless living, have lost or mislaid our silver badge, we still remember the day it came in the mail: the intensity of victory, the sweetness of young fame, a pubescent moment." One of his friends gave him a tip that helped him win his first medal:

> It was a buddy of mine two houses up the block, an observant child named E. Barrett Brady, wise in the ways of the world, who put me on to kindness-to-animals in its relation to winning a silver or a gold badge. Barrett said it was worth while to put plenty of it in. As I look through the back numbers and examine my own published works, I detect running through them an amazing note of friendliness toward dumb creatures, an almost virulent sympathy for dogs, cats, horses, bears, toads, and robins. I was kind to animals in all sorts of weather almost every month for three or four years. The results were satisfactory.

White's prizewinners displayed the clarity and conciseness that have always distinguished his style. Here is the first of them (his first published work), written when he was twelve:

> I awoke one morning in my little shanty to find the ground covered with snow. It had fallen rapidly during the night and was about six inches deep.
>
> I dressed, ate a good breakfast, did some of the camp chores, and set about taking down my snow-shoes and preparing them for wintry weather. Soon I heard a short yelp which reminded me that Don, my pointer, had been left hungry. I gave him some bones and a few biscuits. Then, pulling on my heavy overcoat and buckling the snow-shoes on my feet, we started out in the frosty morning air to pay the forest a visit.
>
> Such a morning! There was a frosty nip to the air that gave life to everybody and everything. Don was so overjoyed at the prospect of a walk that he danced and capered about as if he was mad. Jack Frost was busy for fair! My nose and ears were victims of his teeth.
>
> After a small stretch of smooth ground had been covered we entered the forest.

All the trees wore a new fur coat, pure white, and the pines and evergreens were laden with pearl. Every living creature seemed happy. Squirrels frisked among the branches, chattering because we trespassed on their property. Once in a while we caught an occasional glimpse of a little ball of fur among the fern, which meant that br'er rabbit was out on this cold morning. A few straggling quails were heard piping their shrill little notes as they flew overhead.

. All these harmless little wood creatures were noticed by Don and he wanted to be after them, but I objected to harming God's innocent little folk when He had given the world such a bright, cheery morning to enjoy.[15]

"This precocious anticipation of an editor's needs," White wrote, "is a sad and revealing chapter in my life; I was after results, apparently, and was not writing, or drawing, for Art's own sake. Still, the League motto was 'Live to learn and learn to live.' "[16] And three years later, when he won the gold medal, it was with an attempt to tell an exciting story, free from moralizing. "A True Dog Story" tells how the narrator, his two brothers, and their father, out for a walk one morning in Maine, were saved from a herd of "menacingly" advancing steers by Beppo, their "large Irish setter, with a beautiful red coat, and a loveable disposition." Safely over the stone wall of the hilltop pasture, the frightened people looked back and "saw the whole herd standing on the brow of the hill, with a little ball of red racing madly up and down in front of them."[17]

Not long after eight-year-old Elwyn had discovered that "looking a sheet of paper square in the eyes" made him know where he belonged, he began to keep a journal in which he made daily entries for the next twenty years. Some of the entries he made during the early years of his journal-keeping found their way into *The Trumpet of the Swan,* where they are attributed to an eleven-year-old boy named Sam. Sam's concerns were Elwyn's. He worried about how to be honest with his father and still preserve his privacy. He wondered about such puzzling questions as "Why does a fox bark?" and "How does a bird know how to build a nest?" and often ended his entries with "I wonder what I'm going to be when I grow up?"[18]

The decision to keep a journal, to write something every day, may have been prompted by his ambition to become a writer, to move towards a way of life different from that of his father, whom he had seen tied down and harried by business. As a child he sang a hymn that "advised" him to "Work for the night is coming, when man's work is done," but he soon decided that the advice was not meant for him:

When I was thirteen . . . I made a conscious effort to drop out of the race against night, knowing that for me there could be no such thing, in the conventional sense, as retirement, knowing that whether night arrived soon or late it would find me still flirting with words and with trouble.[19]

ANY TEENAGE BOY in Mount Vernon, New York between 1913 and 1917 might have lived in a world much like that of Willie Baxter, the Hoosier hero of Booth Tarkington's *Seventeen,* published in 1916. But Elwyn White was subject to fears that did not trouble Willie. He was afraid of failure; and his successes were not enough to give him the self-confidence of more fortunate teenagers. Though he had good friends among his peers, could write better poems than his classmates, and could skate, swim, and canoe at least as well as any of them, he was afraid to speak to girls he liked, forgot his speech in a debate, and failed to make the track team. At parties he felt ill-at-ease. The first signs of hypochondria seem to have appeared during his adolescence. In one of White's essays, an adult who consults his doctor about his fears remembers the first time when, as a child, he had entered a doctor's office, "sneaking a look at the titles of the books—and the flush of fear, the shirt wet under the arms, the book on t.b., the sudden knowledge that he was in the advanced stages of consumption, the quick vision of the hemorrhage."[20]

What White remembers best about high school is "getting to and fro, which was on my bicycle"; "the names of a few girls to whom I was attracted"; and the poetry readings of Miss Bertha Brown, a young Canadian teacher who, according to Stanley, had "a silver-toned voice and blue eyes," and with whom "all the boys fell in love." "When she read poetry," White said, "it came alive." But she did not, he said, educate him in literature. He was grateful to her because she made him want to continue his own experiments in writing.[21]

In the classrooms of Mount Vernon High School in 1914,

the desks were bolted to the floor. Whatever the furniture lacked in comfort and charm, you could be sure of one thing: it would be right there in the morning, in the exact same spot. Furthermore, the desk of one scholar was an integral part of the seat of the scholar in front of him. Communication was maintained by sticking your toe through the slot between desk and seat and boring into the behind of your friend or enemy. The ferocity of the thrust was tempered to the state of your relationship. Desks were of black cast iron and dark-brown wood, and every desk had a distinct character of its own— the nicks and challenges of former occupants defacing it and creating a link between generations, the cuneiform record of the interminable hours. Every desk had a pencil groove, a sunken inkwell surrounded by a Devil's half acre of blue-black stain, and a book well.[22]

Like grade school, high school was what separated one vacation from the next. After his freshman and sophomore years, there came, of course, Maine in August. But in 1916, in an effort to get free from his family and to be a more independent seventeen-year-old, he got a job as a caddy, and later as a rod-man for a surveyor, in Lake Placid, New York, where Stanley was working as a landscape architect. In some ways Lake Placid was a more interesting community than any other he had lived in. There he met Efrem Zimbalist and his wife, Alma Gluck, as well as Melvil Dewey, the country's leading librarian, and Marcella Sembrich of the Metropolitan Opera. Victor Herbert lived up the street from Stanley, and the White brothers liked that, though they never met the man whose songs they had played and sung together in the parlor on Summit Avenue. New freedom of movement, new natural beauties, the independence of a wage-earner, and residence in an interesting little colony with class made the summer of 1916 a good one for Elwyn.

In the fall he began his senior year at Mount Vernon High. He was assistant editor of *The Oracle,* the school literary magazine, and a member of a fraternity; he even played the part of an English butler in a Pinero farce. His contribution to the *Oracle* included two stories, an editorial urging nonintervention in the ongoing war in Europe, and a version of *Hiawatha* in which Hiawatha got married to avoid the draft. In November he wrote the editor of *The American Boy* objecting to an article about the trapping of fur-bearing animals for profit. He argued that trapping was cruel to animals and that such articles would encourage boys to trap who did not need the money they received for pelts. He recommended that *The American Boy* publish stories reflecting the humane attitudes of the stories of Ernest Thompson Seton. The editor's reply began: "I have read your very interesting and forceful letter."[23] When he was writing, he was often as happy and self-confident as he was when skating or canoeing. But, according to his own accounts, he was awkward socially:

In the matter of girls, I was different from most boys of my age. I admired girls a lot, but they terrified me. I did not feel that I possessed the peculiar gifts or accomplishments that girls liked in their male companions—the ability to dance, to play football, to cut up a bit in public, to smoke, and to make small talk. I couldn't do any of these things successfully, and seldom tried. Instead, I stuck with the accomplishments I was sure of: I rode my bicycle sitting backward on the handle bars, I made up poems, I played selections from "Aïda" on the piano. In winter, I tended goal in the hockey games on the frozen pond in the Dell. None of these tricks counted much with girls. In the four years I was in the Mount Vernon High School, I never went to a school dance and I never took

a girl to a drugstore for a soda or to the Westchester Playhouse or to Proctor's. I
wanted to do these things but did not have the nerve.

Of one girl who lived four or five doors up the street, he wrote:

> She was the girl I singled out, at one point, to be of special interest to me.
> Being of special interest to me involved practically nothing on a girl's part
> —it simply meant that she was under constant surveillance. On my own part,
> it meant that I suffered an astonishing disintegration when I walked by her
> house, from embarrassment, fright, and the knowledge that I was in enchanted
> territory.[24]

White later described taking this sixteen-year-old girl to a tea-dance at the
Plaza Hotel in New York. (She was Eileen Thomas, sister of J. Parnell
Thomas, who later became famous as the chairman of the House Un-
American Activities Committee.) On the appointed afternoon he walked
her to the Mount Vernon station, where they boarded the train for Grand
Central. The conversation on the way in was strained. From Forty-second
Street they rode the Fifth Avenue bus to the Plaza. There they found their
way to a table, ate cinnamon toast, drank tea, and watched the dancing.
At six they returned to the station, and by seven Elwyn had returned Eileen
to her front porch.

In the winter of 1916–17, however, Elwyn "singled out" another girl
"to be of special interest." Her name was Mildred Hesse, and during the
two following years when she was "under constant surveillance," she was
even less aware of Elwyn's interest than Eileen had been. She was a pretty,
popular, bright, and athletic junior at Mount Vernon High School who
was acquainted with Elwyn White as one of a group of high school
students who skated on Siwanoy Pond, on the outskirts of Mount Vernon,
at the end of the streetcar line. He was one of several boys who took turns
skating with her. Many years later White described the pure bliss of gliding
along with her on the ice:

> Her eyes were blue and her ankles were strong. Together we must have
> covered hundreds of miles, sometimes leaving the pond proper and gliding into
> the woods on narrow fingers of ice. We didn't talk much, never embraced,
> we just skated for the ecstasy of skating—a magical glide. After one of these
> sessions, I would go home and play *Liebestraum* on the [player piano], bathed
> in the splendor of perfect love and natural fatigue.[27]

In his journal for the winter and spring of 1917 White recorded some
of his feelings about Mildred; years later, in reading the entries he made

during that period, he was amused to discover that in the spring of 1917
he had been more preoccupied by his memories of skating with Mildred
than by the fact that America had just entered World War I.

> Springtime and wartime! Of the two, springtime clearly took precedence.
> I was in love. Not so much actively as retrospectively. The memory of winter
> twilights when the air grew still and the pond cracked and creaked under our
> skates, was enough to sustain me; and the way the trails of ice led off into the
> woods, and the little fires burning along the shore. It was enough, that spring,
> to remember what a girl's hand felt like, suddenly ungloved in winter. I never
> tried to pursue the acquaintanceship off the pond. Without ice and skates, there
> seemed no reason for her existence. Lying on my back on the settee in the hall,
> I listened to Liszt on the pianola.[26]

In the fall of 1917, when he packed to go off to college, he took with
him the strip of bicycle tape which she and he had used to hang onto in
their "interminable circuit of the pond" the winter before. As late as
December 1918, when he was already a sophomore in college and home
for Christmas vacation, he wrote a poem in his journal about the girl of
Siwanoy Pond:

> The pines hang dark by a little pond
> Where the ice has formed in the night
> And the light in the west fades slowly out
> Like a bird in silent flight.
> The memory of the sun that's gone
> Is just the glow in the sky,
> And in the dusk beyond the trees
> A figure is skating by.

Commenting on this poem he had found in his old diary, White said:
"I was still in love. The great world war had come and gone. Parlez moi
d'amour."[27]

The memory of his love for the girl on the pond became the central
image of "Liebestraum," part V of "Zoo Revisited." In a discarded version
of this autobiographical poem he praised this "love known, but not once
spoken," because it "sought for nothing it did not have," a characteristic
he described in the final version as "Perfect in deed and wanting no
completion." "Liebestraum" is a memory of an innocent love, free from
all physical realities that would have made not only the love less "pure"
but the lover less free. In addition to images of ice (frozen pure water)

and snow-covered evergreens, the poet made metaphorically significant the early evening hours of winter when the wind had gone down, as well as the location of the pond, "where the town ended and the fields began," and its biological function as "cradle of frogs in the spring, home of the turtle." But though he was unable to make a good poem from these images, the ideas they implied formed the center of his nostalgic view of innocence —cool, calm, lovely, rural, at one with beneficent, fertile nature. Ponds and skating remained charged images for White for the rest of his life. Once he joined the two in a brief allusion to skating on a frog pond under a midwinter moon. He was "conscious of the promise of pollywogs under [his] runners, and [his] thoughts turn[ed] to seeds and the germinal prospect."[28]

During the spring and summer of 1917 his love for Mildred Hesse was not Elwyn White's only preoccupation. America's entry into the war made his future harder than ever to envision, and it forced him to make difficult decisions about what to do immediately. He did not want to enlist, though he thought about it. Perhaps he would join the American Ambulance Corps, since he would "rather save men than destroy them." If he waited till he was drafted, he could go to Cornell in the fall, as he had planned; but how should he spend his summer? He wanted to be independent ("My utter dependence galls me, and I am living the life of a slacker," he told his journal), but he did not know how to break away. His sense of desperate helplessness intensified his lack of faith in himself. He applied unsuccessfully for a job playing the piano at a resort in the Catskills. He planned canoe trips. He bought a Liberty Bond. Finally he decided not to enlist but to spend July working patriotically as a "Farm Cadet" on a farm in Long Island, and in August to go with his parents to Maine. He worried about his lack of purpose and direction.[29]

When he set out for Cornell in September, his self-confidence was not much higher than it had been on July 11, when he cried out to his journal: "My birthday! Eighteen, and still no future! I'd be more contented in prison, for there at least I would know precisely what I had to look forward to."[30]

William Hart, N. A. (1823–1894), E. B. White's maternal grandfather. He was "happy in his work—full of enthusiasm, arising in the morning with eagerness and retiring at night with reluctance."

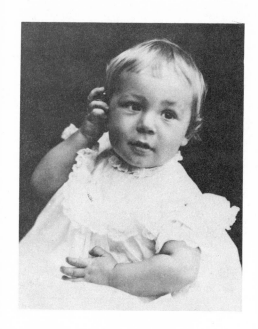

LEFT. *Elwyn White at nine months. "It seems highly unlikely to me that I have unconscious memories of unsatisfied hunger."*

BELOW. *"I played piano, picked at the mandolin, and at one point acquired a three-quarter size cello and took lessons. But I failed to develop musical curiosity . . . and was content to make a noise, whether ragtime or schmalz or Czerny."*

OPPOSITE ABOVE. *101 Summit Avenue, Mount Vernon, New York. The stable faced on Sidney Avenue. "Our big house . . . was my castle. From it I emerged to do battle, and into it I retreated when I was frightened or in trouble." The identities of the figures in the foreground are unknown.*

OPPOSITE BELOW. *Family portrait, 1899. Top row, l. to r. Marion, Albert. Middle row: Jessie, Elwyn, Samuel, Clara. Front row: Stanley, Lillian. "We were a large family and were a kingdom unto ourselves."*

Lillian and Elwyn about 1904.

Studio portrait of Elwyn (note fountain pen) and his mother, who was "loving, hard-working, and retiring."

OPPOSITE. *Elwyn and Stanley, Belgrade, Maine, 1910. Elwyn in the bow, and ELWYN on the bow.*

OPPOSITE. *Elwyn at the controls of his Flexible Flyer, and Lillian as passenger—both impatient with the photographer, their father, a perfectionist.*

Elwyn and his father, about 1914, probably at Camden, South Carolina. "My father was formal, conservative, successful, hard-working, and worried."

Cover and page 2 of a pamphlet made about 1914 for Elwyn's friend Freddie Schuler, who lived across the street in Mount Vernon. Art work, copy, layout, and publication by Elwyn B. White. In the illustration on page 2, the man in the white shirt is Samuel White.

Belgrade Lake

Maine is one of the most beautiful states in the Union, and Belgrade is one of the most beautiful of the Lakes of Maine.

This wonderful lake is five miles wide, and about ten miles long, with many coves, points and islands. It is one

②

resorts of fishermen; for bass, perch, chub, and pickerel are very plentiful.

The beauty of the surrounding country makes tramping a pleasure, and the well packed country roads are fine for bicycling and horse back riding.

The lake is large enough to make the conditions

of a series of lakes, which are connected with each other by little streams. One of these streams is several miles long and deep enough so that it affords an opportunity for a fine all-day canoe trip.

All the lakes are favorite

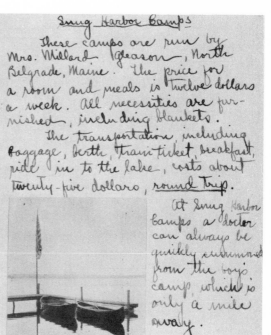

③

④

Pages 3 and 4.

Pages 5 and 6. Elwyn is at the helm of Jessie in the illustration on page 5.

Snug Harbor Camps

These camps are run by Mrs. Millard Gleason, North Belgrade, Maine. The price for a room and meals is twelve dollars a week. All necessities are furnished, including blankets.

The transportation, including baggage, berth, train ticket, breakfast, ride in to the lake, costs about twenty-five dollars, round trip.

At Snug Harbor Camps a doctor can always be quickly summoned from the boy's camp, which is only a mile away.

ideal for all kinds of small boats. The bathing also is a feature, for the deep grow very warm at noon time and make a good swim feel fine.

⑤

⑥

Cornell and Lake Cayuga, about 1914. "A considerable portion of Cornell's power and magic originates from the lake, the hill, the sky above Tompkins County. . . . God Almighty had a lot to do with the success of Ezra's idea—good enough idea into the bargain."

Professor Bristow Adams in his den, "the Navajo-Balinese-walrus room." "In his home I felt a confirmation of my aspirations, a sympathy for my prejudices. I felt encouraged."

Hann Purcell T. Doremus Gillies Thornhill Peel Calvert
Salmon Dietric Teed Bumstead White Taylor Galbreath Joyce
Adams Hoar Stabler Lobrano Gray Hearn Laning

Kappa Nu Chapter of Phi Gamma Delta, 1921. Brothers White, Galbreath, Adams, and Lobrano later shared an apartment in Greenwich Village. "My memory of the presidency [of Phi Gamma Delta] is the sadness of Sunday nights, the foul musty robe, the dim lights, the childish ritual."

Professor William Strunk, Jr., about 1921. "A memorable man, friendly and funny."

Gustave S. Lobrano, 1922. "The nicest guy we ever met in all our life was in the travel business." "Gus had literary tastes and aspirations, a humorous mind, and was great company."

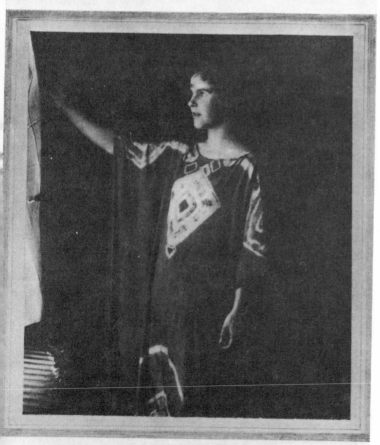

ALICE BIRCHFIELD
Whose simple piquancy adds charm to many a Dramatic Club presentation

Alice Burchfield, 1922. The frontispiece of the "Vanity Fair Issue" of The Cornell Era, *vol. 54, no. 5 (1922), whose editor misspelled Alice's name.*

Camp Otter, Dorset, Ontario, 1921. Note White's first moustache. He is the fourth from the left.

*Andy White
in Seattle, 1923.*

Howard Cushman in Hotspur, in Montana, 1922. "The Model T was not a fussy car. It sprang cheerfully towards any stretch of wasteland whether there was a noticeable road underfoot or not. It had clearance, it had guts, and it enjoyed wonderful health."

CHAPTER III

Cornell

1 9 1 7 — 1 9 2 1

"I'd send my son to Cornell . . . because Will Strunk, Jr. is there, who first hoped to graft me on the tree of knowledge by emphasizing the sanctity of an English sentence. . . . I'd send him there to walk up Six Mile Creek in the early wetness of a recalcitrant Spring."

E.B. WHITE ENTERED CORNELL IN THE FALL OF 1917. His first day on campus was almost his last. Years later he recalled:

I had arrived a few days before the opening of college, to take a scholarship exam. In Morrill Hall I stood waiting in a long line to get an application form, but when I reached the desk where I thought the form was, I reached over and picked up the wrong thing. I was instantly challenged by a man I had never seen before, who turned out to be the registrar. Mr. Hoy coiled and sprang. He roared and railed, called me a thief, and told me to get out and stay out. I was paralyzed with fright, unable to speak, and could hardly believe that it wasn't all a dream. I left the building, went back to my room in Sheldon Court, lay down, and bawled. When I got through, I packed, and prepared to leave Ithaca.[1]

But he changed his mind, unpacked, wrote "Davey" Hoy a note of explanation and apology, and the next day received a reassuring reply. He took the exam and a few days later heard that he had won a scholarship worth six hundred dollars. Since he had already won a Regents Scholarship of four hundred dollars, he entered Cornell financially well ahead. Tuition was then only one hundred dollars a year, and being, in his own words, "a well-heeled little customer" anyway, he actually was not in need of aid.

Sheldon Court, the privately-owned dormitory to which he had been assigned, was off-campus, in noisy Collegetown. The single room he had requested turned out to be "an incredible cell, shaped like a wedge of pie and about the size of a broom closet," and after five days of misery he moved into a conventionally shaped room with a high ceiling and a window looking out over Lake Cayuga, in a new dormitory on the campus.[2]

With his own ability and his father's means Elwyn White could have attended any college or university in the country, but since boyhood he had had his heart set on Cornell, where his brothers, Stanley and Albert, had preceded him. Even if he had seriously considered other possibilities he might still have decided that Cornell was the best place for him. It was situated in the Finger Lakes region of upstate New York, a place of great natural beauty. The university sat high on a hill looking north up the long narrow lake, and west and south towards hills of woodland and cultivated fields, whose rural patterns and seasonally changing colors delighted the eye. Cornell was also a relatively large university, and the size of its community offered some of the virtues of city life that appealed to White —the "queer prizes" of "the gift of loneliness and the gift of privacy" that he later learned to cherish when he lived in New York City.[3] Cornell was less uncomfortably elitist, less discriminatory, less homogeneous than Harvard, Yale, or Princeton. It was coeducational. It had no religious affiliations (though it had a nonsectarian chapel, in whose choir White sang). It offered its students unusual freedom to make their own choices. When Ezra Cornell had founded it in 1864, he said that it was to be "an institution where any student could find instruction in any subject," and its first president, Andrew D. White, an historian, had seen to it that the utilitarian aims of its founder did not dominate the traditional aims of a liberal education. Cornell students were offered courses in theory as well as practice, in science as well as technology, in the humanities as well as in the performing arts; and the university's loose federation of schools of agriculture, engineering, architecture, arts and sciences, law, and medicine helped make Cornell an intellectually open society. Its educational philosophy was not doctrinaire; its characteristic attitude was skeptical. For someone more interested in educating himself than in taking courses, Cornell was an almost ideal community. For the son of Samuel White, from Mount Vernon, New York, Cornell was to be both reassuring and enlightening. Insecure as he was in some respects, Elwyn needed the freedom it offered.

In a nostalgic essay written twenty years after he graduated, White praised his alma mater chiefly for its location and its students. He remembered that "the most romantic journey" of his life was the last part of the train ride from New York to Ithaca, on a spur line of the Delaware, Lackawanna, and Western Railroad, "rolling along with the late afternoon through Catatonk, Candor, Willseyville, Caroline, where September lies curled up asleep in every pasture and life lies curled up in the towers at the end of the line." He remembered that Cornell students were of "both sexes, all colors, all beliefs," and that among his acquaintances were "two men from Hawaii, a girl from Johannesburg, a Cuban, a Turk, an Englishman from India, a Negro from New York, two farmers, three Swedes, a Quaker, five Southerners, a reindeer butcher, a second lieutenant, a Christian Scientist, a retired dancer, a motorcyclist, a man who had known Theda Bara, three gnomes, and a lutist."[4]

When Elwyn turned eighteen, in July 1917, he did not weigh enough to pass the physical examination required of American men who offered to enlist in the army. So when he enrolled at Cornell in September, he did not feel, as some of his classmates did, that he had been unpatriotic to choose to go to college at a time when posters everywhere said, "Uncle Sam wants YOU!" But like most young men six months after America had declared war on Germany, he was at least distracted by the uncertainty of his immediate future. The historian of the Cornell class of 1921, E. B. White, writing for the yearbook in his senior year, remembered how it felt to be a student in the fall of 1917:

> 1921 was the first class to enter Cornell during wartime. Every man that entered had made a decision—he entered only after deciding that he would be more useful, for one reason or another, in college than in the field. To the casual observer this decision savored of the unpatriotic. . . . The explanation that a man could be of service to the nation by remaining in college and completing his course was plausible but not impressive. . . . [1917–18] was a trying year: men studied with one eye on their book and the other on the armed forces of the nation. . . .
>
> The whole atmosphere at Ithaca was military. The technical colleges were offering special war courses. Ithaca was full of cadets training at the Aviation School in the New Armory. Every day came new reports of the sacrifices and heroisms of Cornell men in the fields of battle.[5]

The pattern of undergraduate life, however, did not significantly change until the second semester of the 1917–18 academic year. In September, a few weeks after the first semester had opened, the traditional fraternity "rushing" began. When White was invited to join Phi Gamma Delta, he asked the advice of his sister Lillian, then a student at Vassar. Lillian's reply, urging him to accept the invitation, reveals her awareness of some of his weaknesses as well as some of his solid virtues:

> For Heaven's sake *don't be scared.* . . . You say that you don't know whether to join or not because it seems like pulling such an awful bluff and that you would be continually trying to be what you weren't etc. That is absolutely foolish!! You are just like everyone else underneath only you haven't had enough practice in bringing it out to the surface. This is the very thing that you need. . . .
> . . . Have confidence in yourself. You know that you have a much-to-be-desired brain, that you have fine instincts, that you have a sense of humor and a million other things that most boys want. . . .
> Wear decent clothes. Oh! by the way! I have just learned that people who only take cold showers *never* get themselves clean—you have to take two or three hot soaks and scrub hard with soap. Now will you be clean? And don't call a fraternity a "frat." It's small town stuff. I await developments.
>
> Lill

He pledged Phi Gamma Delta, whose newly acquired house stood high above Fall Creek gorge on the edge of a wooded area thick with evergreens that smelled like the hemlocks and firs of Maine. The fraternity had a good reputation, and several of its members were on the staff of the student newspaper, the *Cornell Daily Sun,* for which he was already a freshman reporter. Elwyn had made a good start. Such good fortune did little, however, to reduce the insecurity and anxieties he had endured since childhood. His journal entry for October 13 read: "My English prof said the other day that bashfulness was a form of vanity, the only difference being that vanity is the tendency to overestimate your worth, and bashfulness to underestimate it; both arising from the overindulgence of self-consciousness. The days are getting colder." And on November 21 he wrote in his journal: "I've been feeling sick for the past week and I think I must have consumption. If I have, I will leave college and travel for my health."[6]

In his freshman year Elwyn took two semesters of English and Spanish, and one semester each of chemistry, music, physiology, and geology. It was not a heavy load; and it became lighter when he was exempted from the requirement of daily themes in freshman English. Even so, he completed the work for only three courses in his first semester, and made a C in geology and a D in English in his second semester. It was not an impressive start for a scholarship winner. From the beginning he was more interested in writing for the *Sun* than he was in studying for his classes.

The academic year ended in May, six weeks earlier than usual, in order to free students for work in war industries. White, however, worked only in the early part of the summer—and not in a war industry but in the credit department of his father's company. In July he bought a second-hand Oldsmobile convertible, a gesture that one of his fraternity brothers, working in a munitions factory in Virginia and about to enlist in the army, found questionable.

The month of August he spent with his parents and his sister Lillian at a resort hotel in Bellport, Long Island. There, his parents hoped, Lillian would meet "some nice young men"; and Lillian hoped, among other things, that her now–not-so-little brother would lose some of his shyness with girls—might at least learn to dance. But there were few young men; and Lillian succeeded only in introducing Elwyn to a girl named Adelaide, with whom he swam and sailed, but whom he felt sure he was not going to marry because she was "too predictable." "The sea washed over me," he wrote twenty years later, "the sun struck down, the wind blew at me, in an attempt to dispel the fearful mists of indecision." His state of mind at that time is suggested in the notes he made for an autobiographical poem:

> uncertainty about war, and whether to go back to school or war, enormous vitality and vitalness of life at that time, all heading toward, pointing at, getting on toward SOMETHING, some point, some thing—and like the vital feeling in his body after salt bathing in surf, when lying in the sun naked in the little men's court at beach.
>> all pointing up toward:
>>> War, school, earning
>>> living, sex expression,
>>> marriage.
> Ponds with duckweed—flower gardens, hollyhocks, coreopsis, how the sumac trees looked, the pale sinewy trunks tropical looking; sailing by moonlight, hitting the stakes, snarl of catboats at Old inlet when wind shifted during bathing hour.
> Girl letting straps down.
> People, guests of hotel, all seemed dead too—had passed magical point.
> Adelaide's breasts, first view he had had, when leaned forward in catboat and dress had pulled away—
> What were the questions in those days? Life, love, war, girls—girls are love.
> Love is girls and girls are breasts, breasts is Love is war is life.[7]

During the whole summer his indecision and a nagging sense of purposelessness plagued him. He asked a brother-in-law in Washington to help him get into the navy, but before his letter arrived all enlistments were stopped in anticipation of universal conscription. On September 12, "with thirteen million other Americans," White registered for the draft.

Before returning to Ithaca for his sophomore year, White learned that the *Cornell Daily Sun* would suspend publication for the duration of the war because too many members of its staff had gone into the armed forces. Upon his arrival, he enlisted in the Student Army Training Corps. The university curriculum had been changed; his new courses were advanced algebra, trigonometry, military law, "War Aims," and drill. Within a month he was made a corporal. Thirty years later one of the men in his squad remembered Corporal White walking home alone on a drizzly afternoon:

> Knees akimbo, as always—especially in tight putees—no goose step. You had original knee action; yours was the plod of the mental man—a thought per step. The drip off your campaign hat and your nose detracted not a whit from the individuality of your bearing. As your moist clothes sagged you were wondering, no doubt—as we all did—why 1918 uniforms draped rather than fitted.[8]

"The enemy," White remembered, "turned out to be an epidemic of the flu—which I met stoically with a bag of licorice drops. I can't remember who told me that licorice fended off flu germs, but he was right."[9] Within a month after the armistice was declared, in November 1918, all the cadets were mustered out. After Christmas vacation students returned to the prewar academic curriculum. White moved into his fraternity house, with his mongrel dog named Mutt.

The university was slow to return to normal life, but fortunately for White the *Sun* soon resumed publication, and in late spring he was one of four members of his class elected to its board of editors. During his freshman year, the *Sun* editors had been impressed by the talent of "Andy" White (he had been so nicknamed after President Andrew D. White). He wrote clear, accurate news stories and brief, informative headlines. His interpretive pieces drew letters of praise from members of the faculty, and his poems and one-liners were funnier than anything anyone else could produce. Though only a few members of the board knew him by sight, and fewer still knew him personally, he won his place easily, because everyone on the board was convinced that he was a better writer than any of his competitors, including a classmate named Allison Danzig, who later became a distinguished sportswriter for the *New York Times*.[10]

In his junior year Andy White lived a very full and interesting life. He was elected editor-in-chief of the *Sun*—probably the high point of his college career. He was also elected president of his fraternity. In his junior year he took Professor William Strunk's famous course, called "English

8." In his junior year he became a "regular" at the weekly "Monday nights" at the house of Professor Bristow Adams, and he became a member of the Manuscript Club, which met monthly at the house of Professor Martin Sampson. He took a European history course with Professor George Lincoln Burr. Among all the elements of his education at Cornell, those that most influenced his later life were his career on the *Sun* and his association with Professors Adams, Burr, Sampson, and Strunk.

Strunk opened fewer windows on the world than the others, but Andy liked his sense of humor and admired his enthusiastic teaching. "English 8" was an advanced course in writing, and though it was an easy course for Andy (in its two semesters he earned two of the A's he made at Cornell), it taught him precepts he never forgot and may have strengthened his hope to be a writer. Strunk was, in White's words, a "memorable man, friendly and funny," who "wielded a kindly lash." White remembered vividly his

> puckish face . . . his short hair parted neatly in the middle and combed down over his forehead, his eyes blinking incessantly behind steel-rimmed spectacles as though he had just emerged into strong light, his lips nibbling each other like nervous horses, his smile shuttling to and fro under a carefully edged mustache.

Strunk's ideas about the "sanctity of the English sentence" were clear and simple. He "loved the clear, the brief, the bold. . . . He scorned the vague, the tame, the colorless, the irresolute. He felt it was worse to be irresolute than to be wrong." His classes used a privately printed forty-three-page pamphlet called *The Elements of Style,* consisting of

> a short introduction, eight rules of usage, ten principles of composition, a few matters of form. . . . The rules and principles [were] in the form of direct commands, Sergeant Strunk snapping orders to his platoon. "Omit needless words!" cries the author on page 17, and into that imperative Will Strunk really put his heart and soul.[11]

Andy got to know Strunk informally at the meetings of the Manuscript Club, founded by Professor Sampson in 1909 for students and faculty who "wrote for the sake of writing" and who liked to read their work to fellow writers. Before Andy's time Morris Bishop and Frank Sullivan had been members. Like Strunk, Sampson was hardly a distinguished scholar, but he was a sensitive and widely read teacher with an infectious enthusiasm for literature. He was a handsome man, somewhat self-conscious about his

looks. When he read aloud in a classroom or at meetings of the Manuscript
Club, he performed. Morris Bishop remembered that in these performances
he would "turn his profile carefully, like John Barrymore." It was Sampson's pleasure in writing and in reading what he had written, as well as
his desire to encourage other amateur writers, that prompted him to lead,
and to be host to, the Manuscript Club for so many years. It met "on winter
Saturday nights" in Sampson's library. In his senior year White described
the club's activities in an article for the *Cornell Era,* an undergraduate
magazine:

> The Club meets at 9:30, listens to its own ebullitions, discusses them sometimes
> sharply, sometimes casually, refreshes itself lightly, lights up its pipe, meditates
> adequately before the fire, and departs after midnight. . . . Refreshments are
> shandygaff, crackers, and cheese—the proverbial meager diet of the pen pusher.
> . . . The Club is held together not by a written constitution but by the spirit
> of its members.
>
> Its traditions are few and simple. In a valedictory item for the budget this
> year, the founder wrote: "To be frank, to use one's brains, to write what is
> in one to write, and never to take oneself too damned seriously or too damned
> lightly—these are the only articles of our creed."[12]

According to Bishop, Sampson "especially loved courtly wit and satire,
the sharp and shining phrase, and he hated spiritual bombast. . . . He also
loved to encourage his juniors to follow in his path." His taste was, as
Bishop said on another occasion, for the antiromantic style of the nineties,
and he encouraged his followers to avoid the expression of excessive
emotion, to understate their feelings in witty or comic statements, and to
aim for the tone of world-weary, supercilious elegance, like that of *Smart
Set* magazine.

American college poets in 1920 were more likely to imitate Oscar Wilde
and William Ernest Henley than Shelley or Tennyson. The prosodic forms
popular among poets in Professor Sampson's group were the sonnet and
the elaborate stanzas of the ballade, rondeau, triolet, and villanelle—forms
popular forty years earlier in Oxford, where Wilde had enjoyed "days of
lyrical ardours and of studious sonnet-writing; days when one solemnly
sought to discover the proper temper in which a triolet should be written;
delightful days, in which I am glad to say, there was far more rhyme than
reason." In Ithaca, New York, in 1920, the young literati knew more of
Algernon Charles Swinburne and Henry Austin Dobson than of T. S.
Eliot, whose "Prufrock" had appeared in 1917, or of Ezra Pound, whose
poems had been appearing in little magazines for the past ten years. In this
academic insularity Cornell was not alone: the Harvard esthetes of 1920

were reading the *Yellow Book* and discussing the harmonies of Walter Pater and the rhythms of Aubrey Beardsley. Up-to-date undergraduate writers were more likely to read *The American Mercury* than *The Dial* or *The Little Review,* which at that very moment was serially publishing James Joyce's *Ulysses.* [13]

A stronger influence on Andy than Strunk or Sampson was Bristow Adams, then forty-five years old, a professor of journalism, in whose house on Fall Creek Drive and with whose family Andy once said he felt more at home than he did with his mother and father in Mount Vernon.[14] As a student at Stanford, Adams had been editor of the campus humor magazine, and between graduation and the time he moved to Ithaca he had been a writer for the U. S. Department of Conservation in Washington. His wife, Louella, had grown up in the West in a family of boys and knew how to be frank and friendly with college men without either losing their respect or reminding them of their mothers. In her vigor and relative youth, Ma Adams was the antithesis of Jessie White. She was practical, sharp, unsentimental, strong-willed, and, like her husband, a hearty laugher. She was also a handsome, attractive woman. She eventually became fond of Andy, who, she remembered, was "like a mouse until you got to know him. If he liked you, he was just as easy as anybody else." She thought Andy was "a wonderful musician, who played the piano for himself, not for other people." On one memorable day when Andy was lonely, he came over to her house and the two of them spent a long afternoon enjoying Gilbert and Sullivan. Andy played the piano and Mrs. Adams sang all the parts, with Andy "chipping in once in a while." On other occasions when he dropped in, it was just for a friendly chat. He used Mrs. Adams not "as a wailing wall," she said, "but as a friend." "He didn't want counseling from anybody." She liked him for many reasons, one being that though he took a strong dislike to some people (including some of his professors), he never criticized them.

Professor Adams invited students in his journalism classes to meet in his living room on Monday evenings after seven-thirty, to talk about anything they chose and to be refreshed by Mrs. Adams's cookies and cocoa. (Cocoa always made Andy slightly sick, but he drank it anyway.) The Monday-nighters included a fair number of the *Sun*'s staff-members. Occasionally a man brought a "co-ed" along, and from time to time a few independent women came by themselves, but the society was predominantly male. The talk was wide-ranging: "from the ethics of newspaper work to the oppression of Korea by the Japanese." Andy admired Adams for "his good humor and his sincerity," and was grateful for his "knack of treating a young man as a companion rather than an oddity." When Andy White walked back over the footbridge to his fraternity house across Fall Creek gorge at midnight, after an evening at the Adamses' house, he felt "all smoothed out and peaceful."[15]

Adams did not, any more than Strunk or Sampson, turn Andy into a reader. He did not give him a literary education, and no one at Cornell, it would seem, aroused in Andy such admiration for the great works of literary imagination as to make him aspire to become a great writer. White seems not to have been capable of the kind of ambition or self-confidence that F. Scott Fitzgerald expressed when, fresh out of Princeton, he said to Edmund Wilson, "I want to be one of the greatest writers who ever lived, don't you?"[16] To be sure, "the sanctity of the English sentence" is something few students discover, but a good literary education leads to other discoveries, wider in scope, among them the discovery that the works of great writers nourish the imagination and augment the wisdom of experience. Andy took courses under professors capable of giving such a literary education, but none seems to have succeeded with him. Bristow Adams encouraged Andy's inclination to be a journalist and strengthened his disposition to believe that there is more fun in the journey than in the journey's end. But neither he nor Strunk nor Sampson was the sort to open up to White the traditions in Western art and culture that were nourishing Pound and Joyce and Eliot, or to reveal the powers of mind and art that were enabling Frost and Stevens to find forms of expression that would "suffice," that would satisfy the needs of the greatest of contemporary artists. None of his teachers, it would seem, was able (if indeed any tried) to give White the confidence needed to aspire to greatness.

Only one Cornell professor, apparently, instilled in Andy White a conviction strong enough to influence him profoundly for the rest of his personal and professional life. That was George Lincoln Burr, an historian and a passionate man. White recalled vividly his experience in Burr's class:

> I wasn't particularly interested in the Middle Ages but I was trying to get an education and was willing to listen to almost anything. The professor [was] a little old gentleman named George Lincoln Burr. He had white hair, and we students used to see him trotting briskly across the campus carrying a big stack of thick books, taller than he was himself. For the first few days, his class in history seemed pretty much like any other college class. But as Professor Burr talked, something began to happen. Somehow I seemed to be transported into another century [and] I began living in the dark days when a few men who still called their souls free were struggling against tyrants and bigots, struggling to preserve what priceless shreds of knowledge and truth the world had at that time managed to scrape together. . . . My chance encounter with George Lincoln Burr was the greatest single thing that ever happened in my life, for he introduced me to a part of myself that I hadn't discovered. I saw, with blinding clarity, how vital it is for Man to live in a free society. The

experience enabled me to grow up almost overnight; it gave my thoughts and ambitions a focus. It caused me indirectly to pursue the kind of work which eventually enabled me to earn my living. But far more important than that, it gave me a principle of thought and of action for which I have tried to fight, and for which I shall gladly continue to fight the remainder of my life.[17]

Though Burr's influence was exerted mainly in the lecture hall, it carried, as sometimes happens, a stronger power and left a more lasting impression than did the personal support of a professor who compensated for his lack of scholarly achievements by his kindness, hospitality, and practical advice. Burr not only reinforced, or gave shape and direction to, Andy's liberal, humanistic convictions about the nature and value of freedom, he "indirectly" pointed him toward a profession in which he could, in his direct, simple, modest style, express those convictions.

When White was elected its editor-in-chief in the spring of 1920, the *Cornell Daily Sun* was one of only two daily college papers published in America. As Ithaca's only morning paper, it was read by nearly everyone in town. It subscribed to the A.P. wire service, and carried international and national news on its front page. Andy took seriously the considerable responsibilities of an editor-in-chief: to be true not only to the best traditions of journalism but to the best interests of his alma mater. He did not think of the paper as a guardian of student interests against the faculty or administration. In fact, he sometimes sounded as if he were above all three of those estates, giving students, faculty, and administration equally nonpartisan and judicious advice. He favored progress by evolution, compromise, and steady effort to reform without damaging traditional values and institutions. There was little of the youthful radical in Andy White.

This editor of the *Sun* thought of a college education as a practical preparation for a career, as well as a training of the mind and a liberating experience; and he understood and respected the demand that colleges should teach students "how to get results." When the dean warned of the dangers of utilitarian notions of education and made a plea for the love of learning for its own sake, Andy gave only qualified assent:

There is no dodging the fact that we live in an intensely material world and the men whose influence is most widely felt are those who are able to meet the world on its own footing. It takes a genius to ignore the material side of education and still leave his mark. And universities aim to develop men and not geniuses.[18]

Here and elsewhere in the editorials of the *Sun* the voice was that of the son of Samuel White, the friend of Bristow Adams, and the disciple

of Professor Burr—not that of a young man who might dare to hope that
there was a touch of genius in him. Among the many fears Andy suffered,
his fear of failure may have been the most debilitating one.

The last two months of White's editorship, February and March 1921,
were largely devoted to achieving a goal he had set in his "Statement of
Policy," published at the time he assumed the position in April 1920. The
goal was to restore some of the "self-government" students had lost during
the war. The first step towards such a restoration, he thought, would have to
be the establishment of a student-administered honor system for reporting
and punishing plagiarism. He wrote editorials on the proposal, moving
slowly at first and recognizing all the arguments against it. He admitted that
at some colleges it had failed, and that Cornell's recent, much-publicized
scandal of widespread cheating on a final examination suggested that its
students were not ready for such an idealistic scheme. But under the constant
prodding of the *Sun* a committee produced a plan for an honor system, and
the plan was finally approved by a student referendum. The proposal was
sent to the faculty, who approved it without a dissenting vote. Andy had
written thousands of words in the campaign, and its success, for which he
was largely responsible, must have been gratifying. The triumph came in
March, just before his term as editor ended. Four days after the faculty vote,
Andy wrote an editorial that tells much about how he felt now that he was
giving up the responsibilities of his editorship, as well as his fraternity
presidency, and many related committees and activities:

> Activity is wont to run riot. It gathers speed with its own momentum: with
> some students it becomes an obsession, out-doing right reason and completely
> withering the contemplative faculties of the mind. Activity is no end in itself
> —it is elemental and instrumental, but not final. It supplies a great interest in
> life. In the balance of things it has its opposite, passivity—equally vital. The
> man obsessed with activity loses his receptive powers: he cannot merely
> "enjoy."
> A man must live as he goes along. Otherwise when he finally comes to the
> point where he decides he is ready to live it, he will find that there is nothing
> left to live. To drown life in a whirl of activity is a folly from which students
> are not exempt.[19]

IN MARCH ANDY was not only tired and, perhaps, bored with his
work in and out of courses: he was beginning to feel other urges. One was
caused by spring, a season whose advent White has celebrated in writing
almost every year of his life. The day after his editorial on activity
appeared, he wrote one on spring.

IT'S COMING ON

Sooner or later we are forced to break down and confess to ourselves that
there is a significance in the queer smell of the air, in the piping noises in the
wet places below the slope, in the higher pitch of the roar in the gorges, in
the sight of small boys on roller skates. Sooner or later we must acknowledge
that the rawness of the wind and the wetness of the mist at nightfall are not
what they used to be. The rawness and the wetness are of a superior quality
—they are almost delicate. . . . Have spring without a struggle; for it's coming
on.[20]

It was spring, and Andy had found a girl. He began at once to sing of
her in a poem he read to the Manuscript Club. It ended:

> If I had time I'd fall in love,
>   Nor do I doubt
> With whom, you know, hi ho—nor do I doubt with whom
>   If I had time.[21]

The girl was Alice Burchfield, called "Burch," a very pretty, bright,
popular junior from Buffalo, New York. She had a happy and outgoing
temperament; her smile was almost a grin; her laugh was generous; her eyes
were lively and blue; her handshake was firm. She was an Alpha Phi and
a chemistry major, but the center of her life was the theater. She had played
the lead in several Dramatic Club productions under the direction of
Cornell's famous professor of drama and gifted director Alexander Drum-
mond. Two days after Andy announced the advent of spring, he saw her
play the part of Columbine in Edna St. Vincent Millay's *Aria da Capo.* She
attended the Adamses' Monday-night gatherings, often in the company of
her friend and fellow-actor James Sumner. She was a favorite of Professor
Adams, who had once, in a gesture of fun, "pinned" her with a little gold
pin he had won as an undergraduate at Stanford.

After spring vacation Andy discovered that he "had the time" to fall
in love—to go walking with Burch along Six Mile Creek and Fall Creek,
and to take her to the movies, and to ballgames. They saw a crew race on
Lake Cayuga from the privileged seats of a launch; and one evening they
watched the sky for falling stars, sitting in the bleachers of an empty
athletic field.

Andy began to write poems to her. Under the pseudonym "D'Annunzio" he published them in the *Sun,* where Burch would be sure to see
them, recognize the author, and get the message. In the first, he compared
her eyes to those of his faithful mongrel Mutt:

O OCULI

I now observe with some surprise
Some facts about the depth of eyes.
I knew a pair a while ago
I thought were deep as deep ones go;
A mongrel owned 'em, as it were,
A very ordinary cur.
With limpid gaze they followed me,
Expressing true caninity.

O oculi, O orbs of old,
Thy depth must still remain untold;
But I've been casting 'round until
I've found some that are deeper still.
One may, by using simple wiles,
Look down for miles and miles and miles
And still fall short. I must confess
The gol darn orbs are bottomless;
And must observe from sense of duty
Their depth surpasses not their beauty.

When I look from a turret tall,
I sometimes feel I'm apt to fall;
O Lord, how frail these earthly ties
When I look down this pair of eyes.[22]

Only six months before, "D'Annunzio" had sung a different sort of tune, a meditation in a trolley car, addressed to no one in particular:

I mused upon the girl who sat
And rambled on of this and that;
She differed not from others there;
She had, I thought, quite pleasing hair,
And surely it was no high treason
To think that there was no more reason
Why she should not—and not another—
Be my future children's mother.[23]

In the words of a popular song that Louis plays in *The Trumpet of the Swan,* "They say that falling in love is wonderful," and they are right. To fall in love with Alice Burchfield was, indeed, a wonderful thing to have happened to Andy. For the first time in his life the object of his love was not someone he could merely adore from a distance, but someone he could actually talk to, look into the eyes of, be close to. Andy was lucky that this happened to him before he left Cornell, lucky that this pretty, petite actress with a disarming openness was attracted by his sense of humor and was flattered by his attentions—the attentions of this "big man on the Hill" who nevertheless seemed a little scared of girls. He was lucky that she had the womanly maturity to encourage his friendship and to make him feel at ease in her presence. For the next two years she was to play the lead in the romantic comedy of Andy's imagination, and to be the subject of many of his poems.

When he left Cornell in June, Andy could, in fact, look back on four years of good luck. He had overcome his initial self-doubt; he had with-stood attacks of anxiety (including a chronic fear that the brakes would fail in the trolley he was riding up or down Ithaca's steep hill and over its deep gorges); he had gained distance from his family and outgrown Mount Vernon; he had formed something closely resembling new family ties with Professor and Mrs. Adams, and had found other friends, young and old, who had made him feel more self-confident than he had ever felt before. He had enjoyed his identification with the institution. He was proud of being a Cornellian, and it had given him pleasure to contribute, when he was still a junior, five hundred dollars to the university's endow-ment fund. Best of all, he had been a clear success as a newspaperman, and had even won the Arthur Brisbane Award for one of his editorials. He had become convinced that journalism was a high calling and that the country needed well-educated and responsible journalists. No profession, except that of an artist, appeared to him more valuable. Moreover, he had become attracted to the life of a journalist and editor. After putting the paper to bed and watching it through the press and seeing the bundles leave the office for their journey up the Hill, he had sometimes stretched out on the flat-bed press and slept till it was time to go to class. He didn't much care for routine reporting, but producing editorials, short features, articles, and poems that would be printed in the very next issue excited him—then and for years afterwards. He had also been successful in influencing public opinion and in fulfilling the responsibilities of executive offices, though of executive duties he had had enough to last him a lifetime.

Professor Sampson had offered to find him an instructorship in English at another university, but Andy knew he did not want to be a teacher. He had already become a journalist, and it must have been clear to him that, however he would have to earn his living, he would always be, among other things, a writer. At Cornell he had acquired skills that he would later develop and that eventually would make him a master of English prose. The most important aspect of his experience at Cornell, however, was not the training he received there but rather the nourishment he found in the physical and social climate of the place, and the reassurance he gained simply in the course of his daily life as an undergraduate.

In the spring of his junior year, Andy had toyed with the idea of making a trip across the continent to California and back during summer vacation; though in an editorial he had advised his readers, who were also wondering how they should spend the summer, to do something "directly or indirectly" productive. He himself finally accepted the offer of a job as a counselor at Camp Otter, near Dorset, Ontario, owned by the director of physical education at Cornell and staffed by other Cornellians. It was a memorable summer. After graduation in June 1921 Andy returned to Camp Otter for a second summer, bringing with him as a fellow counselor his friend Howard Cushman, editor of the Cornell humor magazine, *The Cornell Widow,* and member of the Manuscript Club. The job was perfect for Andy. The camp was "informal and unorganized, and specialized in canoe trips—usually two canoes, each containing a counselor and two boys."[24] White later used his memories of Camp Otter in his account of Louis the swan's stay at Camp Kookooskoos, "on a small lake, deep in the woods of Ontario," where Louis's friend Sam Beaver was a counselor:

> The camp consisted of a big log cabin where everybody ate, seven tents where the boys and the counselors slept, a dock out front, and a privy out back. The woods closed in all around, but there was a bare spot that had been made into a tennis court, and there were plenty of canoes in which to take trips to other lakes. There were about forty boys.

In the evenings round the campfire the boys "sang songs and toasted marshmallows and swatted mosquitoes. Sometimes you couldn't understand the words of a song because the boys sang with marshmallows in their mouths." Some of the comic episodes White ascribes to the time Louis stayed at the camp must have been ones White experienced at Camp Otter and remembered fifty years later. It is even more probable that Louis's rescue of a camper from drowning is a fictional transformation of an episode in which Andy and another counselor saved the life of a boy who became seriously ill on the third day of a canoe trip in the wilderness. They carried the boy back at night over four lakes and three portages. There is some of Andy in Louis as well as in Sam Beaver, and at Camp Otter Andy seems to have spent a good deal of time thinking of Alice, just as at Camp Kookooskoos Louis spent a good bit of time thinking of Serena, his beloved:

> He was terribly in love with Serena, and he often wondered what was happening to her. At night, he would look up at the stars and think about her.

In the late evening, when the big bullfrogs were calling *trooonk* across the still lake, he would think of Serena.[25]

In the last of several letters he wrote Alice Burchfield from Camp Otter, in late August, Andy asked her to go skating with him the following winter, and she accepted—"any night in February is fine." He had included a snapshot taken at camp that made him look, she thought, "half-starved and entirely neglected," and she asked her mother to invite him to come to her house for a good meal, if he phoned as he passed through Buffalo on his way home from camp. She herself would not be at home, having gone back to Ithaca to begin play rehearsals before the new school year began.[26]

When Andy stopped for a day or two in Ithaca on his way to Mount Vernon, he unsuccessfully tried to find a job that would keep him there for the next eight or ten months, during Alice's senior year. The evening of the day he left he walked with Burch to Percy Field, where, she remembered later, she saw her first falling star—at 9:26. Because it got so late that Andy might miss the night train for New York, Burch said that rather than allowing Andy to take her to her sorority house, she'd rather go with him to the Adamses' house, where he had to pick up his suitcase, and then wait with him for the streetcar that would take him to the railroad station. As he said goodbye to her at the trolley stop, he promised to write her as soon as he found a job.

CHAPTER IV

From Sea to
Shining Sea

1 9 2 1 – 1 9 2 2

*"Springtime in the heyday of the Model T
was a delirious season."*

A S SOON AS HE GOT HOME, ANDY BEGAN to look for a job in Manhattan. The first thing he saw was evidence of the widespread unemployment caused by the depression of 1920–21. He tried to be cheerful in his progress report to Mrs. Adams—cheerful and professional. He was an unemployed *writer*:

> There are four hundred thousand of me, and we sit on the park benches and develop a hungry, glassy stare. But I am coming along fairly well, having interviewed the managing editor of the *Post,* the assistant managing editor and the city editor of the *Sun,* the director of the Bureau of Publications of the N.Y. Edison Company. . . . Not to mention the thousands of intervening and short skirted secretaries. . . . New York is a wonderful city . . . but it makes wrecks of men. I see them on the benches—old grizzled men in dusty derbies, asleep in the sun, old broken souls snatching at candy wrappers because the tinfoil brings a few cents when you get enough of it. . . .[1]

When White put an ad in the "Positions Wanted" column of *Editor and Publisher* magazine, its editor was so impressed by the style of the ad that he called White in for an interview. He could not offer him a job, but he could, and did, write letters to the managing editors of the *New York Times,* the *Globe,* the *World,* and the *Evening Mail,* recommending E. B. White as "one of the ablest young fellows" he had met lately.[2] Among the editors who turned him down was Bruce Bliven of the *Globe,* who years later, when White was famous, remembered the occasion and said that in the light of White's achievements as an essayist, he was glad he hadn't hired him as a reporter.

After six days of hunting, and with the help of a former *Cornell Sun* editor, he landed a job with the United Press. Its offices in the Pulitzer Building were near those of several New York dailies where some of his Cornell friends worked. Within a week, however, he was complaining in a letter to Bristow Adams that the U.P. emphasized speed at the expense of accuracy, and within another he had written satirical verses on two evils of cheap journalism: sensational exploitation of human tragedy and indecent invasion of privacy. The verses were published over his initials in Christopher Morley's column, "The Bowling Green," in the *Evening Post* for October 15. A week later he quit, after failing his first assignment as a reporter. He had been sent to Valley Forge to cover the funeral of Senator Philander C. Knox, had taken the wrong train, and had arrived just in time to see the coffin lowered into the grave. His sense of failure was painful, but it was pleasantly mixed with his sense of relief at having regained his freedom. He did not really want to work (or write) for anyone but himself. If he was to be a reporter, he wanted to be free like Thoreau, who had described himself (transcendentally) as a reporter "trying to hear what was in the wind."

Years later, in a piece of fictionalized autobiography, White vividly described the sensations of a man who had left his office for the last time and descended to the lobby of the building where he worked, having just quit his first job in New York. He pictured the man standing in "a doorway in Park Row . . . late Saturday afternoon in the fall of the year . . . slowly eating Tokay grapes and spitting out the seeds":

> He was moodily eating the grapes by way of celebrating, in one inclusive ritual, the failure of his first major maneuver in life and the renewal of his liberty. His inability to cope with the requirements of the job was a stone in his stomach, to which he was now adding ripe grapes; but the sense that his movements were no longer circumscribed by the hands of a clock, the sense of the return of footlooseness, the sense of again being a reporter receiving only the vaguest and most mysterious assignments, was oxygen in his lungs. He stood there a long time, having nowhere in particular to go any more. An important doorway, he had always thought. He had never eaten a red grape since without tasting again the sweet tonic of rededication.[3]

The following week he was once more looking for work. He applied unsuccessfully to the *Greenwich* (Connecticut) *News and Graphic,* the *Mount Vernon Daily Argus,* and the *Grand Rapids* (Michigan) *Press.* Having been turned down by the managing editor of the *New York Times,* he went to see its publisher, Adolph Ochs, but at the interview could not bring himself to ask for a job. Within a few weeks, he was hired by a public relations man to write press releases and to edit the house-organ of a silk mill. He, or the job, lasted only a few weeks.

From his room in his parents' house on Mersereau Avenue, in Mount Vernon, Andy wrote fairly regularly to Alice Burchfield, who had begun to sign her letters "Alice," instead of "Burch." He closed his letters with "Very truly yours, Andy," and allowed himself nothing more sentimental than an allusion to "that night" at Cornell when they had seen a falling star. His letters contained mostly newsy or humorous accounts of his activities. Alice took her cue from his bantering tone but allowed herself to express concern about his disappointments and occasional "gloom." Theirs were not love letters.

In early October Alice asked Andy to come to Ithaca for the Cornell-Dartmouth game, but he answered that he would have to work that Saturday. Two weeks later when she announced that she might come to New York for the Columbia game, Andy's response was not enthusiastic. She and Andy finally managed to make a date for the last game of the season (Cornell vs. Pennsylvania), on Thanksgiving Day, in Philadelphia. On the Monday preceding Thanksgiving a case of the grippe forced Alice to go to the University infirmary, but she got herself out in time to catch the Wednesday-night train for Philadelphia. The game took place in pouring rain, and the meeting between Alice and Andy was awkward and frustrating. Andy described it in a poem he promised Alice he would write for her and then somewhat ungallantly entitled "Payment of Debt":

> One squirrel coat—one dented hat
> One lady and one fella:
> Two minds with but a single thought,
> Two hearts neath one umbrella.
>
> Ten hundred thousand drips of rain
> One field reduced to jelly:
> Two minds with but a single thought
> Two hearts neath one umbrelly.
>
> One dripping purple parasol.
> Two coughs that sounded mellow.
> Two minds with but a single thought,
> Two hearts neath one umbrellow.
>
> One girl that came 200 miles
> A million things to say,

> And couldn't think of more than 3
> 'Twas such a rainy day.
>
> One boy that had it on his mind
> A coupla things to tell 'er.
> And couldn't for the life of him
> Beneath that damned umbreller. . . .⁴

Back at Cornell, Alice wrote Andy a note ending "I wish you were here," and signed "Alice and Burch."⁵

During the fall and winter of 1921–22, one of Andy's greatest pleasures was the company of his sister Lillian, now twenty-seven, still single, living at home, and commuting to her job as a secretary in New York. She was a handsome, redheaded, vivacious woman, intelligent and sophisticated, never lacking male admirers, and like Andy in love with the glamor of New York and bored by suburbia. They often went to dinner and the theater together, but most evenings Andy spent at home alone with his parents, who for all their love and their interest in him could not relieve his loneliness.

Christmas at home this year may have been a melancholy echo of the exciting, childhood holidays in a big family in the house on Summit Avenue; and New Year's Eve Andy spent in the kitchen, where the sound of his typing would not disturb his parents, writing Alice a long letter. He was about to take a new job, his fourth since June: "Three guesses how long I'll keep it." The letter, signed "Yours ploddingly, Andy," was so full of gloom and thinly concealed self-pity and self-contempt that it might have made her wonder why she should continue to write to this self-absorbed, melancholy boy of twenty-two. Yet after a silence of three weeks she sent him a note and a picture of herself, which Andy acknowledged by saying, "Gosh, you're beautiful."⁶

In January he took a job with the American Legion News Service, "in a dingy loft building on West 43rd Street near Eleventh Avenue." (Though he was unaware of it, he worked in the same building with an ex-serviceman and newspaperman named Harold Ross.) His boss was Carl Helm, who liked him, and who taught him how to write press releases. Helm planned to leave before long, and he groomed White to succeed him; but most of the time publicity work "pained" White when it didn't "bore" him. "Publicity is new," he wrote Alice, "and, like other new things, it is overpaid and consequently has been exploited."⁷

To relieve the tedium of his days, Andy wrote at home in the evenings —not only letters to Alice and entries in his journal, but poems to be submitted to New York newspaper columns. In January "The Bowling Green" accepted Andy's fourth poem in four months, a sonnet to a cheap restaurant beginning "O roaring sanctum! 'Neath thy whirling blast," and signed "Elwyn Brooks White." And he won fifty dollars by writing a script for the annual Cornell Masque musical comedy (though his script was never produced). Still, nothing seemed to him to be going right, and he was depressed. Bristow Adams encouraged him to try to find a job he was better suited for, such as "a desk job in the higher realms of editorial writing, criticism, essays, and the like," adding that he was sure Andy would eventually "arrive."[8]

FIVE MONTHS earlier, at Camp Otter, Andy and his friend Howard Cushman had daydreamed about making a real journey together, a foot-loose, wandering journey west that would take them—who knows, they would say, perhaps as far as China. They would earn their expenses as they went along by doing odd jobs and perhaps by selling humorous accounts of their travels. When not camping out they would find free lodgings on college campuses in Phi Gamma Delta or Beta Theta Pi fraternity houses, where they might play and sing popular songs for their supper. Both were in search of "experience," and of adventures that might incidentally provide them with material to write about. When Cushman flunked out of Cornell in February 1922 and came to New York, their plans became concrete, and Andy decided to quit his job and take off with Cush as soon as possible on the much-discussed journey west.

The previous October, a day or two after he had quit his first job in New York, White had bought himself a Model T Ford roadster, which he had christened "Hotspur." Now, in February, the first step in preparation for the getaway was to drive Hotspur to a blacksmith, who would rivet to its left running board strap-iron braces designed to hold an army foot-locker. For the right running board Andy bought a conventional running-board bracket that would accommodate a suitcase. Then, over the next week or so, he and Cush bought gear for the trip, which Andy stored for the time being in his office rather than at home, because he had not yet said a word to his parents about his plans. It would have been hard to explain to Samuel and Jessie why, not liking any of the jobs available, not feeling ready to settle down, and not knowing what he wanted, he had simply decided to hit the road, supporting himself by doing only as much work as necessary. Nor, if his self-frustrating love for Alice Burchfield played any part in the decision, could he talk to his parents about that. All he could do was to follow the road which, years later, he made his fictional hero Stuart Little take, by making him simply decide to "run away from home without telling anybody and go out into the world."[9]

On March 8, the eve of their actual departure, he and Cush drove into the yard of the Whites' house in Mount Vernon and Andy broke the news. The presence of Cush at this delicate moment may have made things easier for everyone. At any rate, years later Cush recalled how gracefully Andy's parents had taken the shock. He remembered Mr. White's "presiding at the dinner table" and playing the piano afterward, and Mrs. White's fluttering anxiety "while the car was being loaded." He especially remembered the Whites' "twinkling gentleness," and looking back he thought that they were much more understanding than he or Andy realized at the time.[10] Samuel White was in fact characteristically supportive. In a thank-you letter for a tie and a sonnet Andy sent him en route for his birthday, he said:

> Well, my boy, we miss you here at home but we can understand the lure of the great outside world that has taken you away. You should not have left us so abruptly—It was all right for you to go but it would have been better to have told us you were going. Mother was shocked by the suddenness of it all and it will take her some time to recover from it. Well, it is a great adventure that you have planned and it may have some point and objective that is not plain to me just now. At any rate we all wish you good luck and hope you will keep us posted from time to time. . . .[11]

The summer before, in response to a gloomy letter Andy had sent him from Camp Otter, Samuel White had encouraged his son to follow his own bent:

> If you feel that you are lacking in ambition, be assured that meditation and contemplation, of which your letter is full, is a more certain joy in life. Anyone can indulge ambition; only those who have the spirit can revel in passive enjoyment.[12]

Samuel White's efforts to understand his uncommunicative son were admirable. Yet, in his efforts to be free, Andy inconsiderately hurt his parents. Before setting out on his journey he told them just to hold any mail addressed to him until they heard from him, but he told others to send mail to Cush's parents, who would be kept informed of the post offices at whose general-delivery windows the transients would call as they moved westward.

Andy and Cush left Mount Vernon sometime during the day of March 9. In a letter to Alice, Andy described the loaded Hotspur as they set out:

> In the back compartment is a big telescopic suitcase full of shirts . . . , two Coronas [portable typewriters], a can of grease, 40 foot of rope, a jack, two

pairs of shoe-packs, and a briefcase. On the left running board is the Army trunk full of sweaters, notebook paper, stationery, Corona tripod, and sixty-two what-nots, including one money belt (Cush's, but he can't wear it because it itches so), one complete lottery set, one hunting knife, eighteen pairs of heavy socks, two journal covers, three issues of the Greenwich Village Quill, and a whetstone. Also on the left running board is a book-box within easy reach of the driver so that he may lean over and bring up the Holy Bible or Putnam's Word Book without slackening the pace. Jammed in in front of the spare on the rear is the bed-roll—our pride and joy—tent, blankets, and ponchos all neatly contained within a buckled duck ground cloth. Hanging one on either side of the windshield are spacious bags—one of 'em is an S bag to catch the eye of Cornellians along the route. These are catch-alls, and incidentally hold such things as percolators, double boilers, grills, pans, and one fiddle.[13]

The "S bags" were laundry bags issued to customers of the Cornell Student Agencies. In the wooden book box (labeled "Dr. Pierce's Pepsin Syrup") were *Webster's Collegiate Dictionary, Lyric Forms from France,* by Helen Louise Cohen, and "a sociological study of America or maybe an anthology—popular at the time."[14] The fiddle, made out of a cigar box, was a relic of the old family musicals on Summit Avenue.

They started out with a little cash, but the vow of poverty within reason was at first hard to keep. Carl Helm sent Andy an extra week's pay, and in Ithaca Andy picked up the fifty dollars the Cornell Masque owed him. To his parents he wrote: "What chance has a poor man to become penniless when ruthless debtors beset him on all sides with payments."[15]

The journey began slowly. Merely to get out of New York State took five weeks, thanks partly to cold weather and partly to hesitation. The first day's drive ended in Poughkeepsie, where they had to put up in a hotel. But the next night they found fraternal hospitality on the campus of Union College, in Schenectady, and by the third night they were back home in Ithaca, where they spent five days. They arrived there on a Saturday night about 9:30, just in time for the meeting of the Manuscript Club at Professor Sampson's house.

In her recent letters, Alice had been referring to herself as "your big sister," "auntie," and "old grandmother-fixit," as she invited him to tell her his troubles and let her try to help him. But Andy had not told her of his plan to wander west, and after he arrived in Ithaca, he behaved in his usual ambiguous and awkward way, and with a disregard for her feelings that must have hurt her. He did not let her know he was in town, although the news was likely to reach her the next morning. And even when, soon after his arrival, the rumor reached him that she had become engaged, he made no move to see her or to talk to her.

Cush and Andy went to the Adamses for "Monday night," told everyone present of their plans, and collected sixty-one cents "for singing a very
brief song, entitled 'Father's a hand-organ man, is he,' "[16] a performance
given to illustrate how these part-troubadors would work their way across
the continent. If Alice had not heard on Sunday or Monday that Andy was
in town, she certainly would have heard it on Tuesday from mutual friends
who were at the "Monday night" reunion. And when she read the *Sun*
on Wednesday morning she might have guessed that Andy White, who
signed himself "HO," and Howard Cushman ("HUM") were the "guest
editors" responsible for one of the columns that appeared in that day's issue
of the paper. She must have been puzzled, or moved in some way, by
finding in it a poem, signed "HO," that could be read as a farewell to her:

PROMISE
I saw the sun once more descend
Behind a certain lovely hill—
And though I follow there, I'll send
My vesper greetings eastward still.[17]

On Thursday, his last day in Ithaca, Andy got up early and drove to
the bridge he thought Alice would cross on her way to an eight o'clock
class. He parked and waited. He intended, he told her later, to ask her to
cut class and ride off with him to a nearby hamlet. His plans were not
definite beyond that, but he wondered whether he would have enough
courage to ask her to leave with him.

As it turned out, Alice had stayed home that morning with a cold. After
the last of the straggling eight-o'clock scholars had crossed the bridge,
Andy cranked up Hotspur, drove back to the house, picked up Cush, and
drove fifty miles to Geneva, New York, where they spent the night at
Hobart College. The next day they drove to the home of Cush's parents
in East Aurora, near Buffalo. There they stayed for almost a month.

In a letter he wrote to Alice after he had left Ithaca he tried to explain
his behavior during his stay there: "Monday morning I developed a funny
looking boil on my nose, and between the two [the news of her engagement and the nose] I quit entirely and spent the rest of the time [till
Thursday, when Cush and I left] trying to convince myself I was having
a fine time 'back at college!' "[18]

When Alice came home to Buffalo for spring vacation, Andy was still in
nearby East Aurora. He called on her and asked her to marry him. She was
surprised by this proposal from a man who thus far had never managed to say
"I love you," much less taken her in his arms and kissed her. Andy was
equally unprepared to hear her reply: she was not engaged to Jim Sumner, as

rumor had it, nor did she think she would ever marry him, because she and he
fought too much. But she was in love with him; and what was more, she did
not think that Andy was really in love with her. When he returned to East
Aurora, he did what he had always done: he put into writing what he did not
trust himself to say in person. In a long letter to Alice he described his
feelings and explained his actions. The letter exists because Alice Burchfield
did what Mrs. Adams advised her to do: she kept every word this promising
young writer sent her. He had wanted to propose a year ago, during Senior
Week at Cornell, he wrote; but he couldn't even bring himself to say he
loved her because he did not "think it was fair [to] say things promiscu-
ously" when he had "no money nor any immediate prospect of getting any,"
and "such a thing as marriage seemed a thousand years away."[19] Reflecting
many years later on his behavior as a lover in this period of his life, White
called it ironically his "immaculate romancing"—and added that it was no
wonder "Alice was confused."[20]

Alice and Andy parted amicably. She kept his fraternity pin, as he asked
her to do, as a pledge of friendship, and told him she looked forward to
following his career as a successful writer. He agreed to write her from
time to time, letters that would "pass any censor," about "the weather and
similar gol darn things."[21] If he had not known it before, he soon came
to realize that it had not been so much his lack of money and of a good
job that had prevented him from pursuing Alice more effectively as it had
been his fear of losing the independence and privacy he could not live
without. Pained as he may have been to see beautiful Alice drift out of
his dreams, hurt as his pride may have been by rejection, and discouraged
as he may have been by what he considered a personal failure, he must also
have felt some sense of relief. He was luckier than he knew. He did still
need years of freedom, and he needed, perhaps, a different kind of woman
for his wife—a woman like the one he finally married, as Alice said years
later.

When Andy and Cush finally left East Aurora in mid-April, the weather
was still too cool for comfort in their open car. (Except once, in North
Dakota, as protection against the sun, they never put the top up.) At the
post office in Cleveland Andy picked up an eighteen-page letter from
Alice, which he answered with a humorous account of recent events, and
closed with a few serious sentences:

> Thank you for some of the things in the letter, and the advice. If at any time
> within the next 60 years you think you would be proud of any thing I do,
> I wish you would. I wish that hard. I've flubbed so badly on three or four
> counts since April 1921 that it's going to take about two decades to even up

my score with myself. . . . I like the idea about our not having any more misunderstandings.[22]

From Cleveland the wanderers turned south to Columbus and the Beta House at Ohio State University. While there, Andy wrote a journalist friend in New York asking him for help in finding newspapers that would buy a daily column containing humorous accounts of his and Cush's travel adventures. The two planned to write and syndicate this burlesque travelogue at the rate of a dollar a day for each subscribing newspaper. The sample column they submitted did not show much promise, and it is no wonder they found no takers. They did not, however, give up the dream of financing the trip from their income as syndicated columnists until Andy had made a quick train trip east from Chicago, in a last but futile effort to secure a contract with a syndicate.

The failure of this cherished enterprise did not dampen their spirits for long. The sense of high adventure that had filled them when they started out kept them going for the next six months. The exhilaration they felt was unforgettable. Andy wrote:

It was spring, and I was young, and my little black roadster was young and new and blithe and gay. Everything lay ahead, and we had plenty of time of day: the land stretched interminably into the west and into the imaginations of young men. Our car seemed full of a deep inner excitement, just as we did ourselves.

The highway was a blazed trail of paint-rings on telegraph poles. It was a westering trace marked by arrows whittled out of shingles and tacked negligently to the handiest tree. In many places the highway seemed non-existent —just a couple of ruts in the plain—but the Model T was not a fussy car. It sprang cheerfully toward any stretch of wasteland whether there was a noticeable road under foot or not. It had clearance, it had guts, and it enjoyed wonderful health.[23]

During the first two months on the road they found lodging in hospitable fraternities at colleges in Ohio, Kentucky, and Indiana, where Andy's piano playing, the music he made on the cigar-box fiddle, and his accounts of their adventures were amusing enough to make both men welcome. In the beginning, while they still had a little cash and the weather was raw, they often ate in restaurants. Andy liked to drive for a while before breakfast, as Cushman once reminded him:

You always did have a sort of sniffing stance, tooling along in Hotspur on a fresh morning—I think it was partly to throw me off with my belly-aching

about shoving off for the next town without breakfast. You just never *would*
retrace a mile in the morning, though the prospect of hotcakes was forty miles
in front of us.

Cush was in a weak bargaining position: it was Andy's car, and Cush
couldn't drive.[24]

They spent about two weeks in Kentucky, camping out most of the
time. There, one night, lying in his sleeping bag, White heard his first
whippoorwill (and never forgot it). In Lexington he won twenty-two
dollars at a horse race; but the following week, in Louisville, he lost his
bet at the Derby. After the race, however, he returned to his campsite near
the municipal dump and wrote a sonnet to the winning horse, which he
sold later that evening "to a surprised but accommodating city editor."[25]
From Louisville he and Cush went to Cincinnati, where three letters from
Alice awaited him, then through Indiana and Illinois to Madison, Wisconsin. In early June, after observing how coeducation at the University of
Wisconsin differed from that at Cornell, they drove to Minneapolis.

When they settled into the Beta house at the University of Minnesota,
they were down to their last seventy-six cents. Andy at once contracted
to write two philosophy papers for a desperate fraternity brother, one on
the "Summum Bonum" and one on "The Problem of Evil." One day he
worked for an advertising agency signing the name "Horace C. Klein" on
a thousand direct-mail advertising letters, for forty cents an hour. For a
few days he sold roach powder from door to door, but gave that up when
he won twenty-five dollars by supplying a last line for a limerick in a
contest sponsored by the *Minneapolis Journal.* He wrote and sold to the
Minneapolis Sunday Tribune an eighteen-hundred-word, serious feature
story comparing coeducation at Cornell, Wisconsin, and Minnesota, and
during a period of five days he wrote twenty other potboilers—or so he
told Alice. To the *Ladies' Home Journal,* he said, he sent "Four Ways of
Making Egg-Timers"; to *Breezy Stories* he sent a piece of fiction "with sex
appeal." For "an outing magazine" he wrote "something on the spirit of
the great outdoors,"[26] which he followed up immediately with a burlesque
on the same subject for *Smart Set.* He answered Alice's latest letters in good
spirits and with affection, but in reply to her suggestion that he come to
Buffalo and get a job there for the summer, he asked: "What could be more
foolish? Granting that I could get a job, I should certainly be taking you
to ten-cent movie shows every night, and then how could I grow to be
worth a million dollars." He sounded pleased with himself, and he reported
that even his parents were beginning to think the adventure a good idea.[27]

Andy and Cush were not the only young flivver tourists on the road
in those days, of course. As Cush remembered it thirty years later, "the

roads were glutted with charming young men in Model T's and every last one of 'em had a . . . ukulele."[28] But from Minneapolis west, on roads that were unpaved and, through North Dakota and Montana, often only "a couple of ruts in the plain," the exciting feeling of being a long way from the east grew even stronger. They followed an itinerary planned with the help of a popular touring guide called the "Blue Book," whose entries, years later, White found powerfully evocative:

> A characteristic entry in the Blue Book went something like this: "38.8—Cross iron bridge, and at forks beyond, bear right, coming into Main Street."
>
> The words are beautiful in my heart. How many times have I crossed that bridge, borne right at the fork, and come into Main Street! I can shut my eyes now and come into Main Street at the wheel of a Model T, can experience again the sense of errantry, the sense of discovery, the excitement of arrival in a strange town.
>
> My left leg is languidly draped over the side, to indicate an easy familiarity with my mount. The hand throttle is at second notch, easing her along at a trickle. A whisper of dust curls in the wake. There are no cars ahead, no cars behind; we are the new arrivals—we have the stage to ourselves. Bystanders give us the eye. Main Street sprawls contented in the sun, and every third vehicle drowsing at the curb is a blood relation of the T.[29]

In Walker, Minnesota, Andy dislocated his right elbow. But a couple of weeks later he was able to type a long and vivid account of the trip from Minneapolis to a ranch near Hardin, Montana, where for three days Cush worked as a hay hand and Andy earned their meals by playing year-old foxtrots on a piano in Becker's Cafe. Then they pushed on, stopping first at the post office in Billings, where they had asked that their mail be forwarded. Andy was rewarded by a letter from home and birthday presents of twenty-five dollars each from his mother and his father. "Green and crisp they fluttered from their cozy envelopes, green and crisp and strong—out onto the counter of White's Lunch," Andy's letter of thanks began. Yet fifty dollars was not enough to support them during their trip through Yellowstone Park. En route, in Cody, Wyoming, they sandpapered a dance floor, washed dishes, and ran a concession during a carnival. As they were leaving Yellowstone, they were threatened with a five-hundred-dollar fine for allegedly not extinguishing a campfire, and they were grimly amused by the knowledge that they had only three dollars between them. Of Yellowstone Park, Andy wrote in his letter home:

> The Park is spectacular beyond my Corona (I should say beyond Cush's Corona—I sold mine [for twenty dollars] to a bystander one time in a moment of starvation), and it is well and unobtrusively policed. But it is so obviously

"on exhibition" all the time. [Names like] "Inspiration Point," for instance— on the rim of the wonderful Yellowstone canyon.[30]

Among the tourists in the Park, Cush remembered a "dizzy Bohemian Greenwich Village couple . . . in the snow flurry" who impressed him because they were "living IN SIN." From Yellowstone they went north to the Dot S Dot ranch near Melville, Montana, owned by a friend of a friend of the Cushmans. It was much like the ranch of Sam Beaver's father, in *The Trumpet of the Swan,* where "guests came to board every summer." Here they stayed for ten memorable days. Cush worked on the ranch and Andy "work[ed] for grub by proving [himself] a factotum." The owners, Harry and Nan Hart, took to Andy. In a Christmas card in 1950 Nan Hart reminded Andy of a poem he had written at the Dot S Dot ranch and quoted the line: "The sweet-grass tumbles down out of the Crazy Hills." From letters he received years later from friends he made along the route, it is clear that he charmed people in ways they did not easily forget. His eyes, his smile, his laugh, his modesty, his wit, his generosity—and his music and poems—were all ingratiating and memorable. Nan Hart was only one of many. In 1937 she wrote Andy: "Here we still think of you as the boy with such good pluck, who with the smashed-up arm and an infernal go of hay fever still could charm us all, and amuse the whole ranch with his poems."[31] At the Harts' ranch, during the ten days or so before Cush was fired and they decided to move on, Andy's elbow responded to treatment with horse liniment but not sufficiently to allow him to do heavy work; and at times his hay fever practically blinded him.

From the ranch they drove north to Great Falls, bought four dollars' worth of food, and pointed Hotspur northwest to Glacier National Park. There, on a five-day, sixty-mile hiking trip, they crossed the Continental Divide at Gunsight Pass and crossed back at Swiftcurrent Pass. From Macleod, Alberta, Andy wrote Mrs. Adams:

I'm right next to an encampment of Blackfeet Indians here. Robbed of his setting the poor old American Indian has left only his dirtiness and his laziness and his inclination to steal ponies. I like to watch the old squaws smoking their strong old pipes and spitting into the fire. If only some of our pale-cheeked maidens could pull upon the dainty WDC's of their boudoir with the same relish!

The rain is increasing, and threatens to make light of my pup tent. Outside I can hear the pounding of horses' feet—the Indians are forever chasing them over here. The plains of Alberta end in a grey mist. I suppose I ought to take our socks in off the line.

I know I ought to end this letter. I know it just as well as I know that I ought to pull the edges of the blankets in from the drip and that I should make myself a cup of coffee. But I sit here and do nothing about any of these things. I go on pounding the Corona, imagining that the rain is just the rain on the Adamses' roof. I even imagine that I am warm and full of cocoa. I even imagine that school children in unborn centuries will be taught to say, "The poet White had a very good imagination."[32]

This may have been the last letter Andy wrote on Cush's Corona. It had to be sold, sharing the fate of Andy's Corona. Though Cush showed up that afternoon with several days' wages, gasoline was fifty-five cents a gallon, and when they blew out a tire they were without a spare and without money. Andy walked thirty-two miles to the nearest town of any size, carrying Cush's Corona; he returned without the Corona but with a new Goodyear.

Back across the border, they drove to Spokane, where seventeen letters awaited Andy, among them one from his father advising him to give up the life of a gipsy, sell Hotspur, and return by "regulation railroad."[33] With the advice came welcome cash, some of which was spent at once for waffles, a spare tire, and a night in a bed at the YMCA. There were also two letters from Alice, in one of which she had enclosed a five-dollar bill she claimed was from her father, sent in response to one of Andy's amusing accounts of going broke. From Spokane they drove south across the Snake River to Walla Walla, and from there to Yakima, where for about a month they picked and packed fruit ten hours a day, for thirty cents an hour. Through friends of Cush's family they met people and enjoyed their first bit of social life since leaving the Beta house in Minneapolis two months earlier.

In a letter written in Yakima, White recorded some of his impressions of the West:

I like it. . . . Everyone is either a Mason, an Elk, or a chiropractic, and no one understands anything subtler than the Saturday Evening Post. The prosperity is astounding. The stupidest [fruit] rancher owns a three-thousand dollar automobile and a player-piano and two or three children. Success seems to be imminent. Newspapers are rotten to the core. Filling stations look like hotel lobbies. The air is free. Every tawdry spot on every highway is labelled "Tourist Camping Ground" and contains a tired woman in khaki breeches sitting in front of a dirty tent, peeling potatoes. The sunsets are marvelous. The dawns equal the sunsets. . . . Everyone is expected to be a "booster." It doesn't matter for what. Irrigation ditches run down the main streets of important towns. Alfalfa produces three crops a year. Bookstores decorate their windows with "How to Concentrate," "Power of Will," "Know Yourself," "Psychoanalysis," "Are You a Ten Thousand Dollar Man?," and "What a Boy of

Eighteen Ought to Know." Houses are painted white, and have pretty little snapdragons and bachelors buttons in the front yard. Sunflowers grow all along the wall. You can buy a horse for twenty-five dollars. Girls are not as pretty as they are in the East, but more spontaneous. Cantaloupe are unexcelled. Sagebrush, jack rabbits, and blanket Indians are not all gone yet by a long shot. Shadows at evening are beyond description. Men wear trousers just to the ankle. Women don't know that long skirts are the thing. A person interested in literature is "queer." Homecooking is featured—justly so. People waltz. Nights are cool, and breakfast is at 6:30. In short, the west is wonderfully and fearfully made, and is a thing to reckon with. It is all very interesting.[34]

On the transcontinental trip Hotspur had been very economical. Worn-out tires and fan-belts had had to be replaced, but the Model T had required no major repairs until Andy and Cush got to Pasco, Washington. There the rear-end went; that is, the pinion gear in the differential was stripped. A new one cost a dollar. As it turned out, however, that was a small price to pay for the story White derived from it. He included it in the nostalgic essay on the Model T Ford that he entitled "Farewell, My Lovely!" and that appeared in *The New Yorker* in 1936. For about ten years half the college freshmen in America learned how that pinion gear got replaced, because the essay became part of many anthologies used in freshman English. Here is the way White told the story:

> One time, on the banks of the Columbia River in Washington, I heard the rear end go out of my Model T when I was trying to whip it up a steep incline onto the deck of a ferry. Something snapped; the car slid backward into the mud. It seemed to me like the end of the trail. But the captain of the ferry, observing the withered remnant, spoke up.
>
> "What's got her?" he asked.
>
> "I guess it's the rear end," I replied, listlessly. The captain leaned over the rail and stared. Then I saw that there was a hunger in his eyes that set him off from other men.
>
> "Tell you what," he said, carelessly, trying to cover up his eagerness, "let's pull the son of a bitch up onto the boat, and I'll help you fix her while we're going back and forth on the river."
>
> We did just this. All that day I plied between the towns of Pasco and Kennewick, while the skipper (who had once worked in a Ford garage) directed the amazing work of resetting the bones of my car.[35]

What White did not tell his readers was that the pinion gear was paid for with part of the five dollars Alice had sent him. He had "choked with embarrassment" when he received it, and had vowed it "would not see the light of day" till he was back in Buffalo, but he had to swallow his pride in

Pasco, when he used three-fifty of it for the gear, some new gaskets, and a square meal. Then, at the end of the long, hot day spent repairing Hotspur, as he prepared to dive from the stern of the ferryboat for a refreshing swim, a silver dollar and a fifty-cent piece somehow fell from his pocket into six feet of the icy water of the Columbia River. "I loved those two coins for both financial and sentimental reasons," he wrote Alice. "They were coins apart." And he dove for an hour, until it grew too dark to see the river bottom, in a futile effort to retrieve them. Late the next morning the ferryboat captain handed him a silver dollar that he said some kids had found while diving early in the morning. Andy did not believe him.[36]

In his letter urging his wandering son to come home, Samuel White had said: "I would seek some way to settle and stabilize my life so that the manifold experiences of these glorious days now past could be turned to profitable and worthwhile achievement."[37] It would be a year before Andy returned and nine years before he "stabilized his life," but when he did finally follow his father's advice, he certainly put the experiences to "profitable and worthwhile" use. He not only drew from it the material for his essay on the Model T, the first of his essays to become famous, but he used the wealth of impressions he had gained on this trip in shaping some of the themes, some of the background, and some of the scenes that appear in two of his children's stories, *Stuart Little* and *The Trumpet of the Swan*. In another, less specific but even more important way, the trip was invaluable to him, as one gathers from the concluding paragraphs of a little essay called "From Sea to Shining Sea":

To an American, the physical fact of the complete America is, at best, a dream, a belief, a memory, and the sound of names. My own vision of the land—my own discovery of its size and meaning—was shaped, more than by any other instrument, by a Model T Ford. The vision endures; the small black roadster is always there, alive and kicking, a bedroll wedged against its spare, a dictionary sprawling on its floor, an army trunk bracketed to its left running board. The course of my life was changed by it, and it is in a class by itself. It was cheap enough so I could afford to buy one; it was capable enough so it gave me courage to start.

Youth, I have no doubt, will always recognize its own frontier and push beyond it by whatever means are at hand. As for me, I've always been glad that mine was a two-track road running across the prairie into the sinking sun, and underneath me a slow-motion roadster of miraculous design—strong, tremulous, and tireless, from sea to shining sea.[38]

When, in the twenties, many American writers—some of whom were to become famous—took off for Europe, Andy White in a "sniffing

stance," behind the wheel of the most American of all automobiles, was
headed west.

After he got to Seattle in mid-September, he looked back with pleasure
on his four weeks in Yakima:

> I never dreamed that there was any country like it. All around it are the
> bare brown sand-hills, sizzling and baking under a relentless sun. Everywhere
> are the ditches—little invisible streams of water tapped from the main flume
> which comes down from the Cascades. Every hillside in the valley is laden
> with fruit, and in the leveller fields grows alfalfa-hay, a rich green crop, almost
> before the previous crop has been stacked. There is no rain. In the mornings
> and evenings the brown hills are streaked with great black shadows and the
> world is cool. Mount Adams and Mount Rainier rise white in the west.

Such memories of sun, sky, light, color, and fruitfulness only made
Seattle seem more dreary. "The days here," Andy wrote Alice, "are full
of mist from Puget Sound and of depression. I find it hard to keep cheerful.
I know what it is to be homesick." Though he had been tempted by offers
of two jobs back east, he was determined not to return home until he had
made a go of something out west. This brought him again to the point
at which he had to set out in search of a job, and he was full of despair:

> There were days in 1917 [his first year at Cornell] that were like these. I
> got over them by chance. Maybe I will these also. It's funny what this past
> year has brought—one darn failure after another. And here I am, precisely as
> I was a year ago today, hunting a job in a rainy city. The way I feel now I'll
> never be able to stay in one place for more than about six days at a time.[39]

CHAPTER V

From Seattle
to Siberia

1 9 2 2 — 1 9 2 3

*"Self is the most interesting thing in the world—if not carried to extremes
—and life would be far less gallant and exciting if men were not
continually absorbed with watching what they're doing with their own
hands and marvelling at the stew which is simmering in their own heads.
I hate people who are not interested in themselves."*

BY THE TIME ANDY AND CUSH REACHED
Seattle, Carl Helm, Andy's former boss at the American Legion
News Service, had moved to Seattle and was working for the *Post
Intelligencer.* He was unable to find work for Cush, who after about
three weeks started back home, but he succeeded in helping Andy land a
job as a reporter on the *Seattle Times,* at a good starting salary of forty
dollars a week. With Cush gone, Andy was left with Carl and his vivacious
wife, Harriet, as his only friends. Evenings at their house on Lake Washington, at the end of a trolley line, were memorable; he envied their
conjugal happiness.

Seattle in 1922 was "a frontier settlement of 300,000 people in the
shadow of Mount Rainier. The mountain never cast any shadow . . . , but
stood ready to. All it asked was an even break." Andy soon grew to hate
the monotony of the city's constant cloudiness and rain, and "missed the
stern tread of the Eastern calendar." "In Seattle there were roses at Christmas, and how we hated roses at Christmas." The spiritual climate of the
city was equally hateful: "Seattle [was] a very young city . . . and
everybody was under the impression that something wonderful was about
to happen to the Northwest—like making a lot of money." And the *Seattle
Times,* he decided, was "very highbrow, very conservative, very rich, and
entirely unreadable."[1]

Andy's relations with his boss, Mr. Johns, the city editor, seem to have been good. At any rate, White referred to him many years later as "one of the gentlest, most soft-spoken men I have ever encountered" and remembered him with gratitude, not only for putting up with the mistakes of a young man not really cut out to be a reporter, but especially for giving him some memorable advice about writing. Once, when Andy "got stuck on a story" and couldn't find a way to express what he meant, he asked Johns how to get around his difficulty. Johns thought for a minute and then said, "Just say the words."[2] It was, White thinks, excellent advice.

But Andy found the work of a reporter no more to his liking in Seattle than it had been in New York. He did not like to be told what to write about, and he disliked many of his assignments, which were often ludicrous, boring, or worse. He once had to write a story about flying low over Lake Washington in a seaplane, hired by the *Times,* to look for the body of a drowned person. That, he thought, was a stunt whose main purpose was to call attention to the *Times.* He "spent many a lunch hour covering the noonday gatherings of fraternal and civic groups," and broke "the hard roll countless times with Chamber of Commerce people, . . . laughed courteously at their jokes and listened patiently to their tales of industrial growth." He was at the time "under the influence of Mencken and Lewis, and felt proud disdain for business and for businessmen."[3] Worst of all was having to report acts of violence. How he covered one such assignment he described in a letter to Alexander Woollcott, several years later:

I was sent to Everett [, Washington,] licketty-cut one rainy morning [in 1922] . . . to report an unusually fine murder that had occurred during the night. It was my first murder, and, if I may make a little joke, the four victims' first, too. They were all Greeks—one Greek man, one Greek lady, two Greek children. All dead as hell. I was taken by a pleased Everett detective to the scene of the crime—a small shanty whose roof and walls were still smoldering and whose smoldering Greek occupants (charred remains is, I believe, the phrase) still lay in the illicit, half burned bed. That is, the adult pair were still there: the two children had been taken, in their innocence, to the rear parlor of a local mortician. The perpetrator of this ugly affair had hit everybody over the pate with a blunt instrument, and had then set fire to the modest little home —following, the detective assured me, an old Greek custom which permits the relative of a defiled woman to take matters pretty much into his own hands. The rambling account of the incident given me by the detective, the smell of the toasted Greeks, the sight of the waxy little corpses in the undertaker's back room, combined with my inexperience in marshalling the shabbier details of murders of this sort, were all, I don't doubt, accountable for the extraordinarily concise report that I gave the Times over the phone. I called the city desk.

"This is White, on the Everett story," I volunteered in a tiny pre-nauseated voice. "What's it like?" asked the city editor, in an attempt, I suppose, to gauge in his mind how much of the front page he better hold open. "It's raining," I said, hung up the line, and vomited.[4]

Even when White did "get the story," he did not always get it in on time. "Every piece had to be a masterpiece," he once recalled, "and before you knew it, Tuesday was Wednesday."[5] And there were other ways, White recalls, in which he was unable to fill the conventional role of reporter:

[City editor] Johns soon realized that in me he had a special problem. Although punctual and neat, I didn't know the meaning of the word "indictment" and was unable to hear anything over the telephone. I could have heard perfectly well over the telephone if the "leg men," as they were called, had simply talked in a natural manner, but they were all keyed up and insisted on spelling out everything in that "B for Boston," "C for Chicago" style. I can't grasp a word when it is spelled out—I have to hear the word itself, and think I am entitled to. Taking a story over the phone, I would get confused and write down the word "Boston" or the word "Chicago" and gradually lose the thread of the narrative. Anyway, Johns saw that his best bet was to keep me away from telephones and courtrooms and let me write feature stories in which you didn't have to know anything except where the space bar on the typewriter was.[6]

Johns's decision to take White off all straight news reporting, and to allow him to write feature stories instead, was a lucky break.

During the nine months Andy stayed in Seattle he lived in the boarding house of Mrs. E. D. Donohue, at 1222 Seventeenth Street, North. It was a rather dreary place permeated by the stale odors of cooking, and even the songs of Mrs. Donohue's canary could not enchant it.

Andy's new acquaintances were, in spite of their friendliness, no substitute for old friends, and he felt intensely lonesome. He was depressed, occasionally sick, often restless. It was a struggle to obey the alarm clock in the morning, and not always a successful one.

To cheer himself up, Andy traded in Hotspur and bought a new Ford coupé, on the installment plan. He bought a new Underwood portable, also on the installment plan. He made himself acquainted with Mr. Knudsen, the keeper of the zoo, and once, instead of going to work, walked five or six miles out to the zoo to find comfort in looking at the animals. He went to concerts and recitals: the Minneapolis Symphony, Josef Hoffman, and Chaliapin. He read W. H. Hudson's *Purple Land,* Carl Sandburg's *Rootabaga Stories,* Christopher Morley's *Where the Blue Begins,* Willa

Cather's *One of Ours*, A. E. Housman's *Last Poems*, and Harry Leon Wilson's *Merton of the Movies*.

He spent Christmas by himself. He strung up cheerful decorations in his room, and on Christmas morning his landlady presented him with a table lamp. He had written many greeting cards and letters, and had sent Cush a copy of *Nonsensorship*, by Heywood Broun. Andy missed his old companion, whose friendship he cherished for the rest of his life, even though after their grand tour they saw each other only infrequently and corresponded only sporadically. In coming years Cushman was not to be as lucky as White. Lacking White's gifts, he was to have an uneventful career in various fields of journalism and public relations. The trip in Hotspur and his friendship with White were high points in his life.

Alice did her best to cheer Andy up with letters and little gifts, but he did not encourage her efforts. "Letters should not become a habit," he warned; and he advised her against sending him cookies, because they might crumble en route. Their correspondence was plagued by misunderstandings and hurt feelings. When Andy wrote Alice a postcard with a post-office pen because he had lost his fountain pen, Alice sent him a new fountain pen, but Andy's thanks were not very warm or gracious. For Christmas she made him some linen handkerchiefs on which she embroidered his initials and sent him a necktie as well. He did not notice the handwork on the handkerchief and wrote her that the tie was "awful." In his next letter he explained that since "the most prominent thing about the tie was that it had a yellow streak," he thought perhaps she was "trying to take some sort of wallop" at him. From September 1922 to September 1923 he wrote her only once a month—letters that were friendly but self-centered, and that failed to suggest that he was in love with her—if, indeed, he still believed he was. He seems to have been so full of self-doubt, even self-dislike, that he was unable to respond to gestures of affection from a woman who, he must have recognized, was wiser, more mature, more generous, and more capable of love than he. Alice even sent him a card to mark the first anniversary of the day he and Cush had set out from Mount Vernon on their great expedition. In his reply he spoke only of being "homesick" for college life and of wishing that one of his fraternity brothers (Mike Galbreath) were around for him "to argue with all night long."[7]

In March Andy's luck and good spirits returned when the publisher of the *Times* asked him to create and conduct a small daily column of his own. Headed "Personal Column," it was to consist of a series of individual items —brief notes, comments, anecdotes, poems, etc. Its layout was to resemble that of the columns in a newspaper's classified ad section: each of its items was to be separated from the one above and the one below by a line, and items that ran longer than a few short sentences were to be subdivided by such lines. It was not a glamorous assignment, nor was White allowed a by-line; still, he would be free to write and edit as he chose, and he was "pleased to have an outlet for poems and paragraphs."[8]

The "poems," of course, would be light verse such as he had written at Cornell for the Manuscript Club or, over the pseudonym of "D'Annunzio," for the *Sun*. The "paragraphs" would be what White once called "capsule essays," that is, very brief prose pieces no more than three to eight or ten sentences long, and usually consisting of comments on things seen, heard, or read. The "paragraph" was a journalistic genre, and a "paragrapher" could write about almost anything, provided he "wrote short"—and could be interesting or amusing.

In the twenties, when there were so many more newspapers than there are today, and when everybody read newspapers, columns of the kind Andy was about to imitate supplied a substantial part of the literary fare of the common reader. They varied greatly in style and quality, but typically they consisted of a collection of short items ("poems and paragraphs") submitted by contributors or written by the columnist, or both. As editor and writer, a columnist was expected, as White said, to be something of a scholar and a poet, and the most successful columnists were gifted writers whose good sense and humor projected a personality, and built a following. Their readers looked forward to daily communications from a familiar voice. Andy White, preparing his "Personal Column," could think of himself as an apprentice in a profession from which had emerged such men of letters as the New York columnists Franklin Pierce Adams, famous as "F.P.A.," Christopher Morley, and Don Marquis.

The influential predecessors of F.P.A. had been the American journalist-commentators of the nineteenth century. Since the days of Eugene Field's column "Sharps and Flats," published in the *Chicago Daily News* from 1883 to 1895, every good newspaper publisher had wanted a good columnist on his staff. (Charles Dana, publisher of the *New York Sun*, never gave up trying to lure Field, the most widely quoted commentator in the country, to his paper.) From 1909 to 1921 "B.L.T." (Bert Leston Taylor) was known everywhere for his column "A Line o' Type or Two," in the *Chicago Tribune*. F.P.A.'s "Conning Tower," in the *New York World*, Morley's "Bowling Green," in the *New York Post*, and Marquis's "Sun Dial," in the *New York Sun*, all known and admired by White, were part of a long tradition which was eventually to include *The New Yorker*'s "Notes and Comment." In such columns can be traced an important part of the history of American literary humor, which had its roots in American journalism, beginning with the newspaper humor of Artemus Ward and including the work of journalists Mark Twain, Petroleum Nasby, and Bill Nye.

Three weeks after becoming a columnist, Andy described his new venture in a warm, happy letter to Alice. He liked its challenge, he told her, partly because Seattle's columnists all depended on "knock-down, pie-throwing humor," whereas he himself hoped "to work into dramatic criticism, book reviews, and whimsy—of a sort that will appeal to persons who can understand words of more than one syllable—a very delicate undertaking." So far, he was "tickled to death with the modicum of success" he had had.

In fact, he never got around to anything so ambitious as dramatic criticism or book reviews. Even when, in spite of the constraints of the column's queer format, he managed to string together eight or ten sentences that constituted a "paragraph," it was a "personal" essay. From the beginning of his long career as a columnist and essayist, White wrote about himself—in the tradition of Thoreau and Whitman. And though he probably did not think in terms of any literary tradition, he may at this time have been considering, more or less theoretically, the question of what a writer's subject should be. He ended his letter to Alice with a remarkably frank and self-revealing statement:

> I ramble terribly when I get talking about myself. We all do. Self is the most interesting thing in the world—if not carried to extremes—and life would be far less gallant and exciting if men were not continually absorbed with watching what they're doing with their own hands and marvelling at the stew which is simmering in their own heads. I hate people who are not interested in themselves.[9]

White never lost his interest in observing himself. It was an interest that served him well throughout his long professional career, for it made him tune his ear to his inner voice, and it supplied him with all the material he needed for his art.

In Seattle in 1923, however, his "Personal Column" did not prove to be the right medium for his muse, and a month after he had written so optimistically to Alice, he wrote that he was "a particularly bad columnist" because he was "not allowed to be sincere." His employer was "a very vain, stupid" person, a "typical successful man." Still, Andy seems to have been pleased with himself. He felt like an "evangelist," he said, in a city that was only fifty years old, because he was, after all, the first man to mention names of books in the *Times*, the first man allowed to devote full time to writing a column, and the first to whom the editor and publisher ever said, "Do you mind if I change this word?" He was so happy he was thinking of buying himself a sailing canoe.[10]

After three months as a columnist he was once again utterly discouraged, "full of grief and empty of ideas." He wanted a "cat-boat and three months' vacation," also "a dog, a new pipe, a new shirt, two new neckties, a new job, a new thought, a new pot of paste, a new climate, a new enthusiasm, a spring overcoat, somebody to play tennis with, more letters from the east, and a new pair of eyes for reading after 9 P.M." He ended this youthful confession to Alice by saying:

> My column has been a failure. I am not so downhearted over that, however, as I might otherwise be, because it isn't humanly possible to make anything else but a failure out of a column in this particular newspaper. . . . Even at that, a failure is a failure, and it doesn't make one bubble with jollity all day long.[11]

During his first job as a humorous commentator White invented some formulas that he later used in *The New Yorker*. One of them was a department headed "We Answer Hard Questions," in which he ran such items as this:

> Sir: How can a man determine how much sugar he is putting in his coffee when using one of those restaurant sugar shakers?
>
> ROUGH ROLLO
>
> Rollo: Pour your coffee into your empty soup bowl, put the desired amount of sugar into the empty coffee cup, and then pour the coffee back, straining the soup particles out through your napkin. ASK US anything at all.[12]

Ten years later, in his "Answers to Hard Questions" in *The New Yorker*, White was wittier:

> Q. When a man does not believe in tipping and is eating in a place where tipping is customary, what should he do?
> A. Tip.[13]

Most of the items in his column, however, consisted of brief notes and comments. In verse as well as prose he quipped about people and events in the news: the mayor, the municipally owned street railway, prohibition, President Harding, Tutankhamen, the Scopes trial, and the press agentry for the Dempsey-Gibbons fight to be held on the Fourth of July in Shelby, Montana.

The column also carried the first comic story White ever told on himself in print:

> YESTERDAY WE encountered a salesman extraordinary. We told him we wanted to buy garters. "Gray is your color," he said, briskly handing us a set. We pocketed them in amazement.
>
> ———
>
> ALWAYS BEFORE when we bought garters the salesman had said, "What color?" and that had thrown us into a panic. We'd try to remember what color we had on, and fail. Then we'd try to go boldly ahead and select a color. It used to take all the pleasure out of buying garters.
>
> ———
>
> BUT NOW we are on solid ground. The next time we buy garters, should the salesman ask us what color, we will promptly shout: "Gray is our color!" and stare at him angrily, as though he should have known without any help.[14]

What White had produced was the kind of anecdote he would later on help to make popular in *The New Yorker.* Just three years later, the then-fledgling magazine accepted White's expanded and funnier version of this original, under the title "Garter Motif." "The proof of humor," James Thurber once said, "is the ability to put one's self on awkward public record."[15]

The poems White published in the nearly eighty columns he turned out for the *Seattle Times,* most of them humorous and topical, were written in the various verse forms used by writers of light verse. On the first day of spring he greeted his readers with quatrains in ballad measure; for Memorial Day he offered a sonnet; and in his last column he ran a quatrain in rhymed pentameter:

JUNE 21 — THE LONGEST DAY

Tomorrow is the longest day of all,
The punctual sun rides brightly into port;
The charms of lengthy days will never pall—
But oh, they tend to make the nights so short![16]

He practiced writing triolets and rondels. Like the journalist poets he admired, he was interested in prosody—in metrical patterns and rhyme schemes—and presumably he consulted the book *Lyric Forms from France,* which he and Cush had carried west with them. In addition to a history of these lyric forms, the book contained an anthology of poems written by the leading practitioners of light verse, including the journalists Eugene Field, F.P.A., and Don Marquis, as well as by poets of greater pretensions, such as Edwin Arlington Robinson and Lionel Johnson. The poems were arranged according to categories of the verse forms, and were followed by a handy chart "for the Construction of the 'Forms' in Modern English Verse," showing for each form the number of stanzas, number of lines, rhyme scheme, position of the refrain, advice about the "envoy," and "special features."[17] White's experiments with the lyric forms from France are not, however, worth quoting.

Two of his pieces from that period, however, are autobiographically interesting because they concern a writer's unceasing struggle to translate into words thoughts and sensations that move him but seem to elude expression. The first of these pieces, a short poem in free verse, one of the best he produced at the time, deals with the ultimate futility of this struggle:

> Capturing a thought
> And hoping to display it in words
> Is like capturing a sea gull
> And hoping to show its velvet flight
> By stuffing it—wings outstretched—
> And hanging it in a window
> By a thread.[18]

The second piece, a "paragraph" or "capsule essay," regards writing as a painful addiction whose victim is forever condemned to search for the words that escape him:

THERE USED to be an old family ritual about "the first drink." When a youth touched spiritous liquor for the first time, he marked his downfall, from which there was small hope of redemption.

_____

BUT WE would like to record another ritual. It concerns "the first scribbling." This seems to us far more abysmal and important than the first drink.

_____

UP UNTIL the time when a youth first seizes a pencil and furtively scratches a thought on paper, he is secure. He rides the top of the world, a normal person.

_____

BUT WITH the first inspired pencil mark, he signs his life away, unwittingly. The door slams shut. He has accepted words as his medium of exchange—and words, more than dollars, are elusive and painful to a degree which the youth yet knows nothing of.[19]

In early May Andy's parents came to visit him for a week. On the day of their arrival his "Personal Column" carried a poem called "To My Specific Mother"; and when he put her on the train as she and Samuel left, he gave her a corsage of roses and violets. But much as he loved her and his father, they both seemed "very old and funny," and he found it a "jolt" to discover that he had nothing in common with them "except a little superficial gossip about the home town and the various branches of the family."[20] Their visit may have intensified both his loneliness and his reluctance to return to New York.

When he was fired, on June 19, White was told that his dismissal was "no reflection on [his] ability." He didn't believe it, but we know what his boss meant: Andy White had talent, wit, style, integrity, and devotion to writing, all of which might sometime make him a good writer, but not of the kind suited to the *Seattle Times*. And so, for the fourth time in about eighteen months, Andy felt the great relief of freedom from a job. No Tokay grapes this time, and no new Ford runabout equipped with special brackets to hold a foot-locker. "I can still recall experiencing an inner relief —the feeling of again being adrift on life's sea, an element I felt more at home in than in a city room." His journal entries for the days following his dismissal, as White said on rereading them years later, revealed "a young man living a life of exalted footlessness":

I was a literary man in the highest sense of the term, a poet who met every train. No splendor appeared in the sky without my celebrating it, nothing mean or unjust took place but felt the harmless edge of my wildly swinging sword. I walked in the paths of righteousness, studying girls. In particular, I studied a waitress in a restaurant called the Chantecler. I subscribed to two New York dailies, the *World* and the *Evening Post*. I swam alone at night in the canal that connects Lake Union and Lake Washington. I seldom went to bed before two or three o'clock in the morning, on the theory that if anything of interest were to happen to a young man it would almost certainly happen late at night. Daytimes, I hung around my room in Mrs. Donohue's boarding house, reading the "Bowling Green" and the "Conning Tower," wondering what to do next, and writing.

My entry for June 15, 1923, begins, "A man must have something to cling to. Without that he is as a pea vine sprawling in search of a trellis." Obviously, I was all asprawl, clinging to Beauty, which is a very restless trellis. My prose style at this time was a stomach-twisting blend of the Bible, Carl Sandburg, H. L. Mencken, Jeffrey Farnol, Christopher Morley, Samuel Pepys, and Franklin Pierce Adams imitating Samuel Pepys. I was quite apt to throw in a "bless the mark" at any spot, and to begin a sentence with "Lord" comma.[21]

After hanging around Seattle for another month, he luckily found a way to do what he had recently announced in a poem he wanted to do—which was to "dribble off" to the Pribilof Islands, lying north of the western tip of the Aleutians.[22] The S.S. *Buford,* out of San Francisco, put in at Seattle as its first stop on a forty-day cruise that would take its passengers to Nome, through the Bering Strait to East Cape, Siberia, and then back to Nome, Seattle, and San Francisco. Andy tried unsuccessfully to sign on as a member of the crew; then, with most of his savings, he bought a first-class ticket that would take him as far as Skagway, Alaska. He later wrote in "The Years of Wonder":

> To start for Alaska this way, alone and with no assurance of work and a strong likelihood of being stranded in Skagway, was a dippy thing to do, but I believed in giving Luck frequent workouts. It was part of my philosophy at that time to keep Luck toned up by putting her to the test; otherwise she might get rusty.

During the first part of the voyage he made copious entries in his journal. Towards his companions in first class he felt some superiority; in fact he had thought that one of the attractions of the cruise would be the chance to observe at close hand the kind of Americans that Mencken and Lewis had taught him to be disdainful of: members of fraternal orders and chambers of commerce. "It was important to me at that time to move among people toward whom I felt aloof and superior, even though I secretly envied their ability to earn a living." Three days out the *Buford* made her first port of call, at Ketchikan, Alaska. White remembered the way he felt at the end of that day ashore:

> I was an extremely callow and insecure young man, but as I examine my record of Ketchikan . . . , I can see that I was not alone in my insecurity; all of us were seeking reassurance of one sort or another—some with mystic rites and robes [the Shriners, who had participated in a meeting of Alaskan Shriners], some with the metaphysics of commerce [the businessmen, who had met with the Ketchikan Commercial Club], some with expensive Indian baskets and inexpensive Indian girls [the ladies, who had gone shopping, and one of the engine-room crew, who had "managed to get ashore and establish trade relations with a half-breed girl"]. I was enraptured with my surroundings— contemptuous of all, envious of all, proud, courageous, and scared to death.[23]

In Ketchikan he bought a handsome string of walrus ivory beads for Alice.

During his first week on board, when he was not dining and dancing in first class or writing in his journal, he sought out some of the ship's officers and tried to talk himself into a job that would allow him to stay aboard after the ship reached Skagway, which was as far as his ticket would take him. But when the ship docked at Skagway, Luck had not yet proved equal to the challenge Andy had set her. He packed his bag, took it and his typewriter up on deck to disembark, and sat down, "delaying until the last possible moment [his] walk down the plank out into the forlorn street of Skagway—a prospector twenty-five years late and not even primarily interested in gold." As he sat there, a girl whom he had danced with during the first week out, the daughter of one of the ship's owners, brought him word that the captain wished to see him. He was given a job as saloon boy, and within a few hours he was serving some of the people with whom he had earlier been on equal first-class terms. Though the job kept him busy from eight in the evening till six in the morning, he continued to write in his journal. One entry was a poem called "Lament," which began:

> Millions of songs are knocking round, back and forth inside my head: songs of praise and wonder. But I canot give birth even to one song.

"An odd statement," White commented, years later. "I was giving birth almost continuously, like a hamster. None of the songs had any merit, but there was no lack of parturition."[24]

On the same day that he managed to get ashore on an island that was "about as far west as a man could conveniently get on this continent," he was ordered to replace a mess boy who had been knifed. "This descent [into the firemen's mess] seemed a difficult but necessary step up life's ladder," he remembered. "I wanted to test myself—throw myself into any flame that was handy, to see if I could stand the heat."[25]

He stood the heat. He also, in high spirits and good health, rode through three days of full gale that made almost everyone else on board sick, crew and passengers alike. In retrospect, that victory seemed crucial and significant:

> I was headed now toward the south and the east, toward unemployment and the insoluble problem of what to do with myself. My spice route to nowhere was behind me; I would soon be host again to the spectre that I commonly entertained—the shape of a desk in an office, the dreaded tick of the nine-to-five day, the joyless afternoons of a Sunday suburb, the endless and ineffectual escapes that unemployed young men practice (a trip to the zoo, a walk in the night, the opium pipe of a dark cinema). The shape was amorphous—I seldom attempted to fill in the outlines; it hung above me like a bird of death. But in the final hours of the *Buford* the gale granted me a reprieve. In the fury of the storm, thought was impossible; the future was expunged by wind and water; I lived at last in the present, and the present was magnificent—rich and beautiful and awesome. It gave me all the things I wanted from life, and it

was as though I drank each towering wave as it came aboard, as though I would ever after be athirst. At last I had adjusted, temporarily, to a difficult world and had conquered it; others were sick, I bloomed with health. In the noise of battle, all the sad silences of my brooding and foreboding were lost. I had always feared and loved the sea, and this gale was my bride and we had a three-day honeymoon, a violent, tumultuous time of undreamed-of ecstasy and satisfaction. Youth is almost always in deep trouble—of the mind, the heart, the flesh. And as a youth I think I managed to heap myself with more than my share. It took an upheaval of the elements and a job at the lowest level to give me the relief I craved.

The honeymoon was soon over; the wind abated, the *Buford* recovered her poise. On September 4th, we docked at Seattle. I collected my pay [seventy-five dollars] and went ashore.[26]

A few days later he reluctantly took his father's advice and boarded a regulation railroad train for home. He rode the Canadian Pacific first class, and for part of the journey he sat beside a girl who eventually appeared in a Whitmanesque poem, called "Walt Sits Beside Me on the C.P.R." In it White begins by rejecting the notion that there were any real differences between the land and people of Canada and the land and people of the United States. The boundary is a "myth of man":

> I cross over boundaries with a cloud, easily: and the clouds
>   and I say that the heart of wheat is in Saskatchewan
>   and in the Dakotas
> The same and equal
> Giving the same shadows of afternoon, and the same chaff
>   into the sunset.

Then, in the second stanza, he says, a little like Whitman, that the girl who sits beside him on the train is part of the land itself and is as lovely as the land; that somehow the rails in their wake, the telephone poles speeding by, the grain fields and harvest hands, the girl's body, the girl's voice, and the "early stars above," are "all one song."[27]

The holistic creed that White expressed in these verses supported him all his life and informed his view of, and love for, the world and all its creatures.

WHAT ABOUT ALICE? As he rode to the C.P.R., he was traveling towards Buffalo, where he had promised to stop to see her on his way home, whenever that might be.

In a letter from back east one of his friends had asked a hard question:

"If I remember rightly, your heart spilled something to me in New York about a girl—Have you looked very hard for love? As you say in your letter you have come clear across a continent, searching for love. I am very bold. But I will ask: Are you not running away from it?"[28] Perhaps Andy did not know the answer. If he did, it could not have been simple. What he wanted most was to find a career, but he had not even a job—not even a good record as a job-holder. Thurber once wrote White that he assumed he would have married Alice if he had had a good job, a clear professional future, and perhaps a little capital. But we cannot be sure, intimate as the two men were for a while, that Thurber drew the correct conclusions from Andy's account of his feelings for Alice.

While Andy was traveling from Seattle to Buffalo, Alice, not aware of his impending arrival, had mailed him a long letter. When they met in Buffalo, Alice did not tell him what she had said in that letter. The reunion was uncomfortable. Alice had tonsillitis, and Andy talked about the weather. What Alice wanted Andy to know and had implied in her letter, but could not bring herself to tell him face to face, was that if he were to propose to her now, she might say yes. After he got back to Mount Vernon he received letters from Alice that made it clear she wanted to be convinced he loved her. By this time, however, Andy had decided that he was no longer in love with her, and in a long letter, written five months after his return, he finally managed to leave Alice no room for misunderstanding. He wrote of his love as if it were a closed chapter:

> If I had been a normal person two years ago [after she had rejected his proposal], I would have either besieged your doorstep, or else I'd have gone off and sent you a polite note saying, "My dear Lady: Having besought your hand without success, I shall consider the incident jolly well closed and hoping you are the same. . . ." But I was more of a dub.

Instead, he said, he and she had kept on corresponding in a noncommital way that had led to misunderstandings. "Failing to understand the game, I should have kept out."[29] It was a self-regarding way in which to say goodbye to someone he must have known he was hurting at that instant.

Back in New York in the fall of 1923, eighteen months after he had set out on his journey west, Andy had little to lift his spirits. His sister Lillian, the human being with whom he was most congenial—whom, perhaps, he loved most—had married in April, and he could no longer count on her for the companionship that had lightened his dreary days during the autumn and winter of 1921–22. In the little house in Mount Vernon, Samuel White, aged sixty-nine, was suffering from severe attacks of rheumatism. Andy moved back into his room there and sat at the desk from which his father had written him one Saturday afternoon ("a holiday from business") the year before, saying that he hoped his son would leave the gipsy trail and "seek some way to settle and stabilize" his life.[30] But how was a writer to support himself, if he was not fit to be a journalist and had no interest in writing fiction or drama?

At the age of twenty-four Andy had little reason for self-confidence. Without the blessing of instant maturity that their participation in the war had given some writers, and without the personal trials that had shaped some others, he had been a long time growing up. There is no point in wondering what would have happened to him had he joined an ambulance corps and gone overseas in 1917, or if in 1922 he had sailed east instead of driving west. Discovering America gave him more joy and provided him with more experience of the kind he had been seeking than discovering Europe would have done—even though he shared some of the critical attitudes of Lewis and Mencken towards his native land. He once said that because of his ignorance of history, Paris and London failed to excite him: "I solve the capitals of Europe by making straight for the nearest boat rental place."[31] Discouraged as he may have been at the end of his *Wanderjahr* in 1923, he had done, hindsight would suggest, just the right thing for him. He had traveled in the right direction.

CHAPTER VI

New York and
The New Yorker

1 9 2 3 – 1 9 2 6

*". . . the enormously important discovery that the world would pay a man
for setting down a simple, legible account of his own misfortunes."*

S|HORTLY AFTER HIS RETURN FROM THE WEST
in the fall of 1923, White found a job as a layout man in the
production department of the Frank Seaman advertising agency in
Manhattan. His salary was only twenty-five dollars a week (he had
made forty at the *Seattle Times*), and the work did not call for any of his
skills as a writer. Once again he lived in his parents' house and once again
he commuted to work, getting up at 6:30 to catch a train in Mount Vernon
that would take him in twenty-five minutes to Grand Central Station, only
a few blocks uptown from his office on lower Park Avenue.

It took a certain amount of pluck to face the days of his dull routine
and the evenings with his elderly parents in the little house on Mersereau
Avenue. There, in what had been his room since high school days, he
encouraged himself by writing in his journal and turning out occasional
poems. One was a nostalgic sonnet about a bantam rooster he had owned
as a boy, a cocky little creature whose spirit he now admired in retrospect.
Christopher Morley published it in "The Bowling Green," in the *New
York Evening Post*, in November; in December he awarded it first prize
for the best sonnet published in his column during 1923; and years later,
when he offered White the editorship of the *Saturday Review of Literature*,
he recalled it with pleasure.[1]

In January White seems to have quit his job, or taken a leave of absence,
to drive his mother and father to Florida for a winter vacation. En route

9 8

he mailed two squibs to F. P. A., who published them in "The Conning Tower," in the *New York World.*[2] When he returned to Mount Vernon in February, he wrote Alice Burchfield that he didn't have a job; but shortly thereafter he returned to his uncongenial work at Seaman's:

> I . . . was unhappy in the advertising world, because I couldn't seem to make myself care whether a product got moved or not; it never seemed to me of any consequence whether a certain ointment (for stuffy head colds) or a certain window-shade material (waterproof, washable) or a certain wrapping material (transparent) got sold. . . . I found it impossible to get out of bed in the morning caring about them one way or another. I would get out of bed in the morning caring about a certain girl, or about the shadows on the lawn below my window, or about my unsuccessful excursions into the field of letters, or about my sixteen-foot canoe, which I was rigging with a sail; but I was little help to Frank Seaman, who expected me to bring myself to a slow boil in behalf of Mentholatum, Du Pont Tontine Window Shades, Du Pont Cellophane, and other items on his list.[3]

One of his more successful excursions into the field of letters was a poem written on the occasion of his twenty-fifth birthday, and published in "The Conning Tower." In it he contrasted the triviality of his days spent in the world of business with the beauty of his nights spent in the natural world of June bugs, lilacs, and starry heavens. Still, he concluded, he'd rather have the world on these less than perfect terms than not be alive at all:

IN RE GLADNESS

At nine my little doings are begun:
I thumb the thumby files, and note the day,
And write—on some small doing that is done—
"O.K."

The owl-faced phone begins its questioning,
My pencil leaves an odd, cubistic track,
And like as not you'll hear me say, "I'll ring
You back."

With blanks and clips I make my tiny fuss,
The tides of memoranda ebb and flow;
How well I know that such and such is thus—
And so!

But soon, at five, my office day is o'er,
And through the dome of blue the bright stars press,

Reminding me that I am funny—more
Or less.

The June bug bumps his head upon the screen,
The lilac blows the last sweet kiss of spring;
Compared with these my doings do not mean
A thing.

Yet though my tasks with stars cannot be matched,
And men and days and hours are all a myth,
I feel it's something just to be attached
Herewith.[4]

During the two years he worked at the Seaman agency, White continued to send verses to F.P.A., who accepted almost everything he submitted. Since "The Conning Tower" was the most prestigious of all literary columns, White was pleased to appear there, in the company of Arthur Guiterman, William Rose Benét, Dorothy Parker, John O'Hara, William Lyon Phelps, and Don Marquis.

What F.P.A.'s "Tower" meant to him in those early days he still remembered vividly decades later:

There are still plenty of writers alive today who will testify that the high point in their lives was not the first check in the mail from a publication but the first time at the top of the Tower looking down in the morning at the whole city of New York. Making the Tower was a dizzy experience. No money changed hands. . . . One wrote for the sheer glory of it. Such times are unforgettable. If you were skilled in French verse forms, you could even make love to your girl in full view of a carload of subway riders who held the right newspaper opened to the right page. It was a fine era. . . . Frank Adams gave a young writer three precious gifts: discipline, a sense of gaiety, and a brief moment in the sun.[5]

Sometimes late at night Andy would squander a nickel on the early edition of the *New York World* and turn its pages in "secret suspense to discover whether some nubbin of poetry had achieved the decent fame [he] hoped it deserved." His literary ambitions continued to be journalistic, and his idols were then chiefly New York wits:

I burned with a low steady fever just because I was on the same island with Don Marquis, Heywood Broun, Christopher Morley, Franklin P. Adams, Robert C. Benchley, Frank Sullivan, Dorothy Parker, Alexander Woollcott, Ring Lardner and Stephen Vincent Benét. . . . New York hardly gave me a living at that period, but it sustained me. I used to walk quickly past the house in West 13th Street between Sixth and Seventh where F.P.A. lived, and the block seemed to tremble under my feet—the way Park Avenue trembles when a train leaves Grand Central.[6]

During the noon hour he sometimes bowled at Thumb's Bowling Alley or lunched with one of his Cornell friends working in the city. Occasionally he stayed in town in the evening and ended up having a drink in a speakeasy with Pete Vischer, Frank Sullivan and others; but as Sullivan recalled, he never stayed very late and was not "a real drinker." He sailed his canoe, rigged with two masts and fitted with sails made of bed sheets, "mostly by night," in Long Island Sound out of New Rochelle. Of the girls he cared about at this time we have a record only of someone who worked in a "dreary section of Fourth Avenue" and whom he waited to catch a glimpse of as she left work at five o'clock—"a glimpse being the only nourishment that [a] bitter day afford[ed]."[7]

IN THE FALL of 1924, when Andy White was contributing light verse to "The Conning Tower," F.P.A.'s old friend Harold Ross was already well along with his plan to publish a "funny" metropolitan weekly. He had hired a general utility man named Philip Wylie and an advertising salesman. He had published a prospectus, in which he promised that his new weekly would reflect life in New York and be "a necessity for the person who knows his way about, or wants to." Its "conscientious guide" would indicate what was "worthwhile" among "current amusement offerings" in theater, cinema, music, art exhibits, and sports events. It would be witty, gay, and satirical, but it "would be more than a jester." It would "hate bunk." It would not try to please, or even be intelligible to, the "old lady in Dubuque" (a famous character in B.L.T.'s column, "A Line o' Type or Two," in the *Chicago Tribune*), but it would attract sophisticated readers nationwide. It would not be what was "commonly called radical or highbrow," by which perhaps he meant to distinguish it from *The New Republic* or *The Nation* on the one hand, and from *Vanity Fair* or *Harper's Magazine* on the other. It was to be called *The New Yorker.*[8]

With the financial backing of Raoul Fleischmann, a young businessman and member of a wealthy family of bakers, Ross began in late 1924 to put together his first issue, on the cover of which would appear Rea Irvin's caricature of a Regency dandy—a Beau Brummel—wearing an antique, curl-brimmed high hat and a tall, wide, starched stock, or cravat, and looking superciliously through a monocle at a butterfly. As it turned out,

Ross thought that the cover, which he recognized as a piece of art, was the only successful feature of the first issue.⁹ Perhaps he knew that it was the only thing that clearly distinguished his magazine from *Life* and *Judge,* the popular humor weeklies that he did not want *The New Yorker* to resemble. Perhaps he saw in Irvin's man of fashion the amused skeptic and the sophisticated connoisseur who would personify the spirit of *The New Yorker* as that of a man of taste, not that of a moralist, a pundit, or a clown. But no one knows what Ross thought at the time. Later on he regretted some of the other characteristics that could be attributed to the dandy—disdain, snobbishness, and frivolity. Uncomfortable as he became with the ambiguity of an image both smart and skeptical, he nevertheless reprinted it on the cover of *The New Yorker* every succeeding February to mark the anniversary of the magazine. Within six months after *The New Yorker's* first appearance, in a series of illustrated pieces called "The Making of a Magazine," written by the humorist Corey Ford and published in *The New Yorker,* Irvin's Beau Brummel was given the ridiculous name Eustace Tilley and thereafter became identified as the mythical New Yorker representing *The New Yorker.*

The first issue of *The New Yorker* appeared on the newstands on Thursday, February 19, 1925. Andy had been on the lookout for the first issue ever since a friend had suggested that the new magazine might be interested in contributions from a writer with Andy's sense of humor, and he remembers vividly the momentous afternoon when he "swung into Grand Central Terminal" on his way to catch the train to Mount Vernon and "laid fifteen cents on the line" to buy his copy of *The New Yorker,* vol. 1, no. 1. Nine weeks later the new magazine published his first contribution, a short piece on the coming of spring. It consisted of six examples of what an advertising copywriter might produce if he took over the VERNAL account. One example:

NEW BEAUTY OF TONE IN 1925 SONG SPARROW

Into every one of this season's song sparrows has been built the famous VERNAL tone. Look for the distinguishing white mark on the breast.

A few weeks later Ross published a four-hundred-word "Defense of the Bronx River," by E. B. White. It was written in a tone of humorous New York chauvinism that suited the purpose of the magazine. It began well: "The Bronx River rises in Valhalla and flows south to Hell Gate." Though few people knew its name until the Bronx River Highway Commission was named after it, it runs, White insisted, "through Woodlawn, West Mount Vernon, Bronxville, Tuckahoe, Scarsdale, Hartsdale, and White

Plains," right alongside the New York Central tracks on which the commuter trains run; and, he concluded, "here is one commuter who wouldn't trade this elegant little river, with its ducks and rapids and pipes and commissions and willows, for the Amazon or the Snohomish or La Platte or the Danube, or the Mississippi, even though the latter does rise in Lake Itaska and flows south to the Gulf of Mexico and is wider."[10]

The first issue of *The New Yorker* sold fifteen thousand copies on the newsstand; the fourth sold only ten thousand five hundred; and by late April sales had fallen to eight thousand. In May Fleischmann sought the opinion of a publisher's counsel and on his advice decided to continue to support the magazine for another eight months and to allocate a considerable amount of money to a promotional campaign designed to convince businessmen of the advantages of advertising in a magazine read chiefly by affluent New Yorkers of sophisticated tastes. Ross and Fleischmann decided to coast through the summer and to throw all their resources, editorial and entrepreneurial, into a fall campaign.[11]

While waiting for this campaign to start, however, Ross himself made two moves aimed at improving the magazine. First he changed the layout of the "front of the book." Up to then, these opening pages had consisted of three "columns" or "departments": "Talk of the Town," a sophisticated gossip column; "Behind the News," short feature stories about interesting people, places, and events; and "Of All Things," *The New Yorker*'s equivalent of an editorial column, consisting of a series of short, mostly lighthearted comments on people and events in the news. Now Ross decided, after some experimenting, to drop the gossip column altogether, to call the entire front of the book "Talk of the Town," to open it with editorial paragraphs under the subheading "Notes and Comment," and to follow "Notes and Comment" with the kind of short feature stories that had previously been headed "Behind the News." The new arrangement was, as one historian of the magazine called it, "an inspired piece of bad makeup." It has endured to this day.[12]

Ross's next move was to hire two new writers: Morris Markey, an excellent feature writer and rewrite man from the *New York World*, to produce the short feature stories that the staff were soon calling " 'Talk' pieces," and a "brilliant young amateur" named Fillmore Hyde, to write the paragraphs of "Notes and Comment." Until he was succeeded by E. B. White, Hyde wrote excellent comment; but as it turned out, Hyde made his most valuable contribution to the magazine, shortly after he was hired, by introducing his neighbor Katharine (Mrs. Ernest) Angell to Harold Ross. Ross hired Katharine Sergeant Angell, also in the summer of 1925, as a part-time reader of manuscripts, but by fall she had become his full-time editorial assistant. "I suspect," White once said, "one of Ross's luckiest [days] was the day a young woman named Mrs. Angell stepped off the elevator all ready to go to work."[13] It quickly became evident that she possessed great energy, intelligence, and self-assurance; a solid education in literature, which Ross, lacking it himself, respected; and a keen eye for the quality of the material she was given to read. Her opinions on whatever pieces of writing were laid before her impressed Ross, and he did not hesitate to give her talents wide scope. Within a few months after her appearance on the scene he entrusted her with chief advisory responsibility for "fiction," which included stories, poems, and everything else that Ross thought of as "literary." Ross soon thereafter asked her to join him and Rea Irvin in the weekly art meetings, at which cartoons were accepted or rejected. In fact, in the early stage of the magazine, according to White, she was "messed up with the whole works"; she was "deep in the dingles of humor, and she was a whiz."[14]

D U R I N G that summer of 1925, Andy quit his job at Frank Seaman's agency. It was a dead end, he was not writing copy, as he had hoped to do, and he was bored. He also decided once again to leave home, this time to live in New York, the city that could bestow "on any person who desires such queer prizes . . . the gift of loneliness and the gift of privacy." He joined three Cornell fraternity brothers in renting an apartment at 112 West Thirteenth Street, in Greenwich Village. Having made these decisions, he entered what he later called a period of "comparative unemployment" and the "only genuinely creative period" in his life. It lasted eighteen months, from the summer of 1925 to the winter of 1926–27, and in the course of it he finally succeeded in finding an answer to the question that had haunted him for at least ten years: How was he going to earn his living?[15]

When he left Seaman's he gave himself a twenty-foot catboat, christened *Pequod,* with "accomodations for one, . . . a simple gaff rig, a marvelous compactness, [and] a one-cylinder Mianus make-and-break engine." Being "rich in leisure" at the time, he loved to make "solitary voyages" in her, "to a remote and lotus-scented land—the north shore of Long Island." On one such voyage he had an unpleasant brush with privilege that he never forgot:

One afternoon we anchored at slack tide off a pleasant spot and swam ashore. We were met by a man with a gun. He explained that it was Mr. [J. P.] Morgan's place and not for people who came up out of the sea dripping. So we swam back, poisoning the waves with bile, and lay anchored all night, debating with ourself the subject of private property: torn between our own great happiness in the ownership of a catboat, and our resentment at Mr. Morgan's happiness in owning such a large chunk of shore. . . .[16]

The furnished walk-up apartment on West Thirteenth Street into which Andy moved in August occupied the third floor of an old four-story house. It consisted of a living room, a hallway, a kitchenette, a bedroom containing two sets of bunk beds, and a bath. The rent was $110 a month. Andy's roommates were Gustave Stubbs (Gus) Lobrano, a close friend with whom he shared memories of the *Cornell Daily Sun,* Monday nights at the Adamses', and Camp Otter; Burke Dowling (Bob) Adams; and Mitchell T. (Mike) Galbreath, the man whose conversation Andy had missed during lonesome nights in Seattle. Lobrano and Adams worked for the Cunard Line, and Galbreath for McGraw Hill. The four young men were congenial. Adams remembers their going together to the Theatre Guild's *Garrick Gaieties,* for which Rodgers and Hart had written such hits as "Mountain Greenery" (1925) and "Manhattan" (1926). On their radio-with-loud-speaker (a step up from radio-with-earphones) they heard together the first Dempsey-Tunney fight, with its long count.[17]

But in spite of his pleasure in their companionship, and in spite of his liberation from suburbia and an unrewarding office job, Andy's life in Greenwich Village, during what he called these "lean and tortured years," was lonely and full of frustration:

those mornings alone in the apartment straightening up after the others had left for work, rinsing the dirty cereal-encrusted bowls, taking the percolator apart and putting it together again, and then sinking down on the lumpy old couch in the terrible loneliness of midmorning, sometimes giving way to tears of doubt and misgiving (his own salt rivers of doubt), and in the back room the compensatory window box with the brave and grimy seedlings struggling, and the view of the naked fat lady across the yard. It had always been a question then of how to get through the day, the innumerable aimless journeys to remote sections of the town, inspecting warehouses, docks, marshes, lumber-yards, the interminable quest for the holy and unnameable grail, looking for it down every street and in every window and in every pair of eyes, following a star always obscured by mists.[18]

In September he began to look for a part-time job that would support him and still afford him enough time to write. He found one with the advertising agency of J. H. Newmark that paid him thirty dollars a week for writing copy about a new automobile called the Star. According to his journal, he was hired on Thursday, October 8, 1925, and spent all the next day "walking, mostly in the rain, by the Harlem River."[19] During the first two months of his employment at Newmark's he found time to write eight pieces for *The New Yorker*. One of them, a definition of *critic,* eventually found its way into Christopher Morley's edition of *Bartlett's Quotations:*

> The critic leaves at curtain fall
> To find, in starting to review it,
> He scarcely saw the play at all
> For watching his reaction to it.[20]

That fall the campaign to save the faltering young *New Yorker* was succeeding. The magazine was improving editorially, circulation was climbing, and the business office was selling advertising. Ross may have given a lucky fillip to the upswing when he decided to take the advice of well-connected Yaleman Ralph McAllister Ingersoll to publish an unsolic- ited article written by the daughter of a socially prominent family and entitled "Why We Go to Cabarets: A Post-Debutante Explains." It revealed the shocking news that young women from families of New York's elite "400" would rather go to nightclubs than to coming out parties, where the men in stag lines were "pretty terrible." According to the legendary history of the magazine, the article "took Park Avenue in a storm of gossip" and was all that was needed to establish *The New Yorker* as a must among those in the smart set of Manhattan. If this rather banal article really did give circulation a boost, it may have done so mainly because three of New York's leading dailies, the *Times,* the *Tribune,* and the *World,* carried front-page stories about the *The New Yorker*'s news from the world of debutantes. Such publicity was more valuable than the most costly advertising. In any case, within a few weeks B. Altman and Company had signed a contract for fifty-two pages of advertisements for 1926, and shortly thereafter Saks Fifth Avenue did the same. Circulation had risen enough to enable the business office to claim an average circulation for the year of over twelve thousand. Ross had dreamed of only ten thousand. In the first-anniversary issue of February 1926, there were ads for Pierce-Arrow, Helena Rubinstein, I. Miller, and The French Line.[21]

No event in the young life of *The New Yorker* was more auspicious, however, than the appearance, in the last issue of 1925, of a 650-word piece signed "E.B.W." It was called "Child's Play," and consisted, as its subtitle stated, of an account of how its author turned "a glass of buttermilk into a personal triumph." Charlie Chaplin called it "one of the best humor things he had read."[22] It tells the story of a waitress in a crowded restaurant who inadvertently spills a glass of buttermilk on the blue serge suit of the author. He reacts in a style reminiscent of the character Chaplin had made famous. He refuses to be embarrassed, pitied, or laughed at; he enjoys making the magnanimous gesture of comforting the tearful waitress and of making a magnificent exit by rising in full view of the silent patrons, putting on his overcoat, and deliberately "strolling" through the long aisle to the cashier's cage, paying his seventy-five-cent check with a dollar bill, refusing the change, and walking out. It was a self-mocking story of a "personal triumph." Ross and Mrs. Angell recognized in it a new and original voice.

White himself was greatly heartened by the success of the story. He realized that in writing it he had "unconsciously stylized the [story's] action, and . . . that at last [he] had produced something that made sense journalistically." What this discovery of an effective narrative voice meant to him and his future he described years later, in the third person, veiling his identity under the name of a fictional character he called Mr. Volente:

Here was Fifth Avenue and the Childs restaurant where the waitress had long ago spilled a bottle of buttermilk down his blue suit. A turning point, he liked to think. He often wondered where the girl was, this somehow invaluable and clumsy girl who had unwittingly shaped his life into a pattern from which it had not since departed. (Mr. Volente had written an account of the catastrophe at the time and had sold it to a young and inexperienced magazine, thus making for himself the enormously important discovery that the world would pay a man for setting down a simple, legible account of his own misfortunes. With the check in his pocket and trouble always at his elbow, the young Volente had faced life with fresh courage and had seen a long vista of profitable confession; and in fact he had stuck it out and done well enough.)[23]

By "confession" he meant "simple, legible accounts of his own misfortunes." And by "misfortunes" he meant almost anything that happened to him. In short, he had found a way to make a living by writing about himself—briefly, and frequently, like other journalist-essayists, beginning with Addison and Steele. He liked to "write short"; he liked the freedom to report whatever most interested him at the time; and he liked to be published promptly.

White was not interested in the works of the most ambitious and accomplished literary figures of his generation. Indeed, he seems to have been hardly aware of them. Now that he was at last living in the Village, on the same block as F.P.A., he was also living only a few doors down the street from the office of *The Dial,* where Marianne Moore was publishing poems by the best poets of the time: T. S. Eliot, William Butler Yeats,

Ezra Pound, Wallace Stevens, William Carlos Williams, Yvor Winters, and D. H. Lawrence. A block to the north, on Fourteenth Street, was the house in which only a few years earlier *The Little Review* had published *Ulysses* in installments. And a block to the south was the house in which Malcolm Cowley, Matthew Josephson, and William Slater Brown had tried to save *Broom*.

In the mid-twenties the Village was full of young artists, poets, novelists, and critics. In September 1923, when Andy began to work for the Frank Seaman agency, Hart Crane, son of a successful candy-manufacturer in Cleveland, resigned from the agency of J. Walter Thompson. Crane lived on Dominick Street, in the Village. E. E. Cummings, John Dos Passos, and Gilbert Seldes were in Paris at that moment, but they would soon be back in the Village—Cummings in his studio on the top floor of 4 Patchin Place, next door to John Cowper Powys. (When White moved to the Village, Cummings was beginning to contribute humorous pieces to *Vanity Fair,* which White probably read. Cummings wrote in praise of Coney Island, and White in defense of the Bronx River; Cummings wrote "Why I Like America," and White "Why I Like New York.")[24] In 1925 Allen Tate, then an assistant editor of a pulp magazine, was living in the Village. And when Andy settled in with his three Cornell roommates in 1925, John Steinbeck had just worked his way to New York on a cattle boat, and Malcolm Cowley and Kenneth Burke were planning a little magazine to be called *Aesthete.*

Cummings once said that in this period of American literature, writers who had not been in the war were outsiders. But what made the literary world of the Village alien to White was simply his temperament and his taste. Though he wanted to be read, he did not seek the approval of the "literary" world. He was not interested in movements, literary or otherwise. He was not, nor has he ever been, devoted to any of the fine arts: "I know nothing of music or of painting or of sculpture or of the dance. I would rather watch the circus or a ball game than ballet." As for literature, he was never so much interested in what had been or was being written as he was in what he was writing himself. To a literary historian he once wrote: "Thurber can write you an informative letter about American letters and trends in same, but I can't, as letters have never been my interest, only my fate. I read farm journals and boating magazines and my favorite authors are people nobody has ever heard of."[25] In 1925 he was not interested in the people who made up the literary world, and he has never ceased to be amused by the pretensions of people who identify themselves as authors, especially those who wish to be thought of as serious poets. Describing himself once as a "non-poet who occasionally breaks into song," White said that the life of a non-poet is an agreeable one because "he feels no obligation to mingle with other writers of verse to exchange sensitivities, no compulsion to visit the Y to read from his own works, no need to travel the wine-and-cheese circuit, where the word 'poet' carries the aroma of magic and ladies creep up from behind carrying ballpoint pens and sprigs of asphodel."[26]

AFTER WHITE had glimpsed that "long vista of profitable confession" in December 1925, it was five months before *The New Yorker* published another piece of his prose. In May he submitted two brief sketches of men whose behavior he had observed. One piece was a sad, ironic description of a hopeless, unemployed derelict in Union Square, the other a cheerful description of a good-natured drunk on a commuter train. Both were in an informal style Ross liked to call "casual"—in the style, in fact, of pieces that eventually were called casuals at *The New Yorker*. Both were like the fiction Katharine Angell admired, short and free from the "heavy burden of plot."[27] It was the second of White's casuals that prompted Mrs. Angell to suggest that Ross offer its author a job as a staff writer at *The New Yorker*. When White took Ross's suggestion that he drop in at the *New Yorker* office, it was Katharine Angell who came out into the reception room where he sat waiting and met him with the question, "Are you Elwyn Brooks White?" That first meeting between Andy and Katharine was to be as rich in consequences for the two of them as for Ross and his magazine.

When Andy met Katharine she was thirty-three years old and a striking woman in appearance and manner. Anyone meeting her for the first time, in her office, might well at the outset have been startled, perhaps even slightly unsettled, by her large, discerning eyes resting intently upon him —measuring him. But she knew how to put her visitor at ease by listening attentively to what he had to say, by answering carefully and to the point, in words that showed her good will and, at times, her humor. She spoke in a clear, pleasant voice, in a Bostonian accent. If a longer conversation ensued and the visitor was—as often happened—a writer whose work was to be discussed, he would quickly discover how intimately she had acquainted herself with it, how unerringly she had noticed whatever were its virtues and weaknesses. John Updike once remarked that she was "gifted with that terrible clear vision some women have (the difference between a good and bad story loomed like a canyon in her vision), yet not burdened by it, rather rejoicing in it and modest and humorous in her firmness." She was "a lovely person—a formidable woman," he added.[28]

The qualities that made her seem formidable, and that lent her, in the words of Brendan Gill, a "touch of blue-eyed augustness," were essentially intellectual—along with her straight-backed, one might almost say regal, carriage.[29] These qualities were softened, however, by her equally evident and appealing femininity, which expressed itself in all the ways that caused Updike to call her not just a formidable but also a lovely person—and which, of course, revealed itself in her looks.

She was small—a fact that prompted her to wear high-heeled shoes most of the time. Her blue eyes were set in relief by her dark hair, some three feet long (it was never cut). She arranged it at the back of her head, where it enhanced her fine Roman profile. She was proud of her luxuriant hair and had had it groomed, ever since her college days, by the Francis Fox Institute for the Scientific Care of Hair, which maintained studios in Boston, New York, London, Paris, and (in season) Palm Beach and Bar Harbor. She liked and wore handsome, elegant clothes. But even without such extraneous aids she would have been a good-looking young woman.

KATHARINE SERGEANT ANGELL came from an old New England family. Her most distinguished ancestor was John Sergeant, a graduate of the Yale Divinity School who went to Stockbridge, Massachusetts, as a missionary to the Mahican Indians about 1730, and there founded the first integrated and first coeducational school in America. The Mission House in Stockbridge, now a museum, was once the Sergeant house. Katharine's less remote ancestors moved to Northampton, Massachusetts, where her father, Charles S. Sergeant, was born. Her mother, Elizabeth Shepley, reared in Maine, was studying art in Boston when she met Charles Sergeant, by then a promising young businessman. Katharine, the youngest of their three daughters, was born in Winchester, a suburb of Boston. Her mother died when Katharine was five, and Charles Sergeant's unmarried sister Caroline came from Northampton to help her brother rear his children. ("Aunt Crully" had "strong opinions on Rights for Women.") By this time Sergeant's financial success as an executive of the new Boston Elevated Railway, which he had helped build, enabled him to own a fine house in Brookline, near the Arboretum.

Katharine's was a bluestocking education. She was sent to Miss Winsor's School in Boston and then to Bryn Mawr, where she majored in English literature and philosophy. In her junior year she became engaged to Ernest Angell, a good-looking Harvard undergraduate about to enter Harvard Law School. He came from Cleveland, where his father had been a lawyer.

At Bryn Mawr Katharine resurrected and became co-editor of a fortnightly campus magazine called *Tipyn o' Bob* (Welsh for "a bit of everything"), which published news, editorials, stories, sketches, and verse. One of her editorial rules was that contributions should be short. As co-editor of the annual literary publication, *The Lantern,* she succeeded in obtaining a poem from Marianne Moore (who later became her friend when Katharine was her *New Yorker* editor).

In her last year of college she was stage manager for the senior class play, *Cyrano de Bergerac* (a favorite play of E. B. White's), which she had persuaded her classmates to produce. The job, she said, called for "tact and firmness"—traits she was amply blessed with. Years later a contemporary of hers at Bryn Mawr remembered "her responsive sensitivity, her humor, and her respect for any and all personalities," as well as "the quiet but definite way she could size us all up—not a bit patronizing, but very sure."[30]

After her graduation in 1914, Katharine worked as a volunteer at the Massachusetts General Hospital under the supervision of a woman studying occupational diseases. She had not settled on a career, though at various times she thought she would like to become a writer, a doctor, or an archaeologist. In 1915 she and Ernest Angell were married in her father's house in Brookline. They settled in Cleveland, where Ernest joined his late father's law firm and Katharine worked for a nurse who was making a survey of the physically handicapped in the area. After the survey was finished, she became secretary of the Consumers' League of Ohio and began a study of working conditions in factories.

In 1917, shortly after America entered the war, Ernest enlisted in the army; and right after his and Katharine's first child, Nancy, was born, he was sent overseas. Katharine felt abandoned, and soon found life difficult having to support an infant on half the pay of a first lieutenant. After the Armistice, in 1918, she moved back to her father's house in Brookline, there to await Ernest's return. Katharine thought bitterly that he was one of the last of the American soldiers to leave France.

After Ernest was discharged from the army in 1919, he and Katharine and Nancy settled in New York City. Although Ernest Angell eventually became a distinguished lawyer and president of the American Civil Liberties Union, the early years of his professional life were slow going. Nonetheless, he and Katharine lived in a pleasant house on East Eighty-first Street and rented as a summer place an old stone cottage in Sneden's Landing, across the Hudson River, a little north of the city.

For about a year, until their son Roger was born, in 1920, Katharine worked at the first job she could find—as an assistant to an interior decorator—and with her earnings was able to employ a cook and a nursemaid. She was not a suffragette, nor was she ever active in women's rights movements. She simply did not like housework and was, in her words, "easily tired and frazzled by the steady care or teaching of children."

Within two years after the birth of Roger, however, Katharine became convinced that her marriage could never be happy. The difficulty was, she said years later, "a matter of having married too young, before we knew what we were going to turn out to be, and a matter of [Ernest's] coming back from World War I with quite different ideas about marriage than before he left for the War." Now more than ever she was determined to find work that not only would buy her freedom from domestic chores but would fully engage her energies and her talents.

Since girlhood she had assumed that she would have a husband, a family, and a professional career, and now she was looking for "work of the mind, not hands, for which [she was] best fitted." She had several temporary jobs. For a short time she tried "putting into English the very Germanic English of a famous woman psychoanalyst" who, Katharine thought, "was as mixed up as her patients were, and more so." (It was a job that left her permanently skeptical of the value of psychoanalysis, especially for artists.) For about a year she helped conduct a fund-raising campaign for Bryn Mawr. It was not until the summer of 1925, when Harold Ross hired her, that she found the work that would become her career. By the time she met Andy, in 1926, she was professionally more successful than her husband, though this had not been her aim. According to her daughter, Nancy, there developed between her mother and father a kind of rivalry that was never to develop between Katharine and Andy, either as editor and writer, or as wife and husband.

A year and a half after she began to work for *The New Yorker,* Katharine could speak of her success in being both a mother and a professional woman —though she could not say she was happily married:

Now after eleven years of marriage I find myself, strangely enough, actually living to some degree the life I visualized for myself fifteen or more years ago. I am married and have two children, five [sic] and nine years old. I live a very full home life, and I hold an editorial position that is as exacting a full-time job as any I see about me.[31]

White could not, of course, have known any of this when he met Mrs. Angell for the first time. Of their interview all he remembers is his awareness "that she had a lot of back hair and the knack of making a young contributor feel at ease."[32] Presumably Mrs. Angell broached the subject

of White's becoming a staff writer for *The New Yorker,* and presumably
White would not commit himself to an office job, even as a writer. In any
case, within a few weeks he had left the country.

One morning at breakfast late in June, White's apartment-mate Bob
Adams, who worked for the Cunard Line, offered him free passage, expenses, and forty-five dollars a week to join a tour of Europe organized
for college students and to write the script for a promotional movie to be
shot en route. The ship was to sail that afternoon at five. Forty years later
White recalled the caper as follows:

> I said I would be pleased to go, but had no passport, no visas, no clean shirts,
> and no money. Bob phoned Washington and arranged a passport, I taxied
> around town on borrowed money, buying shirts and obtaining visas and
> getting photographed. . . . At four I threw the contents of my bureau drawer
> into an old suitcase, and at five the *Andania* with Bob and me aboard dropped
> her lines and proceeded downriver, while a college band played down below
> in College Cabin. . . . For the next five or six weeks, I saw Europe and had
> a ball. The crossing took nine days. We shot Cunard travel movies during the
> day, and danced with the college girls by night.[33]

Before he left, he sent a poem to F.P.A. that appeared in "The Conning
Tower" on July 13, two days after his twenty-seventh birthday, which had
been the occasion for it.

Though the trip supplied him with material for a few publishable
poems, there is little evidence that what he saw of Europe greatly impressed
him. In a letter to Cushman he spoke of

> a dreamlike journey, leaving tiny bright memories: the glint of sun on the
> Avon, late in the day; the Cornish coast in the blue of morning; the melodious
> voice of a concierge in Berne, phoning; the way gravel feels under your feet;
> drinking beer in a garden in Koln; a hayfield above the Lake of Thun; hors
> d'oeuvres for eight francs.[34]

When he returned to New York on August 7, he went directly from
the *Berengeria* to 112 West Thirteenth Street, picked up his mail, walked
to the Child's restaurant on Fourteenth Street, ordered a meal, and, while
he waited for it to be served, sorted out six envelopes from *The New Yorker*
containing checks for a total of $178. It was then, for the first time, that
he felt confident he could do what he had dreamed for twenty years of
doing—earning his living by writing what he wanted to write.[35]

Getting White to join the staff of *The New Yorker* was not easy. There
were lunches with Mrs. Angell and with Harold Ross before he agreed to

take a specific weekly assignment, and there were more negotiations and another lunch before he agreed to accept an office at the magazine's premises and to spend at least a part of each day in it. From the vantage point of his new position he produced an ironic little self-portrait entitled "Life Cycle of a Literary Genius," which *The New Yorker* published in October:

I

Shows precocity at six years of age. Writes poem entitled, "To a Little Mouse," beginning, "Last night I heard a noise in my scrap-basket." His mother likes poem and shows it to Aunt Susie.

II

At fourteen years of age, encouraged by former success, writes short essay entitled, "The Woods in Winter," beginning, "I whistled to my dog Don and he raced and romped as we set out together." Sends this to *St. Nicholas Magazine* and wins silver badge.

V

At forty, encouraged by success, accepts invitation to have lunch with editor of popular magazine. Editor orders exotic dishes and mentions an opening "on the staff!"

VI

Encouraged by success, dies of nervous indigestion right after lunch, leaving an illegitimate son who grows up in obscurity and writes the great American novel.[36]

Ross, suffering from ulcers, did in fact order unusual luncheon dishes, and White had in fact always been vulnerable to attacks of nervous indigestion. Related to White's life and feeling, as dreams relate to reality, the piece veils in humorous hyperbole White's ambition as well as his fears.

So E. B. White filled an opening on the staff, "got a job there," as he once wrote, "as an orderly"; and as time went on he rather liked it because it "reminded him of the fireman's mess on the Buford. "It was only a thirty-dollar-a-week, part-time job, and he did not give up his other thirty-dollar-a-week part-time job with Newmark until after he had been "at *The New Yorker*" for several months.[37]

CHAPTER VII

"We"

1 9 2 7

"We write as we please and the magazine publishes as it pleases. When the two pleasures coincide, something gets into print."

I
N A REMINISCENT MOOD ROSS ONCE WROTE White that in the very first years after he had started *The New Yorker* he had had an incredible run of luck, and that in retrospect the magazine seemed to be really "a whim of God's." White had come along, he said, then Thurber, and along with them Peter Arno and Helen Hokinson and a few more.[1] In fact Arno and Hokinson preceded White by more than a year, and Ross's run of luck started even earlier than that, at the time he hired the artist Rea Irvin, who was largely responsible for the handsome new look of the magazine as a whole. Ross's luck had also included engaging Janet Flanner to write "Letter from Paris," and Lois Long to write the two consumer columns "On and Off the Avenue" and "Tables for Two." Not the least of his luck had been finding Katharine Sergeant Angell.

When he persuaded Andy White, late in 1926, to take a part-time job on the staff, he was looking for someone to edit the funny column-fillers called "newsbreaks," to help with rewriting "Talk" pieces, and to invent or improve captions for cartoons. Within a month he discovered that what he had found was a writer whose style could give the magazine the humorous editorial voice it most needed.

Ross "took to White instantly, sheltered him from the day of his bewildered arrival," according to Ralph Ingersoll, the managing editor at *The New Yorker* when White came aboard. But at first White "found Ross a bit hard to take—he was a very different fish from me," and it took these two men a while to develop the personal and professional friendship that became an important element in their lives—and, of course, in the history of *The New Yorker*.[2]

When they met, Ross was thirty-four and White was twenty-seven. Ross had been on his own as a journalist for about eighteen years before he founded *The New Yorker*. He had covered the waterfront for the *San Francisco Call and Post;* he had worked for twenty-three newspapers during the two years it took him to reach the East Coast; he had been managing editor of *Stars and Stripes* (the American army's enlisted men's newspaper published in Paris in 1918 and 1919); and at the time he started *The New Yorker* in 1925 he had already been editor of three national magazines published in New York City. But for all his professional experience, Ross was, in some ways, as immature as White.

"Ross never really grew up," White once wrote (and added, "Some of the best contributors [to the magazine] never really grew up").[3] His honesty, his self-assurance, his playfulness, his restlessness, his terrible temper, his awkwardness, and his idealism were all expressions of a basic innocence. In general, he didn't like women (or tended to be afraid of them), and he was most at ease in the company of the men with whom he liked to drink and play poker.

Ross's first wife thought him the homeliest man she'd ever met, and remembered him as follows:

> There was certainly a mismating of his head, his hands and his feet to his gaunt, angular body; his hands, though he learned to use them gracefully, were too large; so were his feet, and his ears and his mouth were also oversized; his tongue was a real problem and he was really more comfortable when he let it hang over his loose lower lip, as he did when he was relaxed or was thinking hard. His keen gray eyes were too small—became even smaller as he squinted them when he looked at you intently, as was his habit. The only normal-sized feature of his large-boned face was his nose that sat against a sallow background: no color ever flushed his face. His stooped shoulders and his shambling walk were also characteristic. A chronic restlessness so plagued him that he seemed to be suffering from growing pains—perpetual growing pains—with such symptoms as fidgeting, scratching his head, jumping up suddenly, and walking nervously about as he jingled coins in his pockets.[4]

He was gap-toothed, brushed his mouse-colored hair into a high, stiff pompadour, and wore "old fashioned, high-laced shoes, because he thought Manhattan men dressed like what he called dudes." He didn't like to be spoken to in elevators and didn't like people to whistle in the corridors. In his quest for perfection he strained for efficiencies inappropriate in an organization dominated by artistic temperaments, and his schemes to simplify procedures or eliminate error usually ended in comic frustration. Ross loved to gamble and was sometimes played for a sucker. He liked elaborate practical jokes. He used profane language. He was "terrified of physical violence," and whenever he could he delegated to an assistant such unpleasant confrontations as firing an employee.

But in conversation, Janet Flanner recalled, Ross was a "fascinating character, sympathetic, loveable, often explosively funny, and a good talker, . . . a vitally intelligent man, . . . a magnet for intelligent people." He liked to talk with his writers and was always available in his office. As he listened, he "sat with his head resting in hand, looking thoughtful, sitting quiet, as if he were prospecting his thoughts." He even sought out his writers in their offices:

> He . . . prowled around the corridors in the late afternoon, looking things over and looking in on those who worked for him and about whom he was always paternally curious. He would drop in on them, chat and swear, and usually make them laugh. As an official chief, he was a humanly observing kind of man. He shared himself especially with the new young writers on his staff. He would bang on their doors, walk in, and say "Ross," as his introduction.[5]

He had not had a good formal education, nor was he well read. He sometimes tried to hide his ignorance of literature by exaggerating it ("Who's Willa Cather?"), but there was some truth in White's statement that whenever anyone mentioned a book, Ross and he hadn't read it. Ross loved to learn, and what he most enjoyed reading were reference books. "Facts steadied him, and comforted him," William Shawn has said. "Facts also amused him." Moreover, as White pointed out, "Ross had a thing that is at least as good as, and sometimes better than, knowledge: he had a sort of natural drive in the right direction, plus a complete respect for the work and ideas and opinion of others." His lack of a literary education was not, according to Katharine, a serious weakness. "Ross," she said, "spent all his life reading to catch up and . . . was a natural literary man."[6]

Perhaps no one at *The New Yorker* understood Ross better than Mrs. Angell. Years later, in discussing her relationship with him, she told why he and she were so congenial, personally and professionally:

> Ross and I got on perfectly from the very start but it's true that he did, in moments of frustration, put his hands over his head and exclaim "I am surrounded by women and children." I was the "women," I'm sure. Ross was furious that I was a woman but he soon came to depend on me and accept

me. He delegated work to me with complete freedom and when he sent me back a short story with two or three pages of his famous notes he told me to omit any I thought were foolish. This I did but I could sense the queries that he felt were really important and if I didn't agree with them I would just go to his office and argue it out. From Ross I picked up the habit of swearing occasionally. He used profanities and I do to this day—ones that are unsuitable for a proper New England old lady. Ross confided to me many things about his personal life—perhaps more than he did to anyone else. . . .

I never felt any attraction to Ross as a male. In fact I couldn't see how anybody could bear to be married to him, but we were fond of each other and had complete faith in each other. When he died I felt I had lost my best friend. . . . I respected and dearly loved Ross as a boss. He was fond of me, I think, but he never really expressed it. Once when Ernest and I were going to Paris and Ralph Barton, one of our major New Yorker cartoonists, was living there, Ross gave me a letter of introduction to Barton. It started: "This is to introduce Mrs. Angell, who is not unattractive." This is the highest personal comment I ever got from him. But I loved and admired him and despite his limitations and prejudices I thought he was a brilliant editor.[7]

White described how Ross and Mrs. Angell complemented each other in ways that seemed "to have been indispensable to the survival of the magazine":

She had a natural refinement of manner and speech; Ross mumbled and bellowed and swore. She quickly discovered, in this fumbling and impoverished new weekly, something that fascinated her: its quest for humor, its search for excellence, its involvement with young writers and artists. She enjoyed contact with people; Ross, with certain exceptions, despised it—especially during hours. She was patient and quiet; he was impatient and noisy. Katharine was soon sitting in on art sessions and planning sessions, editing fiction and poetry, cheering and steering authors and artists along the paths they were eager to follow, learning make-up, learning pencil editing, heading the Fiction Department, sharing the personal woes and dilemmas of innumerable contributors and staff people who were in trouble or despair, and in short, accepting the whole unruly business of a tottering magazine with the warmth and dedication of a broody hen.[8]

On another occasion White said that though "no two people in the world could be more different" than Katharine and Ross, "they met at one point (they both thought the same things were funny)." Ross's humor was, Katharine thought, "the best of all his qualities," and humor, in her opinion, was "the rarest of all the great qualities of mind."[9] But something deeper than their shared sense of humor bound Ross and Katharine and

Andy. They all trusted each other's honesty and respected each other's gifts. Ross soon became so convinced of the good sense, good taste, and good will of Katharine and Andy that they became his literary or editorial conscience. After twenty years of working with them both, Ross confessed in a memo to Andy that by nature he had always had to have someone to hold himself responsible to, and that as editor of *The New Yorker* he had always had an instinct to be responsible to Andy and Katharine—more to Katharine than to Andy.[10]

Katharine and Andy in turn gave Ross their loyalty because they admired "his ability and his stamina" and his dedication to the magazine, and they grew to love him because he was a man following a dream— not, as with Andy, a dream of "something he could not name," but still a vision of something unattainable in its full perfection and not always describable in detail.[11]

"Ross's dream," White once wrote, "was a simple dream; it was pure and had no frills: he wanted the magazine to be good, to be funny, and to be fair," and in pursuit of this pure and simple vision he "spent himself recklessly on each succeeding issue, and with unabating discontent."[12]

If Ross needed Katharine and Andy to help him create the particular magazine that *The New Yorker* became, he did not need anyone to tell him how to edit a magazine that was "good" and "fair." To be good the magazine must be well written, which was to say that first it must be written clearly. Ross was "driven by a passion for clarity," a virtue he believed writers should seek by following the rules of Mark Twain: an author "must *say* what he is proposing to say, not merely come near it; use the right word, not its second cousin; eschew surplusage; not omit necessary details; avoid slovenliness of form; use good grammar; employ a simple and straightforward style."[13] To be good the magazine must also publish, in fiction as well as nonfiction, only what seemed to Ross to be "genuine, authentic, real, true," in the words of William Shawn; something in Ross made him feel affronted by writing that was "specious, spurious, meretricious, dishonest."

To be "fair" the magazine must be governed by what Ross called "journalistic integrity." It must never "publish anything for a hidden reason," or anything written from "an ulterior motive, however worthy." Everything it published was to be "published for its own sake." It was, Shawn says, Ross's passion for facts and his dislike of propaganda that made him "suspicious of 'thinking'—his magazine was not to publish either essays or what are called articles of opinion."[14] Ross published only what he liked. As an editor he followed a principle that White once said should govern writers:

[A writer's] concern for the reader must be pure: he must sympathize with the reader's plight (most readers are in trouble about half the time) but never seek to know his wants. The whole duty of a writer is to please and satisfy himself, and the true writer always plays to an audience of one. Let him start sniffing the air, or glancing at the Trend Machine, and he is as good as dead, although he may make a nice living.[15]

Ross would snicker at those who said he had a genius for discovering new talent. According to White, Ross's theory was that "discovering new talent isn't a question of genius—it is a diligence in looking at everything that comes in—every picture, every manuscript."[16] It was, however, Ross's taste for fun and high humor that enabled him to recognize White's talent.

White's first assignment as a member of the staff was to edit "newsbreaks," which were, in his words, "little excerpts from newspapers and other publications—excerpts that were supposed to be funny or instructive because they contained some error of typography or judgement." His job was to select the funniest and to append to them "some slight comment calculated to make people laugh if and when the excerpt itself failed."[17] Newsbreaks were an invention of *Punch,* the venerable English humor magazine, which had used them for at least fifty years as space-fillers at the end of columns. American magazines and newspapers had been using them for years. Excellent ones were rare, and the less-than-excellent (a matter of taste, of course) were worthless. Ross set great store by newsbreaks, and his faith in their potential as a form of high humor was finally justified by what White was able to do with them. To be good they had to express a playful, verbal intelligence.

Here are a few of White's "breaks" from his first years on the job:

NEW SULTAN OF MOROCCO ENTITLED TO FOUR WIVES: PREFERS MAHOGANY
—Headline in the *Omaha Bee-News*
Our preference is for the bird's eye maple.

Saturday Molly bit Galigan Gonzales, 8, 2140 W. 44th Street. Sunday she bit Pedro Menedes, 9, 2138 W. 44th Street. Yesterday she bit William Papenfuse, 2, 2136 W. 44th Street. —*Cleveland Plain Dealer*
She's moving east.

GENT's laundry taken home. Or serve at parties at night.—*Pittsburgh Sun Telegraph*
Oh, take it home.

MAY POST A UNINFORMED GUARD AT SUSPECTED RESORTS—Headline in the *Telegram*
"An," not "a."

Mr. and Mrs. Channing Porter, 306 Concord Street, announce the arrival of their fourth son this morning.—*Framingham* (Mass.) *News*
And they still have the best part of the day ahead of them.[18]

After a while, White began to recognize patterns or types of "breaks," and he established what he called "Departments," under the specific headings of which he could run examples without further comment. For instance:

Neatest Trick of the Week
Her black hair was drawn tight so that her huge forehead bulged and hung twisted into meagre pigtails down her back.—From the *Family Herald*

Uh Huh Department
OF 750 HUNTER GIRLS, ONLY ONE PLANS TO WED—Headline in the *Times*

Other departments that became part of the *New Yorker* tradition were "Letters We Never Finished Reading" and "How's That Again? Department." Out of newsbreaks grew two other genres. One was called "Funny Coincidence Department" under which *The New Yorker* printed examples of plagiarism. The other was called "Answers to Hard Questions," a formula White had invented when he edited his "Personal Column" in the *Seattle Times.* Here are two samples of White's *New Yorker* "answers."

Dear Sir: What does it take to be a successful businessman?—*Letter from Kiplinger* A successful business.[19]

———

Dear Ruth: For the past two years a young man has been dropping in to see me. He never makes a date ahead of time, never calls to say he's coming, but makes it a point to see me at least once a week.
In all that time he has never taken me anywhere—not even for a ride or to a neighborhood movie. He goes away for a month and doesn't even drop me a card. When I subtly make a suggestion, he yawns and tells me he's too tired, or he's not dressed properly, or it's too hot or too cold or something. . . . All he wants to do is sit on the davenport, drink my father's wine and smoke his cigars.
What shall I do?—Letter in Ruth Alden's column in the *Detroit Free Press*
Your father is passing out the wrong kind of cigars. Get the kind that explode. You can get them by mail from the Franco-American Novelty Company. Also, don't serve wine. . . . If all else fails, move away from Detroit. What's so special about living in Detroit?[20]

White remained responsible for newsbreaks until 1982. All told, he must have turned out more than thirty thousand of them.

Pleased as Ross was by the originality of White's repartee in this rather special kind of humor, he was to become even more pleased during 1927 to discover that "there was practically no purpose to which words could be put that White was unable to master."[21] Soon nearly every issue of *The New Yorker* carried ten or twelve of his newsbreaks, five or six of his paragraphs of "Notes and Comment," and one or more cartoons whose captions he had written or rewritten. (Mother to child at the dinner table: "It's broccoli, dear." Child to mother: "I say it's spinach and I say the hell with it.") In the course of the year the magazine published twenty-four of his "Talk" pieces, thirty of his "casuals," fifteen pieces of his light verse, four of his "Summer Theatre" reviews, and ten full-page advertisements he wrote for a *New Yorker* subscription campaign—parodies of well-known ads for courses in culture-made-easy.

THE YEAR 1927 was perhaps the most important in the history of *The New Yorker* because it was the year in which the magazine developed its own distinctive and henceforth consistantly maintained character. It was certainly an important year in White's life, for in the course of it he helped to create a style new in the history of journalism. White once summarized the achievement of Harold Ross by saying that "to a notable extent he changed the face of journalism in his time" and that he did so by "toppling many conventional literary forms." Thinking of himself, among others, White recalled that "young new writers and artists, attracted by the rich odor of innovation, were drawn to the magazine," and "under Ross's guidance, satire and parody flourished, reporting became lighthearted and searching, [and] humor was allowed to infect everything."

Ross thought of "Notes and Comment" and of "Talk" pieces as forms of reporting, and in both departments White was instrumental in effecting the change he later ascribed to Ross's "guidance." Particularly in "Notes and Comment," White's humor infected the reporting of *The New Yorker*, made it "lighthearted and searching." There most of all he helped establish the criteria for Ross's new "journalism." There, too, he expressed the characteristics Marc Connelly referred to when he said that White "brought the steel and the music to the magazine." "I can't remember a piece by anyone but E. B. White that Ross ever really thought just right," Ingersoll once said, recalling those first years of the magazine, and he added, "White was the exception to prove his lack of faith in everyone else."[22]

In "Notes and Comment" White used the conventional editorial "we," and thereby appeared to be speaking for *The New Yorker,* but in fact he did not represent any one's opinions but his own—not Ross's, not the collective opinions of an editorial board, and certainly not those of the mythical dandy Eustace Tilley, on the cover of the first issue. Like a good columnist he spoke for himself, and his "we" was from the start a transparent mask for an "I." He commented on trivial as well as significant topics and events, not in the usual solemn editorial voice, but in a way that he hoped was "merry, wise, and subtle"—and never pretentious.[23]

During his first year as editorial paragrapher for *The New Yorker,* he ribbed President Coolidge, Mayor Walker, the Bureau of Internal Revenue, and societies for the promotion of virtue or the suppression of vice. He made fun of the antics of publicity-seeking authors and publishers— and the very idea of book clubs. But in the same column in which he commented on the frenzy, valor, and faith of window-box gardeners, and the high-jinks of Shriners at their annual convention, he told his readers whom to call to report chimneys illegally belching "black soft-coal smoke,"[24] expressed concern about a disease that was afflicting trees at the corner of Fifth Avenue and Forty-second Street, and alerted his readers to threats to civil liberties—from zealots, politicians, or other meddlers.

Among all the issues he commented on, only those of war and peace were immune to humor. When delegates to the Geneva Conference of 1927 proposed that the relative naval strength of the United States, Great Britain, and France be limited, and fixed at the ratio 6-6-4, he asked why that particular ratio would insure peace better than one of 5-5-3. "When they begin talking about 0-0-0, which we know to be neither practical nor likely, we will begin to listen credulously and attentively. Until then we shall go on considering armament ratios as politically interesting but pacifically insignificant." In the same spirit he objected to a publicity blurb that called the "Pantheon de la Guerre" "a harbinger of Peace." Nothing made him madder, he said, than "the notion that war memorials, battleship maneuvers, war paintings, citizens' military training camps . . . are 'harbingers of peace.' Harbingers of bunk."[25]

The "editorial policy" of *The New Yorker* or, more precisely, the general principles guiding that policy, can be inferred from the way "Notes and Comment" reacted to two subjects of widespread public attention in 1927: the debate on the justness of the trial and verdict in the case of Sacco and Vanzetti, who were ultimately executed in August of that year, and the transatlantic solo flight of Charles A. Lindbergh from New York to Paris in May. *The New Yorker* did not mention Sacco and Vanzetti, though it must have been the only journal of any intellectual pretension that ignored this international cause célèbre. White refrained from commenting on the case since he felt that he did not know enough about its underlying facts to express an opinion, and Ross was content to believe that speculation or debate about such complicated and controversial issues was not the business of his "funny little magazine." *The New Yorker* took many things seriously, of course—books, music, plays, films, and art—and its writers were free to express their opinions on these subjects, but Ross's magazine was not to be a medium for what he called "sectarian" opinion. He would not support causes or take sides in politics.

Since the opinions expressed in "Notes and Comment" were not the official opinions of the magazine but the personal ones of the man who wrote them, White enjoyed great freedom as an editorial writer—a freedom he once described as follows:

> George Seldes, in the Saturday Review, says he has never known of an editorial writer who wrote as he pleased. This makes us a kept man. We often wonder about our life in our bordello, whether such an existence erodes one's character or builds it. An editorial page is a fuzzy performance, any way you look at it, since it affects a composite personality with an editorial "we" for a front. Once in a while we think of ourself as "we," but not often. The word "ourself" is the giveaway—the plural "our," the singular "self,"—united in a common cause. . . .
>
> At any rate, we have evolved (and this may interest Mr. Seldes) a system for the smooth operation of a literary bordello. The system is this: We write as we please, and the magazine publishes as *it* pleases. When the two pleasures coincide, something gets into print. When they don't, the reader draws a blank. It is a system we recommend—the only one, in fact, under which we are willing to be kept. . . . Of course, a good deal depends on the aims of a publication. The more devious the motives of his employer, the more difficult for a writer to write as he pleases. As far as we have been able to discover, the keepers of this house have two aims: the first is to make money, the second is to make sense. We have watched for other motives, but we have never turned up any. That makes for good working conditions, and we write this as a sort of small, delayed tribute to our house. Anytime Mr. Seldes wants to see writers writing as they please, he can just step off the elevator [the offices of the *Saturday Review* were located in the same building as those of *The New Yorker*] and take a gander at us.[26]

White's editorial comments on Lindbergh's flight, and on the ecstatic public reaction to it, may not now seem as remarkable as they did in 1927, but they will illustrate the humor that infected editorial policy and practice at *The New Yorker*. The Lindbergh story was almost a week old by the time White's first comment on it could appear. In the meantime the newspapers had been flooded with reports, feature articles, and editorials on the event to the exclusion of almost anything else.

When Lindbergh landed at Le Bourget, on Saturday night, May 21, the newspapers and radio had already hailed him as a hero, an idol, had made him into a paragon. He was the personification of "the spirit of unconquerable youth"; this "young Viking" was also "this man of the lion heart." On Sunday morning the newspapers were filled with elaborations on the few facts of the flight, the pilot's reception in Paris, and the worldwide response to his stunning success. The first six pages of the *New York Times* were devoted entirely to Lindbergh.

For editorial writers and other commentators the event may have seemed beyond comment—certainly it challenged their muses. The column-long lead editorial in the *Times* was headed "Lindbergh Symbolizes the Genius of America," and in a solo flight all his own its author proclaimed:

> Lindbergh is, indeed, the Icarus of the twentieth century; not himself an inventor of his own wings, but the son of that omnipotent Daedalus whose ingenuity has created the modern world.

In his column in the *New York World* Heywood Broun flew even higher and claimed Lindbergh not as the son of American ingenuity, but as a member of the wonderful family of man:

> A pretty fine lot we are—I refer to human beings. Nature can't bully us indefinitely with wind and wave and peril of vast oceans. One of our boys has put the angry sea in its place.

Such self-satisfied boasting may not have sounded so foolish at the moment as it would sound later—even a few days later. And editorial-writer White had the advantage of an extra day to wait for something to occur to him to say.

But the editorial writers of other weeklies had the same advantage; while White was pressing to meet his deadline, a paragrapher at *The New Republic*, for example, was trying to give the event another perspective— a sober, *New Republic*–like perspective—by saying:

> His flight was probably of small scientific value; as a precedent for transatlantic aviation it was less useful than would have been a trip by a big plane with more than one motor, and with several persons on board. . . . Lindbergh's achievement, after all, lies in the realm of pure spectacle.[27]

White put the whole affair in perspective, but he did not belittle the hero or the achievement, nor did he preach a little sermon in the midst of a celebration. His first observation was that in two respects Lindbergh had been most un-American:

The lonely Mr. Lindbergh made the hop without a cup of coffee. This fact alone startled fifty million Americans who have never been able to get through a working day without one. Furthermore, the flyer came down in France without saying that he did it for the kiddies—un-American and unusual. We loved him immediately.[28]

White's further observations, though both "lighthearted and searching" were satirical as well:

We noted that the *Spirit of St. Louis* had not left the ground ten minutes before it was joined by the Spirit of Me Too. A certain oil was lubricating the engine, a certain brand of tires was the cause of the safe take-off. When the flyer landed in Paris every newspaper was "first to have a correspondent at the plane." This was a heartening manifestation of that kinship that is among man's greatest exaltations. It was beautifully and tenderly expressed in the cable Ambassador Herrick sent the boy's patient mother: "Your incomparable son has done me the honor to be my guest." We liked that; and for twenty-four hours the world seemed pretty human. At the end of that time we were made uneasy by the volume of vaudeville contracts, testimonial writing and other offers, made by the alchemists who transmute glory into gold. We settled down to the hope that the youthful hero will capitalize himself for only as much money as he reasonably needs.

After all, trying to get into the act, trying to feel the warm glow of the hero's glory, was only a harmless human weakness that made the whole world kin. And noticing it could make the whole world smile. But the rush to transmute glory into gold, however human, was a sad, not a merry, spectacle.

The truth of White's comments was the chief source of their value, but the modesty of their tone enhanced that truth; and such modesty was what characterized the humor that White allowed to infect everything. Five weeks after his first comment on Lindbergh was published, he wrote a "Talk piece" on Lindbergh as author—as the author of *We*—with the same self-effacing merry irony:

In Putnam's window, in Forty-fifth Street, are displayed six pages of manuscript written in longhand by Charles A. Lindbergh, or more properly, "us" —Lindbergh and his fountain pen. These, we learn by carefully reading the signs, are sample pages of the book entitled "We." The display shares the window with Walter Scott, Robert Burns and wedding invitations. How near Putnam's came to ruining the entire sale of this book in Southern California is made clear by perusing one of the pages. "I went to San Diego," wrote the young author, "to place the order, and remained in California, with the exception of three trips to Los Angeles, during the entire construction of the plane." Then his sense of geography apparently crushed his sense of humor for he crossed out the words "with the exception of three trips to Los Angeles."

From the many revisions and fresh starts in the manuscript, we gathered that Lindbergh does not write easily, and we felt a spirit of kinship immediately.

His hand is cramped and sketchy—the sort you find in persons whose last interest on earth, probably, is literary composition. His spelling is debatable. He spelled "occasion" with a double "s." According to the publishers, this is the only book (of many published) which was written by the Colonel and in which he has a financial interest. Sixty thousand words is what they say it contains. We assume he wrote it in his spare time.[29]

The humor that won Ross's approval was as various, of course, as the people whose writing and cartoons he chose to publish, and it would be difficult to define. But White's humor, or one of its distinctive qualities, is not beyond description. In fact, in 1946 he came very close to defining it himself:

> Somebody, perhaps suspecting that we were having an affair with Humor, sent us the following passage from Proudhon. We reprint it in free translation, with pride and embarrassment—the sort of mixed feeling you have when walking with a pretty girl and the girl is whistled at:
>
>> Liberty, like Reason, does not exist or manifest itself except by the constant disdain of its own works; it perishes as soon as it is filled with self-approval. That is why humor has always been a characteristic of philosophical and liberal genius, the seal of the human spirit, the irresistible instrument of progress. Stagnant peoples are always solemn peoples: the man of a people that laughs is a thousand times closer to reason and liberty than the anchorite who prays or the philosopher who argues.
>>
>> Humor—true liberty!—it is you who deliver me from ambition for power, from servitude to party, from respect for routine, from the pedantry of science, from admiration for celebrities, from the mystifications of politics, from the fanaticism of the reformers, from fear of this great universe, and from self-admiration.
>>
>> Come, sovereign, turn a ray of your light on my fellow-citizens; kindle in their soul a spark of your spirit, so that my confession may reconcile them to each other and so that this inevitable revolution may come about with serenity and joy.
>
> Proudhon's word is "l'ironie," which we have translated "humor," possibly too loosely but at any rate with serenity and joy. After so many summers and winters living with Humor as our mistress and credit manager, seeing her blow hot and cold, running her unreasonable errands, taking her lip, we find our

affection undiminished. The attachment strengthens, even as it grows more troublesome. Come, sovereign, give us a kiss. And deliver us, right this minute, from self-admiration.[30]

The "humor" or *l'ironie* that White so loved was once described by Thomas Mann as "blithe skepticism, a mistrust of all schemes and subterfuges of our souls":

Once roused and on the alert, it cannot be put to sleep again. It infiltrates life, undermines its raw naiveté, takes from it the strain of its own ignorance, . . . inculcates the taste for understatement . . . for the deflated rather than for the inflated words, for the cult which exerts its influence by moderation, by modesty. Modesty—what a beautiful word!"[31]

When White said that Ross "allowed humor to infect everything" he used words that implied his own idea of the nature of humor. That is, he did not say, "Ross allowed writers to inject everything with humor." White regards humor, as a quality that slips into a writer's discourse; and just as he prefers to be thought of not as a writer but as a man who among other things writes, he dislikes being called a humorist. His notions about humor are much like his notions about thoughts—at their best both are involuntary. A writer is like a hunter who sits in a blind and waits. He waits for thoughts, and if he stays awake (to use Thoreau's word), his patience may be rewarded. The kind of humor-infected writing that Ross and White admired could not be willed into being. Once, in a paragraph for "Notes and Comment," White revealed his method of hunting for something to say:

While thirty students of a mission school in Bombay were dying from having eaten soup into which a poisonous lizard had fallen, fifty school children of New Brunswick, New Jersey, were giving a party to a horse which had produced in nine years enough anti-toxin serum to protect thirty thousand children from diphtheria. We read these items at the breakfast table, and subsequently spent some little time trying to resolve them into their components, hoping that a small moral or a few grains of irony would be deposited on the test-tube of our thought. The task was too great for us, our equipment too meagre. We found ourself spellbound by the items, rather than genuinely interested in them. We ended by clipping them out and sending them to Arthur Brisbane. He'll know how to handle them.[32]

What he meant by a "small moral" or a "grain of irony" was what in another paragraph he called "little granules of essential thought," which he said were always involuntary, and were "usually a by-product of loneliness. They come pricking through when the blood is rich; or, if they are found at all by anyone searching, it is in unlikely places—under the radiator in the hall, in a pocket of an old coat." On another occasion he said that writing "is something that raises up on you [like] a welt"; and he once said that a book was a sneeze. Humor is, if anything, even more involuntary.[33]

White has never been much interested in theory about anything, and not till well along in his career as a writer did he try to express his notions about the art of writing. But in 1927 he knew that in general he agreed with the intuitionist philosophy of Henri Bergson, which he had been exposed to in a philosophy course at Cornell. Bergson's intuitionism was attractive to most artists, and it expressed in fairly simple terms an epistemology that writers had for some time endorsed. As skeptical about the scientists' claim to truth as he was about the claims of other rationalists, White must have been pleased to read, as a senior at Cornell, Bergson's doctrine that

> philosophy is a direct vision of reality . . . in the literal sense of the word, an intuition, [that] there is something in the universe analogous to the creative spirit of the poet, a living, pushing force, an *élan vital* . . . which approaches nearer to the essence of things than reason. This divine sympathy is . . . essentially free, and . . . is inhibited by the brain except in rare moments of disinterest. . . . Only when we are not trying to remember will this creative memory, feeling, essential thought produce spontaneously its unwilled, its involuntary gift.[34]

In the same semester in another course, White might have heard about Thoreau's notion that "only by observing for the sake of observing and not for the sake of acting, will the Absolute reveal itself." Thoreau believed that "no mere willful activity whatever, whether in writing verses or collecting statistics will produce true poetry or science." In fact—and here he defined a kind of humor—Thoreau said: "Not by constraint or severity shall you have access to true wisdom but by abandonment, and childlike mirthfulness. If you would know aught, be gay before it."[35]

Gaiety, mirthfulness, abandon—these were the ways to wise humor and humorous wisdom. *Delight* and *fun* are other words for the state of mind Thoreau recommended, and the first of those words is the one White once used in praising Don Marquis, who, he said, "wound himself up at the beginning of a paragraph, leaped high in the air, and dissolved in pyrotechnical delight."[36] White's power to perform such acts himself came from a sense of fun that John Updike remembers vividly:

What struck me in [White's] walk, in the encouraging memos he once or twice wrote me, and in [what he wrote for "Notes and Comment"] was how much more *fun* he had in him than us younger residents of those halls [of *The New Yorker*]. Not loud or obvious fun, but contained, inturning fun, shaped like a main spring.[37]

The birth and development of *New Yorker* humor, it should not be forgotten, occurred as White said, "under Ross's guidance" and in those "dingles of humor" wherein dwelt not only Katharine Angell, who was "a whiz," but James Thurber, of whom White said, "The whole world knows what a funny man he was, but you had to sit next to him day after day to understand the extravagance of his clowning, the wildness and subtlety of his thinking and the intensity of his interest in others. . . ." Finding Thurber was part of Ross's "run of luck" in 1927; meeting him was lucky also for White. Within a year of their meeting White wrote in his journal, "one of the persons I like best in the world is Thurber."[38]

JAMES GROVER THURBER was born in 1894, five years before White, in Columbus, Ohio, of a ne'er-do-well father and a stage-struck mother.[39] Neither parent had much formal education, but both were readers and understood their son's desire to be a writer. His earliest literary aspiration was to become a paragrapher as good as Robert O. Ryder, the nationally known editor of the Columbus *Ohio State Journal.* In 1913 he entered Ohio State University, where his gifts were soon recognized by a teacher and by a few fellow students, and where, during his on-again, off-again college career, he joined a good fraternity, wrote for the university's daily newspaper, *The Lantern,* and edited the *Sun-Dial,* the humor magazine. He was active in the dramatic society, and was eventually elected to an honorary society for campus leaders. But in June 1918, at the end of his fifth academic year, at the age of twenty-three, still needing one more year's work before he could graduate, he left college and took a job as code-clerk in the American Foreign Service. After living for a little over a year in Paris, he returned to his parents' home in Columbus and found a job as reporter on the *Columbus Dispatch.* In 1922 he married Althea Adams, a handsome, popular Ohio State senior, daughter of an army doctor and a professor of home economics. By 1924, though he enjoyed writing his weekly column, he had become bored as a reporter, and he decided to move to New York, try to support himself and his wife by free-lance writing, and enjoy the literary society of Greenwich Village. But at the end of six months Jim had failed to sell anything he had written, and he and Althea had to return to Columbus, where for a short time he

earned a living as a press agent. In the spring of 1925 Althea became
convinced that Jim would find himself, or that the literary world would
find him, if he went to France, where all the other ambitious young
American writers then seemed to be. While crossing the Atlantic on the
Leviathan they met White's newly married sister Lillian and her husband,
Arthur Illian. Lillian told Jim that she had a brother named Elwyn Brooks
White who also hoped to be a writer.

In France Thurber went to work for the Paris edition of the *Chicago
Tribune,* first in Paris and later in Nice. He kept the job for about a year,
and at the same time he succeeded in selling feature stories about life and
people in France to various American newspapers. Much encouraged when
he sold a piece to *Harper's Magazine,* he returned to America, in the
summer of 1926, without Althea, who was not yet ready to give up her
good time in France but promised to come home a little later.

In New York he settled in a room on West Thirteenth Street and
worked hard, writing and submitting various short prose pieces to, among
other publishers, *The New Yorker.* He tried once to meet "Elton" Brooks
White at his *New Yorker* office, but White was not in.

In the fall of 1926, about the time Andy returned from his six-week
European tour, Althea came back to Jim, and the Thurbers moved into a
basement apartment in the Village, near the Ninth Avenue elevated subway
—and near the apartment of old friends from Columbus, Kate and Russell
Lord. Lord and White, both admirers of Professor Bristow Adams, had met
at Cornell. Lord and Thurber had become acquainted at Ohio State, where
Lord had gone to teach journalism. White and Thurber finally met at the
Lords' apartment early in 1927.

In background and experience the two men had much in common. Their
parents had not gone to college. Each had been given as a middle name
the name of a Protestant minister. The middle-class culture of Mount
Vernon, New York, was not much different from that of Columbus, Ohio.
Both had been editors of university newspapers, though Thurber had not
been editor-in-chief. Both had read their poems to fellow members of a
literary society, and both had practiced the meter and rhyme schemes of
lyric forms, though White's triolets and rondeaus were not, as Thurber's
were, "scandalous."[40] Both had written scripts for campus musicals. Neither had shown much ability to write fiction; both admired the great
American paragraphers.

Thurber and White had both matured slowly. Each had first secretly
worshipped a girl at a great distance and then fumbled through a long,
unhappy romance. Neither had gone to war. Both had left home for about
two years and then returned at the age of twenty-four to spend two more
years with their parents. Neither had enjoyed his experience as a reporter.

Both admired the humor of Robert Benchley and Don Marquis above that of all other American humorists, including Mark Twain. Both were born with a comic spirit; both were skeptics; both hated know-it-alls. Both loved parody and other forms of satire.

In other ways they were different. Whereas White was a quiet, reserved, and private person, modest about his talents and careful to say or to write no more than he meant, Thurber was voluble, gregarious, and sometimes extravagant. Unlike White, Thurber read constantly, and he remembered and thought about what he read—not just newspapers and magazines, but fiction and history. He admired Henry James above all other novelists. He was a literary person. Thurber had suffered semiblindness since he had lost the sight of one eye at age six, and he had been under the threat of total blindness ever since. He had been poor. He had been unsuccessful. He knew more than White about the rages of the human heart, both tragic and comic. He imagined more. His humor was wild, his love was large, his resentments ran deep. People loved Jim who only admired Andy—partly because Jim could express his affection easily, partly because he seemed to need to be loved.

Shortly after White and Thurber met, early in 1927, White told Lord that Ross was looking for staff writers. When Kate Lord heard that news, she walked over to the Thurbers' apartment on Hudson Street and passed it on to Jim, who went at once to White's office at *The New Yorker*. After a few minutes of conversation White took Thurber to Ross's office and introduced him. Ross decided to hire him as an assistant editor. Within six months Thurber had succeeded in proving his incompetence as an administrator, and Ross relieved him of this job and asked him to write "Talk" pieces. From that time on Thurber and White shared one of the few, tiny offices at *The New Yorker*.

"We got on fine together, and from the first we loved each other's stuff," White recalled. Though from the first White found Thurber one of the most self-centered men he had ever known, and noticed that he was "often broody because he was troubled by Althea and his marriage," they shared so much of their humor, revealed so much of themselves to one another, and each admired in the other the particular gifts he himself lacked, that they soon established a friendship strong enough to survive several shocks caused by Thurber's erratic behavior during the last unhappy years of his life. After Thurber's death White said, "There never was a kinder, nicer friend—when he was sober." Thurber's widow, Helen, has said that with one exception Thurber loved White more than any other man in his life.[41]

When White wrote Thurber's obituary in 1961, he dwelt on the early joys of their friendship:

I am one of the lucky ones; I knew him before blindness hit him, before fame hit him, and I tend always to think of him as a young artist in a small office in a big city, with all the world still ahead. It was a fine thing to be young and at work in New York for a new magazine when Thurber was young and at work, and I will always be glad that this happened to me.

It was fortunate that we got on well; the office we shared was the size of a hall bedroom. There was just room enough for two men, two typewriters, and a stack of copy paper. The copy paper disappeared at a scandalous rate— not because our production was high (although it was) but because Thurber used copy paper as the natural receptacle for discarded sorrows, immediate joys, stale dreams, golden prophecies, and messages of good cheer to the outside world and to fellow-workers. His mind was never at rest, and his pencil was connected to his mind by the best conductive tissue I have ever seen in action. . . . You had to sit next to him day after day to understand the intensity of his interest in others and his sympathy for their dilemmas—dilemmas that he instantly enlarged, put in focus, and made immortal, just as he enlarged and made immortal the strange goings on in the Ohio home of his boyhood. His waking dreams and his sleeping dreams commingled shamelessly and uproariously. Ohio was never far from his thoughts, and when he received a medal from his home state in 1953, he wrote, "The clocks that strike in my dreams are often the clocks of Columbus." It is a beautiful sentence and a revealing one.[42]

It took Thurber six months to learn how to write a "Talk" piece that would move Ross to tell him, "Now you've got it." That he got it was, as Thurber often said, due to White. "Thurber was a good critic and a good reporter," White once said, "but he was perhaps too emotional to be a great reporter. What made his casuals pure Thurber was his marvelous sense of the incongruous, the unexpected." It was for an understanding of the elements of style, according to Thurber, that he was indebted to White:

Until I learned discipline in writing from studying Andy White's stuff, I was a careless, nervous, headlong writer. . . . The precision and clarity of White's writing helped me a lot, slowed me down from the dogtrot of newspaper tempo and made me realize a writer turns on his mind, not a faucet. . . . White was the first guy to write perfect Talk pieces, and everybody has in a sense imitated him.

As Thurber got the hang of it, however, White gradually wrote less "Talk"; Thurber became the chief "Talk" writer and rewrite-man, and eventually gave the department his own distinction. According to Robert Coates, a friend and fellow *New Yorker* staff writer, "It is no more than simple fact to say Thurber 'made' the department." For the next ten years, the front of Ross's book was essentially White and Thurber.[43]

If it is true, as Burton Bernstein says, that in 1927 "the White effect began to show up in all Thurber's work," as Thurber's "casuals got funnier, sharper, less forced, and, as they were increasingly set in the first person, more original,"[44] it is also true that the Thurber effect began to show up in White's work. Knowing that the two men were friends working in the same office, one can't help recognizing Thurber's kind of comic madness in the series of ten advertisements White wrote as part of a circulation campaign *The New Yorker* ran in the summer of 1927. Each advertisement consisted of a photograph of "Sterling Finny" and his wife, "Flora," about 350 words of text, and a subscription coupon to be filled in and sent to *The New Yorker*. Sterling and Flora were window-display mannikins that White borrowed from Wanamaker's department store and dressed and posed in a variety of situations. The ads were, in White's words, "parodies of a certain kind of 'culture-made-easy' advertising that was prevalent in the Twenties and Thirties."[45] In one of these ads the war between the sexes furnishes the lead: " 'Good Morning, Stupid!' That was the way he always greeted her at the breakfast table. . . ."[46] And in another appeared the following Thurberesque exchange between Sterling and Flora on the golf course:

"Why do you hand me a niblick, my husband?" she asked. "The hole is four hundred and eighty yards away."

"I hand you a niblick, my wife, because no matter what club you use, you do not hit the ball, and I would rather have you destroy the niblick than the driver. Does that answer your question?"

"It does, but it does not answer our previous question, Why has the caddy left us to ourselves and gone back to the clubhouse?"

(The truth was the caddy had stood their conversation as long as he could.)

If, the ad went on to say, you have friends who are too dull for caddies to associate with, why don't you send them a subscription to *The New Yorker*? Reading it will enable them to attract caddies simply by "conversing brightly and exchanging badinage on topics of sport, current events, and the arts."[47]

For all his own extraordinary talents and achievements, Thurber always looked up to White and never ceased to feel indebted to the friend who had found him his job, disciplined his writing, helped him with his first important casual, "Menaces in May," discovered him as an artist, and collaborated with him on his first book. Helen Thurber once said that after 1934, whenever he wrote letters to White it was as a "student writing to his master."[48]

In 1927, in their flat on Hudson Street, and a little later, on West Eleventh Street, the Thurbers lived within a few blocks of White, of their mutual friends the Lords, and of some other old friends, Robert and Elsa Coates. Thurber had known Robert Coates in Paris in 1925, and shortly after Ross hired Thurber, Thurber persuaded Ross to hire Coates as art critic. Coates had been a member of the board of the *Yale Literary Magazine,* and in Paris, between 1921 and 1926, he had known Dos Passos and Fitzgerald, and had introduced Hemingway to Gertrude Stein. Soon another of Thurber's old friends, Joel Sayre, who had worked with Thurber on the *Columbus Dispatch,* moved to the Village, and he too became a *New Yorker* writer. Before long, Gertrude Lynahan, a friend of Alice Burchfield's who had been women's editor when White was editor-in-chief of the *Cornell Sun,* rented a flat on Twelfth Street and became part of this group of *New Yorker* writers; later she married Joel Sayre. Jap and Helen Gude, other friends of Thurber's, soon joined this circle, of which Thurber seems to have been the center. They all became friends of Andy's, and later of Katharine's.

Harold Ross. The "official protrait," taken about 1925. "He was determined that neither money nor influence would ever corrupt his dream or deflower his text."

Ralph McAllister Ingersoll, whom Ross made his managing editor in the summer of 1925 when Ingersoll was twenty-five years old. "My closest friends on The New Yorker," Ingersoll wrote years later, "were Jim Thurber and Andy White. The most fun I had was with Andy."

Harold Ross.
An informal picture taken in
the thirties.

Katharine Sergeant (Mrs. Ernest) Angell,
about 1928.

Katharine Angell, James Thurber,
and Jeanie, the mother of Katharine's
Scottie, Daisy, at Sneden's Landing,
February 1929.

An unpublished drawing by James Thurber. Many ideas for paragraphs in "Notes and Comment" came from members of the staff of The New Yorker, *including Harold Ross.*

"I Was Never So Embarrassed!

Just when I wanted to be so proud of you, you sat there all evening without saying a single word"

"AREN'T you a bit harsh?"

"Not in the slightest. Couldn't you think of *anything* to say?"

"No, I couldn't. How was I to get in on that kind of conversation?"

"And what did you expect them to talk about—business?"

"Really, Ja——"

"Oh, I'm so ashamed! I wanted to be proud of you, Ted. You are cleverer and more successful than any man who was at that dinner tonight—but you acted as though you were afraid to open your mouth."

"I was, dear! What do I know about that philosopher they were talking about—what was his name?—Nietzsche. I couldn't even follow their conversation, half the time . . ."

"You should read more. It's pitiful! Why, you didn't contribute one idea or opinion all evening. I was so embarrassed!"

"I'd like to read more, but you know how much time I have!" He helped her into the cab, then turned to her with a smile. "But you made up for both of us tonight, Jane! You were wonderful! How did you ever find out so many things to talk about?"

Busy People Enjoy This Way of Becoming Well-Informed

Jane glowed, flattered by her husband's praise. "Do you really think I made a good impression on those people, Ted?"

"I should say you did!" he laughed. "You seemed to know about everything. Well, you have plenty of time to read."

"Is that so!" she retorted. "I have even less time to read than you. I found all that information in Elbert Hubbard's Scrap Book."

"What's that?"

"You must have heard about it. It's quite famous. Now don't tell me you don't know who Elbert Hubbard was! One of the most versatile men America has ever known—a writer, craftsman, orator, business man—a many-sided genius. Well, he began keeping a scrap book when he was quite young, and he kept it throughout life. He put into it only the things that inspired him most, choice bits from the best minds—the *highlights* of literature."

"Great idea! Tell me more about it."

Elbert Hubbard's Scrap Book Selections from 500 Great Writers

All the way home she told him about Elbert Hubbard's Scrap Book, and urged him to use it as she had.

"Imagine, Ted! In that one great Scrap Book are all the ideas that helped Hubbard most, all the wonderful bits of wisdom that inspired him—the greatest thoughts of the last four thousand years! He did all your reading for you! You don't need to go through long, tiresome volumes—you can get at a glance what Hubbard had to read days and days to find. Promise me you'll read in it every day for five or ten minutes, dear! It will make you so well-informed—you'll never need to feel embarrassed or uncomfortable in company again."

"It sounds great," he said, as the cab drew up at their door. "Why didn't you tell me about it long ago!"

Sent FREE for Examination

The Elbert Hubbard Scrap Book is a unique volume made up of ideas, thoughts, passages, excerpts, poems, epigrams—selected from the master thinkers of all ages. Selected by *Elbert Hubbard*, himself a master thinker. There is not a commonplace sentence in the entire volume. Only the *best* of a lifetime of discriminating reading has been included.

This Scrap Book is a fine example of Roycroft bookmaking. The type is set Venetian style—a page within a page—printed in two colors on fine tinted book paper. Bound scrap-book style and tied with linen tape.

Please examine it at our expense! The coupon entitles you to the special five-day examination privilege. Just send it off today, and the famous Elbert Hubbard Scrap Book will go forward to you promptly. When it arrives, glance through it. If you aren't inspired, enchanted—simply return the Scrap Book within the five-day period, and the examination will have cost you nothing. Otherwise send only $2.90, plus few cents postage, in *full payment*.

We urge you to act now. We want you to *see* the Scrap Book and judge it for yourself. Mail this coupon TODAY to Wm. H. Wise & Co., Roycroft Distributors, Dept. 84, 50 West 47th Street, New York City.

An example of the culture-made-easy advertising that White parodied in his Sterling Finny ads for The New Yorker.

"Our Little Son Must Never Know!"

STERLING FINNY grasped his wife's hand. "Good-bye," he said, "it is better for me to leave now than to have our boy grow up in the knowledge that his own father is not interesting."

"God bless you," sobbed Flora.

"God bless you, too!" said Sterling. His very reply showed lack of originality. It was just that that was breaking up their home.

Only the week before, a neighbor had said to Mr. Finny, "I hear that the American wing of the Metropolitan Museum of Art is very entertaining." And all Sterling could answer was: "I, too, hear that the American wing of the Metropolitan Museum of Art is very entertaining."

The neighbor moved away.

Not Fit to be a Father

"We must think of Junior," Flora insisted. "It isn't fair to have him come under your influence."

"You are right," answered Sterling. "When my little boy gets to be a man, I want him to join in the conversation, everywhere. I better go."

"Oh, that our happy love might have turned out differently!" sobbed Flora.

"Oh, that our sweet love might have," said Sterling as he departed,—varying his answer a little but not enough to make it interesting.

* * * * *

Perhaps you, too, have a dear baby who will soon be old enough to know what an ass his father is! Are you going to leave home, or will you take simple measures to get bright? THE NEW YORKER is written entirely by fathers and mothers whose children are proud to know them. Browse for a few minutes between its covers each week—you will quickly acquire so much culture that even your children will be glad to have you around the house! How would you like to return from work at night and have the little ones run and greet you with, "Good evening, my cultured, cultured Daddy!" Not a bad welcome, eh?

Well, it's not only easy, it's pleasant. You merely sign your name in the little space below and every week new vistas of this enchanted isle will be opened up gently and firmly before your surprised eyes.

The New Yorker
Drawer 7293-C
25 W. 45 Street,
New York City.

☐ 1 Year $5.00
☐ 2 Years $7.00

Postage: Canada, 50c.; Foreign, $1.00 additional per year.

Dear Sirs: Junior is beginning to get wise to me. please enter my subscription to The New Yorker for—

☐ Remittance enclosed
☐ Send bill

Name ....
Address ....
....

One of a series of ten advertisements White wrote for a subscription campaign in the spring of 1927. Copyright © 1927, 1955 The New Yorker Magazine, Inc.

WE noted that the *Spirit of St. Louis* had not left the ground ten minutes before it was joined by the Spirit of Me Too. A certain oil was lubricating the engine, a certain brand of tires was the cause of the safe take-off. When the flyer landed in Paris every newspaper was "first to

have a correspondent at the plane." This was a heartening manifestation of that kinship that is among man's greatest exaltations. It was beautifully and tenderly expressed in the cable Ambassador Herrick sent the boy's patient mother: "Your incomparable son has done me the honor to be my guest." We liked that; and for twenty-four hours the world seemed pretty human. At the end of that time we were made uneasy by the volume of vaudeville contracts, testimonial writing and other offers, made by the alchemists who transmute glory into gold. We settled down to the hope that the youthful hero will capitalize himself for only as much money as he reasonably needs.

One of three paragraphs White wrote for "Notes and Comment" on the occasion of Lindbergh's non-stop, solo flight New York to Paris, May 20–21, 1927. Illustration by Otto Soglow. Copyright © 1927, 1955 The New Yorker Magazine, Inc.

33. OPPOSITE.
E. B. White and James Thurber, 1929.

White designed and did the lettering for the dust jacket for the first edition of Is Sex Necessary? *The drawing is Thurber's.*

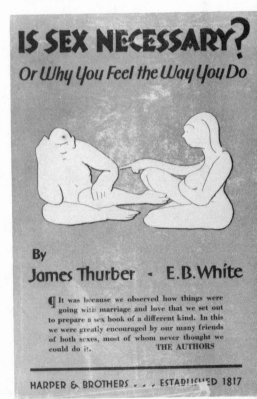

Monsieur a fait an entrée!

One of a series of fourteen drawings entitled "La Flamme and Mr. Prufrock," which Thurber gave Katharine and Andy as a wedding present. In the words of Katharine, they are "hilariously uninhibited."

E. B. White and son Joel, 1931. "I feel the mixed pride and oppression of fatherhood in the very base of my spine."

THE TALK OF THE TOWN

Notes and Comment

WE looked up Mr. Eustace Tilley this week, on the eve of his departure from the city—his "maiden" departure, as he pointed out. The elegant old gentleman was found in his suite at the Plaza, his portmanteau packed, his mourning doves wrapped in dotted swiss, his head in a sitz bath for a last shampoo. Everywhere, scattered about the place, were grim reminders of his genteel background: a cold bottle of Tavel on the lowboy, a spray of pinks in a cut-glass bowl, an album held with a silver clasp, and his social-security card copied in needlepoint and framed on the wall. We begged the privilege of an interview for The Talk of the Town (or what the French call "Murmures de la Ville"), and he reluctantly granted it.

When we inquired about his destination, Mr. Tilley was evasive. "I should prefer to be grilled on that," he remarked, bitterly.

So we grilled him, naming over all the fashionable watering places, without success.

"Would you say you were going to a spa?" we ventured.

"It has a little of the spa in it, a little of the gulch," replied the renowned fop.

"Oh, the White Mountains," we cried.

"Let it go. Ask me about things of moment, such as the ever-normal granary." Mr. Tilley pulled the plug in the sitz bath, sat down at a dressing table, and began to do his hair.

"Why are you leaving town?" we asked.

"I should say that my departure was in part a matter of temper, in part of expediency."

"You mean you're beating the purge?"

Mr. Tilley let the comb drop into his lap, and turned half around, his magnificent profile etched in light from the window.

"We live in a new world," he said. "St. Bernards are killing little girls. Books, or what pass for books, are being photographed on microfilm. There is a cemetery I want to see," he continued, "a grove where ancient trees shelter the graves and throw their umbrage on the imponderable dead. The branches of these trees, my dear young man, are alive with loudspeakers. I believe Upper Montclair is the place. That is one reason for my departure— I have certain macabre pilgrimages to make, while the lustiness is still in my bones. And besides, the other day I received a letter." He gave us a cryptic glance.

"You mean it contained a threat?" we asked.

"Oh my, no," said Tilley. "It came from the office of a division manager, and began: 'Dear Mr. Tilley, Take two pieces of metal and rub them together for a few seconds.' You see, it is time I took my leave." A waiter carrying a guinea fowl aspic entered the room and buzzed about Mr. Tilley. A fly buzzed about the waiter.

"And then, there are things I want to think about, things on which I can more readily concentrate when I am not in town. I want to think about the Will Rogers memorial."

"Why?" we inquired.

"I don't know why," said Tilley, petulantly. "I simply know what are the things I like to think about, and the Will Rogers memorial is one of them. I want time to examine the new English divorce law, the ever-normal granary (which you forgot to ask me about), the new Knopf book about a man who had a good time, the grasshopper invasion, Hitler's ban on all art that he doesn't understand. I shall perhaps enter a putting tournament, using my old brassie, of course. And I have a strong desire to hear again the wildest sound in all the world."

"You mean timber wolves?" we said.

"I mean cockcrow," snapped Tilley, who by this time was becoming visibly agitated. "I want time to think about many people, alive and dead: Pearl White, Schoolboy Creekmore, Igor Sikorsky—I couldn't begin to name them. I want to think about the custom of skiing in summertime, want to hear a child play thirds on the pianoforte in midafternoon. I shall devote considerable time to studying the faces of motorists drawn up for the red light; in their look of discontent is the answer to the industrial revolution. Did you know that a porcupine has the longest intestine in Christendom, either because he eats so much wood or in order that he may? It is a fact. There must be something to be learned by thinking about that. Take a person employed by a broadcasting studio to close contracts with mountain people who sing folk songs over the air—what will such a person develop, in the course of time, to correspond to a porcupine's long intestine? Ah, well, it's time to be off."

The elderly eccentric rose, phoned

White's farewell to New York and The New Yorker *in the character of Eustace Tilley, in the issue for 7 August 1937. The drawing by Otto Soglow depicts the departure from the Plaza, at Fifty-ninth Street and Fifth Avenue, in a Victoria.*

Wolcott Gibbs, who took over "Notes and Comment" from E. B. White in 1938.

John McNulty (on the left) in front of Tim Costello's bar on Third Avenue. After White moved to Maine some of his most entertaining letters came from McNulty, whose writing was beautifully "funny and touching."

CHAPTER VIII

Katharine

1 9 2 8 — 1 9 2 9

". . . the most beautiful decision of his life."

I N 1927 RAOUL FLEISCHMANN REJECTED AN offer of three million dollars for *The New Yorker*. By the end of the year its circulation exceeded fifty thousand, it was making a profit, and its advertising department was about to raise its rates. E. B. White made about ten thousand dollars that year, or more than six times as much as the year before; what he remembers most vividly about this time of his life, however, is the sheer joy of writing and of being a part of Ross's lively enterprise. He knew that he was lucky to be paid well for doing what he liked to do. All in all, he had a splendid year professionally.

His work at *The New Yorker* did not immediately affect his private life. He continued to live in his third-floor walk-up on West Thirteenth Street with his Cornell friends, and he continued to see Mary Osborn, a southern girl with whom he had fallen in love a year earlier. But as the year 1927 neared its end, so did his romance with her. The course it took is suggested by some of White's poems and other writings of the period. Among them, none reveals more about White as a lover than the following two poems. The first, written shortly after he and Mary met, shows them standing in the moonlight in Washington Square, the poet unable to accept her proffered kiss because, as he says self-mockingly, he is embarrassed by the wide-eyed stare of a watchful statue nearby. The sonnet, addressed "To the Bronze Bust of Holley in Washington Square," ends with this sestet:

> Could your cold silent stare, my heart deterring,
> Effect a cold constraint as hard as this:
> That when I felt a hand in my hand stirring
> And read the breathless proffer of a kiss
>   I could not then unbend to claim my prize
>   Simply because you would not close your eyes?[1]

The second poem, presumably also addressed to Mary, and written at the close of 1927, sounds like a rueful farewell. In it the poet confesses that his courtship has failed because he has loved "aimlessly" and with "too small a heart, too large a pen":

BELATED CHRISTMAS CARD

> If I have said in sundry ways
>   What I may never say again,
> It is because myself obeys
>   Too small a heart, too large a pen.
>
> And if I have not said it well,
>   Or even loud enough to hear it,
> That is because I cannot tell
>   How much I like, how much I fear it.
>
> And if to love you aimlessly
>   Is small divertissement for you,
> Please be assured that it can be
>   As small for this poor ingrate, too![2]

The lines of this poem sum up not only White's romance with Mary but his earlier affairs of the heart as well. He had been in love off and on ever since his boyhood, when he had taken Eileen Thomas tea-dancing at the Plaza and had skated with Mildred Hesse on Siwanoy Pond. In his college days there had been Alice Burchfield, and after Alice there had been others, whom he referred to years later as his "Supreme Girls." By now, at twenty-eight, he had loved more than one woman he could have won. But he did not wish to win—or to be won by—anyone. He had been in love with the idea of being in love, but he had been wary of love's power to bind the lover. For White, the most compelling of his needs, overriding all others, was his need to keep himself free, uncommitted. It was the need of an egocentric young man, a need that at times was apt to lead him to actions that must have appeared thoughtless, even callous, and incomprehensible to those close to him. But it was also the need of a talented young man afraid that by giving up his independence he might diminish the self that nourished his talent.

Such independence was costly. He had to pay for it the price of loneliness—of which he could have said that he did not know how much he feared and how much he liked it—and of frustration. Thus he chose to be an aimless lover because, as he said in a poem at the time, he shunned fulfillment in all his enterprises lest it "try his pride" or "glut his soul:"

PORTRAIT

He goes his way with a too cautious stride
That checks him safe just short of every goal;
Seeks not conclusions lest they try his pride,
Claims not fair booty lest it glut his soul.
If it be love, he finds it unrequited,
And seasons it with sadness to the taste;
If it be fame, he finds his name is slighted,
And turns his luck aside in conscious haste.
Frustration tickles his most plaintive strings
And satisfies his bent for somber living;
He daubs with mystery the obvious things,
And holds fulfillment off—always contriving
From life (held very gingerly) to press
The fine musk odor of unhappiness.[3]

White's problem was not unusual; certainly artists are not alone in wishing to be responsible only to themselves. He was not exceptional in wanting love, and a mate, and possibly a family, without having to say, "I promise." But he was slower than most in coming to terms with that dilemma, and more inhibited than he would have liked to be. He felt more confident talking to his beloved from a distance, in rhymed verse, than he did face to face. And his humorous awareness of that fact did not help him to overcome it.

But in 1927 two persons gradually changed the color and complexion of his life. One was James Thurber, whose wit, wild humor, and extravagant flights of fancy delighted him. The other was Katharine Sergeant Angell, the magazine's literary editor, to whom White found himself increasingly drawn in admiration and affection.

The earliest record of his attraction to Katharine may be the following verses, presumably addressed to her, which he signed with the pseudonym "Beppo" (the name of the Irish setter his family had owned when Elwyn was a child). They appeared in *The New Yorker* at the very start of 1928 and must have been accepted for publication by Katharine herself:

NOTES FROM A DESK CALENDAR

Monday

Now grows my heart unruly
    At mention of your name,
And if I love you truly
    Is anyone to blame?
        (No answer required.)

Tuesday

Suppose the glance you gave me
    While standing by my chair
Struck home, could aught then save me?
    And am I one to care?
        (No answer desired.)

Wednesday

The persons who have seen us
    Together—have they guessed
There stands so much between us
    Which has not been confessed?
        (No answer requested.)

Thursday

Does earth, with each new sun-up,
    Abundantly proclaim
My heart in yours is done up?
    And do you feel the same?
        (No answer suggested.)

Friday

The trays upon my table
    Are labelled "Out" and "In";
Was ever man less able
    To have his day begin?
        (No answer projected.)

Saturday

Were I more plain and artless
    In setting forth this love,
Could you continue heartless
    In re the lines above?
        ("No" answer expected.)[4]

The poem shows a hesitant, tentative approach. There was good reason
for his hesitation. It was addressed, not to another adorable girl like those
who had fired his imagination and prompted his muse in the past, but
to a mature and rather formidable, if most attractive, young woman

whose remarkable professional achievements were daily before his eyes, and who, moreover, was married, had two children, was seven years his senior, and was his "boss"—as he called her in a letter to his brother Stanley. And yet, when he says, "there stands so much between us which has not been confessed," we gather that Katharine had not shown herself indifferent to his feelings. She must at least have felt flattered by the admiration of this gifted and engaging young man. Quite possibly she felt herself strongly attracted to him. But whatever their feelings, expressed or unexpressed, Andy could hardly have hoped that they would lead to anything more than another instance of his loving "aimlessly."

As it turned out, however, "Notes from a Desk Calendar" was the opening movement of the long and intricate mating dance that led finally to their marriage. It is no wonder that the persons who saw them together could not always guess its meaning—or that a biographer some fifty years later would not be able to describe its complete choreography, much less interpret it. For one thing, though Mary had left the scene, another woman had appeared who seems to have attracted Andy's ardent attention. With her, for four or five months, he danced a lively divertissement with an abandon he could never achieve in his pursuit of Mary. She was a nineteen-year-old secretary at *The New Yorker* named Rosanne Magdol. She was small, pretty, and pert, with lively eyes and an artless, provocative way of talking. She was quick, candid, uninhibited, and ambitious. She had broken away from what she felt to be the stifling atmosphere of her Russian Jewish immigrant family by setting herself up in the Village and finding a job in the office of the liveliest magazine in New York. She admired writers and wanted to meet interesting people. She is the girl referred to in Ralph Ingersoll's account of the first annual beer party given for *The New Yorker* staff in Webster Hall:

> The office help had a really fine time, getting looped among the great and near great. My favorite memory is of a tiny secretary approaching Mr. Gene Tunney, then heavyweight champion of the world, and announcing in a clear voice, "Sir, I introduce myself because it has always been my ambition to rub elbows with the great."[5]

White wrote a casual based on that episode, and *The New Yorker* published it in June 1927. It was called "Rubbing Elbows," and it began: "My wife is at her best when she is rubbing elbows. Literary people have the elbows she likes best, then come artists' elbows, then prizefighters', then aviators'. . . ." It ended with this bit of dialogue:

"What about Senator Underwood, F. Scott Fitzgerald, Mayor Walker, and Gene Tunney?" asked my wife. "I would like to rub elbows with them, and then we can go home."

"Mr. Tunney is standing by the head of the stairs," I said, "with his arms akimbo. Maybe if you were right slick about it you could rub elbows with him without his knowing it. Otherwise you will have to talk about books, and then where will you be?"[6]

Rosanne Magdol remembers her days at *The New Yorker* with great pleasure, remembers with a grin being kidded about rubbing *shoulders* (not *elbows*) with Tunney, who was standing alone at the party looking shy and uncomfortable. She simply went over and did what came easily to her, introduced herself and led him into a conversation. She remembers Andy White with great affection. He too seemed shy when she first knew him. He told funny stories about his canary and was inclined to find something funny in most things that happened to him. She enjoyed talking to him, but he didn't seem much interested in girls. Rosanne grew to like him, he soon was drawn to her, and for a while they were on intimate terms. He didn't really "take her out," as she remembers it; he preferred just going for walks. One night she and he climbed over the fence enclosing the private garden of Gramercy Park, but she does not now remember that he wrote a good poem about that little caper. (It appeared in *The New Yorker* two months after "Notes.") She was puzzled by his driving her out one afternoon to his parents' house in Mount Vernon. By that time she knew him well enough to realize that his elderly parents would never approve of his being serious about her. As it turned out, they were not at home and Andy and Rosanne drove back to the Village.

One night he came to her apartment and insisted that she come out with him. When she told him she would have to tell the man who was staying with her that she was going out for a while, Andy was terribly upset—even after she explained that the man was a lot older than she and just a good friend down on his luck and in need of a place to stay. At one point, she seems to remember, he wanted her to run off with him but didn't say anything about marriage. He was, she says, "afraid of being hemmed in."

Rosanne was interested in yoga and once took Andy to a lecture on the subject. (White wrote, and published in the same issue in which the poem "Gramercy Park" appeared, a satirical account of such a lecture.) When in the late spring of 1928 she decided that she would like to go to a yoga camp for several months, Andy lent her two hundred dollars, and gave her a golden figurine of a lamb and a copy of *Walden*. When she returned to New York in the fall, Mrs. Angell helped her find a job at another magazine. White says that he was briefly in love with Rosanne but knew that marriage with her would not work.[7]

Marriage was on Andy's mind in those days, as it had been for a long time, but his ambivalent feelings towards it were, as usual, not far away. Now, more than ever before, he worried about the effects of marriage on an artist, and in the spring of 1928, in a *New Yorker* piece called "Bye Low Baby," he explored the subject in a dialogue between himself and his male canary, Baby, who speaks from the point of view of a singer, a musician, and a poet. Baby has recently acquired a wife, Justa, who, as the dialogue opens, is asleep in her nest "on five sea-green eggs, . . . and the blessed event is not far off." To White's inquiry into Baby's new way of life, Baby replies:

"Marriage?" he said, "well, it's difficult. I knew it would be. Still, a man owes it to himself—even an artist." "Do you mean your art is suffering?" I asked.

"Don't let's put it that way," he replied. "It isn't fair to Justa. She's a good girl. But there are things a woman simply can't get hold of. She's so diligent for success—that's what ruins a union like ours. Have you ever noticed her trick of digging up the white seeds and leaving them on top where I can get them easily?"

"I know," I said, "you'd rather she wouldn't."

"Certainly. But in order to enjoy the nobility of self-sacrifice, she merely assumes the advisability of it. It has never occurred to her that I might like to dig white seeds for myself. One of my happiest ideas for a tremolo came to me one time, in the old days, when my head was buried to the hilt in that seed cup. Take away an artist's troubles and what has he?"

"Still," I said, "those first few days with Justa: you were never in better voice. Marvellous, those love lyrics. More of the blue sky in them than I gave you credit for knowing about in such a dark apartment."

"Yes," said Baby, "but it wasn't a pure form. That throat-bulging song that ripples my feathers and shakes my frame, that song of desire and love and conquest—it's life, but it isn't art. It's like writing for a medium. I've watched you at that typewriter—always thinking about how it's going to look in print. Attenuated stuff, all of it. Most of my love warblings were that way; I discovered which notes Justa preferred and gave them to her. I knew what I was doing. After all, it's not much of a trick to make a woman love you, once you put your mind to it. Sometimes I get thinking about the old days, when there was nothing to keep me company but the cuckoo clock—the damn little wooden nightingale! . . .

"There used to be times when I was alone in the cage, in the old days, times when life seemed to have stopped—an unutterable dreariness in the room, just the ticking of the clock, the sense of desolation in the cage, water cup empty, trapeze hanging idle, all material things disembodied, the sort of feeling you get sometimes on a holiday in town when nobody is around and the weather is gray and even the 'L' sounds unreal. And I'd sit there on the lower perch, silent and puffed out. Times like that my spirit used to grow and expand, definitely. I could feel it. The way you can see a bulb develop in the gloomy wetness of a bowl. After such periods my song was appreciably better. A man needs those moments, you know? But nowadays . . . well, the other afternoon I was just getting into the doldrums when Justa came over and said: 'Hop down and take a drink of water, you'll feel better.' I could have wrung her little yellow neck! . . .

"Of course, marriage has its compensations. I won't pretend I don't like the little sleepy noise she makes late in the afternoon when she's on the nest. Art isn't everything. Soon there will be a stirring in the eggs, a pipping incomparable. Haven't we brought something into the apartment? Spring requires vindication—you've got to translate April. A lonely singer, however good his art, looks a little silly when the thaw comes. What was that line you read me one time "Look at songs, hidden in eggs." Life goes on. What time is it getting to be, anyway?"

"Almost ten o'clock," I said.

"Put that night-blanket over the cage; I want to recapture old twilights. Sometimes, in my artificial dusk, I hear mighty choruses—the primordial bands of robins, improvising the first great lullaby for the red sky of a hot and early world. I don't mention a thing like that to Justa, she might not get it."

"No," I said, "she might not."

"She'll make a good mother, that bird. Maybe one of the fledglings will take after me."[8]

The piece may have been prompted by Andy's recent experience with Rosanne, though the character of Justa, the canary's wife, seems only to typify an artist's view of women in general. Katharine Angell, however, was different from the type in one important way: she understood an artist's need for freedom to "hear mighty choruses—the primordial bands of robins, improvising the first great lullaby for the red sky of a hot and early world." She also understood that "the song of desire and love and conquest" is life, and whatever she may have felt about Andy's involvement with Rosanne, her instincts told her to keep herself in Andy's thoughts and feelings. During the late spring and early summer of 1928, Andy resumed writing poems to Katharine which he sent her by way of "The Conning Tower" and *The New Yorker*.[9]

The various duties he performed for the magazine kept him at its offices, and he was thus never far from Katharine for long. His Thursdays were mostly taken up with writing his weekly "Notes and Comment"; on Wednesdays he took part in the "art meeting," at which Ross, Rea Irvin, and Mrs. Angell decided which cartoons to publish; and on the other weekdays he came to the office to rewrite the work of "Talk" reporters and to do newsbreaks. Out of the office he roamed the city. In his pieces for *The New Yorker* that year we can trace the paths he took in these wanderings. He wrote about the orchid show, the Statue of Liberty, and a visit to Magistrates' Court for traffic violations. He recorded a trip to Sheepshead Bay to fish from one of the boats that take anglers out for a day's excursion, another one to Forest Hills to see Helen Wills play, another to Newark Airport to fly over New York Harbor in a Ford trimotor, and another to the Ambrose Lightship.

These accounts were in a form White had practiced in his column in the *Seattle Times* under the heading "Little Journeys." Artistically they reached a level above that of the conventional feature story. One written in May of that year, after a trip to potter's field, is a good example of the distinction White gave to this kind of prose:

New York's pauper dead are buried in a sandy hill on the north end of Hart's Island in Long Island Sound, a mile from Execution Light. They lie in big graves, tier on tier, unclaimed. It was blowy the day we went out there to see the field, and the low storm-swept island looked particularly weather-beaten. Michael Breen, warden of the island prison, met us, smiling broadly, glad of a visitor.

Twice a week the boat comes up from Bellevue. The prisoners bury the dead, solemnly and without ceremony, one hundred and fifty to a grave, one white headstone for the lot. It is a beautiful spot—the sweep of the Sound, the restless clang of the bell buoy at the point. . . .

Mr. Breen allowed us to look at the record books, and we glanced at a few entries: a baby found in the parcel room of the Penn Station, a man picked up in the Fifth Avenue sewer, page after page, six thousand a year. There is a single monument to honor them—a small cross bearing the inscription: "And He shall call His own by name."

As we stood there a gull wheeled and circled above our head. From the far side of the island the wind brought the smell of tide flats, the incessant sounding of the bell. And rather vaguely we heard the fine Irish voice of Michael Breen: "Thim horsechissnut trees will be all full o' blossoms soon—pretty as a picture!"[10]

In paragraphs like these White achieved the art that Baby aspired to, improving upon what Baby called songs of life. The flight of the gull, the rich smell of marine life, and the certainty of the return of the seasons, attested to by the horse-chestnut tree, are gladsome evidence of unseen but hoped for providence.

In the late spring of 1928 Andy knew, like Baby, that art isn't everything, that a poem can only "translate April," and that "a lonely singer looks a little silly when the thaw comes." But Andy was not in the mood for spring that year. "I'll not go along this time," he wrote. "I'll wear September like a charm all spring."[11] He saw no promise in his private life. And his professional life was no longer as exciting as when he first began to work for *The New Yorker*. Now that he had mastered all the kinds of writing the magazine asked of him, he felt he had arrived at a dead-end. In such moments of desolation or frustration Andy had long since learned the trick of quitting his job, or taking a long vacation; and this time he made plans to go to Europe with Gus Lobrano, who was sailing June 1 on the *Corinthia*, partly on Cunard Line business and partly to try to forget a girl to whom he had been engaged. Andy's reasons for going abroad were not uncomplicated; one of them was that he hoped to see Katharine in Europe.

Ernest and Katharine Angell, their children Nancy and Roger, aged ten and seven, and Katharine's sister Rosamond, with her husband, John S. Newberry, were all going to Paris for a month. Ernest would see an old flame from World War I days; Katharine, now deeply in love with Andy, would see Andy; and perhaps, Ernest thought, he and Katharine, by being sensible and modern, could save their marriage.[12]

Andy and Katharine kept their rendezvous in Paris—they had not crossed on the same ship. Andy took her canoeing on the Seine, near Bougival, and sometime later they went to St. Tropez and then to Corsica. Andy never forgot the island's "good small hotel called Hôtel des Étrangers with a pretty garden full of lizards and sweet smelling vines" at which they stayed. He remembered "the sound of someone practicing the piano in the dead afternoon [and] the red rocks of Pianna, and Vizzavona, and Calvi, and . . . trying to ride a bicycle after too many cups of beautiful white wine and landing in a cactus coppice."[13]

The Corsican interlude, as he later called it, found its way into White's poetry:

Once I felt a garden hold me,
　Orange trees and long vines clinging—
I could not escape its fragrance,
Break loose from the strong vines—
　Orange trees and swallows winging,
　　Noon and sunny paths and lizards
　And a slow voice singing.

> Earth was full of flowers and giving;
> I was full of life and living.[14]

And toward the end of that year he seemed to allude to Corsica when he wrote:

> Yet I still dwell
>   In a strange land,
> Beholding your life,
>   Possessing your hand.[15]

But the Corsican interlude had a bittersweet ending. Back in New York in August, the lovers agreed not to see each other except in the office of *The New Yorker.* Looking ahead, they saw their affair leading inevitably to pain and frustration, the way to marriage apparently blocked by Katharine's reluctance to leave her children, by her apprehension lest she be "scorched twice," and, more than anything else perhaps, by her awareness of Andy's deep-seated resistance to any irrevocable commitment. They decided therefore to be sensible.

Only a few weeks after their return Andy told Katharine how he felt about that decision in the following poem:

SOLILOQUY AT TIMES SQUARE

> The time for little words is past;
> We now speak only the broad impertinences.
> I take your hand
> Merely to help you cross the street
> (We are such friends),
> Choosing the long and formal phrase
> Deliberately.
> At dinner we discuss, rather intelligently,
> The things one should discuss at dinner. So.
> How well we are in tune—how easy
> Every phrase! The long words come, fondling the ear,
> Flattering the mind they come. Long words
> Enjoy the patronage of noble minds,
> The circumspection of this sanity.
>
> How much is gone! How much went
> When the little words went: peace,
> Sandwiched in the space between madness and madness;
> The quick exchange of every bright moment;
> The animal alertness to the other's heart;

The reality of nearness. Those things went
With the words.

Suppose I should forget, grow thoughtless—
What if the little words came back,
Running in upon me, running back
Like little children home from school?
Suppose I spoke—oh, I don't know—
Some vagrant phrase out of the summer!
What if I said: "I love you"? Something as simple
And as easy to the tongue as that—
Something as true? I'm only talking.
Give me your hand,
We must by all means cross this street.[16]

And out of his loneliness came another poem, written at the end of that
year, in which he tried to remember all the things that had always sustained
him in the past, and that he prayed would continue to do so in the future:

THIS IS A PRAYER BEFORE I SLEEP

. . . this is a prayer for small things only
To a jealous God from a man that's lonely:
Remembered things of my life I'll weave in,
Ask of the God I half believe in—
Giver of grass and the wind that blows it
And the man that mows it.
    This is a prayer.

Keep most carefully alive in me
Something of the expectancy
That is somehow likeliest to be
    In a child waking,
    A day breaking,
    A robin singing,
    Or a telephone ringing.

Give me again the strange thrill
Of a boy climbing a Maine hill,
    topping the rise,
Coming on the farmer's band of sheep:
Give me the terrible surprise
Of their raised heads, their startled eyes. . . .

And once, in a ship, in a frozen sea,
I glimpsed a thing that was really me.

In at the death
Let me draw the same courageous breath
I drew the day I looked on Unalaska. . . .

Guard the most difficult part of me
That has fattened me not, but has left me free.

Now grant me, and may I keep forever
Unharmed, the memory of those ways
Walking with love, hand on her shoulder,
    Happily together.
Never allow me to forget
That which was once a kiss
And is now a phrase.

That is the prayer, and now I'll sleep,
With a lay-me-down and a soul-to-keep.
    I hadn't prayed in a long time.[17]

By the beginning of 1929 White was thinking seriously of running away from this situation. In his journal for New Year's Day he wrote: "Walking twice around the reservoir this afternoon in the fog, resolving a problem: whether to quit my job and leave town telling no one where I was going."[18] "No one" included Katharine, presumably. Yet two days later he thought of one of Thurber's funny drawings, remembered how much he liked Thurber's company, and decided to hang around for a while longer. The next day "The Conning Tower" carried another verse epistle to Katharine, "Rhyme for a Reasonable Lady," which ended with the words:

Only alone, at peace, at night,
    Have I the simple will to say
The words I love, and love to write,
    For you to read, alone, by day.[19]

On January 21, his problem still unresolved, Andy decided to resort simultaneously to four well-tried remedies: he would make a journey; he would drive his brand new Model A Ford roadster; he would go to Maine; and he would skate. Years later he remembered the excursion as follows:

Wanting to get by myself and think about many things, I left New York by car, headed in a general northerly direction. (I hated office work and occasionally just up and beat it when I had had a belly full.) I went to Belgrade, persuaded Bert Mosher to take me in for a few days, and spent about a week happily skating on Great Pond. . . . I let a lot of cold fresh Maine air blow through my brains and then returned to New York.[20]

And went back to work, and Katharine.

On a sunny Sunday afternoon in February, the day after the fourth birthday of *The New Yorker,* Andy and Jim Thurber visited Katharine in her new residence, the Angells' little summer house at Sneden's Landing, on the west bank of the Hudson River. Only a week or so before, she had decided that a divorce would be less harmful to her children than continued exposure to violent quarrels between their parents. Having arrived at that decision, she had walked out of the Angells' house in uptown Manhattan and gone to the Thurbers' apartment in the Village, where she had stayed for a day or two, until Jim and Andy had been able to help her move some of her possessions to the summer house. She intended to live in it until she could make arrangements to go to Reno for a divorce. Jim Thurber was about to move to bachelor quarters, his marriage to Althea having likewise failed irreparably. Andy was equally alone and uncertain of the future. These three *New Yorker* bachelors, "feeling good about being together," made a pact to have a reunion at the same place twenty-five years later. They each put a dated newspaper clipping in their wallets as a reminder (White and Thurber still had theirs twenty-five years later—but the reunion never took place).[21]

The next two months were deeply disturbing and distressing to Katharine because of the pressures exerted on her from various sides to abandon the thought of divorce and return to her family. Ernest, full of remorse and professing his love, entreated her to change her mind. He even "summoned" Thurber more than once to enlist his help in persuading her to reconsider. Relatives implored her to stay with Ernest for the sake of the children. Katharine, however, remained adamant. Only a quick, clean break, she thought, would bring her and ultimately her children the necessary relief from discord.[22]

On May 1 Harper and Brothers published *The Lady Is Cold: Poems by E. B. W.* It contained sixty-four poems written between 1923 and 1929, all but a dozen of them first published in "The Conning Tower" or *The New Yorker.* The title refers to the female figure in the fountain in front of the Plaza Hotel, at the corner of Fifty-eighth Street and Fifth Avenue. The six small drawings in the book were made especially for it by Ernest F. Hubbard, a friend of Katharine's who drew for *The New Yorker.* Eugene Saxton, another friend of Katharine's, was White's editor at Harper. It was a good-looking volume. Granville Hicks, in the *New York World,* called White "unpretentious, competent, and versatile," praised him for "poems rich in emotion and beauty," but concluded that he seemed to have "accepted the role of a minor poet and to be determined to get as much fun out of it as possible."[23]

Ten days after *The Lady Is Cold* was published, Ross and White put Katharine Angell on the posh Twentieth Century Limited, bound for Chicago, en route to Reno, where she could get a divorce in three months. She left New York without knowing where she would live when she returned, and without even being sure that she wanted to go back to *The New Yorker*. She was exhausted.

Having seen Katharine off at four o'clock in the afternoon, Andy returned to his apartment and fell into a deep sleep from which he was roused a few hours later by a telephone call from Gertrude Lynahan, who lived in the same building and had called to invite him for cocktails the following afternoon. When he fell back to sleep, he dreamed that Katharine was calling him from Albany to say that it was all over between them. When he awoke much later that night, he confused the telephone call in his dream with the call from Gertrude, and was convinced that he had heard from Katharine before he fell asleep. Unwilling to accept what he thought was Katharine's decision to make a clean break with him, he chartered a small plane and took off from Curtiss Field, on Long Island, "in an attempt to overtake his vanishing beauty" in Chicago.[24] There he found Katharine at the house of friends whom he knew she had planned to visit en route to Reno. Reassured that his dream was unrelated to fact, he returned to New York by train. White's dreams, in those days at least, were vivid and compelling, and in more than one instance he acted on an assumption that what he had dreamed had really happened.[25]

In Chicago Andy and Katharine had renewed a pledge not to write to each other, but Katharine broke it as soon as she settled in at the Circle S Ranch, where she spent the three months of residence in Nevada required for obtaining a divorce in that state.

During her first month in Reno, Katharine's letters were brave, unsuccessful efforts to put a cheerful face on her misery. Her sisters and Ernest's family continued to press her not to go through with the divorce and accused her of heartlessly abandoning her children. She had arrived in Reno physically and emotionally run down, and she was, of course, very lonely. Before she left New York she had asked Andy to visit her in Nevada, but he had not yet decided what he wanted to do during his vacation; among other things, he was thinking of going to Europe with Gus Lobrano. In one of her first letters from Reno she renewed the invitation, suggesting that he bring Ross along—that all three could have "such a good time." But Andy replied at once that he wasn't coming; he was afraid of getting hay fever out there. Katharine felt that he had not wanted to discuss his real reasons. What she assumed them to be is revealed in the following part of her response:

> Your letter came saying you couldn't come to Nevada. I'd been looking forward to it so, but you're certainly right *not* to come if you don't want to. I doubt if hayfever would bother you here. There's almost no pollen from vegetation—the land is like Corsica. . . . I wouldn't want you to come if I didn't really believe it was a perfectly natural and comfortable thing. . . . As for ourselves, you may assume that it would complicate us still further, get us involved in endless pros and cons of behavior, make me take for granted more for the future. Well, it wouldn't. I'm living right now in a state of suspended animation—with no past and no future and all I want is a little companionship to help the present. . . . Also, of course, I do want to see *you,* and want you to see me when I'm healthy and normal so that you can forget the abnormal half mad woman I was those last months in New York.

If he came, she said, she was sure they wouldn't get "all mixed up just from saying good night," as he had "once put it," and there would be no "talk about whether you and I should get married."[26]

Andy did not go to Reno, but he did fulfill another of Katharine's requests. He found her an attractive apartment in Greenwich Village to move into upon her return in August. In her letter informing him that she had decided to follow his advice and sign a two-year lease, she added that she could hardly stand the idea of returning to New York or to *The New Yorker,* which was "poison" to her: "Now when I begin to feel I may be able to live again, I realize *The New Yorker* was an escape from the life I didn't like." Katharine knew that Andy himself was disenchanted with New York and *The New Yorker,* and perhaps she wanted him to know that she shared his feelings. But she knew likewise that she would have to earn her living and that she could not easily find another job as good as the one she had. Under the circumstances, she said, all she could do was to go back determined to reduce her responsibilities and her working hours. She may have wished to assure Andy that if they did marry she would not be so fully preoccupied by her job as she had been before her divorce.[27]

White's letters to her during this period, if they exist, are not available. He did not, it seems, write as frequently or at such length as Katharine. But her letters often reflect pretty clearly what Andy had written her. One of them, written on June 21, is of particular interest since it reveals a great deal about Andy's state of mind at the time as well as about Katharine's understanding of him:

Friday, June 21—

Dear Andy:

I've been thinking a lot about what you've written as to your [thirtieth] birthday and the decision you must make for your future. You're the only person who can decide and my thoughts on the subject may not interest you —either you'll think I'm impertinent to write them or that I'm biased or not clearly thinking on the subject, so maybe I ought to shut up but please don't feel that way and let me write away from the detachment of Nevada. It would be a lot easier to talk—or maybe it wouldn't—I'm not usually good at expressing myself in either medium.

You say you're a failure at the writing racket and that you could be contented in your present job if you didn't mind being just a hack. I know what you mean by this even if I don't agree and I admire you for not being content to do what seems to you, just a small thing in writing, well. You feel that in thirty years you haven't produced a really important book, poem or piece of prose—Most people haven't by then. It seems to me, though, that you are preeminently a writer—everything you do has a certain perfection that is rare. You have made the Comment page of the New Yorker the most distinguished part of that magazine—this is not just my opinion; many people who did not know who wrote that page and whose opinions I value have said so to me—Charles Merz for example—He picked out Notes and Comments and the newsbreaks as the two real achievements of the magazine aside from the drawings and drawing captions. Your comments grow better and better—this last year's have been more important than the year's before—Aside from that you've written some of the best prose and poetry we've published (I am *not* biased, this I thought long before I knew you well or had an affection for you). You've written most of your best poems in the last year and a half so far as I can see. Now I quite understand why you don't want to go on writing what you call "palpitating paragraphs" all your life and appreciate your feeling that writing is fun when you don't have to do it, when you do it as an amateur and not because you must sit before a typewriter and turn out so many words a week. Whether you should keep the New Yorker job I can't say,—certainly you shouldn't if it prevents you from writing things you care about more but it seems to me that that job, properly held down so you control it and not it you,—so you don't give all your life to it and allow it to harass and burden you, seems to me to have a lot to be said for it for the next few years anyway. After all it's a pretty pleasant job as things go,—allows you to live a comparatively gracious and free life. Your hours are your own with certain exceptions, you have some fun out of it you must admit; you have, I should guess, a life that would please you more than another sort of office job would give you. You might go into farming, ferryboating what not and write when you felt like it. That has a lot to be said for it, too, but I do know this: there's no real freedom or happiness in life for the person who just vagabonds, throws over the idea of being a responsible member of society and says "This year I can live on 50¢ a day and work my way to the coast." Everyone of your temperament should do that once in a while but a lifetime of it would leave you pretty blank after a year or two. I discussed this with Thurber in relation to his own rebellions against the job etc. He said that of course he talked a lot but that he realized that for himself or anyone the best freedom and happiness came from living a somewhat regular life with responsibilities and continuities and that the romantic urge to hop to Europe to run around indefinitely was not an honest or sensible modus vivendi. This is true for Thurber—not necessarily for you. If you do keep on the New Yorker job, why not limit yourself definitely to, say, three days in the office,—and give yourself a real break in writing something you want to, the rest of the time—or not writing at all if you don't want to. For you to give up writing now would be like a violinist so good that he could always be the Concert Master of one of the four or five leading orchestras of the world, giving up fiddling because he couldn't be Heifetz. Perhaps you'll never be a Heifetz, perhaps you will, I can't say—Perhaps you won't be Willa Cather, but there's a good chance you might be (she, by the way, never wrote a book anyone noticed till she was almost forty —she worked on magazines). But it doesn't seem sensible for a concert master to throw over music, the thing he most loved in the world, because he can't be Heifetz. The least you'll ever be, in my estimation, is a concert master. You know there's a kind of vanity in underestimating yourself. Also, the frustration motif continued for a lifetime doesn't give anyone much happiness. There's a certain satisfaction in it, but not the best kind. Oh, stop preaching, Katharine. I ought to be the last person in the world to hold forth on how to arrange one's life, I having made a pretty disgusting mess of my own and other people's—Do please forgive me—I'll bet on you whatever you do. And I'm with you more heartily than I can say in being against success that is economic only, and against loading one's life with possessions, routines and riches of one sort or another, that only tie one down and keep one from really living. How I long for a *simple,* decent life of my own,—with a few things for the soul to feed on. You can have it anyway, my dear,—and *please* don't be unhappy or worried now. At least don't create unhappinesses for yourself where they don't exist—there are enough necessary ones around for everyone.

Do just tell me once you forgive me for this letter—or that you don't, as the case may be.

I'll have to write you later about the horses—Oh, it was swell, except that yesterday I almost got a sunstroke sitting on the corral fence in the first really hot sun of the summer here—had to spend the afternoon in bed.[28]

Eight days after she had written that remarkable letter, and only a day after she had mailed Andy a long, cheerful report on her recent activities, (which included finding a lake where she could shed her swimming suit and sunbathe in the nude), Katharine heard from someone in New York that White had resigned from *The New Yorker*. She telegraphed Andy asking him to telephone her at the Riverside Hotel in Reno on Sunday. He called on Monday, and Katharine apparently was reassured—Andy was only about to take a leave of absence of indefinite duration. She wrote later that it somehow made her feel good to know that he was "quit of *The New Yorker* for the time being at least."[29]

The next day she received Andy's reply to her letter of June 21 on the subject of his dissatisfaction with his life. Apparently he had badly misunderstood her. Katharine was hurt, as she made clear in her response:

> I am more shocked and overwhelmed at the part in your letter about my letter to you, than I can say. If you can think those are my ideas, if I wrote so badly that you can misunderstand me, I give up. I thought perhaps you were the one person in the world who understood that ease, safety, income and locality were so little a part of my own desires for life that I'd never recommend them to anyone else. Andy, do you honestly think I meant or said that?[30]

During her last month in Reno Katharine wrote only four letters to Andy, all cheerful and relatively impersonal, except for the last, written on July 29, in which she allowed her brave front to fall: "Will you be back when I arrive on the 23rd of August? Probably not." The twenty-third, she explained, would be a Friday, and she would face an August weekend in an unfurnished apartment in an empty city. Her children, in the care of her family (aunts and sisters), would be away till after Labor Day. She thought that if Andy were around maybe she'd ask him to take her out on that "empty Sunday" for the canoe trip on the Sound she'd been promised for so long. "Maybe Jim and Althea would let me go to Silvermine and see the poodles—for I must plan to be very busy I can see when I get back and not just sit home and mope."[31]

But Andy was not around when Katharine returned. Before he received her last letter from Reno he had left New York for Camp Otter, in Ontario, from where he had sent her the following pencilled note:

> Dear Katharine,
>
> I'm starting in about 10 minutes for Cache Lake with Hubbard. Wish you were going. It's marvelous up here—same as ever; and its good to see food bags of rice, prunes, and corn meal,—and blanket packs, again. I've been here about 4 days and have been fishing most of the time on a lake near here with some people from Ithaca—up at dawn and too tired at night to do anything but sleep.
>
> Much haste—yrs
> Andy

In fact, Katharine's letter may not have caught up with him by the time he wrote his next letter to her from Camp Otter, for in it he made no mention of her plea for his companionship when she returned to New York. His letter was hardly what she had hoped for:

> If my calculations are correct (one arrives at the day of the month by taking shots at the stars and computing from old newspapers discovered in the privy) you are on the way home. Probably none too soon. I have an anguished letter from Ross that sounds as though he could only hang on three days longer. He takes things too hard. If he thinks the New Yorker is complicated he ought to see a boys' camp. Lost blankets, heart-aches, fallings-in-the-lake—a marvelous confusion, always comical because kids are so funny. . . . I haven't heard from you in a dog's age, but my mail seems to be scattered around a bit anyway. I have succeeded in losing track of about everything—people, dates, friends, mail, jobs, home. And it feels good. . . . Things are much as they were in the days when I was here before—the clanging gong that gets you up, the kids trading desserts for nickel candy bars, the still shore where you brush your teeth, the little lakes nearby where you can watch blue herons catch frogs, the lumber camp and the peat bog. Ontario is wonderful (haven't you been up here, I seem to remember that you have). I envy Hub his job even though it is a lot of work and a lot of responsibility. . . .
>
> There's a marvelous doubles game going on right outside, making it impossible to write. It's impossible to write up here anyway. Love to everybody, and keep the home fires burning.
>
>   Andy[32]

At about the same time Andy wrote Ross as follows:

> Dear Ross:
>
>   Report on me, as requested in your letter of uncertain date.
>
>   I am getting back to New York later than I expected due to the fact that I'm acquiring an interest in this camp, and that takes time. My mild participation in the belles lettres of New York will probably be less this year than formerly (I'm working out a tentative schedule of 10 minutes a week for poesy, 25 minutes for prose, and a half hour before breakfast for answers to hard questions), a consummation designed to improve the state of the local b.l. as well as my own general condition. On account of the fact that The New Yorker has a tendency to make me morose and surly, the farther I stay away the better. I appreciate very much your extraordinary capacity to endure, and in fact cope with, my somewhat vengeful attitude about The New Yorker and my crafty habit of slipping away for long intervals (these intervals wouldn't have cost you a cent if you hadn't been a damn fanciful bookkeeper—this last

one has cost you some $420, but if you insist on being ridiculous, it's out of my control). Next to yourself and maybe one or two others, I probably have as tender a feeling for your magazine as anybody. For me it isn't a complete life, though, and that's one reason why returning to this place where I worked during the summers of 1920–21 has been such a satisfying experience. In ten years Dorset hasn't changed—it's almost the only place I've ever come back to that hasn't given me an empty feeling from discovering that nothing can be the same again. The fellow that I first came here with is now running the camp, and we're working on a plan for going in business together. At the moment I don't know just what this amounts to, but it's a lucky break for me because it's a realization of an old desire of mine. . . . I don't know exactly when I'll be in New York.

I'm worried about old man Thurber and hope you can make him take a decent vacation. He needs fancy bookkeeping more than I do, who don't need it at all. . . .

This report on me is a bit sketchy, but you asked for it and it's the best I can do in the hour between breakfast and the time I have to row over and get the milk.

Yrs with love,
White[33]

One reason why he didn't know exactly when he'd be back in New York was that he was planning to take the "handsome new canoe" that had been built for him in Dorset to a point on the Erie Canal, and from there he wanted, as he said, to "paddle my shiny new canoe down the Erie Canal and Hudson to surprise central New York people and to give myself a good time."[34] Andy was vigorously ignoring his having passed his thirtieth birthday.

Though she dreaded coming home to an empty apartment and longed to see Andy, Katharine had spoken the truth in her last letter from Reno when she had said she was "thrilled at the thought of getting back." First of all she wanted to see her children, but "even the thought of New York pavements and New York offices" made her nostalgic. Katharine was never a person to endure hopelessness for long. She tended to believe that she could do something about imperfections of many kinds. Her life consisted of all sorts of "editing." She may have been more deliberate than casual when she added as a P.S. to her last letter to Andy: "Maybe it's as well I'm leaving—I was discovered naked on Pyramid beach by an Indian today. It's their lake, too."[35]

Andy stayed on in Canada well into September. He decided to invest about eight thousand dollars, a good part of his savings, in Camp Otter. He was thinking of making a drastic change in his life, for the reasons he had spelled out to Katharine in the long letter she had so carefully answered. Four months earlier, in "Notes and Comment," he had described the chief one: the dilemma of a professional writer who has to be inspired on schedule. Few writers caught between the desire to be free and the need to write for a living "have the courage to buy a country newspaper, or even quit a city writing job for anything at all."[36] Running a boys' camp in Ontario would not be just anything at all; it would be a dream.

By late September Andy and Katharine were both back at *The New Yorker,* but, true to his word to Ross, Andy produced only three "Talk" pieces and four casuals during the rest of 1929. Nor did he publish anything in "The Conning Tower."

In November 1929, however, nine days after the stock market crash, Harper and Brothers published *Is Sex Necessary? Or Why You Feel the Way You Do,* by James Thurber and E. B. White.

Eight months earlier the authors had begun to think about collaborating on a parody of some of the works on sex produced by "heavy writers" (doctors, psychiatrists, and "other students of misbehavior") with which the market had recently been flooded. They had decided that the way to collaborate was "to get thinking about the same thing in the same way, and then [for] each [to] withdraw into [his] separate orbit and write it."

Thurber wrote the Preface, and White wrote the Foreword, which opened as follows:

> During the past year, two factors in our civilization have been greatly overemphasized. One is aviation, the other is sex. Looked at calmly, neither diversion is entitled to the space it has been accorded. Each has been deliberately promoted.
>
> In the case of aviation, persons interested in the sport saw that the problem was to simplify it and make it seem safer. They introduced stabilizers and emergency landing fields. Even so, the plain fact remained that very few people were fitted for flying.
>
> With sex, the opposite was true. Everybody was fitted for it, but there was a lack of general interest. The problem in this case was to make sex seem more complex and dangerous.[37]

Half the chapters were by White, half by Thurber. The book was illustrated by Thurber, whose drawings had never before been published. Thurber had offered cartoons to *The New Yorker* at various times in the past, but Ross had never recognized their art or their wit and had never published them. It had been White's idea to illustrate the book with drawings by Thurber. During the two years the two men had shared an office at *The New Yorker,* Andy had watched Jim fill yellow sheet after yellow sheet with lightly penciled drawings of men, women, and dogs, and then toss them, sheet after sheet, on the floor. As White said in the account of his discovery of Thurber as artist, "They were more a problem of disposal than anything else."[38]

A day or so before he and Jim took the typescript of the book to the publisher, they selected a few drawings that were lying around the office and Thurber drew a few more specifically for the book. Then White spent hours retracing them with India ink. When they spread them out on the floor of the office of Eugene Saxton, their editor at Harper, he said: " 'These, I take it, are the rough sketches from which the drawings will be produced?' 'No,' [White] said cheerfully, 'these are the drawings themselves.' "[39] And with that White and Thurber left. Saxton finally decided to rely on White's judgment and advice in the matter, and to include the drawings in the book. They contributed so much to its humor that they made Thurber an instant success as a cartoonist and launched him on a new career. From that time on Thurber's genius was recognized in his cartoons as well as in his writing. For a second time White had helped Thurber achieve the recognition he deserved. Ross was embarrassed by the reviewers' praise of the drawings of a man whose art he had not taken seriously, and within a few weeks Thurber became a fairly regular contributor of cartoons to *The New Yorker.* In his later books, of course, Thurber revealed his world in pictures as well as in words.

White not only discovered Thurber the cartoonist, he also wrote the first appreciation of Thurber's art, in a note in *Is Sex Necessary?*

When one studies the drawings, it soon becomes apparent that a strong undercurrent of grief runs through them. In almost every instance the man in the picture is badly frightened, or even hurt. These "Thurber men" have come to be recognized as a distinct type in the world of art; they are frustrated, fugitive beings; at times they seem vaguely striving to get out of something without being seen (a room, a situation, a state of mind), at other times they are merely perplexed and too humble, or weak, to move. The women, you will notice, are quite different: temperamentally they are much better adjusted to their surroundings than are the men, and mentally they are much less capable of making themselves uncomfortable.

It would be foolish to attempt here a comprehensive appreciation of the fierce sweep, the economy, and the magnificent obscurity of Thurber's work, nor can I adequately indicate the stark qualities in the drawings that have earned for him the title of "the Ugly Artist." All I, all anybody, can do is to hint at the uncanny faithfulness with which he has caught—caught and thrown to the floor—the daily, indeed the almost momently, severity of life's mystery, as well as the charming doubtfulness of its purpose.[40]

As for the apparent irrelevance of some of the drawings to the text, White said, "Just how some of the animals shown in these pages 'come in' is not clear even to me—except in so far as any animal may be regarded as sexually relevant because of our human tendency to overestimate what can be learned from watching it." The book was, in fact, dedicated to two live Thurber dogs—Scottish terriers named Daisy and Jeanie. (Daisy, a daughter of Jeanie, was a gift from the Thurbers to Katharine, and had lived with Andy while Katharine was in Reno.) White designed the dust jacket for the book and did the lettering for it.

In the history of the publisher it was an important event, for Harper subsequently published all but one of White's books and ten of Thurber's best books. The reviews were excellent, and so were the sales. During the first five months Harper made eleven printings with a total of forty-five thousand copies. By the end of the year the printings numbered twenty-one.

On Wednesday morning, November 13, 1929, Andy White walked down Fifth Avenue to Katharine Angell's apartment to renew with her, before she left for the office, the discussion they had been conducting for some weeks on whether to get married or not. The breakthrough occurred when Katharine said something about ivy. White wrote years later:

> I don't remember how ivy got into the discussion but potted plants have never been far removed from Katharine's thoughts. Anyway, when I heard the word "ivy," I said petulantly, "Oh, let the ivy rest!" K's whole manner changed. Instead of slamming the ball back over the net at me, she replied in a mild and thoughtful voice: "That sounds like the name of an English country house."
>
> At this point, I decided that she was the girl for me and the hell with the obstacles. So, after some badgering, she agreed to it, and we spent the rest of the day getting married—no mean feat.[41]

Before they could go down to City Hall for the marriage license, Katharine had to phone John Mosher, her assistant editor for fiction, and call off her dinner date with him that night, and she had to let her part-time housekeeper, Josephine Buffa, know that she need not come in that afternoon to cook "a company dinner for two." Since Josephine would not be in, Daisy could not be left at home all day and had to go with them. First they stopped at the Guaranty Trust Company to pick up Katharine's divorce papers, which they would need to obtain a marriage license. On the way back up Sixth Avenue from City Hall they stopped at a cheap jewelry store and looked at rings, but Katharine decided to use her college ring and give Andy time to buy her the kind of ring he liked. They had lunch at Louis and Martin's, a favorite speakeasy in the West Forties, where they encountered the writer Emily Hahn, whose work Katharine had been the first to recommend to Ross and whose editor at *The New Yorker* she had been ever since.

After lunch, Andy, Katharine, and Daisy drove north about fifty miles to Bedford Village, where, failing to find a justice of the peace, they persuaded Dr. A. R. Fulton to marry them in the Presbyterian church. Branches of autumn-colored leaves, left over from a funeral the day before, were banked along the front of the platform. Daisy was left in the minister's house next door, and during the ceremony she and the minister's police dog got into a noisy scrap. Back in Manhattan the married couple had dinner in a back room of Marta's, an Italian restaurant on Washington Place.[42]

They both were back at work the next day. On Friday, Walter Winchell's column, "On Broadway," in the *New York Daily Mirror*, announced their marriage:

> News that couldn't wait until Monday: E. B. White, of *The New Yorker*'s comical department and one of the better wits in the town, and Katharine Angell, the managing editor of *The New Yorker*, eloped Tuesday and were sealed up-state.
>
> The groom recently co-authored a book titled (heh-heh): "Is Sex Necessary?"[43]

When Nancy Angell, then not quite twelve, heard of her mother's marriage from her aunt, who had read about it in the papers, she was terribly upset. She and her brother, Roger, had met White only once, a year or so earlier, when he had come to dinner at the Angells' house on East Ninety-third Street. Since Katharine's divorce, the children, now in the custody of their father, had been spending weekends with their mother at her apartment, and it was there that they met their new stepfather on the first Saturday following the wedding.

Andy's marriage to a divorcée who had given custody of her children to their father probably hurt his parents. Only a few weeks earlier they had been distressed by *Is Sex Necessary?*, about which Andy had overheard his father say to his mother, "Well, I don't know what *you* think about it, but *I'm* ashamed of it."[44] Still, this was not the first time Andy had surprised them with a decision they found incomprehensible. Within a few months, however, in time for their golden wedding anniversary, they would hear that Katharine was pregnant; and before long they would meet Nancy and Roger and soon consider Andy's stepchildren as part of his family, to be remembered on their birthdays and at Christmas.

A day or so after their marriage Andy sent Katharine by interoffice memo a recent *New Yorker* cartoon by Rea Irvin. It showed a man sitting deep in thought, and its caption consisted of a quotation from Einstein: "People slowly accustomed themselves to the idea that the physical states of space itself were the final reality." Andy had replaced the original caption with one that read: "E. B. White slowly accustomed himself to the idea that he had made the most beautiful decision of his life."[45]

During the second weekend after their marriage Andy stayed in his old apartment on West Twelfth Street, hoping that Katharine's weekly reunion with her children would be a happier one if he were absent. On Saturday night he wrote his wife the following letter:

Dear Katharine (very dear):

I've had moments of despair during the last week which have added years to my life and put many new thoughts in my head. Always, however, I have ended on a cheerful note of hope, based on the realization that you are the person to whom I return and that you are the recurrent phrase in my life. I realized that so strongly one day a couple of weeks ago when, after being away among people I wasn't sure of and in circumstances I had doubts about, I came back and walked into your office and saw how real and incontrovertible you seemed. I don't know whether you know just what I mean or whether you experience, ever, the same feeling; but what I mean is, that being with you is like walking on a very clear morning—definitely the sensation of belonging there.

This marriage is a terrible challenge: everyone wishing us well, and all with their tongues in their cheeks. What other people think, or wish, or prophesy, is not particularly important, except as it tends to work on our minds. I think you have the same intuitive hesitancy that I have—about pushing anything too hard, and the immediate problem surely is that we recognize & respect each other's identity. That I could assimilate Nancy overnight is obviously out of the question—or that she could me. In things like that we gain ground slowly. By and large, our respective families had probably best be kept in their respective places during the pumpkin weather—and gradually, like the Einstein drawing of Rea Irvin's, people will become accustomed to the idea that etc. etc.

I'm just writing this haphazard for no reason other than that I felt like writing you a letter before going to bed.

I love you. And that's a break.[46]

On the following Saturday night he was in Toronto on business connected with his purchase of an interest in Camp Otter. From the King Edward Hotel he sent Katharine this poem:

NATURAL HISTORY

The spider, dropping down from twig,
Unwinds a thread of his devising:
A thin, premeditated rig
To use in rising.

And all the journey down through space,
In cool descent, and loyal-hearted,
He builds a ladder to the place
From which he started.

Thus I, gone forth, as spiders do,
In spider's web a truth discerning,
Attach one silken strand to you
For my returning.[47]

The Whites had decided to postpone their honeymoon until spring, when they would go to Bermuda. They went to Boston for Christmas, to visit Katharine's sister Rosamond Newberry on Beacon Hill. During the visit, Andy wrote a paragraph for "Notes and Comment" reporting that while ice-skating in the Public Garden, "in the cool winter dusk with the green light from the Ritz shining in the clear sky, our shoes were stolen from under the bench where we left them. That left us on skates in Boston —on skates, in a strange city, alone, with night coming on."[48] The old *Liebestraum* of Siwanoy Pond faded out in laughter, just as Katharine and Andy's long and happy marriage had begun in laughter. Katharine said to a friend at the time, "If it lasts only a year, it will be worth it."[49]

CHAPTER IX

"Quo Vadimus?"

1 9 3 0 — 1 9 3 5

*"What the changing times will do to Comrade Tilley's rather formal hat
. . . is a matter of conjecture. Already it shows the dents of rioting."
—From an editorial in the ninth-anniversary
issue of* The New Yorker *(17 February 1934)*

A FTER THE WEDDING A N D Y MOVED INTO Katharine's pleasant apartment, which he had leased for her while she was in Reno. It was at 16 East Eighth Street, a few doors from Fifth Avenue and its double-decker buses, five minutes' walk from Andy's old friend the Sixth Avenue Elevated, and handy to subway stations. Their third-floor, three-room apartment backed on Washington Mews; it had windows facing in three directions: east, west, and south. Shortly after they were married, the Whites increased their living space by renting the apartment directly above them and connecting the two apartments by an interior stairway. In 1933 the Whites paid three hundred dollars a month for their six rooms.

Josephine Buffa, Katharine's housekeeper and cook, was the first of many domestics who were to ease, and to complicate, the lives of the married couple. Though Andy, like Katharine, had been accustomed to servants since childhood, he resented at times—after he had become head of his own household—the complexity they added to daily life. Nonetheless, Josephine Buffa, like others who later worked for the Whites, was beloved and nearly indispensable. She was the original for a character named Antoinette, whose portrait White drew nostalgically ten years later in "Memoirs of a Master." There he recorded some of the comic aspects of life in the White household:

Left to my own devices, I believe I would never employ a domestic but would do my own work, which would take me about twenty minutes a day. However, all matters pertaining to the operation of the home are settled agreeably and competently for me by my wife, who dearly loves complexity and whose instinctive solution of any dilemma like marriage is to get about four or five other people embroiled in it. Although the picturesque and lurid role of householder saps my strength and keeps me impoverished, I must admit it gives life a sort of carnival aspect, almost as though there were an elephant swaying in the dining room. And then, once in a lifetime, some thoroughly indispensable and noble person walks casually into one's home, like Antoinette Ferraro, who proceeds to become a member of the family, blood or no blood. . . . I am perfectly sure that when I draw my last breath, Antoinette will still be somewhere about the premises, performing some grotesquely irrelevant act, like ironing a dog's blanket. . . .

I marvel that we go on paying Antoinette anything. It takes her two hours and a half to dust one side of a wooden candlestick, and even then she forgets to put it back on the mantelpiece and our Boston terrier carries it to the cellar and worries it in the coalbin. All we gain from the arrangement is Antoinette's rich account of the little adventure, including a perfect imitation of the dog. "He so hoppy," she will explain. "Holding in mouth, like beeg cigar, *mais* never dropping. Oh, he barking, he jomping. . . ."

Because our hours interfere with the proper functioning of her own domestic establishment, she has given up cooking for us and prepares food now only for our dog, kneading raw meat and carrots with kindly red hands and adding a few drops of "colliver oily" as cautiously and precisely as a gourmet fussing over a salad dressing. There have been times when I have looked into the dog's dish with unfeigned envy, for the instant Antoinette's hand touches food, it becomes mysteriously delectable.[1]

In May Katharine learned she was pregnant. White, who had long looked forward to fatherhood, was deeply moved by the news but seems to have been unable to tell his wife in person what was in his heart. At any rate, he tried to express his feelings by writing her a letter in the name of their dog, Daisy:

White has been stewing around for two days now, a little bit worried because he is not sure that he has made you realize how glad he is that there is to be what the column writer in the Mirror calls a blessed event. . . . What he feels, he told me, is a strange queer tight little twitchy feeling around the inside of his throat whenever he thinks that something is happening which will require so much love and all on account of you being so wonderful. . . . I know White so well that I always know what is the matter with him, and it always comes to the same thing—he gets thinking that nothing that he writes or says ever quite expresses his feeling, and he worries about his inarticulateness just the same as he does about his bowels, except it is worse, and it makes him either mad, or sick, or with a prickly sensation in the head. But my, my, my, last Sunday he was so full of this matter which he couldn't talk about, and he was what Josephine in her simple way would call hoppy, and particularly so because it seemed so good that everything was starting at once—I mean those things, whatever they are, that are making such a noise over in the pond by Palmer Lewis's house, and the song sparrow that even I could hear from my confinement in the house, and those little seeds that you were sprinkling up where the cut glass and bones used to be. . . .

White didn't seem to be able to tell you about his happiness, so thought I would attempt to put in a word.[2]

In the summer of 1930 Katharine rented a house in Bedford Village where she could be alone with her children. She hoped, of course, to hold their love and to be able to ease the hurt she had caused them. Andy's presence in the house, she feared, would make matters more difficult, since the children knew that their father despised him. As it turned out, they were pleased by the prospect of their mother's having another child. Nancy's hostility toward her mother abated considerably in the course of the summer, and ten-year-old Roger seemed a happy boy.

How Andy felt about the arrangement, especially in view of Katharine's pregnancy, we can only guess. But he bought a 1922 Pierce Arrow touring car in June, and in July he drove to Camp Otter, where he stayed till the end of August. One day, while Thurber was visiting him there, he and Jim photographed a loon's nest with a movie camera mounted on a tripod Katharine had given him for his birthday. He wrote her of the expedition with the same excitement that Sam Beaver, the eleven-year-old character in *The Trumpet of the Swan,* might have felt:

When we got round the other side of the island, the mother was on the nest. I got the canoe in close and she came off like a streak and I could see the day-old chick and the unhatched egg. Then the loon, calling at the top of her lungs, splashed up and down right in front of the camera, trying to attract us away from the nest. I got a lot of shots and then the chick, hearing his mother crying, came off the nest and set out on his first big trip. His mother joined him (all this just a few yards away from the canoe where I could photograph everything that went on) and together they beat it down the lake. I don't see how I can wait to see the picture.[3]

Andy's letters to Katharine were full of what excited him: the camp, the boys, Thurber, a motorboat, a sailboat, canoes, a fire in a lumber mill.

They read like letters from a boy at camp (who could see and write like E. B. White), but they also conveyed his excitement at the prospect of being a father and eventually sharing such boyish pleasures with a son. "It is foolish of you to be anywhere but here," he wrote Katharine, "with your tumultuous little Joe whom I love so and who must hear the great frogs of July at their love-making and see the lights in the north."[4]

Two days after Andy had returned from camp and had joined Katharine in Bedford Village, he was taken to St. Luke's Hospital with a paratyphoid infection. Soon after his recovery, they drove over one morning shortly after sun-up to the Danbury Fair, parked the Pierce under a tree, and enjoyed a day that Andy described in a "Talk" piece:

Nothing much had started. Freaks and crystal gazers were still asleep in the back seats of old sedans. They slept with their clothes on. Grass in the tents was still green, untrampled. . . .

The smells, when we arrived, were just starting to taint the air; the food booths were just starting to smear the first layer of terrible grease on their grills; the faces of the prize dolls were just starting to compete with "your choice of any pretty lamp." . . .

They drank in the sights and sounds around them: "a bull having his hair clipped, . . . trotting horses, the driver hunched over their rumps, . . . in the poultry house, birds full of dawn songs, cocks in fighting trim." "It was a long, untroubled day," White reminisced. "There is nothing like it. All beginnings are wonderful." They rode home in the evening.[5]

Some of Andy's joy in being married to Katharine is recorded in an essay written years later for the *Bryn Mawr Alumnae Bulletin*:

Bryn Mawr graduates, in their appearance and their manner and their composition, are unlike all other females whose minds have been refined by contact with the classics. They have long hair that flows down over their bodies to below their waist. They rise early, to sit in the light from the east window, brushing their tresses with long, delicious strokes and then twisting them into an intricate series of coils and loops and binding them with pins made from the shells of tortoises or, more lately, from the plastics of Du Pont. The husband's day thus begins with the promise of serenity, of order. But there is nothing static about Bryn Mawr. As the day advances, the pins grow (as though nourished by the soil of intellect), thrusting up through the warm, lovely hair like spears of crocuses through the coils of springtime. When fully ripe, the pins leap outward and upward, then fall to earth. Thus does a Bryn Mawr girl carry in her person the germinal strength of a fertile world. . . .

Bone hairpins are not the only things that fall, or pop, from a Bryn Mawr graduate. There is a steady cascade of sensible, warm, and sometimes witty remarks, plus a miscellany of inanimate objects, small and large, bright and dull, trivial and valuable, slipping quietly from purse and lap, from hair and ears, slipping and sliding noiselessly to a lower level, where they take refuge under sofas and beds, behind draperies and pillows—pins, clips, bills, jewels, handkerchiefs, earrings, Guaranty Trust Company checks representing the toil of weeks, glasses representing the last hope of vision. . . .

I have known many graduates of Bryn Mawr. They are all of the same mold. They have all accepted the same bright challenge: something is lost that has not been found, something's at stake that has not been won, something is started that has not been finished, something is dimly felt that has not been fully realized.[6]

Joel McCoun White, Katharine and Andy's son, was born on December 21, 1930, in the Harbor Hospital, at Sixtieth Street and Madison Avenue, by Caesarian section. As White remembered it:

The Caesarian section was an emergency operation and the consensus of doctors and nurses was that Katharine was going to die. They were wrong. A taxi driver was called in off the street and gave a blood transfusion, and she bounced back after a nurse had whispered in her ear, "Do you want to say a little prayer, dearie?" "Certainly not," she replied in her clear Boston voice.[7]

On New Year's Eve, with Joel and his mother still in the hospital, White again let Daisy convey his love—this time to his son:

Dear Joe:

Am taking this opportunity to say Happy New Year, although I must say you saw very little of the Old Year and presumably are in no position to judge whether things are getting better or getting worse. . . .

White tells me you are already drinking milk diluted with tears—in place of the conventional barley water which they used to use in the gay Nineties; so I take it life is real enough for you, tears being a distillation of all melancholy vapors rising from the human heart. . . . I imagine a few tears in the diet are all right, as I am a great believer in lean living otherwise you get eczema, and I would not worry about that ounce that you failed to make on the scales because as I always say it isn't what you weigh it's who you're with. . . .

I walked around the block with White just before he went to the hospital with Mrs. White so you could be born, and we saw your star being hoisted into place on the Christmas tree in front of the Washington Arch—an electric star to be sure, but that's what you are up against these days, and it is not a bad star, Joe, as stars go. . . .

The tree that holds your star will be shedding its needles very soon—they will drop down like rain, and the electric light in the colored bulbs will be turned out, but I have noticed that new things always spring up somewhat methodically and for every darkened Christmas tree ornament there is a white flower in spring. Or, in this particular apartment, even before spring. There are some here now called Narcissus, so come home and see them Joe, and wishing you a very Happy New Year I am

Faithfully yrs,
Daisy[8]

In the spring of 1931, the old Pierce Arrow having proved to be expensive to maintain, White bought a new seven-passenger Buick sedan, big enough to "truck children, bitches in whelp, victrolas, ferns, boxes of books, comforters, skis, and go-carts." It could, and did, carry everything from a "baby's play pen to a 9 1/2 foot dinghy."[9]

In July Andy drove Daisy and Mrs. Lardner, the cook, in the heavily loaded car to Blue Hill, Maine; Katharine, Joe, and a nursemaid followed by train. As in summers to come, White interrupted his vacation by a return to New York to do some work. He liked the city in the summer doldrums, and he did not suffer so severely from hay fever in Manhattan as he did in Maine. Katharine kept working for the magazine in Maine, as she did wherever she was.

In the fall of 1931 she resumed her full-time work at the office, and Joe was attended by his nursemaid and his doting father, who was soon sending him poems by way of "The Conning Tower." In the first of them, called "Apostrophe to a Pram Rider," we sense the "mixed pride and oppression of fatherhood" that he told Gus Lobrano he felt "in the very base of his spine." Part of his fatherly advice ran as follows:

> Some day when I'm out of sight
> Travel far but travel light!
> Stalk the turtle on the log,
> Watch the heron spear the frog,
> Find the things you only find
> When you leave your bag behind;
> Raise the sail your old man furled,
> Hang your hat upon the world! . . .
>
> Joe, my tangible creation,
> Happy in perambulation,
> Work no harder than you have to.
>   Do you get me?[10]

White now wanted many things that made it impossible to travel light. He wanted a family, and a summer retreat, and a good car in which to get to the retreat, and a good-sized sailboat, and leisure to enjoy them all. They all cost money, and Andy had to work hard to pay for them. During Joe's first year he continued to write "Notes and Comment" every week; he wrote many "Talk" pieces, an article on helicopters, a "Profile" of the king of Siam, and seven casuals.

The best of White's work in 1931 was in a genre he later called "Preposterous Parables." During his career he wrote about fifteen such parables, including "The Morning of the Day They Did It" (1949) and "The Hour of Letdown" (1951). The first of these, written in 1928, after his and Gus Lobrano's trip to Europe, concerns a minister on a transatlantic liner who is the sole survivor when the ship hits an iceberg and sinks. It ironically exposes the spiritual shallowness of a smug and jovial clergyman. It was one of the few pieces of White's that Ross ever rejected. He said he couldn't understand it. Two years later it was accepted by John Middleton Murry for his new quarterly *The Adelphi,* in London, where it appeared in the same issue with work by George Santayana, Katherine Mansfield, and Robert Hillyer.

White's second satirical parable, written during his first year of marriage, was about a man who goes up to people on the street and asks them "Quo Vadimus?"—translating the question when necessary: "Where the hell are you going?" One man replied:

> I'm on my way to the Crowbar Building . . . because I forgot to tell Miss Cortwright to leave a note for Mr. Josefson when he comes in, telling him he should tell the engraver to vignette the halftone on page forty-three of the salesmen's instruction book that Irwain, Weasey, Weasey & Button are getting out for the Fretherby-Quigley Company . . . instructing their salesmen how to approach people to sell the Quigley Method of Intensive Speedwriting, which in turn will enable girls like Miss Cortwright to take Mr. Josefson's dictation when he has to send a memo to the engraver telling him not to forget to vignette a halftone in a booklet telling salesmen how to sell shorthand courses.[11]

When asked what he really wants, the man admits that what he really wants is "a decent meal when it comes mealtime" and "a warm place to sleep when it comes night." When the questioner asks him whether he doesn't think he is pretty far from the main issue when he goes to tell a Miss Cortwright to leave a note etc. etc., the man replies by turning the tables and suggesting that the questioner is on his way to write "a story about 'complexity' . . . so a person like Miss Cortwright will have something to read, and not understand, when she isn't busy with dictation." In all his satires White implicated himself.

The second year of Joe's life, 1932, was one of White's leanest as a full-time *New Yorker* writer. He turned out "Notes and Comment" faithfully every week, but he published only a few "Talk" pieces and a few signed pieces. His best among them were on domestic topics. In "Obituary" he eulogized Daisy, killed by a Yellow cab that had skidded up over the curb and hit her as she was "smelling the front of a florist's shop." "She never grew up," he said, "and she never took pains to discover, conclusively, the things that might have diminished her curiosity and spoiled her taste. She died sniffing life, and enjoying it."[12] They were a congenial pair, Daisy and White.

The third year of Andy's and Katharine's marriage may have been the happiest of their years together. It was the last during which both were completely healthy and able to enjoy fully their professional and private lives, in the city they both loved. Their social life was never demanding, but they liked the company of good friends and were generous hosts. They saw less of Thurber as time went on and as he began to drink too much, talk too much, and boast of his success. They enjoyed the theater and the little restaurants White later recalled so lovingly in a celebration of Manhattan called "Here Is New York." Andy didn't like to dance, but he and Katharine both liked popular songs (many from musical comedies and revues they had seen), and occasionally they went out in the evening to places where there was music and people were dancing. White described one such evening:

> About two o'clock the other morning we looked in on the Greenwich Village Ball in Webster Hall. We had just left Russ Columbo crooning softly to the slow dancers on the floor of the Waldorf's elegant Empire Room; our fat capitalistic paunch was full of paté de foie gras and our tarnished old soul dripped with microphone love. "You're my everything," Mr. Columbo had whispered into his little amplifier, his lips parted ever so slightly, his eyes half closed in Latin ardor, his Adam's apple sliding in and out of his wing collar like a check-valve. The kaleidoscope spot had shimmered across the faces and low backs of the dancers, decorum and desire tilting everywhere in the room.
>
> Webster Hall was surrounded by a ring of taxis a mile long. At the door, little groups of gate-crashers slunk about, drunk but hopeful. Inside, the familiar Webster Hall smell came drifting to meet us: sudden illness and old merriment. . . . Squiring a dark beauty, we circled the floor madly with her once, and gave her over to a man who had taken off his shoes. Then, full of weariness at both hotel dancing and hall dancing, we walked home, played a gavotte on the pianoforte, bowed to an imaginary lady in crinoline, and went sadly to bed.[13]

At *The New Yorker* Katharine continued to be Ross's chief editorial advisor, but by now it was in her role as fiction editor that she had proved to be most valuable to him. For it was she, probably more than anyone else, who had persuaded him that the magazine should publish short stories that were just as distinctive, original, and contemporary as its cartoons, its "Talk of the Town," its casuals, and its reviews. She was interested in new writing, and her ambition was to attract the best of it to the pages of *The New Yorker.* Her taste in fiction played an important part in fostering a kind of story that became identified with the magazine—one free from the burden of plot, and devoted to subtle development of character and situation. Katharine's preference for this kind of story was not unlike Ross's preference for the casual, but hers was a literary taste, and thanks to it Ross was able to add an extra dimension to the magazine that he had not at first envisioned.

In the course of the development of twentieth-century American literature, Katharine may have exercised more influence than any other editor of a literary magazine. Once when she was asked to name some of the writers whose work she thought she could take credit for having been the first to publish, she replied that it was Ross, not she, who had the final say on whether a story was to be accepted; moreover that a story had often been read by three people before it ever got to her; and that it would be ridiculous to say that she personally had started on their career any of the writers whose work she had recommended for publication and whose editor she had been. But she would admit that she was the first *New Yorker* editor to buy a work by the following writers: E. B. White, Frank Sullivan, James Thurber, Vladimir Nabokov, John O'Hara, Nancy Hale, Clarence Day, Emily Hahn, J. F. Powers, S. N. Berhman, John Updike, Mary McCarthy, Marianne Moore, Jean Stafford, Morris Bishop, Ogden Nash, William Maxwell, Irwin Shaw, John Cheever, and "countless others." Some of them were already well-known writers at the time they began to contribute to *The New Yorker;* others were not. She bought John Updike's first piece when he was still a senior at Harvard. Phyllis McGinley once said that Katharine had changed her style of writing by a comment she made on the first poem of hers she accepted: "But why do you sing the same sad song most women poets do?"[14]

No doubt Katharine was paid a substantial salary. It was Ralph Ingersoll's guess that in 1934 she made about eleven thousand dollars and that she owned by then between one and five percent of the stock of the F-R [for Fleischmann and Ross] Publishing Corporation. Whatever she got she earned every penny of it. As White once said, though he'd "always been ready to bleed and die for the magazine," Katharine's attachment was "much more solid, steadier" than his.[15]

In the early thirties it was Ross, Katharine, Andy, Thurber, and Wolcott
Gibbs (who had joined the staff in 1928) whose work essentially shaped
The New Yorker's character and to whom the magazine largely owed its
success.[16] In 1934 the circulation reached 125,000 and the profits were over
$600,000.[17] Right through the Depression *The New Yorker* (and Katharine
and Andy White) could not help prospering.

Most of White's income came not from his salary as a staff member but
from his writing, for which he was paid at a rate that he does not now
remember. Ingersoll guessed that White's total income from *The New
Yorker* was somewhat over twelve thousand dollars in 1934; but it must
have been nearer twenty thousand, because he wrote so much. Whatever
it was, it was enough to enable him to speak casually of having lost money
on bonds and of having made some good buys in stocks. It was sufficient,
together with Katharine's income, to rent a house in Bedford Village for
a summer, or a cottage in Maine for a month, and to charter sailboats out
of Blue Hill in the summers of 1932 and 1933. It was enough for him to
start dreaming of moving to Maine.

Andy and Katharine first saw the farm that was to become their home
in Maine from the deck of *Alastor,* a thirty-one-foot yacht, in the summer
of 1933. On a little cruise out of Blue Hill they anchored one night in Allen
Cove at a point from which they could see, up beyond the flats and a
pasture full of stone outcroppings, the barn that *Charlotte's Web* would
make famous. The following day, as they drove along a road running south
from Blue Hill, they passed a house with a FOR SALE sign in front. It was
connected, Maine-fashion, to the beautiful barn they had spotted from the
boat. The Whites bought the twelve-room house (built "shortly before
1800"),[18] the barn and other outbuildings, and forty acres of land that ran
down to the cove, from a teacher at the Juilliard School of Music, in New
York, for eleven thousand dollars. White retained Howard Pervear, who
had served the previous owner as caretaker and handyman, and he engaged
Captain Percy Moore to build a new dock. In late December he received
a progress report from Captain Moore which, in its content and style, must
have reminded him of the contrast between the characters and the concerns
of his friends in Maine and those of the New Yorkers whose lives he was
satirizing in his "Preposterous Parables":

Dear Mr. White
    You will be surprised to learn that the distance on your shore from crest
of shore to low water mark on a low run of the tide is 300 feet by actual
measurement. The section nearest shore drops off about 1 foot in 10 ft. The
lower part of the beach is very gradual—only about 6 ft. in a run of nearly
200 ft.—less than 1/2 in. to a foot of run. . . .

Even with an inshore crib and your outer crib it is going to require 15 set of A frames to give you any kind of a landing. . . . It seemed advisable for me to let you know what my measurements were, as the added number of A frames will mean increasing my order of iron and this I did not feel like doing until I again heard from you.

I plan to get a price on the iron in Bangor. I questioned the B Smith in town on prices, labor and material and he figures 8¢ a pound for material which I think is too high.

I sincerely hope that the Christmas season found all well with you and yours and may the New Year be the best ever.

Yours truly,
P. T. Moore[19]

Shortly after White bought the farm in the fall of 1933, he alluded in his writings, on two occasions, to the Cornell Medical Center, in New York City. He may have been undergoing diagnostic tests there to discover the cause of his chronic gastritis. His stomach had always been easily upset (though he was never seasick), and towards the end of 1933 he seems to have again been depressed by his failure to write anything larger or more substantial than pieces for Ross's "funny little magazine." As he looked out the window of his office on the thirteenth floor of 25 West Forty-fifth Street, over the roofs of the New York Yacht Club, and dreamed of Allen Cove, he may have felt imprisoned by his ambition and pained by doubts about the limits of his power as a writer. At any rate, in *The New Yorker* of November 25 his humor did not conceal his melancholy:

As the year goes into its dying phase, the thing that most distresses us is the paucity of our literary output. Other than these few rather precise little paragraphs, into which we pour the slow blood of our discontent, we never get around to writing anything at all, in a world where not to write is considered irregular. Though we brood a good deal about writing plays and books, and speak of it familiarly at lunch to our friends (as though we were in the middle of it), a careful search of our premises at the end of a year reveals no trace of a manuscript—merely a few notes on the inside flap of paper-match packs. When we look around and see the output of other writers we grow faint. Both President and Mrs. Roosevelt, to name only two other literary people, have published a book in the past year; and to realize that they, who are really busy, can do it, while we, who seldom have anything pressing on hand, cannot, is extremely discouraging. Literary jealousy is probably at the bottom of many of our anarchical impulses.[20]

It was not only the "paucity of his literary output" that was distressing; it was the character of his "rather precise little paragraphs" of "Notes and

Comment." White was beginning to be uncomfortable about editorials that ignored the cruel realities of the Great Depression. In January 1933 he had written a casual, "Swing Low, Sweet Upswing," that tried to be hilarious at the expense of economists and other deep thinkers who were proposing schemes to bring back prosperity. It opened:

> I have been asked to interpret the recent tailspin of pig iron. In a technocracy such as ours, one must go behind the facts. . . . It is marvellous back here behind the facts—just like being backstage at the theatre. Walter Lippmann is here, and George Soule, and Stuart Chase, and Howard Scott, and John Maynard Keynes; in short, all the big people of the depression. . . . Hundreds of facts have been piled together to form a curtain, and all of us are busy writing. It is warm here, and comfortable, and I wish I had found this place a lot sooner. . . .[21]

Economists were harder to make fun of than the sexologists whom he had ridiculed in *Is Sex Necessary?* just a month before the stock market crash of 1929. As a subject, the dismal science of economics lacked some of the advantages of sex, one of them being that whereas everybody knows something about sex, only a few know anything about economic theory —and White (who had gotten a D in his one economics course at Cornell) was not one of them.

Four months later, however, ignoring the difficulties of the subject, his own ignorance of it, and the unfunny plight of the victims of the Depression, White undertook a three-part satirical essay on the U.S. economy that he called "Alice Through the Cellophane."[22] In it he took issue with various theories advanced for remedying the Depression. To the economists who held that prosperity could be regained only by restoring the consumers' buying power, he said that "man's buying power is one of the least noble of his powers and should not be the arch that supports his peace and well-being." Efforts to stimulate production too, he believed, were misguided. Pointing to the excess of unnecessary goods already being manufactured, and to their consumption by people whose demand for them had been artificially stimulated, he advocated buying nothing—or at least no more than absolutely needed. He proposed, on the contrary, to decrease production, and to do that by means of a paradoxical scheme: by paying the highest executives the lowest wages and the lowest-ranking employees the highest salaries. Such a pay scale would provide no incentive to climb the ladder, and those finding themselves by mischance at its top would have no desire to stay there and produce more goods.

White concluded the essay by calling up the memory of Henry David Thoreau, who "had rejected the complexity of life," and by urging his fellow men to imitate Thoreau. His final words were:

The hope I see for the world, even today, is to simplify life. . . . Nature (whose course we are about to prevent her from taking) is, I grant, complicated; but it is only on the surface that her variety is baffling. At the core is a simple ideal. You feel it when lying stretched out on warm rocks, letting the sun in. It is just possible that in our zeal to manufacture sunlamps at a profit, we have lost forever the privilege of sitting in the sun.[23]

The piece had its funny moments, but the satire lacked a cutting edge, and the sober plea for simplicity was quixotic.

In the letter he had written Katharine in 1929 just before his thirtieth birthday, he had said that he wanted to be more than a successful *New Yorker* writer. Now, four years later, still hoping to produce a major work, he had in mind something he referred to as his "magnum opus." And in 1934 he seems to have made at least one concerted attempt to get it under way. In mid-January 1934 he went to Camden, South Carolina, to the same resort hotel he had been taken to by his father in 1911. He went there "to work on a piece away from the distractions of office and home."[24] But while he was there he saw a polo match, made friends with a fox terrier, rented a bicycle, walked ten to twenty miles a day, wrote several charming letters home, and reported that he felt fine; and he returned to New York after five days.

Six weeks later he went to Florida to recuperate from the flu, staying with his sister Lillian and her family in Palm Beach. During that vacation he rented a bike, wrote Katharine amusing letters about his "gorgeously lazy life," and reported that "any grip[pe] germs remaining [were] taking an awful beating from [his] antibodies."[25] But after a week of such good health, he concluded a letter with the following report:

Last night in the middle of this letter I began to feel queer in the head (the letter probably shows it) & when I touched my forehead it felt as soft as a piece of putty. I examined it in the mirror & the whole front of my head was swollen like the breast of a pigeon. "Tumor of the brain," I told myself, & collapsed on the bed in one of my panics. The Illians had gone to the movies, so I prepared for the end—wrote a brief note to you, unlocked the door to save the hotel people the trouble of breaking in and went to bed, full of flatulence, dizziness & fear.

Next morning, when a doctor told him he had a sunburn, White was unconvinced, having been sunburned before without such dire results; but he managed to end his report to Katharine with a show of humor that served to cover his anxiety:

Don't worry about me—it is just my last attempt to round off a perfect winter in a blaze of foolishness. It makes me mad as the devil because I've been feeling so grand down here, up until last night.

The doctor experience was a honey—the perfect last act in my medical farce. He was an eye, ear, nose & throat man (he would be), studied under Craig, is the darling of the winter colonists because of a perfect throat-side manner; and when I presented my bulb-like face to him he pried my mouth open, peeped at the tonsils & said—'They've got to come out!'

Some winter, heh baby?

I still love you & my dying thoughts last night were of you. Kiss Joe.

Andy[26]

Throughout the first nine months of 1934, a period of illnesses, fears, flights, and retreats, White managed to write a substantial amount—including all of "Notes and Comment" for nearly every issue. In a variety of places, but mainly in *The New Yorker,* he published thirty poems, casuals, and other pieces. Of these, one was a satire directed at the rich. "Dusk in Fierce Pajamas," which Louis Untermeyer called "one of the neatest bits of relayed savagery"[27] he had ever read, plays with the manners, morals, and taste of the high-fashion world as reflected in the pictures and prose of *Vogue* and *Harper's Bazaar.* Copies of these magazines supplied the narrator with material for fantasies:

In fancy I am in Mrs. Cecil Baker's pine-panelled drawing room. It is dusk. . . . I have on a Gantner & Mattern knit jersey bathing suit with a flat-striped bow and an all-white buck shoe with a floppy tongue. No, that's wrong. . . . I am in Mrs. Baker's dining room, mingling unostentatiously with the other guests, my elbows resting lightly on the dark polished oak of the Jacobean table, my fingers twiddling with the early Georgian silver. . . . I am at Mrs. Jay Gould's teakwood table in a hand-knitted Anny Blatt ensemble in diluted tri-colors and an off-the-face hat. . . .

How barren my actual life seems, when fancy fails me. . . . Why am I not to be found at dusk, slicing black bread very thin, as William Powell does, to toast it and sprinkle it with salt? . . . Why don't I learn to simplify my entertaining, like the young pinch-penny in *Vogue,* who has all his friends in before the theatre and simply gives them champagne cocktails, caviar, and one hot dish, then takes them to the show?[28]

But good as they were, such sketches did not satisfy his ambition as a writer, and probably nothing he could write for *The New Yorker* would.

Already suffering from a variety of physical symptoms whose cause could not be discovered by his doctors, already aware that his poor health was probably related to his sense of failure as a writer, and now more than ever tied to *The New Yorker* by his responsibilities as father and husband, White was moving toward a crisis in his personal and professional life, and the movement was accelerated by his growing awareness that the world around him was also moving closer and closer to a crisis. Even if he did not think of the world around him in quite such grand terms, he nonetheless took seriously the changes that were threatening the comfortable world he had been born into on Summit Avenue, in Mount Vernon, in 1899. He did not write about these changes, but in 1934 he must have been aware of how the Depression had called into question certain easy assumptions about the American dream, of how the rise of Nazism in Germany could threaten the peace of the world, and even of how the American character seemed to have lost some of its integrity and strength.

For *The New Yorker*'s ninth-anniversary issue, with its familiar cover portrait of Eustace Tilley, White wrote:

> It is fine to be nine. These are more vigorous times than we bargained for when 1925 was young. They are more stalwart times, with royalists storming the Empire Room of the Waldorf, wild dogs roaming the Ramapos, pigeons on the grass, alas, and the price of a used conference table down to eight dollars. In many ways we like these days better than the days when Trader Horn was the foremost national figure and when the soft-coal smoke menace seemed the only vital issue. What the changing times will do to Comrade Tilley's rather formal hat, for which he still feels a sentimental though embarrassed attachment, is a matter of conjecture. Already it shows the dents of rioting.[29]

In August 1934, while Tilley was still conjecturing about the fate of his top hat, Henry Luce's *Fortune* magazine published a long article on *The New Yorker* by Andy's old friend Ralph Ingersoll, now the editor of *Fortune*. In it Ingersoll blamed White for *The New Yorker*'s failure to take strong editorial stands on the social issues confronting the country during the ongoing Great Depression. It was severe criticism from an old friend. *The New Yorker* had, indeed, made it its policy from the start to stay away from solemn discussions of the great issues and problems of the day, on the grounds that such discussions did not belong in its humorous pages. At the time that Ingersoll's article appeared, White had already begun to feel somewhat uncomfortable about the magazine's adherence to this policy, and his discomfort may have increased when he read what Ingersoll thought, in this and other respects, of the magazine and of him:

> It would not be unfair to say that if Ross created the body, Thurber and White are the soul of *The New Yorker*. . . . Of the two, White is the more

typical humorist. He is shy, frightened of life, often melancholy, always hypochondriac. . . . The record of E. B. (Andy) White's absorptions is written for all to see in "Notes and Comment": first his Scottish terriers, then his guppies, more recently a serious interest in economics—his crusade is against the complexity of life—and a continuation of his long campaign against war.[30]

But such condescension was not so hard to take as what followed:

> If you complain that *The New Yorker* has become gentler and gentler, more nebulous, less real, it is the Whites' doing: Andy's gossamer writing, in his increasingly important "Notes and Comment," [and] in his flavoring of the whole magazine with captions and fillers, Katharine's . . . civilizing influence on Ross.

Being called a hypochondriac by someone who was himself as hypochondriacal as Ingersoll was one thing, but the criticism implied in the word *gossamer* was another. White did not have to read much farther to realize that his old friend considered *The New Yorker*'s editorial policy irresponsible in ignoring the issues of the Depression, or in touching upon them with only a light pen, and that he put much of the blame for that irresponsibility on White himself, as the magazine's editorial writer. Instead of speaking out forcefully against poverty, greed, and injustice, *The New Yorker* had battled, according to Ingersoll, "nobly if ineffectually . . . with its delicate barbed quill" against a world that was "far from perfection."[31] As an example of *The New Yorker*'s noble if ineffectual battling, Ingersoll cited White's editorial comments on the hue and cry raised against a truth-in-advertising bill proposed by Rexford Tugwell, a member of President Roosevelt's "brain trust." White had written as follows:

> Mr. L. B. Palmer, of the Newspaper Publishers' Association, says there is a conspiracy in Washington to change the philosophy of advertising—"in fact, to prohibit any advertising that is not literally true." It is rather revealing to observe the ferocity with which the advertising fraternity is fighting for the privilege of remaining ambiguous.
> Well, even if the New Deal demands truth in advertising, we will still remain loyal to it. . . .
> Mr. Palmer's aversion to the Brain Trust is typical of what you hear everywhere, nowadays. "Tyranny!" everybody is crying. "Let us alone, will you!" . . . The *Saturday Evening Post* announces that "the grown-up part of the country wants to put away childish things." In spite of all these fierce cries, we still cherish the idea of Mr. Roosevelt's plan; we are loyal to it in the same way we were once loyal to an old gasoline engine long after it became obvious

that it wasn't going to work very well. It had a kind of beauty of spirit which we admired in the face of its faulty functioning.

Mr. Lorimer's [Saturday Evening] Post demands, in its campaign to put away childish things, "an opportunity for everybody and anybody to accumulate honestly and without special privilege." Honest accumulation is the keynote of the rebellion against the tyranny of regimentation. As we sit here at our typewriter, honestly accumulating, a flood of old memories surrounds us like hungry pigeons—memories of the great days of honest accumulation, when industry was free as a bird and liberty stalked through every transaction, the days when almost the entire wealth of the country seemed in a fair way of getting itself honestly accumulated by a few sharp old gentlemen with a knack for that sort of thing. Those memories are fading, but they are still strong enough to keep us faithful to the efforts of an administration which, however clumsily, is trying to prevent a recurrence of the unsocial consequences of unbridled enterprise.[32]

In Ingersoll's opinion, this "frank espousal of Tugwell principles" was hardly apt to upset any of the bill's opponents, since it was "so carefully swathed in whimsey that not even the staunchest Tory could take affront."[33]

Already half-sick with nagging physical symptoms and dissatisfied with his progress as a writer, White was in no shape to hear his old friend describe his "barbed quill" as capable only of spinning gossamer and playing with whimsy. Ralph Ingersoll's criticism may not have offended White, but it may have added to his dissatisfaction with himself and to his growing desire to quit *The New Yorker*—and New York.[34]

On October 4, Harper published *Every Day Is Saturday,* a selection of White's paragraphs written for "Notes and Comment" between 1928 and 1934. The reviews should have encouraged White to go on. Among them was one that must have pleased him particularly: it was by his old teacher Professor Strunk. William Rose Benét's review in *The Saturday Review of Literature* praised White's charm, humor, and style, and in the *New York Times,* Robert Van Gelder noticed the strength of his intellectual integrity. The most perceptive of the reviews, however, was a thousand-word essay called "E. B. White, the Perfect Modern Skeptic," by William Soskin, in the *New York American.* It opened with a history and definition of pyrrhonism, a "philosophic doctrine which holds that absolute knowledge is unattainable, and which promotes an attitude of . . . suspended judgment":

The good skeptic, like the essayist Montaigne, is merely open-minded and disinclined to accept religious or other organized bodies of thought. In any age true skepticism is likely to produce the most satisfactory and civilized literary artists. . . . It takes a more profound wit, however, and a harder mental constitution and a more catholic composition of sensibilities to write skeptically and amusingly [than it does to write, like G. B. Shaw, for example, from a doctrinaire point of view].

The Pepysian man, the Montaigne man, the gentle ironist and the genuine Pyrrhonian must be "regular" in the peculiar sense of the word which suggests an ability to steer between the doctrines, to understand and not to capitulate to the various religions, to maintain a virile and decently restrained exterior even when the heart and the emotions are genuinely disturbed. . . .

But the real beauty of these pithy pieces and the punch in the entire project of *The New Yorker*'s editorial department are due to something more than a generally skeptical attitude. Mr. White writes with constant and patient attention to form, with a cutting conciseness, with an inventive and infinitely varied sense of situation, with a sweet gift for the precise and nice phrase. . . .[35]

White had never before had a reviewer who so fully understood the essence of his achievement in the literary form to which he had given the greatest part of his writing life. Nor could he have asked for a better answer to Ingersoll.

During 1935 he did not once fail to produce his weekly "Notes and Comment," which Ross told him at the time was "among the best stuff being written today, by a god damned site."[36] He continued to spend a good deal of time with his son, who attended nursery school at the City and Country School from 1934 to 1936 and kindergarten at Friends Seminary the following year. Joe was a bright, active boy, and an acquaintance of the Whites' remembers the atmosphere of affection and confidence in their home.

Nineteen thirty-five was also a year of painful losses. In August Andy's father died. Just a year before, he and Jessie had visited Andy and Katharine during their first summer at the farmhouse in Maine. In a letter of condolence, dated from the Pomfret School in September 1935, fifteen-year-old Roger Angell said that he thought Andy's father "must have been a kind and generous, as well as a remarkable man." Roger had appreciated his kindness in sending him presents and greeting cards, and remembered that he, Roger, had "had a very good time with him in Maine last summer."

In September Katharine had a miscarriage. She had hoped to prevent it by staying behind in Maine, resting there quietly, after Andy had to return to New York at the end of summer. When she informed him of the bad news, she added that she was not discouraged and that she wanted to "try to start fresh on a little Serena."[37]

There were also losses among friends. Jim Thurber, having been divorced by Althea the year before, had married Helen Wismer in June, and he and his new wife now lived in Connecticut. He had left the staff of *The New Yorker* and seldom visited its offices. Jim never lost his great affection and respect for Andy, and wrote him many long, warm, amusing letters, but Andy was never again to enjoy the companionship that had nourished him in earlier, happier days. And in December Clarence Day, a good friend of the Whites, had died. Andy had much admired the man's courage, his humor, and his writing.

Other less serious but nonetheless disheartening events occurred. In 1935 White finally abandoned a long, unpleasant, and fruitless effort to save some of his financial investment in Camp Otter. The *Atlantic Monthly* rejected a sonnet, saying it had no need for "the lighter veins of verse." Both the *Atlantic* and *Scribner's Magazine* turned down an essay about living in New York, and Oxford University Press declined his proposal for a book about New York.

In 1935, having outgrown the apartment on Eighth Street, the Whites moved uptown to a house in Turtle Bay Gardens, a block of brownstone houses between Second and Third Avenue and Forty-eighth and Forty-Ninth Street, whose gardens were a delight to all whose back windows looked out upon them. In their new house Joe had a room of his own, and there were rooms for live-in servants; but the Whites were reluctant to leave the Village, and Andy was not happy about a move that would strengthen his ties to New York right at a time when more than ever he hankered to move to Maine.

Encouraged by the critical success of his first book of prose pieces, *Every Day Is Saturday,* in which he had revealed himself as the author of *The New Yorker*'s "Notes and Comments," White now attempted to persuade Ross to relieve him of his duties as an anonymous editorial writer, to move "Notes and Comment" from the opening page, and to allow him to sign his name to his own column. His reason, he had explained in a letter to Gus Lobrano, was that it was

> almost impossible to write anything decent using the editorial "we," unless you are the Dionne family. Anonymity, plus the "we," gives a writer a look of dishonesty, and he finds himself going around, like a masked reveler at a ball, kissing all the pretty girls.[38]

But Ross firmly rejected White's proposal. Arguing, as he confessed, from the standpoint of the magazine, Ross said that "Notes and Comment" set the keynote for the magazine and that moving it from its long-established position on the magazine's opening page would be a most serious step— and one he would oppose. Moreover, he believed that White's paragraphs were stronger as an anonymous expression of an institution than they would be as the expression of an identified individual. All Ross would concede was that probably White and other anonymous workers should be recognized by having their names printed somewhere in the magazine.[39] They never were, because Ross couldn't settle on a good place to put them. But White did win one concession. Henceforth he himself, rather than an editor, would decide in what order his "paragraphs" would be arranged in "Notes and Comment." This concession gave White the opportunity occasionally to develop loosely structured essays from a series of self-contained paragraphs, all more or less related to one theme. In "Notes and Comment" for October 10, 1936, for example, he played in this way with the theme "man has had his day":

> THE bitter pill that is Sunday afternoon had stuck halfway down our throat; the living room, colliding with time itself, sprawled at our feet, a foul mass of half-read supplements. Mechanically we stumbled on into the book section and began reading a review of a volume of poems by Prokosch. "And here, also, are those manifestations of a dying civilization—superstition, perversion, nostalgia, defeatism—in symbol and image." We gazed mournfully out of the window. A leaf wrenched itself loose from a small, sickly tree, spun to the pavement. "Man has had his day," we read, turning back to the review. The paper slipped from our grasp and fluttered to the moldering carpet. We fell into a deep, dreamless sleep.
>
> NEXT morning the theme recurred: we couldn't get it out of our head that man had had his day. Normally it is our pleasure to defend the noble destiny of the race, at least through breakfast; but this time we just couldn't carry it off. In the middle of orange juice a phone call came from a brisk lady who said it was time we came in for the semi-annual cleaning of our teeth. "Sorry," we replied, "but we have had our day. Let's stop this pretence of prophylaxis; everywhere we find impressions of a warm, overripe beauty, decay. Why should we try to stop decay, even in our teeth?" The lady hung up, in what seemed honest alarm, and we returned to the table to stare at a poached egg. . . .
>
> THE thing got to the point where we felt we had to buy Prokosch's book to decide for ourself whether man had had his day. So we picked up a copy on our way to lunch Wednesday and carried it to the restaurant. We ordered liver and bacon, opened the book to the first poem, and started slowly to read:
>
> > O summon out of memory
> > Into understanding
> > So that all may fear it
> > From the blood and fever

> Of our passionate and forever
> Unregenerate spirit. . . .

At this point the restaurant proprietor, who had been fiddling with a radio, began to get the first premonitory sounds of a ball game. In another minute, the Yankee lineup wove itself inextricably into the poem:

> O love
> Remember Alexander,
> Alcibiades,
> Crosetti, shortstop
> Achilles: more slender
> Than the slenderest of these,
> Rolfe, third base,
> Yet lovelier, still more haunting
> Of voice, feature and form,
> Di Maggio. . . .

We closed the book and finished the liver, conscious that whether or not man had had his day, the day of the person who wants to read in a restaurant was pretty well gone by.

Our considered opinion is that poets, although the most valuable of prophets, are now and always have been hypersensitive to decadence. Their art owes a great debt to the cloying beauty of things past their prime.

A more immediate question is whether democracy has had its day. While 42,000 celebrants who were under the illusion that they were citizens of a democracy were watching the New York Giants bring in four runs in the eighth; . . . while Mrs. Eleanor Roosevelt, wife of a democratic President, was attending the opening of Todhunter School; while matrons were giving teas and doormen were walking other people's puppies around the block . . . while all these manifestations of democracy were taking place, the chief of police of Terre Haute, Indiana, was obligingly jailing Earl Browder on a charge of vagrancy. This, reader, makes vagabonds of us all. If Mr. Browder is a vagrant, then so are we, so is Mrs. Roosevelt, so is Carl Hubbell; and we are all doomed to wander perilously in a land whose capital is Terre Haute, whose overlord is a man named James C. Yates, and whose undersecretaries are Mr. Messmore Kendall of the Sons of the American Revolution and Mrs. Lambert Fairchild of the National Americanization League.[40]

Such pieces elicited congratulations from readers who thought, as one of them put it, that White's editorials would redeem *The New Yorker* from charges of triviality.

The year 1935 brought nonprofessional pleasures. Andy was able to help his best friend, Gus Lobrano, find a job on *Town and Country* magazine, which meant that Gus, who had been running a travel agency in Albany for the last seven years—a job most uncongenial to him—would be back in New York. And in 1935 arrived the first of many letters from Howard Pervear, the caretaker of the Whites' place in Maine, who reported facts White liked to think about: facts about the farm, such as that Pervear had butchered the pig and shipped the smoked ham and bacon to Turtle Bay, or that he had repaired the cedar-post fence, or bought a license for the truck, or sent a mailing carton full of fresh eggs, or planted the garden. And, finally, among the pleasures of the year had been the purchase in April of *Astrid,* a thirty-foot double-ended cutter.

Andy sent a picture of her to his mother, who in turn sent her son, as a birthday present, twenty dollars with which to buy something for his new boat. "Now," she wrote in a characteristically proud and loving letter, he had "a charming wife, an adorable! Son, a beautiful Farm and a Yacht. Now what more could a fellow wish for?"[41] She omitted only the handsome, newly painted, papered, and furnished house in Turtle Bay Gardens, eight blocks from an office that he didn't have to go to every day.

CHAPTER X

Mr. Tilley's Departure

1 9 3 6 – 1 9 3 8

"I spent a solid year once experimenting with idleness and finding out exactly what it was like to occupy myself with nothing at all over a wide range of country. That year now seems to me one of the most sensible twelvemonth periods I ever put in; I have not lost the feel of it—it comes back whenever I need it."

I N 1936 WHITE CONTINUED TO SUFFER FROM poor health and periods of depression. He was able to produce his weekly editorials for *The New Yorker,* but he did not write much else. In the spring, nine months after the death of his father, his mother died of cancer, in Washington, D.C., where she had been staying with her daughter Clara. Andy was with her during her last days. His parents had died before he had fulfilled his promise as a writer, and now, in his mid-thirties, he seemed not even near to producing a work that would endure.

In the fall he began to have spells of dizziness, which he described in a casual entitled "My Physical Handicap, Ha Ha":

It is an unhinging of the equilibrium, a condition of the body which gives rise to queer street effects, dreams, and fancies. I will be walking along the street, say, and will take three normal steps in a forward direction; then, as I am about to set my foot down for the fourth step, the pavement moves an inch or two to the right and drops off three-quarters of an inch, and I am not quick enough for it. This results in my jostling somebody on my left, or hitting the corner of the Fred F. French Building a glancing blow. It was fun for a few days, but I have recovered from the first fine ecstasy of dizziness, and am getting bored with it. Once I sidled into a police horse, and he gave me back as good as I gave him.[1]

In the spring of 1937, in "Notes and Comment," he issued a bulletin suggesting that his illness was psychogenic:

> Partly by stealth, partly by cunning, a doctor gained entrance to our middle ear last week, hoping to discover there the secret of the dizziness from which we suffer. He blew and he blew, setting up Eustachian williwaws of seeming great intensity. The ear must be the very vestibule of the mind, for as we sat there bracing ourself, it seemed as though all the great winds of the world were rattling at the door of the skull, and that the next squall would explode the partition and carry our Intellect away. We still have a ringing in the ear— a globule of Thought, caught in a sea puss; and we still yaw about when we try to hold a course through the streets. . . .
>
> Physicians on the trail of a man's dizziness are explorers of a hardy sort. They are ready to go anywhere, on short notice, travelling light. They speak of "toxicity," and set out for the Yukon. Yet there are undoubtedly toxic secretions in a man which the medical fraternity know very little of. A writer, detecting signs of decay in his own stuff, secretes internal poisons which would make even a diseased tonsil sit up and take notice.[2]

When he wrote that report, he had already decided to take a year's leave of absence from *The New Yorker*. Even some of his friends, having read "My Physical Handicap, Ha Ha," had advised him to give up, for a time at least, the responsibility of meeting deadlines. Russell Lord blamed Andy's trouble on *The New Yorker*, and Andy's brother Stanley urged him to break free from the constraints of journalism and find a "more monumental medium than a newspaper column."[3]

That spring Ralph Ingersoll may have aggravated White's distress when he accused him of "gentle complacency" in the face of widespread human misery caused by the Depression. Ingersoll's criticism was prompted by an editorial in which White protested against Roosevelt's determination to save his New Deal legislation by "packing" the Supreme Court. When the Court had declared unconstitutional certain important parts of that legislation, early in 1937, Roosevelt had proposed to reconstitute the Court by requiring justices over seventy to retire and by increasing the number of justices on the bench from nine to fifteen. These changes, had Congress authorized them, would have enabled him to appoint several new judges who shared his social philosophy and who presumably would not have raised constitutional arguments against the implementation of his New Deal programs. This proposal to tamper with the system of checks and balances among the administrative, legislative, and judicial branches of the government was met with instant, vigorous, and widespread opposition. Roosevelt, however, was undaunted, and in his speech of March 4, 1937

—the speech in which he pointed to "one-third of the nation ill-nourished, ill-clad, ill-housed"—he urged that these ills be remedied *now*, and charged that those who opposed his plan to reform the Supreme Court were "essentially the same elements" that had all along opposed the New Deal itself, i.e., the economic "royalists."

White was not the only supporter of the New Deal who was affronted by the unfairness of Roosevelt's charge, but no editorial writer responded to it with more indignation than he:

> This is balderdash. The opposition to his plan to bring the judiciary into line is from people who care not about their property, their profits, and their old Lincoln limousines, but who care about their freedom from authority—which was what started the first big doings in this country and may well start the last. We ourself applauded Mr. Roosevelt's program four years ago, but we decline to follow a leader, however high-minded, who proposes to take charge of affairs because he thinks he knows all the answers. Mr. Roosevelt is not ambitious personally, but he has turned into an Eagle Scout whose passion for doing the country a good turn every day has at last got out of hand. His . . . remarks were a giveaway—the utterances of a petulant saviour. America doesn't need to be saved today; it can wait till tomorrow. Meanwhile, Mister, we'll sleep on it.[4]

A few days later *Time,* in its story on Roosevelt's speech, took notice of *The New Yorker*'s editorial stand:

> Among U.S. journalists, no more facile penman exists than the New Yorker's famed E. (for Elwyn) B. (for Brooks) White. Grave, smallish writer White, whose devotees consider him the nation's ablest humorist, is generally content to muse on minor human foibles. . . . Last week, however, connoisseurs recognized an unusually earnest thrust from the White rapier in a *New Yorker* paragraph which gave the President and his court plan a pinking far more effective than the bludgeonings of his customarily solemn critics.[5]

Time then went on to quote White's paragraph. Before the *Time* story had gone to press, White had learned that he was to be identified in it as the writer of the *New Yorker* editorial, and he had protested on the grounds that *Time* ought to respect the anonymity of editorials. *Time* editor Manfred Gottfried considered White's argument but concluded that *Time*'s behavior was not unfair since, he explained, he didn't "know offhand of any dinner table in New York where Notes and Comment would not be credited" to White if the question were raised.[6]

On May 17 White received the following letter from Ralph Ingersoll:

Dear Andy,

I have not yet heard how the TIME boys have decided your fate but, in the meantime, I got hold of a copy of the *New Yorker* and read the paragraph. It is indeed well turned.

I am no one to defend Roosevelt whole—too many things about him enrage me. But, so does your gentle complacency. "Let us sleep on it. . . . " Andy, Andy!!

Doesn't that well-fed stomach of yours ever turn when you think what you're saying? Let us sleep on suffering, want, malnutrition. Let us sleep too on young men who are so fond of phrasing things exactly that humanity never troubles them.

Yours,
Mac[7]

White's reply missed Ingersoll's point, as Ingersoll's next letter showed:

Dear Andy:

For your letter, thanks. I wasn't picking on the way you stood on the Supreme Court. I was made angry by the kind of complaisance which I am sure you are not conscious of but which keeps you emotionally always a reactionary. I agree with you about the complaisance of know-it-alls. But I have more sympathy for them than you. Fascists, Communists, New Dealists all seem to me persons who have been so tortured by the horror of the world today that they have simply been unable to live amidst so much that is unsolved, and so cling to the first logic that appeals to them.

The problem that I see is keeping the world intensely aware that there is a problem.

I hear George Lincoln Burr [the Cornell history professor whose love of liberty had inspired Andy as a student] was quite a fellow. I wonder how he would have felt if he had been one of 200,000 people working for the U.S. Steel who, as the head of a family, was earning an average of $12 per week for six years through the Depression.

What I think I believe in is the dignity of man. And I know starvation is a very undignified thing. So is that kind of callousness that the gentle and the delicate and the very old have in common—a willingness to hide behind the philosophy which excuses them from feeling or doing anything about the suffering of the world.

Regards,
Mac[8]

Behind Ingersoll's attack on White there may have been hurt feelings, the reason for which can only be guessed at. Ingersoll may have been defensive about his working for the powerful empire of the Republican Henry Luce, and he probably had been stung by Wolcott Gibbs's savaging "Profile" of Henry Luce in the pages of *The New Yorker* the preceding fall. But he may simply have been irritated by a trait he disliked in an old friend.

Apparently, the argument between White and Ingersoll was essentially the liberal-conservative one about the right to freedom versus the desirability of social justice, or about the right to social justice versus the desirability of freedom. White disapproved of what he considered to be Roosevelt's willingness to sacrifice integrity to expediency and to justify his illegal means by his benevolent social aims. Ingersoll, like Roosevelt, was impatient with the slow progress of the country's economic recovery, and felt indignant towards those who would not risk the freedoms claimed by the Constitution, and protected by the courts, for the sake of relieving the misery of the unfortunate.

How much White was hurt by Ingersoll's indignation we do not know. What we do know is that by the end of May White had decided to stop writing editorials on anything and to take a year's leave of absence from *The New Yorker*. He told no one what he planned to do during this period, not even his wife, to whom he wrote the following letter:

My dear Mrs. White:

It has occurred to me that perhaps I should attempt to clarify, for your benefit, the whole subject of my year of grace—or, as I call it, My Year. Whenever the subject has come up, I have noticed an ever so slight chill seize you, as though you felt a draught and wished someone would shut a door. I look upon this delicate spiritual tremor as completely natural, under the circumstances, and suggestive only of affectionate regard, tinged with womanly suspicion. In the world as now constituted, anybody who resigns a paying job is suspect; furthermore, in a well-ordered family, any departure from routine is cause for alarm. Having signified my intention to quit my accustomed ways, I shall do you the service of sketching, roughly, what is in my heart and mind—so that you may know in a general way what to expect of me and what not to expect. It is much easier for me to do this in a letter, typing away, word after word, than to try to tell you over a cup of coffee, when I would only stutter and grow angry at myself for inexactitudes of meanings (and probably at you, too, for misinterpreting my muddy speech).

First, there is the question of *why* I am giving up my job. This is easy to answer. I am quitting partly because I am not satisfied with the use I am making of my talents, such as they are; partly because I am not having fun working at my job—and am in a rut there; partly because I long to recapture something which everyone loses when he agrees to perform certain creative miracles on specified dates for a particular sum. (I don't know whether you know what this thing is, but you'll just have to take my word that it is real. To you it may be just another Loch Ness monster, but to me it is as real as a dachshund.)

Now there comes the question of *what* I am going to do, having given up the job. I suppose this is a fair question—also the question of what I intend to use for money. These matters naturally concern you, and Esposito [their grocer], and everybody. Dozens of people have asked: "What are you going to do?" so strong is their faith in the herb activity. I know better what I am *not* going to do. But I won't try to pretend (to you, anyway) that that is the whole story either. In the main, my plan is to have none. But everyone has secret projects, and I am no exception. Writing is a secret vice, like self abuse. A person afflicted with poetic longings of one sort or another searches for a kind of intellectual and spiritual privacy in which to indulge his strange excesses. To achieve this sort of privacy—this aerial suspension of the lyrical spirit—he does not necessarily have to wrench himself away, physically, from everybody and everything in his life (this, I suspect, often defeats him at his own game), but he *does* have to forswear certain easy rituals, such as earning a living and running the world's errands. That is what I intend to "do" in my year. I am quitting my job. In a sense, I am also quitting my family—which is a much more serious matter, and which is why I am taking the trouble to write this letter. For a long time I have been taking notes—sometimes on bits of paper, sometimes on the mind's disordered pad—on a theme which engrosses me. I intend to devote my year to assembling these notes, if I can, and possibly putting them on paper of the standard typewriter size. In short, a simple literary project. . . . If, at the end of the year, I have nothing but a bowlful of cigarette stubs to show for my time, I shall not begrudge a moment of it and I hope you won't. They say a dirigible, after it has been in the air for a while, becomes charged with static electricity, which is not discharged till the landing ropes touch the field and ground it. I have been storing up an inner turbulence, during my long apprenticeship in the weekly gaiety field, and it is time I came down to earth.

I am not telling people, when they ask, that I am proposing to write anything during My Year. As I said above, nothing may come of it, and it is easier to make a simple denial at the start, than to invent excuses and explanations at the end. I wish you would please do the same. Say I am taking a Sabbatical and doing nothing much of anything—which will come perilously near the truth, probably.

When I say I am quitting my family, I do not mean I am not going to be around. I simply mean that I shall invoke Man's ancient privilege of going and coming in a whimsical, rather than a reasonable, manner. I have some pilgrimages to make. To the zoo. To Mount Vernon. To Belgrade, and Bellport, and other places where my spoor is still to be found. I shall probably spend a good deal of time in parks, libraries, and the waiting rooms of railway stations—which is where I hung out before I espoused this more congenial life. My attendance at meals may be a little spotty—for a twelvemonth I shall not adjust my steps to a soufflé. I hope this doesn't sound ungrateful, or like a declaration of independence—I intend it merely to inform you of a new allegiance—to a routine of my own spirit rather than to a fixed household & office routine. I seek the important privilege of not coming home to supper unless I happen to. I plan no absences, I plan no attendances. No plans.

The financial aspect of this escapade does not seem portentous, or ominous. I'm going to have Arty send me the money which comes in from my securities. I'm going to sell the P.A. [Pierce Arrow], which should bring $2,000, of which you get $1500. My taxes are paid, and I have enough money in the bank to continue in the same fifty-fifty arrangement with you in all matters of maintenance, recreation, and love. My luncheons will be 50 centers, instead of the dollar and a quarter number, and I will be riding common carriers, not Sunshine cabs. Instead of keeping a car on service at a garage, I would like your permission to keep the Plymouth nearby at some cheap lodging. I don't anticipate laying in a cellar of wine, or buying any new broadloom carpets. I think if I pull in my ears and you watch your artichokes, we can still stay solvent. I think it is better to do it this way than to try some possibly abortive rearrangement of our way of living, such as letting out the top floor to a Bingo society, or going to France to take advantage of the cheap wines. I notice Joe is already starting to sell his paintings.

Well, this about covers My Year. I urge you not to take it too seriously, or me. I am the same old fellow. I hope I shall give and receive the same old attentions and trifles. I don't want you tiptoeing around the halls telling people not to annoy me—the chances are I won't be doing anything anyway, except changing a bird's water. But I do want you to have some general conception of my internal processes during this odd term of grace. I want you to be able to face my departure for Bellport on a rainy Thursday afternoon with an equanimity of spirit bordering on coma.

> Yrs with love and grace,
> Mr. White

P.S. This letter is rather long, but I didn't have time to make it shorter, such are the many demands on me these days from so many points of the compass. I realize, too, that the whole plan sounds selfish and not much fun for you; but that's the way art goes. You let yourself in for this, marrying a man who is supposed to write something, even though he never does.
P.P.S. Unnecessary to answer this communication. Would be a drain on your valuable time. Just signify your good will with a package of Beemans—one if by land, two if by sea.
PPPPPS. Will be glad to answer any questions, or argue the whole matter out if it fails to meet with your approval or pleasure. I do not, however, want to discuss the literary nature of the project: for altho you are my b.f. and s.c., I will just have to do my own writing, as always.[9]

The Pierce Arrow, for which his "best friend" and "severest critic" was to get fifteen hundred dollars, was a brand new, Eustace Tilley–like, eight-cylinder, convertible roadster, custom-painted in two shades of "Dovetone" and upholstered in tan.

White's farewell to readers of "Talk of the Town" appeared in *The New Yorker* for August 7, 1937. It took the form of a whimsical account of Eustace Tilley's departure from New York, and its significance was clear only to those who had heard beforehand of White's decision to take a leave of absence. Among those in the know was someone at *Time,* who reported that "Elwyn Brooks ('Andy') White, not elderly (38), not eccentric, but melancholy and increasingly troubled about the world," was leaving "Notes and Comment" and *The New Yorker* for a year, "maybe a dozen," to "give himself time to think about progress and politics, whether to get out of their jumpy way or try to catch up with them."[10]

The first thing White did with his new freedom was to go cruising in Maine waters for twelve days on his boat *Astrid* with an old Cornell friend and experienced sailor, Charles Muller. They were fog-bound for six of those days, but in such places as Burnt Coat Harbor, Pulpit Harbor, Tenants Harbor, Port Clyde, and Sylvester Cove, being fog-bound can be pleasant. In Tenants Harbor and in Thomaston they spent afternoons watching ballgames.

In September Andy stayed on in Maine for another month after Katharine and Joe had returned to New York. He settled down as faithfully as he could to writing a long poem on what he had called "a theme which engrosses me." The poem presumably was "Zoo Revisted: Or the Life and Death of Olie Hackstaff," and presumably he saw himself in Hackstaff. In its six parts, or episodes, the poem alludes to some of the "pilgrimages" he had warned Katharine he intended to make during his year off, all of which had taken him back to the scenes of his youth. The first of these had led him to the zoo, where in the first section of the poem Olie identifies himself with a bison (an example of a vanishing species) and his "seminal imperative in the suspended globe" (i.e., testicle), standing "incarcerate . . . in the twilight of his desire . . . with torrential need."

White's second pilgrimage, which had furnished the material for the poem's second section, had taken him to Mount Vernon, where Olie recalls the little private zoo of "Kenny Whipple" (Elwyn's grade-school friend Kenny Mendel) on Summit Avenue and his adolescent curiosity about sex.[11] The pilgrimage to Mount Vernon included Siwanoy Pond, and memories of the *Liebestraum,* which became the subject of the fifth section of the poem. The third pilgrimage, the one to Belgrade Lake, undertaken in the fall of 1937, does not figure in the poem, though it was perhaps the most fruitful of all in that it produced a beautiful letter to his brother Stanley full of a kind of Proustian ecstasy.[12] Bellport, the destination of his last pilgrimage, became the setting for the third part of the poem. The "pilgrimage" that reflected the final section of the poem, "The Hospital," White had already made in the spring of 1936, when he had gone to Washington to visit his dying mother. Through the poem run the motifs of Olie's relationship to his son, the feeling of sexual frustration, and the awareness of melancholy ironies. Nothing very clear, however, emerges from "Zoo Revisited." White's ambitious effort to communicate by indirection had failed. Anyone fully acquainted with his life would recognize the source and significance of almost all his images, but other readers would be left more puzzled than moved or enlightened by them. In fact the poem was too allusive, too private. The only things that come through the imagery clearly are sexual desires in the midst of reminders of age and death. White kept the poem in a drawer for seventeen years before he published it, in a collection of his prose and verse.

Katharine's letters to Andy during September, while he was in Maine and she in New York, were informative, humorous, affectionate, wifely, and feminine. "I don't think I ever missed you so much," she wrote, "but I like to think of you there." She told him of trying out a new cook, of hearing from her doctor that she would not have to have an operation, of talking with people who came into her office to ask about him. "Gibbs is healthy and sober, Mac [McKelway] fat and sober." At Bloomingdale's she bought some "replenishing" bulbs for the Turtle Bay garden. Should Joe take music lessons? She urged Andy not to come back "a minute earlier than [he had] to—it's too good a chance to see winter approach on Allen Cove." She had tried last night to shorten the sleeves on a new blouse but failed. She had left "a jug of French perfume" on her bureau in Maine, and when he came down he "might bring it along." And after reporting an important event in the private life of one of the magazine's staff members, she added: "I am in a mood from this and other items that gives me a distaste for this town. Everyone is in *such a mess!*"[13]

Andy worked at his writing fairly steadily in Maine for a while, but he soon gave up and was back home on Forty-eighth Street in October. Wolcott Gibbs had earlier written him a doleful letter about how his departure had affected *The New Yorker*:

Dear Andy:
    We all try very hard to keep Notes & Comment up there where you put it, but I'm afraid it is pretty gummy at best. . . . Anyway, I think it's a crime that you should be out of this book altogether, and wish to God you'd write something—verse, casuals, fables, anything at all. I thought you were going to do some more fables, [i.e., "Preposterous Parables"] and so did Ross, who often speaks about it, with his fingers in his hair.

"He just sails around in some God damn boat," he says.

I think you would find this pitiful if you could hear him. You would also find the forthcoming issues of *The New Yorker* pitiful if you could see our plans for them. . . . My own book is a perfect example of NYer writing at its silliest—not a social dilemma in it that my six-year-old niece couldn't solve by walking across the room. And so is Thurber's. Whole magazine has begun to smell of jasmine if you'll notice, and it is going to smell a lot funnier before another spring.

Kinkead and I were put out of the Fire Island tennis tournament by a couple of children this weekend. We smelled too, though not of jasmine.

W.G.[14]

Katharine might have prompted Gibbs to write that letter to Andy, for Andy's sake as well as for the sake of the magazine, but Thurber needed no prompting from her to try to persuade Andy to keep on writing. Thurber and his wife, Helen, had gone abroad in the fall of 1937, and it was from Italy that Thurber, in several long letters, commented at thoughtful length on White's sense of failure. In September 1937 he invited White to join him and Helen in France. White replied on a postcard from Maine: "Impossible join you till wood is all cut, cranberries harvested. . . . I'm not a writer any more myself, and there's a laugh there, too,"[15] To this Thurber replied: "You may be a writer in farmer's clothing but you are still a writer. . . . This is not a time for writers to escape to their sailboats and their farms. What we need is writers who deal with the individual plight. . . . You are not the writer who should think that he is not a writer."[16] In what Thurber called White's "fine, but faintly sad"[17] reply, White called himself "the second most inactive writer living, and the third most discouraged." He agreed with Thurber that "the individual plight" was "the thing":

I knew it when I stayed with my mother while she died in a hospital in Georgetown. I knew it day before yesterday when Joe (looking suspiciously like me) stood up in meeting house and recited the 117th psalm before the elementary school. You beget a son when your mind is not on that at all, and seven years later he is there in a clean white shirt, praising the Lord. You spend your days chuckling at the obstinacies of French waiters and Italian cooks, but always knowing that much of life is insupportable and that no individual play can have a happy ending. If you have the poetic temperament you go on groping toward something which will express all this in a burst of choir music, and your own inarticulateness only hastens the final heart attack. Even when an artist has the ability and the strength to assemble something of the beauty and the consternation which he feels, he is usually so jealous of other artists that he has no time for pure expression. Today with the radio yammering at you and the movies turning all human emotions into cup custard, the going is tough. Or I find it tough.[18]

Thurber again suggested that White join him and Helen, who were about to settle in a villa at Cap d'Antibes: "you could take an Italian ship —the Rex, say."[19] But Thurber's descriptions of their adventures and their pleasures were not enticing to White, who replied in a post-Christmas letter:

The Rex, either twinkling against Vesuvius, or not twinkling at all, would suit me fine, but I don't think I had better leave these shores under the circumstances. I have made an unholy mess out of this "year off" business. I haven't produced two cents worth of work, have broken my wife's health, my own spirit, and two or three fine old lampshades by getting my feet tangled in the cord. Kay is restless when I go away, and I am no bargain when I am around, either. Gibbs quit his desk job rather abruptly, and Kay has had a lot of extra work deriving from that. She got grippe before Christmas, and I got it, and we celebrated the 23rd of December by fighting over what Xmas was all about anyway. This left us in a limp beaten state—one of those periods from which one can't escape by merely taking a boat and watching somebody balance a 20-gallon water jar on her head. We're going to have to balance our own jars for a while. I took Joe to Maine last week for his holidays, and stayed in the white, peaceful village of Bluehill, listening to the beat of tire chains against cold mudguards, studying tracks where the deer had pawed the snow under the little apple trees, sliding down hill, and ushering in the new year by going to bed and letting the Baptist church ring twelve clear holy strokes for me. It was a fine trip and we had real winter weather, almost Currier and Ives in its purity. The woods, after a snowstorm, were lovelier than any cathedral, and we went in on a bobsled with some men, and helped jig out some firewood. It was birch. The horse had a bell on.

I've felt a lot better since coming back but Kay is still shot to pieces and I think will have to take some time off. We may go to [Bermuda]. The lease on this house expires on October 1, and one of the things that is getting us down is trying to decide whether we will renew it (in which case I would have to go back writing my weekly sermon for the NYer) or whether we will chuck the city and go live in Maine maybe. Problems like that, which are easy to solve if you do them quick, or if you have no children, become increasingly intricate and demoralizing if you take to brooding on them and if you have to fit schools and so forth into the picture. . . .

P.S. . . . I forgot to tell you that my "Memoirs" were rejected by a man named Joseph Bryan III—a coincidence which has done as much as anything to destroy me.[20]

White had submitted an essay called "Memoirs of a Master" to the *Saturday Evening Post,* where Bryan, an old friend of White's and Thurber's, was now an editor.

Thurber's reply was long and rambling. Relevant here are only the passages in which Thurber tried to dispel White's sense of failure by stressing the importance of laughter during bad times and the importance of White's providing some of it:

> Never has there been so much to laugh at off and on. Those of us who are able to do that must keep on doing it, no matter who or what goes to hell, if only because Joe Freeman [a Communist literary critic] and his gang says we should not. It is the easiest thing in the world nowadays to become so socially conscious, so Spanish war stricken, that all sense of balance and values goes out of a person. Not long ago in Paris Lillian Hellman told me that she would give up writing if she could ameliorate the condition of the world, or of only a few people in it. Hemingway is probably on that same path, and a drove of writers are following along, screaming and sweating and looking pretty strange and futile. This is one of the greatest menaces there is; people with intelligence deciding that the point is to become grimly gray and intense and unhappy and tiresome because the world and many of its people are in a bad way. It's a form of egotism, a supreme form. . . . How can these bastards hope to get hold of what's the matter with the world and do anything about it when they haven't the slightest idea that something just as bad and unnatural has happened to them? . . .
>
> I don't think the barricades is an answer, nor giving up appreciation of and interest in such fine, pleasant, and funny things as may still be around. . . . It remains for a few people to stand and watch them and report what it all looks like and sounds like. Among such persons there isn't anybody better qualified for the job than you. . . . You shouldn't submit your mind to Joe Bryan and the rest of those guys on the Post for the God's sake. . . . Of course, it is my carefully arrived at and calmly studied opinion that *The New Yorker* is the best magazine in the world. I think that, of such intelligent people as there are, most of them read *The New Yorker.* More than read anything else. There is, on the other hand, I imagine, nobody of any importance at all in the United States of America who reads *The Saturday Evening Post.*
>
> Of course, it does no good to reason with you in these matters, but still I keep on trying. I not only feel, but know as a fact, that anyone who can write the way you do has to keep on writing. I don't mean any crap about the Urge or anything like that. I mean it is a point of moral necessity.

Thurber then turned to White's question of whether to renew the lease on his house in New York or "chuck the city life and go live in Maine maybe":

New York life gets everybody. I don't mean "city life," I mean New York City life, two different things. There is nothing else in all the countries of the world like New York City life. It does more to people, it socks them harder, than life in Paris, London, or Rome, say, possibly could. Just why this is I have been very interested in pondering over here. I know it is a fact, but I am not sure just why it is. Perhaps Gibbs gets close to it in the Comment of January 8th when he speaks, rather more easily and naturally than bitterly, of "our horrible bunch." He means, of course, their horrible life. And God knows it sometimes is. People have to run away from it, broken or screaming, at the loveliest times of year, on fete days, just before parties, on Christmas Eve. It has been interesting to see the perfect picture drawn in a few sentences in each letter we get of New York life. "There has been a steady traffic to Foord's [a sanitarium resorted to by some members of the staff of *The New Yorker*] among the . . . unstrung group." If I got out my letters from everybody else and put all such sentences together it would be an amazingly vivid and accurate picture of that city and its life. . . . It has to be seen now and again, visited, lived in for short periods, but I swear that all the laws of nature and of the constitution of man make it imperative not to live there. Not, at least, in our horrible bunch. . . .

P.S. I finished all the foregoing off last night after midnight and here it is 3 o'clock of a fine summer, or maybe spring, afternoon. I can see, in this new light, that your problem about the city house is not so easy. What's the matter with renewing the lease and kind of living there half the time, Maine the other half? . . . I also think you should go back to Comment, without letting it depress or kill you, because it was the best column in the country and something to find satisfaction in doing—with periods off now and then. I also think the magazine will rot from the base up if you never do any more newsbreak lines.[21]

Thurber had recognized, and sympathetically considered, the connection in Andy's mind between where he lived and what he wrote. To renew the lease on the house in Turtle Bay Gardens would mean to return to *The New Yorker* and "Notes and Comment." And to return to the magazine as his medium would involve a return to New York as his home. Andy was, to be sure, dissatisfied with his own life, and that dissatisfaction probably colored his view of life at *The New Yorker,* life in New York, and life in Turtle Bay Gardens (where, after his years in the Village, he had always felt alienated). But even if he had not been discouraged by his progress as a writer, New York would have depressed him.

As he had told the *Time* reporter, he was "troubled about the world" of 1937; and much of what troubled him he could see all too vividly in the cosmopolitan metropolis of New York, a place where "there seemed less and less integrity . . . and more people easing off on their principles for some little advantage. There was this or that that they didn't believe in, but if it made things easier for a little while they'd give in."[22] He was not talking here about the compromises made by politicians who let their ends justify their means, but about something more elusive and pervasive, the kind of dissimulation often covered by the justification that "everybody's doing it." White was not a puritanical person, nor was he easily upset by instances of the milder forms of mendacity that help make the world go round. But now, in 1938, distressed by the growing power of Nazism and Fascism, he was becoming sensitive to what he called "moral fraudulence" in the behavior of Americans. The "palpable fraud" in American advertising, for example, bore "a curious family resemblance," he thought, to the propaganda that sold Nazism in Germany: "Here the propaganda is a loose, sprawling lie covering a multitude of hook-ups; there it is a tightly knit lie with a burning purpose."[23]

At a later time, after he and Katharine had finally decided to move to Maine, White tried to explain his "removal from town," which he regarded as "an abdication." "What was it?" he asked in an essay. "What did it? What finally was too much to bear?" And his answer in part was as follows:

A certain easy virtue in everyone, myself included, and the willingness to accept the manner and speech of the promoter and the gossip writer. A certain timbre of journalism and the stepping up of news, with the implication that the first duty of man is to discover everything that has just happened everywhere in the world, as though one couldn't scratch his own mosquito bite till he had first discovered who won the tennis in the antipodes. A certain idiocy of the newsreel and the glorification of acrobatic eccentricity which always seemed to reach its zenith in an outboard motorboat pounding its bottom out on a Florida sandspit. . . . A hardness and brightness of the materials from which the world about me was being constructed: the steel that tarnishes not, neither does it rust, but simply hits you in the eye twenty-four hours of the day with hollow splendor. . . . The acceptance, by individual and state, of the ideal of publicity, as though the sheer condition of being noticed were the ultimate good. . . .

These things combined to create something from which I shrank and do shrink, in a city which I loved and do love. It is a little hard to get on paper, but I smell something that doesn't smell good. There is a decivilizing bug somewhere at work; unconsciously persons of stern worth, by not resenting and resisting the small indignities of the times, are preparing themselves for the eventual acceptance of what they themselves know they don't want.[24]

Like some other poets, White tended to see the large in the small, the general in the particular—in the small lies, the small subterfuges, the small indignities he saw the large, general wrong.

As he reported to Thurber, he had taken seven-year-old Joe to Maine for a happy week right after Christmas in 1937. They had stayed at the home of Captain Percy Moore in Blue Hill, not far from the Whites' farm in North Brooklin. Joe had been ready to go skiing at five o'clock the first morning, and within a couple of days Captain Moore had built him a sled. Andy had written Katharine every day, and every letter was full of delight:

> Yesterday, riding through the countryside and catching glimpses of blanketed pastures and ice makers on the frozen Kennebec and mittened boys on a snowy hilltop and houses snug under hemlock boughs I wondered again why we crucify ourselves on the spiky ruins of New York. Sick as I was, the minute I stepped into the Boston & Maine Pullman and saw those pleasant faces, I felt better.[25]

It was not just the beauty of the region or the romantic, Christmas-card combination of snow scenes and cozy houses that made him think again about moving to Maine; he was drawn to its people, people like Captain Moore. On January 1, White's letter to Katharine took the form of a "local news" column in a town newspaper. He called it "Saturday Night Gazette." Here are some of its items:

> A car driven by Dr. R. V. N. Bliss slightly grazed a coupe this P.M., at the foot of Pleasant Street. Interested witnesses of this encounter were Capt. P. T. Moore & his guest E. B. White, of New York City & North Brooklin.
> Sometimes on these snowy afternoons the only sounds you hear are the slapping of the tire chains and the cases of whooping cough.
> Many deer tracks are visible on the Theodore Keller place.
> Mr. Fred Paige caught one smelt today, which he gave to Joel White, a young friend. . . .
> Midnight silence on New Year's Eve was broken by the clock on the Baptist Church. It struck twelve.
> Joel & E. B. White enjoyed a basket lunch and skate on the White estate. After a flashy performance on the smooth surface of the frog pond, luncheon was served in the tonneau of Capt. Moore's powerful Dodge tourer, which had been loaned to the party for the day. Sub zero conditions and general larkishness made it a memorable occasion. . . .
> The Christmas cactus at Rena Paige's house is a riot of color. The cyclamen is doing good, too. No blooms of any kind were in evidence this week at the E. B. White cottage, but a couple of Chinese lanterns still showed through the snow.[26]

During this week in Blue Hill and North Brooklin, Katharine wrote Andy several letters. In one of them she said:

> I was thinking that on Jan. 1 you have still one half year plus one month of your year off left,—what would last year at this time have seemed like aeons of time, so don't despair of not getting done some of the things you want to do. It's what I care most about, that things should be right for you, even though I seem to show it in curious and disagreeable ways. I know I can do better from now on. I have the feeling now that 1938 can be a very exciting or at least a very good year for us, whether it brings a wholly new way of life, or continues with the old one improved, and I'm not worrying about it at all. It begins to me to seem good to be alive in these queer times, which is a big gain. . . .[27]

On March 1, 1938, White wrote his brother Stanley that he and Katharine had "decided to give up the New York house and go live in Maine, where it is more fun, cleaner, and less wearing," and he added a second piece of news: "Am undergoing change of life today—changing from one publishing firm to another. It's more delicate than changing wives, so I've been told by persons who have been through both experiences."[28] What he was referring to here was a further decision he had made in connection with his move to Maine: he had decided to give up his anonymous weekly column in *The New Yorker* and to take on instead the writing of a signed monthly column in *Harper's Magazine*. It would be entitled "One Man's Meat," and the first installment would appear in the October issue. White's "solid year of experimenting with idleness" was really only about eight months long, from August 1937 to April 1938. During that time he wrote only three casuals and four poems for *The New Yorker*. In April he began to contribute to "Notes and Comment" occasionally and to write casuals and other things more frequently. Nonetheless, he remembers 1936–37 as "one of the most sensible twelve-month periods" in his life.

The agreement with *Harper's* was confirmed in June: White would write one column of about twenty-five hundred words a month for three hundred dollars. When White informed Ross of having made this agreement, Ross did everything he could to persuade White to keep on contributing to *The New Yorker*. White agreed to continue to edit newsbreaks for a salary of seventy-five dollars a week; and in return for promising to contribute an occasional piece to *The New Yorker* (at an increased rate of twenty-five cents a word), he was to be paid at the end of each year fifty shares of F-R Publishing Corporation stock, then worth about twenty dollars a share. Since there was nothing in his contract with *Harper's* to prevent White from continuing to contribute to *The New Yorker,* he did not in fact "switch publishers" so much as switch his primary commitment from *The New Yorker* to *Harper's.*

It was a characteristic move. It looked like liberation from weekly deadlines, an opportunity to write as he pleased. It was not a reckless or very risky move financially, for by 1938 Andy and Katharine, though not wealthy, were fairly well off. The income from their investments, Katharine's *New Yorker* salary for the part-time editorial work she intended to do in Maine, and Andy's income from *Harper's* and *The New Yorker* (and from other writing) would be sufficient for their needs. In 1936 his *New Yorker* essay "Farewell, My Lovely!" had brought him a greatly increased readership, a large payment from *Reader's Digest* for permission to publish a condensed version of it, and an invitation from the editor of *The Saturday Evening Post,* the highest-paying magazine in the country, to submit future pieces. Since the fall of 1937, when publishers learned of his leave of absence from *The New Yorker,* White had turned down several offers to write for other magazines. Moreover, decisive as the move to Maine and to *Harper's* seemed to be, it was not irreversible. Both Whites were in the prime of life and reputation, and they knew that if their new way of life should prove unsatisfactory, they could easily return to New York and their old work, or to other work. In 1936 Christopher Morley had tried to persuade White to accept the editorship of *The Saturday Review of Literature,* and early in 1938 Raoul Fleischmann, wanting at this point to fire Ross, had offered Katharine and Andy the joint editorship of *The New Yorker.* (They had told him not to be foolish.) But if the move did not involve great financial risk, or a professional threat to Andy, it was nonetheless costly to Katharine, who may have believed that, as Brendan Gill says, she was "giving up the best job held by any woman in America."[29] The part-time work she did on the farm in Maine was not nearly as satisfying to her as the first twelve years of full-time work in her New York office. And when, five years later, the Whites returned to New York and *The New Yorker*, Gus Lobrano had long since taken her place as head of the Fiction Department, and she could not regain her previous influence on the magazine. Years later White said that he was not sure he would have pulled out of New York in 1938 if he had known how hard it would be for Katharine to leave her job. As it was, he did what he says he has always done—he followed his hunch, and his hunch was that it was time to get out. In starting "up the road that led toward the north," he felt like Stuart Little, who, in the last line of the story, knew that he was "headed in the right direction."

Possibly Katharine herself had not fully imagined how hard the break would be for her. What she cared about most was that "things should be right" for Andy, and Maine seemed right for him. It may also have seemed right for Joe—Andy thought public school could give him certain advantages that rich little boys could not find in private school. Even for Katharine herself, year-round life in the country offered escape from some aspects of life in New York that she had grown to dislike, and since childhood she had enjoyed animals and gardening. When she and Andy went to Bermuda in April, the holiday was a celebration of their agreement to try a new kind of life, and they may have hoped that, like their honeymoon trip to Bermuda nine years earlier, this one would celebrate a wise decision.

Katharine's father had recently died, and shortly after she and Andy returned from Bermuda his will was probated. She wrote Andy in Maine that she had inherited enough to pay for the repairing and remodeling of their farmhouse, on which work had already begun. White could not stay in New York for any long stretch of time while such exciting work was in progress, and he made several trips to North Brooklin to enjoy watching it. The following letter, written in early May, expresses his elation:

Dear Kay:

On a day like this it is inconceivable that we should live anywhere but here. The spring really began yesterday afternoon: I was working down by the cow shed in the pasture (the turkey house, I mean) and suddenly the frogs began. The wind dropped, the sun concentrated on my back; from the woods came a thrush's pure composition; & into the cove sailed a vessel & came to rest in the calm illuminated evening. Today was a continuation, with warmth, new green, NW breeze blueing the bay, & in the afternoon a sun shower and rainbow.

My structural doings over the week-end constitute a tour de force. On Saturday, tired of mooching sheepishly around the place trying to look as though I understood chimneys, I drifted down to the turkey house where I could be alone in a building I thoroughly understood. The pasture got into my blood, & in almost no time I had determined to convert the turkey shed into a brooder house & install 100 day-old chicks. This project is now three days old. During this period I have worked steadily by day, schemed at night. Tomorrow my labors will come to a head with the arrival of a coal brooder stove—& perhaps the chicks. Mr. Willis is due tomorrow, but if he wants to talk he'll have to come down to the pasture—where I have a little chimney of my own devising & where 100 lives hang in the balance. . . .

Kitchen chimney has risen to Roger's room. Contains 2 tile flues. No sunroom yet. . . . But forsythia is out in the bantam yard, & bluebirds are looking for holes in fence posts.

Lots of love to you & Joe. I'll be home as soon as I can.

Andy[30]

The house the Whites settled into in North Brooklin, Maine, in the fall of 1938 was handsome, well-appointed, comfortable, and spacious. The front room in the northwest corner became Andy's study, and across the hall the room in the southwest corner became Katharine's study, where she would continue her professional life as half-time editor for *The New Yorker*. In back of the living room and dining room was a large country kitchen, which had been modernized but still contained its massive old wood-burning iron range and a rocking chair. Connected to the house by a woodshed, full of neatly stacked firewood, was the barn, a retreat for Andy that surpassed all his previous retreats—Summit Avenue stables, Central Park, the Bronx Zoo, the reservoir, Grand Central Station: "There is no more satisfying structure in the whole world than a well-built old American barn, just as she stands."[31] In addition to the barn were numerous smaller buildings: an old icehouse, a henhouse, a rangehouse, a cowshed, and a garage with an attic big enough to serve as a place for solitude and occasionally for writing.

The setting for house and barn was equally satisfying, as Andy indicated in a letter to Stanley:

> The country in which all this elegance is located is, I suspect, unfamiliar to you. It is Belgrade tempered with a certain bleak, hard-bitten character which the sea gives to the land. Our woodlot is full of hemlock, spruce, birch, juniper, and all the aromatic sweetness of a Maine pasture; yet it dips right down to the tideflats, where gulls scream their heads off and hair-seals bark like old love-sick terriers. There is a twelve to sixteen foot rise and fall of tide. In the east Mount Desert rises high and formidable. Many days are startlingly clear and blue, many are thick a-fog. The fog shuts in fast, catching you short when you are sailing. It settles like a cloud down around the hackmatack swamp and the frog pond, and makes the earth mysterious and enticing. Off the coast are hundreds and hundreds of outlying islands, some tiny, some very big. . . . The prevailing winds are from the south-west, and they make up strong in the afternoon and blow smokey.[32]

CHAPTER XI

"One Man's Meat"

1 9 3 8 — 1 9 4 3

*"Individualism and the first person singular
are closely related to freedom, and are what
the fight is about."*

THE MOVE TO MAINE WAS MORE THAN A
retreat from New York City, where there seemed to be "less and
less integrity"; it was a positive move toward the fulfillment of a
child's dream. The forty-acre farm was a life-size toy, as White once
suggested when he compared his fitted lambs to "some wooden lambs that
had come with a toy barnyard in another period of American history"—
that period being 1905 to 1910, and the toy barnyard the one under the
Christmas tree at 101 Summit Avenue. Now the artificial "sun, moon, stars,
and clouds" that his mother remembered as part of the Christmas tree set
were replaced by real skies, winds, rains, snows, fogs, and sea that he could
feel, hear, and smell.[1]

It was, White said, "not really a farm at all but merely a private zoo."
A year after moving in, White reported the following census:

I have fifteen grade sheep; also own one-half of a full-blooded Oxford Down
ram with another fellow. Two of the sheep are dungy tails; two are snotty
noses; one is black. In general their health is good, no ticks. The ram is gentle.
I have 112 New Hampshire Red pullets in the henhouse and 36 White
Plymouth Rock pullets in the barn, a total of 148 layers, I have three Toulouse
geese, the remnants of a flock of four, one having been taken by a fox. I have
six roosters, celibates, living to themselves. There is also a dog, a tomcat, a pig,
and a captive mouse.

And under "Denizens of Woods and Fields" he listed:

> Skunks, woodchucks, weasels, foxes, deer, mink, rabbits, owls, crows, hair
> seals, coot, whistlers, loons, black ducks, squirrels (gray and red), chipmunks,
> porcupines, coons, hummingbirds, moles, spiders, snakes, swallows, martins,
> toads, snails, and frogs. One night a wild goose stopped over on our pond en
> route south. There are songbirds in large numbers at certain moments of spring
> and fall.[2]

On this farm that excelled the fairest dreams of childhood, in a world
he later immortalized in *Charlotte's Web,* E. B. White lived year-round,
from 1938, the year before the outbreak of World War II, till 1943. It was,
he later said, "just about the best period in my life—best because at that
time I could be almost continuously active without fatigue."[3]

Shortly before he left New York and *The New Yorker* for Maine and
Harper's Magazine, one of White's friends had said, "with an ugly leer,"
"I trust . . . you will spare the reading public your little adventures in
contentment." There was little chance that White would write the kind
of romantic accounts of returns to the soil that were then popular. In fact,
in the spring of 1938 he had written a parody of such accounts, merrily
satirizing the pretense of an author who thought of himself as a farmer
though he was clearly supporting himself on royalties and income from
his wife's investments, and who had carried his culture and his cocktails
to a farm. Nor did White mean to lose himself in the role of a farmer.
He was a writer, and he hoped that life in Maine would allow him to
produce works less ephemeral than he felt his verse, casuals, and "Notes
and Comment" for *The New Yorker* had been. He would earn his living
from his writing (mostly for *Harper's*); and his column, "One Man's
Meat," would be more like a journal than installments in a book of
adventures in rural contentment. He was amused to remember that when
he was a boy there had been a book on the library table in his parents' house
called *Wet Days at Edgewood,* a book consisting of journal entries written
on a farm in Connecticut by Donald Grant Mitchell and originally published in *Harper's Magazine* in the eighteen-fifties. Now, seventy years
later, E. B. White would write a similarly public journal that would be
mainly, as he told Ross, "description and narration . . . based on what is
happening to me where I am."[4]

At first, he found it hard to make the change from *New Yorker* commentator to *Harper's* essayist. His experience with his very first column was
troublesome. When he submitted the copy for it, it was six hundred words
short of the twenty-five hundred needed to fill his space, and he was

dissatisfied with what he had managed to write. He asked his editor, Lee Hartman, whether he couldn't postpone his debut for a month. Hartman reminded him that *Harper's* was running an extensive advertising campaign to publicize the magazine's "new program," of which White's column was to be an important part. *Harper's* could not disappoint its expectant readers. He suggested that White enlarge his column by substituting a new opening for the one he had submitted, which had read:

> This life I lead, setting pictures straight, squaring rugs up with the room— it suggests an ultimate symmetry toward which I strive and strain. Yet I doubt that I am any nearer my goal than I was last year, or ten years ago, even granted that this untidy world is ready for any such orderliness.[5]

Hartman said the paragraph was "a delightful bit, but hardly robust enough to head the procession on this opening occasion." The editor was probably right, but White's opening paragraph was in the personal vein he had looked forward to working, and the "robust" opening he finally supplied was much like a *New Yorker* "Comment." It consisted of five paragraphs on the invention of television; he concluded that "in this new opportunity to see beyond the range of our vision we shall discover either a new and unbearable disturbance of the general peace or a saving radiance in the sky."[6] The first "One Man's Meat" was, however, well received. And the magazine's publicity campaign, too, proved to be a success. Three weeks after the October issue appeared, *Harper's* had gained 11,200 new subscribers and had increased newsstand sales by 20 percent. Such results may only have increased White's anxieties about his new undertaking.

Having committed himself to this new mode of writing, having at last won the chance to write a long column under his own name, in the first-person singular, and having relieved himself of the pressure of weekly deadlines, would he be able to make good use of these opportunities? Would his monthly essays prove to be more substantial, less ephemeral, than his weekly paragraphs? Would his new column lead him out of the dead end he felt he had reached as a writer of light verse and *New Yorker* casuals?

He was more than ever convinced that he had reached such a dead end by the reception given to two collections of his writings that appeared within six months of each other, just as he was beginning to settle into his new work for *Harper's*. Neither book was discussed in the press in a way that could give him great encouragement. The first, a collection of his verse entitled *The Fox of Peapack* and published in October 1938, sold eighteen hundred copies during its first three months, but none of its reviewers took

its author seriously as a poet. The second, a collection of his satirical pieces
called *Quo Vadimus? Or the Case for the Bicycle,* published in March 1939,
received favorable reviews: White's prose was distinguished by "a certain
clarity of style, a certain distinction of mind," and "an apparent effortless-
ness in humor that makes some of his pieces impossible to forget" *(New
York Times);* he was a "rare essayist" who had "influenced for the better
the style of a whole generation," and could be called "the Master of the
Sentence" *(New York Tribune);* he "still considers being a humorist no
laughing matter" *(Time);* and his old admirer Christopher Morley, in *Book
of the Month Club News,* praised him for his "low-pitched savagery" and
his exquisite balance of "gaiety and intelligence." In spite of all these words
of praise, White knew that *Quo Vadimus?* was, as Morley called it, a "study
of contemporary jitters." It was the product of a phase in his own and in
his country's history that was almost over; new jitters were on the way,
and the tone and genre of White's satire might soon be outmoded. Sharing
Morley's views, and having no reason to believe that he had a gift for
writing plays or novels, he regarded his new column for *Harper's* as a test
of his talent as an essayist.

As his anxieties about meeting this test began to abate, White began to
worry about other aspects of his new professional life. He discovered that
the new schedule of deadlines was in some ways more burdensome than
the old. Deadlines that impended, as they now did, for as long as a month,
cast longer shadows than weekly ones. Moreover, the interval of seven
weeks between the time he had to deliver his column to *Harper's* and the
time it appeared in the magazine's pages was too long to allow him to be
as topical as he had been at *The New Yorker.* Within a year he was telling
Ross and others of his dissatisfaction with his new medium; and one
wonders, from the tone of his letters, how he stuck it out as long as he
did—for fifty-five months.[7]

Most of all, however, the enemy was distraction. He discovered, White
said, that he was suited physically to be a writer but psychologically to
be a farmer; and life on the farm offered so many opportunities for
enjoyable activity that he found it harder than ever to sit down to write.
His daily life, to be sure, furnished him with much to write about, but the
pleasures of that life were sometimes tinged with the uncomfortable
knowledge that he ought to be writing about them instead of simply
enjoying them. In response to a letter from a schoolteacher expressing her
envy of a "guy who can make a living by telling what he thinks and sees,"
White replied:

> A person who writes of this and that stands in the same relation to his world
> as a drama critic to the theater. He is full of free tickets and implied obligations.

He can't watch the show just for the fun of it. And watching the show just for the fun of it, once that privilege is forfeited, begins to seem like the greatest privilege there is. The next time my Michigan correspondent is visited by a Thought, or stands in the presence of a Sight, she should give thanks that she can stay right there and doesn't have to grab her hat and sneak up life's dark aisle to a waiting typewriter.[8]

However, as he once said, with reference to Thoreau, occasionally "something good and even great results from the attempt of a troubled spirit to reconcile" his urge to do his duty as a writer and his equally strong urge to watch the show for the fun of it. He had long ago discovered that "writing of the small things of the day, the trivial matters of the heart, the inconsequential but near things of this living, was the only kind of creative work" that he could accomplish "with any sincerity or grace." Occasionally in such writings he had "the exquisite thrill of putting his finger on a little capsule of truth and hearing it give the faint squeak of mortality under his pressure—an antic sound."[9]

"One Man's Meat" soon drew a large readership, but in his skeptical way White was inclined to attribute its popularity as much to the needs of his readers as to the fare he was providing. He once speculated about why people read his column:

> Don [Marquis] knew how lonely everybody is. "Always the struggle of the human soul is to break through the barriers of silence and distance into companionship. Friendship, lust, love, art, religion—we rush into them pleading, fighting, clamoring for the touch of spirit laid against our spirit." Why else would you be reading this fragmentary page—you with the book in your lap? You're not out to learn anything, certainly. You just want the healing action of some chance corroboration, the soporific of spirit laid against spirit. Even if you read only to crab about everything I say, your letter of complaint is a dead give-away: you are unutterably lonely or you wouldn't have taken the trouble to write it.[10]

It is true that in "One Man's Meat" White expressed what Irwin Edman called the "poetry of observation and the philosophy of shrewd, usually gentle, sometimes biting moral insight,"[11] but it was not the poetry and philosophy in his essays that his readers most valued. White came nearer to explaining the attraction (and later the fame) of his essays when he referred to the companionship they provided to the reader whenever he succeeded in breaking through the "barriers of silence and distance." "One Man's Meat," his readers told him, spoke not only for them but to them —almost with them—in a way that comforted them and encouraged them as well as entertained them. In that sort of vicarious companionship, what counted was not only what he said but what kind of man he seemed to be. The E. B. White who gave his readers a little bit of himself in the dark days and nights from the Munich Pact (1938) to the Allied landings in Italy (1943) projected the character of a sensitive, thoroughly honest, decent, and reliable human being with a sense of humor that was modest, self-knowing, and good-natured. The author of "One Man's Meat" did not sound like someone who thought of himself as a writer or a literary person. He was simply a busy, thoughtful man who, when writing, was snatching time from something else. Years later White told an interviewer: "I don't care about being known as a writer. I just want to be thought of as a reliable man." His readers thought of him as both, and he may have reminded some of them of Thoreau, who on the first page of *Walden* said:

> I should not talk so much about myself if there were anybody else whom I knew as well. . . . I require of every writer, first or last, a simple and sincere account of his own life.

As they read White's accounts of what he was doing and thinking, or of what was happening around him, they saw him in the roles of amateur husbandman, professional writer, husband, father, neighbor, and citizen. They learned how he built shelves in the town library for the childrens' books that his wife had donated, how his eight-year-old son liked his one-room country school, how wartime rationing affected his family, how he served as a blackout warden and plane-spotter. One essay, "Memorandum," took the form of a long letter to himself about all the jobs he should get at—there must be a hundred of them, all clearly more fun than the hard work of writing an essay. Readers were even given a rough idea of White's annual expenses on the farm.[12]

Some columns were written in the form of entries in a journal. For example, "A Winter Diary" contained this entry:

> *Saturday.* Last fall I hauled rockweed up from the shore and spread it to a depth of five or six inches on the dirt floor of the sheep shed and covered it with straw. Now the sheep droppings are accumulating on this rockweed base and forming a rich dressing for the land. There is no doubt about it, the basic satisfaction in farming is manure, which always suggests that life can be cyclic and chemically perfect and aromatic and continuous.[13]

"My Day" (written in June 1941) was a twenty-five-hundred-word journal entry for a single day. It took its title from that of a syndicated column written by Eleanor Roosevelt. It began: "With Mrs. Roosevelt's permission, I shall describe my day. I woke at six and lay till quarter past, slowly turning my head from side to side to test my neck, which has less play in it than it once had." As he went on, he interspersed the report of his activities on that particular day with the meditations they prompted, such as the following:

> A man sometimes gets homesick for the loneliness that he has at one time or another experienced in his life and that is a part of all life in some degree, and sometimes a secluded and half-mournful yet beautiful place will suddenly revive the sensation of pain and melancholy and unfulfillment that are associated with that loneliness, and will make him want to seize it and recapture it; but I know with me it is a passing want and not to be compared with my taste for domesticity, which is most of the time so strong as to be overpowering.

At the end of the day, he says:

> I filled a bucket with oats and continued on to the range where the pullets are, the air here smelling of blossoms with a trace of skunk. . . . I returned to the house and got the terrier and put him in the garage and then let the big red dachshund out and then in again and then the little black dachshund out and in again and I set up the fire screen in the living room and closed the door of the woodshed and turned out the lights one by one through all the rooms and ascended and brushed my teeth and pulled the window curtains and looked in at the sleeping boy to see if he was covered, and undressed and got into bed and tried my neck again and changed position from the right side to the left side and heaved a great long sigh. . . .[14]

Almost half the columns he wrote for "One Man's Meat" are twenty-five-hundred-word essays. Of these, many are not about his life in Maine. "Walden" is a report of a visit to the pond, in the form of a letter to Thoreau. "On a Florida Key," an essay on Jim Crow, sounds like a letter from a man in Florida on a winter vacation. "Once More to the Lake" is a meditative account of his return, with his son, Joe, to Belgrade Lake. And one is an essay on children's books, written just after Katharine had completed her pre-Christmas omnibus review of new children's books.[15] Others were, inevitably, about the war.

IN 1938 AND 1939 the news from Europe unsettled him, as it unsettled his fellow countrymen. In the columns of "One Man's Meat" White recorded the evolution of his attitude towards the approaching war, towards its outbreak, and towards the part America should play in it. In the fall of 1938 he wrote about the Munich Pact:

I stayed on [the roof of] the barn, steadily laying shingles, all during the days when Mr. Chamberlain, M. Daladier, the Duce, and the Führer were arranging their horse trade. It seemed a queer place to be during a world crisis. . . .

I'm down now; the barn is tight, and the peace is preserved. It is the ugliest peace the earth has ever received for a Christmas present. Old England, eating swastika for breakfast instead of kipper, is a sight I had as lief not lived to see. And though I'm no warrior, I would gladly fight for the things which Nazism seeks to destroy.[16]

White excelled as a commentator on the war because he reported the thoughts and feelings of a man who had to do his chores—of one who depended on the dailiness of daily life to keep himself sane and effective. For White and his readers a farm was not a queer place to be during a world crisis, nor the roof of a barn a bad place to look at the world from. In fact, his comments attracted readers who had tired of the opinions and the rhetoric of the statesmen and the pundits. All White communicated was what his readers felt—a sense of helplessness in the face of forces too great for an individual to resist or influence, and a compensatory sense of the power to make decisions and do the work at hand. His observations were reassuring because they suggested that war news and local news were equally significant. He told his readers what his family did on Sunday, September 3, 1939, the day England declared war on Germany. They decided to go to church—"a solemn place for a solemn hour":

The minister, a young fellow I recently sold some hens to for a dollar apiece, said he believed the meek would inherit the earth. We sang "Am I a soldier of the Cross, are there no foes for me to fight?"

After church White went out to the barn and worked till dinner, during which the family listened to the broadcast of King George's speech. "The words came with painful slowness, and we all sat and chewed. Thus began the second war for democracy."[17]

For White, as for most Americans, the war was a necessary defensive action against Hitler's threat to freedom, but for him the freedom that mattered most was personal freedom rather than national freedom. The freedom of an individual, he knew, depended on the legal protection it received from the government of his own country. Yet the threat of one nation to another did not preoccupy him so much as did "the individual plight" of people threatened by Hitler's ideas and ambitions. He managed to make that clear at the end of an account of a day, early in September, spent lobstering with his friend Charles Henderson:

It struck me as we worked our way homeward up the rough bay with our catch of lobsters and a fresh breeze in our teeth that this was what the fight was all about. This was it. Either we would continue to have it or we wouldn't, this right to speak our own minds, haul our own traps, mind our own business, and wallow in the wide, wide sea.[18]

In early April 1940, near the end of the so-called phony war, Eugene Saxton, White's editor at Harper and Brothers, tried to interest White in writing a "primer for American youth, which would in . . . substance be a statement of the case for American democracy and the American way of life, and would explain to young readers what the real heritage of this country was and why it deserved to be cherished." It would, he said, be "immensely valuable, and might have a spectacular sale."[19]

White informed Saxton in June that he had decided to accept his proposal to write the little book on freedom; and less than two weeks later he was holed up in a room in the Grosvenor Hotel, in New York, hard at work on it. He developed an outline, drafted an introduction and a first chapter, and sent Saxton three tentative titles. But two days after submitting those titles, he informed Saxton that he could not write the book: he was "ill-equipped for the job"; it was "out of his field":

> I think I am cracking up, anyway. This has been the devil of a spring, even in this free country, and the way I feel now I'd better relax for a while or I'll burst. . . . A man has to quit when nature gives him the wink. . . . I seem to be suffering from a case of brain fag, and am incapable of organizing myself for even the simplest intellectual hurdle.

Back in Maine he wrote Saxton again: "I know that I was ill-equipped for the job. These are tough days for minor poets and lackwits and we tend to get out of our field."[20]

From the wreckage of his efforts to write a primer on freedom he salvaged "enough to make a respectable piece" for *Harper's*. "One Man's Meat" for the September 1940 issue was, in fact, a good column; when he reprinted it later, he called it simply "Freedom." Into it he put the ideas he had been forming and drafting for two months. It is organically whole, its prose has the good White rhythms, its humor is subtle, and its message is strong, serious, and moving. Ross thought it "a beautiful and elegant thing, probably the most moving item [he] had read in years, worthy of Lincoln and some of the other fellows that really went to town."[21] In it are sentences on freedom quoted in an earlier chapter of this biography: "For as long as I can remember I have had a sense of living somewhat freely

in a natural world. . . . I traveled with secret papers. . . . My first and
greatest love affair was with this thing we call freedom, this lady of infinite
allure, this dangerous and beautiful and sublime being who restores and
supplies us all." White made a clear distinction, as well as implied a
relationship between, "the instinctive freedom [a person] experiences as an
animal dweller on a planet, and the practical liberties he enjoys as a
privileged member of human society," and concluded with an expression
of confidence in the power of writers to be of help in the cause of
preserving freedom. In *Mein Kampf* Hitler had said to "all knights of the
pen" that " 'one is able to win people far more by the spoken word than
by the written word. . . . The greatest changes in this world have never
yet been brought about by a goose quill!' " To this statement White
replied: "[Writers] are feared by every tyrant—who shows his fear by
burning the books and destroying the individuals."[22]

In December 1940 White wrote a devastating review of Anne Morrow
Lindbergh's *The Wave of the Future*. It was the strongest of his essays on the
war and one of his most closely argued. *The Wave of the Future* was at the
time a widely read and popular book that presented the case against
America's entry into the war. Its author was not only the wife of a hero and
the mother of a child whose kidnapping and murder made his parents the
object of nationwide sympathy, but the author of other widely-admired
books. There is no way to measure the influence of this book or of White's
criticism of it, but no review was so widely read and quoted as his. It was
effective because White took the book seriously, read it carefully, systemati-
cally attacked the logic of its arguments, and communicated the reviewer's
passion as well as his intelligence, decency, and honesty. His attack was civil
but unrelenting, and it was unrelieved by humor. It was enhanced by the
narrative frame he set it in, a journal entry that began, "Tuesday. Arose at six
on a cold morning and by truck alone to Waterville to keep an appointment
with a medical man." While waiting to see the doctor he bought *The Wave
of the Future* and "read it sitting in the truck."

Quotations can scarcely suggest the cumulative force of White's argument, but the following passage illustrates the force of his style:

> Many of her statements, although accurate enough in themselves, are followed
> by an inferential remark which a logician would find inadmissible. She tells
> me that the German people are not innately bad, which is correct and is not
> even news as far as I am concerned; but then she draws the inference that
> therefore the star the German people are following is good, which I think is
> illogical and a perversion of the facts. And she tells me that life is nothing but
> change, which is correct; and then implies that change is on that account

beneficial, which I doubt in many cases. And she tells me that the fascist push originated in frustration and injustice, which I say is true and correct; and then infers that because the push stemmed from human misery it bodes good for the world, which I feel is fallacious, for I know a lot of things can start with human misery and not bring anything except *more* misery.[23]

White seldom wrote so seriously and persuasively about political and moral questions. He seldom commanded the patience and the intellectual staying-power needed for arguments involving a knowledge of history and the formulation of complex ideas. He seldom so completely avoided the skepticism that weakens arguments, seldom so completely kept his eye from wandering from the play to the critic who was "watching his reactions to it."

Among the various pieces of mail White received in response to his review of *The Wave of the Future* was one on which he commented in print:

I received some letters to-day commenting on the remarks I made about Mrs. Lindbergh's book, including one letter . . . from a man who said that my sudden championship of democracy was characteristic of die-hard capitalists who are trying to buy off the future and who refuse to see in the present struggle the obvious birth pangs of socialism. . . .

So I sat around for a long time in a self-doubting mood, wishing that I knew some way of earning a living except by writing, and wondering whether there was any "purpose" behind history which I was unconsciously serving by resisting revolutionary processes and whether I really felt about capitalism the way many of my detractors think I do. So this made me quite sick, and I began having stomach pains and I asked my wife if she thought I was a bloated capitalist and she said, No, just bloated. And I doubted that there was any purpose shaping men's affairs on this planet, however much men like to think so. Economists often see a purpose behind men's struggles, and so do revolutionaries; but I doubt if biologists do.[24]

A Subtreasury of American Humor, an eight-hundred-page anthology edited by E. B. White and Katharine S. White, was published in November 1941, in time for the Christmas trade. Andy and Katharine had worked long and conscientiously in search of its nearly two hundred selections from the works of American humorists—beginning with Benjamin Franklin, Washington Irving, and James Russell Lowell, through Mark Twain and Artemus Ward, to Don Marquis, Ring Lardner, and S. J. Perelman. About one-third of the pieces had appeared in *The New Yorker:* seven of them were by Thurber, six by Wolcott Gibbs, and four by White. Though the Whites had been thinking about the project since 1938, when a publisher had suggested it, they had not done much work on it until the spring and summer of 1941.

The anthology reflects a wide knowledge of the literature and a sure, consistent taste, and its virtues are those of a marriage of complementary minds and skills. In the Preface White lets us have a glimpse of the way he and Katharine worked together:

> Quite a large amount of the material in here was published first in *The New Yorker.* This discovery should surprise nobody. My wife and I happen to own a complete file of the bound volumes of *The New Yorker,* and after a long evening with George Horatio Derby or somebody or other who wrote the best light verse during the McKinley administration, it would often be our stealthy custom to pull out a volume at random and dip up a nice funny piece before going to bed.

The arranging of the selections into categories (e.g., "Fables and Other Moral Tales," "Parodies and Burlesques," "Satire—Broad and Otherwise") was largely Katharine's work, as was most of the labor involved in getting permission to reprint. White's work included writing to friends asking for nominations from their own or others' works, and writing the Preface and headnotes.

In the first half of the Preface, White explained the anthologists' principles of selection, the chief of which was to please themselves:

> In this collection of American humor, Katharine S. White (who shall hereafter be known as my wife) and I have tried to select some things we like ourselves, and have made no attempt to throw in anything to please anybody else. This is a subtreasury designed for the safekeeping of our own valuables. Anyone else who wants to pay his way in is at liberty to wander about, criticizing the contents of the vaults and looking for trouble. This is part of your money's worth. There are some well-known pieces in here, and some that are not well known, and two or three old chestnuts for roasting over an open fire these crisp fall nights. One thing you may not find in here is your favorite humorist, and we strongly advise you not to look for him, poor fellow. We passed him on the street the other day and he seemed far from well.[25]

The second half of the Preface is a little essay on humor. It states White's concept of his own art and his fate:

> One of the things commonly said about humorists is that they are really very sad people—clowns with a breaking heart. There is some truth in it, but

it is badly stated. It would be more accurate, I think, to say that there is a deep vein of melancholy running through everyone's life and that a humorist, perhaps more sensible of it then some others, compensates for it actively and positively. Practically everyone is a manic depressive of sorts, with his up moments and his down moments, and you certainly don't have to be a humorist to taste the sadness of situation and mood. But, as everyone knows, there is often a rather fine line between laughing and crying, and if a humorous piece of writing brings a person to the point where his emotional responses are untrustworthy and seem likely to break over into the opposite realm, it is because humorous writing, like poetical writing, has an extra content. It plays, like an active child, close to the big hot fire which is Truth. And sometimes the reader feels the heat.

The world likes humor, but it treats it patronizingly. It decorates its serious artists with laurel, and its wags with Brussels sprouts. It feels that if a thing is funny it can be presumed to be something less than great, because if it were truly great it would be wholly serious. Writers know this, and those who take their literary selves with great seriousness are at considerable pains never to associate their name with anything funny or flippant or nonsensical or "light." They suspect it would hurt their reputation, and they are right.

He quotes with approval F. P. A.'s observation that the most successful writers often have no sense of humor at all, because "in writing, emotion is more to be treasured than a sense of humor, and the two are often in conflict." White explains:

The conflict is fundamental. There constantly exists, for a certain sort of person of high emotional content, at work creatively, the danger of coming to a point where something cracks within himself or within the paragraph under con-struction—cracks and turns into a snicker. Here, then, is the very nub of the conflict: the careful form of art, and the careless shape of life itself. What a man does with this uninvited snicker (which may closely resemble a sob, at that) decides his destiny. If he resists it, conceals it, destroys it, he may keep his architectural scheme intact and save his building, and the world will never know. If he gives in to it, he becomes a humorist, and the sharp brim of the fool's cap leaves a mark forever on his brow.[27]

Humor is a handy tool on a critic's workbench. The truth is, almost every good humorist is a critic of sorts. A knave like Ogden Nash, who is classified [in the anthology] as poet and wit, is certainly at heart a critic, who attends life's every opening night; and Mark Twain apparently never had more fun than when he was taking something or somebody apart.[26]

Humorists fatten on trouble. They have always made trouble pay. They struggle along with a good will and endure pain cheerfully, knowing how well it will serve them in the sweet by and by.... We need hardly assure the reader, as he dips into the coming section ["All Sorts of Dilemmas"], that beneath the sparkling surface of these comical dilemmas flows the strong tide of human woe.[27]

The book was favorably reviewed, and by December 15 sales had reached fifteen thousand. In the following spring the Book-of-the-Month Club printed 240,000 copies for distribution as a dividend to its members.

In June 1942 Harper and Brothers published *One Man's Meat,* a collection of the columns that White had thus far written for *Harper's.* In his Foreword, White said that he thought of the book as a "sort of informal journal of the three years before the war" and suggested its relevance to the war as follows:

> The first person singular is the only grammatical implement I am able to use without cutting myself. As a matter of fact, this quality in the book is a thing which perhaps gives it some relation to the war. It is a book of, for, and by an individual. In this respect it is anathema to our enemies, who find in individualism the sign of national decay. It is the "I" in a man which Hitler has set out to destroy. I don't know what he proposes to substitute for it and I don't think he does. Individualism and the first person singular are closely related to freedom, and are what the fight is about.[28]

It was, as Katharine had predicted, his best book so far, and when it appeared it received excellent reviews. The most perceptive among them were those by Irwin Edman in the *Herald Tribune* and Diana Trilling in *The Nation.* Edman, a popular professor of philosophy at Columbia, recognized White's essentially poetic genius for expressing abstract concepts in concrete metaphorical terms, for uniting the general with the particular in ways that made each illuminate the other. White's "I," he said, was "touched with poetry" and "tethered to truth." "He finds in a wry image or a homely incident the expression of themes that have passed through all contemporary minds that are not asleep and contemporary spirits that are not dulled." In excellence of style, Edman concluded, White was a modern approximation of Montaigne and Thoreau. He called White "our finest essayist, perhaps our only one."[29]

Diana Trilling's praise in *The Nation,* equally perceptive, stands the test of time as well as does the book she reviewed:

> The kinship with Thoreau is explicit throughout this book but there is also Mr. White's implicit kinship with Montaigne. Obviously, compared to the great humanist, Mr. White's powers are on a minor scale; in the matter of style, real as his gifts are, we question whether his felicity has not sometimes been achieved by going around rather than over intellectual hurdles. But as we read

the diary he kept in the First World War, we recognize how compellingly the humanistic tradition had already claimed him, even as a young man. Perhaps this isn't remarkable—young men often reach a kind of climax of intellectual decency in their college years, after which their development is a steady retrogression justified in the name of "reality"—but what is remarkable is that Mr. White has held fast to this heritage into maturity and through a period in the world's history in which, on the liberal as well as the reactionary front, it has been so tempting to pervert mind to the uses of power. . . .[30]

The first edition sold about 12,000 copies. A "New and Enlarged Edition," containing ten columns published after February 1942, appeared in 1944. It sold about 20,000 copies during its first two years. In 1945 the Council on Books in Wartime, in cooperation with the Office of War Information, published an "Armed Services Edition" of 150,000 copies, as well as two "Overseas Editions," one in French and one in German, each of 50,000 copies.

CHAPTER XII

"The Wild Flag"

1 9 4 3 — 1 9 4 6

"In wartime the writer almost inevitably becomes propagandist and advocate, and although he may not realize it, he is operating against the grain, for the deepest instinct of a creative person is not to promote the world's cause but to keep the minutes of his own meeting."

ROSS HAD DONE ALL HE COULD TO HANG ON to White after he left *The New Yorker* and began to write for *Harper's,* and as a matter of fact, White never really "left" *The New Yorker.* During the years he wrote "One Man's Meat" his annual income from *The New Yorker* was greater than that from *Harper's.* But Ross wanted White as a regular contributor, and he had been unrelenting in his efforts to persuade White to return to "Notes and Comment."[1] As early as October 1938 he begged White to agree to contribute just an average of one paragraph of "Comment" a week. Nine months later he wrote that he was thinking of "kicking the God damned Comment page to hell out of the book," but before he did so, he wanted to know whether he could count on White for, say, one "Comment" a week for thirty weeks a year. And while he was at it, Ross ventured to ask flatly whether there was any chance of White's dropping "One Man's Meat" and agreeing to do a monthly piece for *The New Yorker.* He thought White was writing for *Harper's* "because of a psychological situation"; he knew it would be better for *The New Yorker* if he left *Harper's* and suspected it would be better for White. White's answer to the second question was no; but to the first he replied that he would set for himself a goal of one "Comment" a week, "a shining goal." (As it turned out, White contributed only thirty-three paragraphs during the next three years.)[2]

In May 1940, nine months after war had broken out in Europe, Ross

asked White whether he would agree to write "Comment" for three weeks
in order to relieve Wolcott Gibbs, who had been writing the column
steadily for a long time and needed a break. It would also, he said, be good
to have White back in the magazine "if only by the thimble-full." Ross
said that as both an editor and a human being he continued to be disappointed at White's having practically ceased to write for *The New Yorker,*
but in neither role would he nag White—or, at least, not much. He had,
he said, a deep understanding of a writer who did not want to work.[3]

White replied that he could not take over "Comment" for the next
three weeks. But in June, when France fell to the Germans, he was glad
of the chance to speak out, and he wrote *The New Yorker*'s editorial:

> To many Americans, war started (spiritually) years ago with the torment
> of the Jews. To millions of others, less sensitive to the overtones of history,
> war became actual only when Paris became German. We looked at the faces
> in the street today, and war is at last real, and the remaining step is merely
> the transformation of fear into resolve. . . .
>
> We are of the opinion that something of a total nature is in store for this
> country, and we don't mean dictatorship or vigor. We mean a total rejection
> of the threat with which we are faced, and a total moral resistance to it.
> . . . Democracy is now asked to mount its honor and decency on wheels, and
> to manufacture, with all the electric power at its command, a world which
> can make all people free and perhaps many people contented. We believe and
> shall continue to believe that even that is within the power of men.[4]

The editorial did not, to be sure, call outright for American interven-
tion, but it tilted *The New Yorker* towards supporting the Allies and
thereby signaled the end of the magazine's policy not to take positions on
political questions. Ross himself did not believe that America should
become involved in the struggle in Europe, nor did he think the time had
come to reconsider his magazine's editorial policy.

A year later Ross still thought *The New Yorker* should not advocate
anything, even though he had become convinced that America would
soon, for better or for worse, be at war. He knew that White now believed
not only that America could no longer "dodge the fight," but that *The
New Yorker* should say so. But in a long letter to White, Ross defended
his policy of silence on the grounds that he did not know anyone who
knew enough to advise him what stand to take. He thought that at the
moment the thing for American publications to do was to follow President
Roosevelt, who was himself keeping quiet and marking time. Ross said
that even Thurber, who favored America's going to war at once, doubted

that *The New Yorker* should try to become a leader of opinion "at this time." There were, Ross thought, enough leaders of opinion already, from Dorothy Thompson, Walter Winchell, and the *Evening Post* on down. Ross hoped that White would contribute to "Notes and Comment" even though he disagreed with Ross's opinions in these matters.[5]

In his reply White sympathized with Ross: "I am as bewildered as anyone else." But if he wrote any "Comment," he would have to be true to his own beliefs insofar as they bore on the news: "Sometimes this 'moral' frame [of belief] seems incompatible, or inconsistent, with skepticism. A skeptic doesn't like to believe anything, for fear it will ruin his intelligence (or his backhand drive), and on the other hand, a believer can't be too skeptical or it affects his faith." Ross would simply have to print what he believed in and "throw the rest to hell."[6]

In November, White's editor at *Harper's* asked him to go to Washington and if possible to write a "Letter from the Nation's Capital" for his next *Harper's* column. White agreed, and when he got to Washington he was issued a permit to attend one of President Roosevelt's press conferences as a nonparticipating guest. He went to the conference with his friend Richard L. Strout, correspondent for the *Christian Science Monitor*, but hardly had the conference begun when White suffered an attack of nervous stomach and dizziness so severe that he nearly passed out and had to leave the Oval Room in a hurry.[7] Back in Maine he wrote Allen that he had failed to get a story out of his trip.

In December he told an old friend that though his reason told him to stay in Maine, produce as many eggs as possible, and write "One Man's Meat," Maine seemed "too remote to satisfy [his] nervous desire to help in a bad situation," and he thought he might "try for a job in Washington, in the high realms of propaganda." Shortly thereafter he wrote a Cornell classmate, John Fleming, then deputy director of the Office of Facts and Figures in Washington, offering his services as a writer. A few days after Fleming had replied that everybody in the Office was "enormously pleased" at his offer to help, President Roosevelt asked the Office of Facts and Figures to prepare "for the widest possible publication" a pamphlet on "The Four Freedoms" that Roosevelt had enunciated in his State of the Union address in 1941. Archibald MacLeish, the director of OFF, asked White to collaborate in this venture, and White agreed.[8]

Early in 1942, at a meeting in Washington attended by all the participants in the project, it was decided that Reinhold Niebuhr would write on freedom of religion, Max Lerner on freedom from fear, Malcolm Cowley on freedom from want, and White on freedom of speech. Moreover, White was to rewrite the entire manifesto on all four freedoms from notes he would keep of the committee's conference, as well as from drafts written by Niebuhr, Lerner, and Cowley.[9]

In a letter to Katharine, White reported that much of the talk which took place in the meeting ("in vague terms as far as the job went, but in the most awful intellectual detail") went over his head. White kept quiet throughout the meeting, though the others seemed to be waiting for him to say something about freedom of speech. All he managed to do was ask how long his part was to be and when it would be due. No one knew. White was tempted to ask why the committee couldn't simply ask Roosevelt what he meant. But more than the folly of the procedure, the behavior of his colleagues upset White:

> It is always sobering to encounter the intellectual idealists at work, for they seem to live in a realm of their own, making their plans for the world in much the same way that any common tyrant does. The conversation today reminded me a little of the early New Deal period when Wallace was talking about one God and one king—and it all seems so far removed from the people, who are all full of tiny faults and virtues and whose name is Schmalz and Henderson.[10]

At the end of the two-day conference Andy wrote Katharine that "the nervous strain of the preliminary rounds was too much for [his] stomach," and "all the old dizziness and vapors returned to plague" him.[11]

From Washington White went to New York and settled in at the Hotel New Weston with a briefcase stuffed with "thousands of untranscribed notes—the kind of thing you scribble on your program in a dark theatre." He dreaded the job ahead of him because it was so demanding and uncongenial. His work had to "suit the President and the Supreme Court Justices and Mr. Churchill," it had to "explain to a great many young men why they are about to get stuck in the stomach," and it had to "reconcile Max Lerner with Felix Frankfurter and [himself] with God." He knew he was a good rewrite man, but this job would tax the most skillful professional; he would have to patch together four little essays on abstractions, by four very different writers. He wrote Katharine from New York about his chief problems:

> I haven't written a word on this, largely because of the way MacLeish arranged the whole thing. I always write a thing first and think about it afterward, which is not a bad procedure, because the easiest way to have consecutive thoughts is to start putting them down. But with this project there have been mountains and oceans of talk, and dozens of people and shades of opinion. The manuscripts turned in by the experts are pretty forbidding and dreary.

Only White's sense of duty kept him at this "very sobering assignment," and he approached it with caution:

> It is dangerous to get playing with words on the very highest of planes, because they become (unless you are careful) like checkers men and eventually take charge. But I am determined that there will be no pretty writing, and an absolute minimum of statements which I do not fully understand myself.[12]

White completed the job in a little over three weeks. The document reads like the work of White, or at least has some of the virtues of White's writing. It does not say more than it should, and its simple eloquence makes its argument persuasive. MacLeish and everyone else were pleased with it. Whatever White thought of the results, the experience helped him decide not to try henceforth to contribute his services to a bureau, in Washington or anywhere else.

A month after he finished *The Four Freedoms*, White proposed in a *New Yorker* "Comment" that the various information bureaus in Washington be unified and that the news commentator Elmer Davis be put in charge of the new central bureau.[13] The idea was taken up by several influential people, and within a few months Davis was appointed director of a new agency called the Office of War Information. Three months later, when White responded to a cry for help from Ross by writing another paragraph of "Comment," Ross replied by saying, "It saved our life," and by renewing his effort to get White to agree to write "Notes and Comment" every week. In fact, he made White a tangible, concrete proposition: that White take over the subject of the war in "Notes and Comment." He argued shrewdly that by contributing to the column White would be doing something important for the war effort—something a lot more important than writing for MacLeish. "If opportunity ever cried for a man," Ross said, it was crying for him. White himself had built the prestige of "Notes and Comment," Ross pointed out, and White should take advantage of that prestige and of the magazine's large readership: "The world sees it, if we run it, and sees it quick." Ross was using the right arguments.[14]

White replied that in one respect he would like to cover the war for *The New Yorker* because it furnished "a more immediate outlet" than his monthly column, which was published seven weeks after he had written it. But he did not see how he could write weekly, up-to-the-minute comment on the news so far away from the editorial offices of the magazine. And there was another reason why he could not accept the offer.

> I think the comment page, as presently managed, is discouraging for a writer.... I believe that an editorial page should be one of two things: either

a signed page, for which one man would take the responsibility, or an unsigned page designed to express a sort of group opinion and which would be considered sufficiently important to warrant the managerial staff's meeting and discussing it each week, to give aid and counsel and ideas, and where opinions would generalize in group fashion. . . . When I write something I like to be out in the open—either as an individual or as the interpreter for an articulate group. . . .

Lately I haven't felt sympathetic enough toward the NYer to make me hot to produce anything. Sometimes it says things that annoy me—usually not because of what they are but because of the way they are said. And other times it fails to say things that seem to need saying. The war is so damn near that it is no longer possible to use printer's ink in place of blood in a man's circulatory system, and Tilley's hat and butterfly return to plague us all. I couldn't bounce off a paragraph a week on the subject of the war, full of "we's" and "us's," when I wasn't sure what key we were all trying to play in.

Writing anything at all is a hell of a chore for me, closely related to acid indigestion, and I take it seriously enough so that I don't want to maneuver myself into any literary stance which is as indistinct and badly defined as comment-writing, because I know it would make me quite sick, and probably my readers, too. Harper's isn't as much fun, and I sometimes feel like a stranger and lonely, but at least I seem to know who is writing and it isn't Jack Frost.

Thanks again for the offer, which I set store by.

White[15]

Three months later, however, White told Ross that he "intended" to write at least one paragraph a week for "Notes and Comment." Ross called the news the best he (and "the office") had heard in weeks. White had no idea, he wrote, how important his decision was for *The New Yorker.* A seventeen-year test had established the fact that there was "only one White." If Ross could do anything at all to facilitate White's contributing, would White please let him know.[16]

It was good news to Katharine, as well. She knew that Ross had not exaggerated the plight of the magazine, and that even a little White would make a difference. She hoped, we may guess, that Andy's decision to contribute regularly might lead, as it did, to a decision to move back to New York. For some time she had been torn between a desire to be back there at her office desk and a desire to be where Andy wanted to be. A year earlier, in a letter he wrote her during a brief stay in New York, Andy had referred to the "baleful tension that has beset us all year," and in February, while Andy was working on "The Four Freedoms" in a hotel room in New York and she was reading "two long manuscripts from Gypsy Rose Lee and editing a Strachey," Katharine wrote Andy that she wished they had taken a furnished flat in New York for part of the winter so that she and Andy could both have done their work in offices *The New Yorker* had always made available to them. She wished there were at least a defense factory near Brooklin, she said, where she could help make tanks or planes for Russia, which was then fighting for its life against the German onslaught. She was sick of zero weather, leaking pipes, blown fuses, and three dogs, and she was depressed by the news of the war ("The Pacific war seems about lost to me in my present mood"). She was convinced that she could make her greatest contribution to the war effort by working again full-time for *The New Yorker*. [17]

Not for almost a year, however, was Katherine able to return to her *New Yorker* office and to full-time work. During the winter of 1942–43 the Whites stayed in Maine, where Andy wrote both "One Man's Meat" and his weekly contribution to "Notes and Comment." It was their last winter in Maine until they moved back permanently in 1957.

For the first six months after White resumed writing editorials for *The New Yorker,* his comments were not predominantly on the war, though some dealt with aspects of it. In his most forthright piece he rebuked *Life* magazine for an editorial that had undertaken to tell the English people what they would have to do if they wanted the American people to come to their aid:

> *Life* magazine set out last week to speak for the American people in an open letter to the people of England. This week *The New Yorker* would like to remind the people of England that there are quite a few Americans (an estimated 134,000,000) for whom *Life* does not speak. Among that happy company is ourself. Our experience in publishing has convinced us that no magazine, no matter how elated with a moral idea, can speak with any assurance or accuracy for a large group of people. It can mumble a bit, and enjoy a momentary glow of power and prescience, but next day the letters flow in, clearly indicating that the people have in no sense been spoken for. Certainly there must have been many people besides us in America last week who resented *Life*'s sudden assumption of the role of spokesman and who thought its letter was patronizing and peremptory. "We Americans are a strange people," wrote the editors of *Life,* whirling rapidly in their chairs. "But you can't understand us at all unless you realize how much *principles* mean to us." We cringe when we think of the unprincipled multitudes in England trying to swallow that one.
>
> In addition to implying that Americans were persons of stronger principles than Englishmen, the editorial seemed to imply that unless England did pretty much as the editors of *Life* prescribed, she would find us missing from her strategy, which was an irresponsible and mischievous suggestion. It also implied that England was alone to blame for the lack of a second front. For a long while we have suffered rather patiently under the strain of *Life*'s posses-

sive attitude about this country—its trick of taking a couple of snapshots of somebody somewhere and announcing that "This is America." We have never thought it was America and do not think so now. Neither do we think that the open letter the editors wrote is a letter which Americans would have written to Englishmen. Our guess is such a letter would be somewhat less bumptious, and a whole lot friendlier.[18]

That particular piece was written on a Sunday afternoon in Maine, in immediate response to reading the *Life* editorial, and was sent by telegraph from Blue Hill in time to get it to the composing room early Monday morning for the issue that would be on the newsstands three days later. *The New Yorker* was a better medium than *Harper's* for a writer who had been a journalist before he became an essayist. It was also read by more Englishmen than either *Harper's* or *Life.* The piece produced a flood of congratulatory mail.

Like most employers at the time, Ross began to suffer from loss of manpower, and at one point he wrote the Whites that he was thinking of publishing only biweekly. That news increased the pressure on Andy and Katharine to return to New York and to full-time work for *The New Yorker,* but it was not until March 1943 that Andy decided to give up "One Man's Meat," and that he and Katharine decided together to devote themselves to helping Ross get out his magazine. They were both temporarily in New York when they made these decisions, and were both severely depressed. Katharine was in a hospital recovering from a hysterectomy, and Andy was under the care of a new doctor, who had prescribed strychnine to treat his symptoms of depression. They returned to Maine for the summer, but for the next three winters they were to live in furnished apartments in New York.

In his letter of resignation to *Harper's*, written on March 13, 1943, while he was "living in a hotel during alterations in [his] character,"[19] Andy explained his reasons for taking this step in the following way:

> The truth is I have had great difficulty, all along, writing essays of this sort. . . . I feel a peculiar disappointment, almost a defeat, in this. . . . It ought to be the most congenial job in the world for me, and the fault is entirely mine if it isn't. . . . For the present, I have farm work and editorial work enough to keep me busy if not solvent, and I am hoping that my health (which has been rather sketchy lately) will improve by my cutting out this regular chore.[20]

White did not tell his *Harper's* editor that he was thinking of pouring all his energies into "covering the war" for *The New Yorker,* nor that he planned to write editorials advocating world government. To his *Harper's* readers he revealed somewhat more. In his last column for the magazine, written only a few days before he mailed his letter of resignation, he spoke to them about the thoughts that he now felt the need to translate into action. He told them of his "worry about the planet's pantry after this meal of war," of his concern about how, when, and where it could be replenished; and, after leading them through scenes resembling a wasteland, he finally arrived at his ideas and plans for "a new and higher level of government," a union of nations. He presented his material, however, in such elliptical ways that his readers might not have been able to grasp its meaning. The piece took the form of a monologue—set in Central Park —in which the speaker digressed in various directions, all seemingly unrelated to his theme.[21]

This curiously undisciplined exercise in indirection was laced with such favorite images of White's as ducks, babies, young women, young lovers, birds, mammals, an ice-covered pond, and a zoo. In its failure as a work of art it was an ominous opening to White's career as a political thinker. It expressed the sources of his faith, but it failed to reveal how they were related to the staggering reality of nationalism and other causes of war.

When Ross heard that White had resigned from *Harper's,* he asked him to take on full responsibility for "Notes and Comment." He had, he said, no new arguments, but the moment was "golden," and he hoped for the sake of all concerned, including the people of the United States, that White would seize it. Ross was sure, of course, that White would be more useful at *The New Yorker* than at any place else he might choose.[22]

A few days later, trying not to sound aggressive and thereby scare White away, Ross added that he was willing to listen to any proposal White might make, as "an old-time associate and contributor, and common "stockholder." Perhaps White would prefer the freedom of the old agreement, Ross said, but if White would agree to write, say, a minimum of four hundred words of "Comment" for, say, a minimum number of forty weeks a year, the magazine would pay him not only twenty-five cents a word but an additional twenty percent bonus at the end of year, or about five thousand dollars annually for "Comment" alone. (The annual bonus was warranted, Ross said, because of the savings to the office in expense, work, and apprehension that White's return would effect.) He would be obliged, he said, if White would earnestly consider his proposal; and he concluded by saying, "Please accept the assurance of my admiration for the piece you sent in this week, and to hell with Harper's magazine."[23]

The day after Ross mailed what he called his "big scheme," he began to worry about the way White might react to such a specific proposal, and he dashed off a memo saying that White should get the annual bonus no matter how much he wrote. God knew that White was worth a premium on anything from twenty-seven words up, regardless. Ross was not trying to "jam" White—he was "just trying to make a step forward."[24] When White sent him in reply a "statement of intention" to write about four hundred words a week for about forty weeks a year, Ross was "greatly cheered," and, to allay White's fear that other writers or staff members at *The New Yorker* might be treated inequitably, Ross declared his intention to demand of Fleischmann that all contributors be paid a dividend at the end of the year. A few weeks later, after White had agreed in principle to Ross's terms, Ross decided to raise the bonus to 40 percent, which meant that if White wrote a minimum of four hundred words a week he would be paid thirty-five cents for every one of his words that the magazine printed.[25]

White's statement of intention enabled Ross to face the future with more confidence, but not much more. So many staff members had left or were about to leave for the armed services that he did not know how he was going to get out the magazine. He dared ask for more: would White come to New York for the winter? He could have Ross's house in Connecticut if he liked. It would be "simply ducky, as a social as well as a business matter."[26] A month later, when he heard that *Reader's Digest* was trying to get White to fill the space left vacant by the death of Alexander Woollcott, Ross dashed off another memo: "You can have any damned thing you want around this place."[27] White was pleased with Ross's good financial offer but what pleased him most was simply regaining his old forum, the opening page of *The New Yorker*.

White's decision to give up writing monthly essays for Harper's and to resume writing weekly editorials for *The New Yorker* was one of the most critical in his professional career. With *One Man's Meat*, he had established his reputation as a man of letters. When he decided to go back to "Notes and Comment," he chose to give up the freedom to write the kind of meditative essays that had persuaded Irwin Edman that White was America's "finest and perhaps its only essayist." It would be five years before White would recover the leisure and confidence he needed for writing anything as substantial as the best of the essays in *One Man's Meat*. And these were years in the prime of his life. But his was not the only career interrupted by the war, and it was the war that made inevitable his return to work as a writer of editorials. For he had decided that the best place for him to publish what he wanted to write was not in a monthly essay in *Harper's* but in weekly editorial paragraphs in the *The New Yorker*, where his observations could be both reflective and timely—and widely read. He hoped to use this platform not only "to cover the war" but to draw attention to a subject that had caught his imagination some years before and that had increasingly preoccupied him since: the need for a world government, or—as he later called it—a supranational government to which all nations would surrender their individual sovereignty, and under which they would unite. He believed that such a government was the only possible means to prevent the recurrence of war. So convinced was he of the need for world government and of the need to consider seriously how it might be achieved that he suppressed his characteristic skepticism towards grand schemes and was willing to act on faith, willing even to make himself a spokesman for this kind of new world order.

It was a departure for him. Trying to "save the world," advocating a "cause," and assuming the role of a "thinker" did not come naturally to him; he knew he was ill-prepared for such undertakings, and he was apprehensive. But as a writer he had always written about what interested him most at the moment, and he was not about to change his ways in this respect. What interested him now was "government on a higher level."

DURING THE PREVIOUS two years, in "One Man's Meat," White had occasionally written about world government, but it was not until after he began to write full-time again for *The New Yorker* in 1943 that he made a concerted effort to persuade readers to consider the arguments in its favor. Beginning with the issue for April 10, 1943, and continuing for the next four years, nearly one-third of White's weekly "Notes and Comment" included at least one paragraph on the subject.

White had talked about it for the first time in his *Harper's* column written three days after Pearl Harbor. There he had stated his thesis in a simple and personal way: we must somehow find a way to make us love the world more than we love our country.

The passionate love of Americans for their America will have a lot to do with winning the war. It is an odd thing though: the very patriotism on which we now rely is the thing that must eventually be in part relinquished if the world is ever to find a lasting peace and an end to these butcheries.

To hold America in one's thoughts is like holding a love letter in one's hand —it has so special a meaning. Since I started writing this column snow has begun falling again; I sit in my room watching the re–enactment of this stagy old phenomenon outside the window. For this picture, for this privilege, this cameo of New England with snow falling, I would give everything. Yet all the time I know that this very loyalty, this feeling of being part of a special place, this respect for one's native scene—I know that such emotions have had a big part in the world's wars. Who is there big enough to love the whole planet? We must find such people for the next society.[28]

In his *New Yorker* editorials White advanced no new arguments in favor of world government, nor did he contribute any new ideas about how to solve the problems involved in its implementation. He simply gave eloquent expression to the aspirations of all who hoped against hope that the dream of a world without devastating wars could be realized. And he kept reminding his readers of the futility of settling for anything less than supranational law enforced by a supranational government. Anything less would prove as ineffectual as the former League of Nations.

As an undergraduate he had taken an active interest in the national debate on whether, and under what conditions, America should join the League of Nations, and he had come to doubt that the League as finally constituted would prove capable of preventing future wars. Now, twenty years later, he was, like everyone else, convinced that the world needed some better peacekeeping organization than the old League, and he found himself in sympathy with the ideas advanced by Clarence Streit, whose book *Union Now* had proposed, in 1938, the immediate formation of a union of the democracies of the North Atlantic, which might eventually incorporate other nations and might finally grow into a universal world government. White's own ideas on the subject derived mainly from Streit.

White was aware of the obstacles that stood in the way of persuading nations to cede even part of their sovereignty to a supranational government, but he believed in the possibility that the power of a great dream, what he called "today's fantasy," might overcome these obstacles and become tomorrow's reality. The spirit and power of nationalism might not prove to be insuperable. Perhaps a passionate devotion to our earth could become more compelling than a jealous love of our own turf. Among the people of the earth at that very moment there were many whose supreme loyalties transcended their patriotism:

> Although internationalism often seems hopelessly distant or impractical, there is one rather encouraging sign in the sky. We have, lately, at least one large new group of people to whom the planet *does* come first. I mean scientists. Science, however undiscriminating it has seemed in the bestowal of its gifts, has no disturbing club affiliations. It eschews nationality. It is preoccupied with an atom, not an atoll.

Then, in a passage reminiscent of Thoreau, White went on to say:

> Before you can be an internationalist you have first to be a naturalist and feel the ground under you making a whole circle. It is easier for a man to be loyal to his club than to his planet; the by-laws are shorter, and he is personally

acquainted with the other members. A club, moreover, or a nation, has a most attractive offer to make: it offers the right to be exclusive. There are not many of us who are physically constituted to resist this strange delight, this nourishing privilege. It is at the bottom of all fraternities, societies, orders. It is at the bottom of most trouble. The planet holds out no such inducement. The planet is everybody's. All it offers is the grass, the sky, the water, and the ineluctable dream of peace and fruition.[29]

Inherently White was more an ecologist than a political scientist, and his concept of the universe was more geocentric than anthropocentric.

As a first practical step towards the formation of a world government, White's *New Yorker* editorials called for a meeting of the representatives of the twenty-six allied nations. "The essence of the spirit of community is a willingness to meet, whether in a grange hall, a town hall, a marble hall, or a hall bedroom." Seeing no possible excuse for delaying any longer "the corporeality of the U.N. of W.," White proposed that such a meeting, to be known as "Meeting Number One," be called at once.[30]

And in the 1943 Christmas issue of *The New Yorker*, in the season for promises of peace, he recounted to his readers an extraordinary dream he recently had dreamed: "After the third war was over . . . there was no more than a handful of people alive, and the earth was in ruins and the ruins were horrible to behold." In his dream the few surviving people sent representatives from their eighty-three countries "to talk over their problems and to make a lasting peace, which is the customary thing to make after a long, exhausting war." To the meeting all but one of the representatives brought the flags of their nations. The exception was the delegate from China (at that time not yet a Communist country), who brought (in a shoebox), instead of a flag, a flower that "looked very much like an iris." It was a wild flag *(Iris tectorum)*. China had adopted it because it was "a convenient and universal device and very beautiful and grows everywhere in the moist places of the earth for all to observe and wonder at." The delegate proposed that "all countries adopt it, so that it will be impossible for us to insult each other's flag." There were objections. When one delegate said that he did not "see how a strong foreign policy [could] be built around a wild flag which is the same for everybody," the Chinese replied that that was one of its virtues; and when another feared that "the wild flag, one for all, [would] prove an unpopular idea," the sponsor pointed out that now, with only a few hundred people left alive on earth, the word *unpopular* had lost most of its meaning. "At this juncture we might conceivably act in a sensible, rather than a popular, manner," the delegate from China suggested. "The next day," White concluded, "the convention broke up and the delegates returned to their homes marveling at what they had accomplished."[31]

Not until the fall of 1944, however, did "Meeting Number One" (the Dumbarton Oaks conference) take place; and when it did, it was hardly the kind of meeting White had hoped for. Although it had been called to draw up plans for a new international peacekeeping organization, it was attended by the representatives of only the Big Four powers (the U.S., the U.K., the U.S.S.R., and China), no one else having been invited.

Its proceedings, moreover, were disheartening. From the very first, ominous disagreements appeared between the U.S. and the U.K. on one side and the U.S.S.R on the other—the most ominous of which concerned a proposal to extend to each of the Big Four the power to veto the decisions, and thereby to override the collective will, of all the other members of the organization. The conference ended in a stalemate. A decision on the "veto problem" was postponed. But White said at once that if the proposal were adopted, it would defeat the purpose of the organization. During the months leading up to the United Nations Conference in San Francisco in May 1945, at which the Charter of the United Nations was finally to be drafted, White continued to comment on the very folly of the concept of a veto power, as well as on the folly of leading the people of the world to believe that without a legally-based world government any universal bill of "human rights" could be more than a pious expression of vague aspiration. Still he tried to maintain the hope that the delegates to the Conference might "manage to bring the United Nations out of the bag, full blown, with constitutional authority and a federal structure having popular meaning, popular backing, and an overall authority greater than the authority of any one member or any combination of members."[32]

In April 1945 *The New Yorker* sent White as its accredited correspondent to the San Francisco Conference, which was to give birth to the new United Nations. He was delighted at the prospect. His accounts of the proceedings would appear under the heading of "A Reporter at Large." A day or two before he left New York for San Francisco, White wrote *The New Yorker*'s editorial on the death of President Roosevelt, which had occurred on April 12. In it he said:

> The President was always a lover of strategy: he even died strategically, as though he had chosen the right moment to inherit the great legacy of light that Death leaves to the great. He will arrive in San Francisco quite on schedule, and in hundredfold capacity, to inspire the nations that he named United. . . . The guns that spoke in the Hudson Valley last Sunday morning,

and Fala's sharp answering bark, were the first salvo of his new fight—for freedom, human rights, peace, and a world under law.[33]

White's reports from San Francisco were written in the "Talk of the Town" style he had helped create twenty years earlier. They included humorous or ironic details that carried the rhetorical force of understatement. Edward Stettinius, the U.S. Secretary of State, was ensconced in a "ten-room suite complete with mosaic baths and a library of books including *Forever Amber* and [Wendell Willkie's] *One World.*" But White also allowed himself to use a solemn tone, as in the concluding sentences of his first report:

> The rich and ribald spectacle of these pre-Conference hours neither conceals nor removes the sense of destiny and the sense of obligation which haunt the citadel. The accusing eye of millions of homesick young soldiers, the hungry gaze of millions of famished children, are trained on this hill tonight. Theirs is a fixed stare, which no one can evade. It waits for every delegate in the bottom of his glass.[34]

To be sure, while the "architectural apprentices" were looking at "a neat and precise blueprint labeled the Future,"[35] Churchill and Truman, as we now know, were looking at a map of Europe showing how far west Stalin had managed to move the Soviet frontiers; and today, in retrospect, it is easy to wonder at the naïveté of the planners and their supporters, who hoped that mankind could devise the means to prevent future wars. On the other hand, it is equally easy to wonder at the prescience of a dreamer who, before the advent of nuclear weapons, envisioned a destroyed earth, on which its few survivors might no longer be so concerned with maintaining their national flags as with assuring their individual survival.

For over a year after the birth of the United Nations, White continued to report or to comment on events in its young life: its meeting in London; its search for a home in the U.S.; its meetings in temporary quarters at Hunter College, in the Bronx; its trouble over the question of admitting Argentina; and its weakness in dealing with an Iranian crisis. And he continued to write paragraphs on other topics of international concern: the Nuremberg Trials, the Bikini atom bomb test, and the absurdity of protesting against Russia's spying ("A nation that doesn't spy today is not giving its people an even break").[36]

In the early spring of 1946, Paul Brooks, an editor at Houghton Mifflin, proposed to publish a collection of White's *New Yorker* editorials on world government. White's initial response was to say no, partly because he was always uneasy about claiming authorship of pieces that had appeared anonymously in "Notes and Comment," and partly because he was a little fearful. As he wrote his brother Stanley, to make a "debut as a *Thinker*" in these days was like "stepping up on the guillotine platform wearing a faint smile."[37] But his editorials had elicited such praise from a wide range of readers—civilians and soldiers, politicians, judges, and international lawyers—that *The New Yorker* had already reprinted a selection of them in an anonymous twenty page pamphlet entitled *World Government and Peace: Selected Notes and Comment, 1943–45*, to be distributed to advertisers as a promotional device and, while the supply lasted, to others who requested copies.[38] Ross had, in fact, encouraged White from the very beginning of his editorial campaign in support of world government. White's paragraphs were, he had said, "excellent leadership-of-thought stuff," and though he himself was convinced that after the war the world would return to the status quo, he nevertheless admired Andy's energy and his capacity for hope for "better international arrangements." Moreover, he argued, though the future would confirm the soundness of his own pessimism, White's readers were currently hearing a "true doctrine," and, in the future, historians would find White's pieces an important part of the record of the period.[39]

But White continued to have qualms about expressing his personal opinions through the mask of the magazine. When, in 1944, he had said he was afraid he was turning *The New Yorker* into a "crank publication," Ross had tried at once to set his mind at ease. Probably the magazine *should* be cranky, if the crankiness was sound—and there was no question that White was sound. Besides, even if the people of the world did not finally get "a new set-up," they were for the present getting "a very remarkable line of writing and thinking." Ross thought that White's pieces were the most eloquent he had ever written and, what was more, Ross believed that if White was able to move him, who had been a cynic about such matters ever since 1922, he must be moving many others as well. In fact, Ross felt sure that White was having some influence on the delegates who were soon to attend the Dunbarton Oaks conference. He pointed out that even President Roosevelt had released the text of the proposals to be discussed at the conference, after White had suggested that they be published so that the people of the world could formulate their opinions. Anyway, Ross concluded, White had made the "Notes and Comment" page what it was, and it was White's to use as he wished. That, Ross had said, was not only the right way to look at the matter but "very sound business."[40]

So with Ross's blessing White agreed to the publication of a collection of his editorials on the subject of world government, in a book to be called

The Wild Flag and to be published in the fall of 1946. In its Preface White thanked Ross in these words:

> Most publications, I think, make rather hard demands on their editorial writers, asking them to be consistent and sensible. *The New Yorker* has never suggested anything of the kind, and thus has greatly eased a writer's burden —for it is easier to say what you think if you don't feel obliged to follow a green arrow. *The New Yorker* is both aloof and friendly toward its opinionated contributors, and I am grateful for this.

In the remainder of the Preface, White acknowledged the possibility that to discuss world government when no means existed of establishing it might be not only futile but dangerous, and explained why he thought that a theoretical discussion of the subject was nevertheless justifiable. He concluded with this paragraph:

> These editorials will be too purely theoretical for the practicing statesman, who is faced with the grim job of operating with equipment at hand, and too sweetly reasonable for the skeptic, who knows what an unpredictable customer the human being is. (A worker in the next stall has just informed me that world government is impractical because "there are too many Orientals.") But theory and sweet reason are all right in their place; and if these topical paragraphs add an ounce to the long-continuing discussion of nationalism, and throw even as much as a flashlight's gleam on the wild flag which our children, and their children, must learn to know and love, I am satisfied.[41]

The Wild Flag had an advance sale of fifteen thousand copies, including an order of three thousand from *The New Yorker*. Andy inscribed Katharine's copy with these words:

> Here is the flag that took my eye,
> Rattled my head unmercifully,
> Who will be here when it passes by?
> Not you and I, not you and I.
> When all the other bright flags are done,
> This will catch color from the sun.

The book was treated with respect by most reviewers and with applause by some, but Isaac Rosenfeld, in *The Nation,* took the occasion of its appearance to attack *The New Yorker*'s newly found conscience, "which where the middle class is concerned is best defined as the fear of dispossession." The essence of his contempt for the book was expressed in one paragraph:

We have world government praised and national sovereignty denounced on every page, but nothing about actual politics. It is *bon ton* to mention fascism and racism and come out against them. But capitalism, imperialism, world markets, the profit system, exploitation, revolution, socialism—these words have a sweaty air; they suggest crowded downtown East Side meeting halls with their folding chairs and smoke in the dingy room, the stain in the armpits of the excited speaker. . . . A fundamental revision of society, a practical consideration of the revolutionary measures necessary to the establishment of world government are in bad taste—and small wonder. The bourgeoisie will never give up its tone without a struggle.[42]

The crux of Rosenfeld's argument was the old paradox that one who takes no position has taken a position. "There is no such thing as urbanity without partisanship," Rosenfeld had said, and he had reproached *The New Yorker* for being partisan to the middle-class values of capitalism. Yet White knew that when he had advocated the adoption of a supranational government, he had done so not in order to make the world safe for capitalism, but in the hope of preserving its peace; and that when he had suggested that such a government be arrived at by way of mutual consent rather than by "revolutionary measures," he had done so not because he thought the latter "in bad taste" but because he believed that if the world were united under a red flag, instead of a wild flag, the plight of the individual would not be mitigated but only intensified.

In the anniversary issue of *The New Yorker* in 1945 White had acknowledged the obvious change that had taken place in the tone of "Notes and Comment" within the last years:

Twenty years ago this week, The New Yorker put out its first issue. Our intentions were innocent and our foresight dim. We armed ourself with a feather for tickling a few chins, and now, twenty years later, we find ourself gingerly holding a glass tube for transfusing blood. Perhaps we should have expected this sort of adventure, but we feel like a man who left his house to go to a Punch-and-Judy show and, by some error in direction, wandered into "Hamlet." . . .

We have been in a good position to observe the effect on writers and artists of war and trouble. Many times we have wanted to fold the magazine up; it is hard to remain seated on the low hummocks of satire and humor in the midst of grim events. A satirist at breakfast may get a firm grip on his day's work from the front page of his newspaper, only to have the whole thing drop out from under him when his eye reaches the casualty list. He then spends the remainder of the day avoiding a typewriter. In wartime the writer almost inevitably becomes propagandist and advocate, and although he may not realize it, he is operating against the grain, for the deepest instinct of a creative person is not to promote the world's cause but to keep the minutes of his own meeting. When this instinct is disturbed, deep emotional and functional changes take place in writers and scare the daylights out of editors, who still face the same old problem of getting out the next issue.[43]

White preferred the uptown meetings of the United Nations to Rosenfeld's "crowded downtown East Side meeting halls," it is true. But as he said in this apologia, what he really wanted to do was "to keep the minutes of his own meeting"; and in becoming a "propagandist and an advocate," in choosing to "promote the world's cause," he had violated his "deepest instinct," with consequences that "scared the daylights" out of him.

On the dust jacket of *The Wild Flag* there was a caveat, probably written, certainly approved, by the author:

> Mr. White does not regard himself as a Thinker and says he feels ill-at-ease writing editorials on massive themes. He regards himself as a clown of average ability whose signals got crossed and who found himself out on the wire with the Wallendas.

But the facetiousness of the disclaimer scarcely concealed the already painful sense of embarrassment and frustration with which his dream of world government had left him. He never forgot it. In 1960, when the American Academy of Arts and Letters awarded him its Gold Medal, he wrote an acceptance speech to be read at the ceremony, in which he expressed doubt about being a man of letters, hesitation about accepting an award for "literary merit," and perhaps some regret over the injuries he had sustained while bearing his wild flag:

> If you are willing, I think I can accept one for bravery. Once, many years ago, while working for an indulgent weekly, I spent a long period wrestling with a subject that was already too big for me. Some of the injuries I sustained in that encounter are, I am afraid, permanent; they account for my being absent today. The subject—the need for government on a higher level—is even livelier and more urgent than ever, and I hope writers and artists will work hard to illuminate it, against the day when statesmen will give it form.[44]

Ten years later, however, in response to an interviewer's request for his views about "the writer's commitment to politics, international affairs," White expressed his creed as a writer with special reference to his advocacy of supranationalism. He drew a fine but clear line between writing because you feel obliged to try to change your readers' opinions and writing because you feel obliged simply to write well about what you believe:

A writer should concern himself with whatever absorbs his fancy, stirs his heart, and unlimbers his typewriter. I feel no obligation to deal with politics. I do feel a responsibility to society because of going into print: a writer has the duty to be good, not lousy; true, not false; lively, not dull; accurate, not full of error. He should tend to lift people up, not lower them down. Writers do not merely reflect and interpret life, they inform and shape life.

For a number of years, I was thinking almost continuously about the needless chaos and the cruelty of a world that is essentially parochial, composed of more than a hundred parishes, or nations, each spying on the others, each plotting against the others, each concerned almost solely with its own bailiwick and its own stunt. I wrote some pieces about world government, or "supranational" government. I didn't do it from any sense of commitment, I did it because it was what I felt like writing. Today, although I seldom discuss the theme, I am as convinced as I ever was that our only chance of achieving an orderly world is by constructing a governed world. I regard disarmament as a myth, diplomacy as a necessary evil under present conditions, and absolute sovereignty as something to outgrow.[45]

The number of White's readers increased enormously during the period from 1938 to 1946. The circulation of *Harper's Magazine* averaged 106,000 in 1942, and that of *The New Yorker* was 276,000 in 1946. In 1945 the Armed Services Editions of *A Subtreasury of American Humor, Quo Vadimus?,* and *One Man's Meat* were available to hundreds of thousands of servicemen around the world. In 1945 *The New Yorker* was published in a special edition for the armed services. In it White was being read by numberless soldiers, sailors, airmen, and marines all over the globe— hundreds of whom wrote him letters thanking him or asking his opinion about such things as the prospects for a lasting peace.

After the war many honors were bestowed on White. In 1945, for *One Man's Meat,* he was awarded the Limited Editions Club's Gold Medal, given every three years to the American author of a book considered most likely to attain the stature of a classic. In 1946 the Newspaper Guild awarded its Page One Award to *The New Yorker* "for general editorial excellence . . . especially as exemplified in . . . the editorials of E. B. White." He accepted the awards, but he declined the invitations to attend the ceremonies at which the awards were made. In the same year he was offered membership in the National Institute of Arts and Letters, but declined the offer, saying that he felt it was too early in his life to join an institute of letters because in his "present condition" he could "barely keep up with letters themselves."[46]

CHAPTER XIII

Stuart Little

1 9 4 4 — 1 9 4 5

"A person who is looking for something doesn't travel very fast."

WHEN HE QUIT "ONE MAN'S MEAT" IN THE SPRING of 1943, White complained of "sketchy health" and a lifeless feeling. Katharine had just undergone a hysterectomy. Joe was about to leave home for boarding school. White had exhausted the possibilities of the *Harper's* medium and was dissatisfied with his writing. He was about to return to his job as an editorial writer and, with some misgivings, to take up a cause—to try "to tidy up a world" that he "knew very little about." He had decided, or was about to decide, to return to winters in New York and to a desk at *The New Yorker*—a step backward, as he said to Ross. He had failed to produce the "original work" he had hoped to write. He hated to leave his lovely farm.

During the summer of 1943 he had a "nervous crack-up," but by October he was able to speak of it as if it were a thing of the past:

> I never realized nerves were so odd, but they are. They are the oddest part of the body, no exceptions. Doctors weren't much help, but I found that old phonograph records are miraculous. If you ever bust up from nerves, take frequent shower baths, drink dry sherry in small amounts, spend most of your time with hand tools at a bench, and play old records till there is no wax left in the grooves.[1]

In February 1944, while Katharine and Andy were living in the furnished apartment on East Thirty-fifth Street that *The New Yorker* had found them when they returned full-time to the staff, Andy wrote a poem that might have interested any psychiatrist alert enough to ask about the meaning of "mice in hiding." The following is a shortened version of it:

> Home is the place where the queer things are:
> Hope and compassion and objets d'art.
> Home is the strangest of common places,
> Drenched with the light of familiar faces.
> Home is the proving ground of sanity,
> Brick and ember, love and vanity,
> Paper and string and the carpet sweeper,
> And the still form of the late sleeper.
>
> Ever at home are the mice in hiding,
> Dust and trash, and the truth abiding.
> Dark is the secret of home's hall closet—
> Home's a disorderly safe deposit.
> Home is the part of our life that's arable,
> Home is a pledge, a plan, and a parable.
> Ever before us is home's immensity,
> Always within us its sheer intensity.[2]

In March White decided to see a doctor about his head, "as there seems to be a kite caught in the branches somewhere." He took "one of those neurological tests" and "passed it without extending" himself: "I never would have believed that someday my head would get overcharged, like a battery on a long drive." Back in Maine at the end of the month he felt much better, though the spells of "knocking" recurred. During the summer, troubled by "mice in the subconscious and spurs in the cervical spine," he several times consulted a Boston doctor who was a summer neighbor and friend. The doctor was interested in White's remark that his mind was full of mice, but he was at a loss to explain White's symptoms, physically or psychologically, and advised White to come to see him in Boston in the fall if the symptoms continued.[3]

In September, in very low spirits, White humorously expressed his sense of defeat in a letter to Gus Lobrano:

> My bad health is now more than a year old, and alternately angers and frightens me. I long ago got reconciled to not feeling good, but am still not reconciled to turning in a bad performance all the time, or no performance —it seems to be mostly that. My nerves are better than when you trundled me to Boston last fall, but something seems to have hold of me by the top of the spine and is giving me the double twist. The details are boring and unconvincing.

[Daise Terry, Katharine's secretary at *The New Yorker*,] is on the phone, trying to sell my wife a house in Turtle Bay, from the sound of things. They are yelling at each other—the loudest real estate transaction I have ever heard. It seems Dorothy Thompson owns the house and there's not a stick of furniture in it, not a stick. What the house needs, obviously, is a stick of furniture. Well, it was 1937 that I began fighting my way out of Turtle Bay, and it looks like I've lost. We'll be back if Terry's voice holds out and the gas furnace in the cellar really works. Remind me to get hold of a stick of furniture.[4]

But Katharine did not buy Dorothy Thompson's house, and the return to Turtle Bay was postponed for a year.

In October, when he went to see his doctor friend in Boston, he learned that he had "too many red cells" and heard, apparently for the first time, that his "head trouble" may have been caused by hyperventilation, a common psychosomatic phenomenon.[5] It was not news to White that his physical troubles were related to his state of mind, and his mind was not at the moment working very well. Instead of bats in the belfry, he had a mouse in his mind. In a poem called "Vermin" he wrote:

> The mouse of Thought infests my head,
> He knows my cupboard and the crumb.
>   Vermin! I despise vermin.
> I have no trap, no skill with traps,
> No bait, no hope, no cheese, no bread—
> I fumble with the task to no avail.
> I've seen him several times lately.
> He is too quick for me,
> I see only his tail.[6]

During the first week of November the Whites moved into a furnished apartment on West Eleventh Street. Andy was now only a block away from where he had been living when he married Katharine; he was back in the Village, in the heart of "the closest written page in the book of his life."[7] Within a week or two of settling in he wrote a happy, healthy poem:

VILLAGE REVISITED

(A cheerful lament in which truth, pain, and beauty are prominently mentioned, and in that order)

> In the days of my youth, in the days of my youth,
> I lay in West Twelfth Street, writhing with Truth.

I died in Jones Street, dallying with pain,
And flashed up Sixth Avenue, risen again.

In the terrible beautiful age of my prime,
I lacked for sweet linen but never for time.
The tree in the alley was potted in gold,
The girls on the buses would never grow old.

Last night with my love I returned to these haunts
To visit Pain's diggings and try for Truth's glance;
I was eager and ardent and waited as always
The answering click to my ring in the hallways,
But Truth hardly knew me, and Pain wasn't in
(It scarcely seemed possible Pain wasn't in).

Beauty recalled me. We bowed in the Square,
In the wonderful westerly Waverly air.
She had a new do, I observed, to her hair.[8]

In returning to the Village, White, like Antaeus, had touched his invigorating earth or, like Proust, had made contact with charged memories. He saw himself again in the terrible beautiful days of youth, devoted to his "interminable quest for the holy and unnameable grail, looking for it down every street and in every window and in every pair of eyes, following a star always obscured by mists."[9] In this auspicious circumstance it took him only eight weeks after he had settled into the Village to complete the manuscript of *Stuart Little,* his first children's book, which had had its beginnings many years earlier. White's own account of the writing of *Stuart Little* is as follows:

Stuart Little . . . came into being as the result of a journey I once made. In the late Twenties, I took a train to Virginia, got out, walked up and down in the Shenandoah Valley in the beautiful springtime, then returned to New York by rail. While asleep in an upper berth, I dreamed of a small character who had the features of a mouse, was nicely dressed, courageous, and questing. When I woke up, being a journalist and thankful for small favors, I made a few notes about this mouse-child—the only fictional figure ever to have honored and disturbed my sleep.

I had eighteen nephews and nieces. As a young bachelor-uncle I used to be asked now and then to tell a story. At this task I was terrible. Whole minutes would go by while I tried to think of something. In self-protection I decided to arm myself with a yarn or two, and for this I went straight to my dream-mouse. I named him Stuart and wrote a couple of episodes about his life. I kept these stories in a desk drawer and would pull them out and read them on demand. As the years went by, I added to the tale. . . .

In 1938, having decided to quit New York, I began tidying up what I called my "affairs." One of these was the Stuart Little adventures, now grown to perhaps a dozen episodes. At the suggestion of my wife, I carried them to a publisher (not Harper) and left them, to see whether they might be acceptable if expanded. The answer came back No, and I left for Maine, taking my rejected child along.

Seven years later, in the winter of 1944–45, I returned to New York to spend a few months in a furnished apartment and do some work for *The New Yorker.* I was almost sure I was about to die, my head felt so queer. With death at hand, I cast about to discover what I could do to ease the lot of my poor widow, and again my thoughts strayed to Stuart Little. My editor at Harper's, Eugene Saxton, had been urging me to finish the narrative, and I determined to put it off no longer. Mornings I sat at a top-floor window looking out into West 11th Street and there I completed the story. I turned it in to Harper and then took a train to San Francisco, to join Stettinius, Molotov, Lawrence Spivak, and that crowd, for the formation of the U.N. Another springtime, another journey! . . .[10]

To this account may be added other interesting facts about the history of *Stuart Little.* On his trip to the Shenandoah Valley in 1926, White had seen the school attended by Mary Osborn, with whom he had just fallen in love; and in the dream on the train back to New York, Stuart appeared to him "all complete, with his hat, his cane, and his brisk manner." In 1935 Katharine showed Clarence Day a typescript of some of the Stuart Little stories White had told his nieces and nephews, and Day told Katharine: "Don't let Andy neglect Stuart Little—it sounds like one of those *real* books that last." Neither Oxford University Press nor Viking, however, was encouraging when they returned the manuscript of these early episodes.[11]

In the late fall of 1938, while Katharine was at work on her annual pre-Christmas review of children's books for *The New Yorker,* Andy wrote a few paragraphs for "One Man's Meat" on the subject of children's stories and concluded, "It must be a lot of fun to write for children—reasonably easy work, perhaps even important work." In response to these published remarks Anne Carroll Moore, the children's librarian at the New York Public Library, urged him to write a children's book that would "make the library lions roar," and his editor at Harper asked for a copy of the Stuart stories that he had heard about from Katharine. By March 1939 Stuart was reported to have "taken everybody into camp" at Harper, and White's editor said they all looked forward to the remaining chapters soon. White replied that he hoped to finish the book in time for fall publication, and to Thurber he wrote that it was "about half done." But his hope of finishing was not fulfilled, and the book remained "about half done" until the winter of 1944–45, when White brought it quickly to completion. It went to press in 1945.[12]

Stuart Little is a story about the adventures of the youngest son of Mr. and Mrs. Frederick C. Little of New York City. He is only about two inches tall, looks "very much like a mouse in every way," and has the "pleasant, shy manners of a mouse." Except for his size and his appearance, however, he is clearly a human being living in a full-scale world. In some episodes he seems to be a boy, in others a young adolescent. At the end he is a very young man. But this is not a story about growing up.

In the opening chapters we delight in his ingenuity as he copes with the disadvantages of his size and succeeds in making virtues of them. He lets himself be let down a bathtub drain on a string to retrieve his mother's ring; he pushes Ping-Pong balls out from under radiators; he releases stuck piano hammers inside the baby-grand piano—even while his brother is playing the "Scarf Dance." What we notice most about his life at home is his independence: he gets up in the morning before anyone else, does his setting-up exercises, and in the family bathroom can turn on the light and the water and wash himself and brush his teeth before he dresses for the day's activities. Though his size makes him vulnerable to dangers that do not threaten his full-scale older brother, George, his life is not abnormally risky, and he asks no favors because of his size.

The plot of *Stuart Little* has three main parts. In the first part, Stuart sails a model sailboat to victory in a race on the pond in Central Park. In the second he falls in love with Margalo, "a pretty little hen-bird, brown, with a streak of yellow on her breast," whom Mrs. Little found near death on the window sill and brought into the house to recover. When Stuart is accidentally carried out to sea in a garbage scow, Margalo rescues him. Back home, and deeply in love with Margalo, he discovers that Snowball, the cat, plans to eat Margalo. He saves Margalo's life by shooting the cat in the ear with an arrow. But shortly afterward Margalo discovers that another cat plans to eat her, and "without saying anything to anybody" she flies away.

The last part of the story begins when Stuart decides to "run away from home without telling anybody, and go out into the world and look for Margalo," and while he's at it, seek his fortune. The story of the journey is interrupted by two self-contained episodes: a day Stuart spends as a substitute teacher at an elementary school, and a brief but frustrating encounter with a girl his own size whom he meets in a lovely New England town. The book ends as Stuart resumes his quest for Margalo, driving north in his car, confident that he is "headed in the right direction." It is this third part of the story, the journey and its episodic interruptions, that gives *Stuart Little* its significance and makes it a book that moves adults as well as children. It is the part that White wrote when he was forty-five, the part in which the fiction bears the most meaningful relation to his own experience and expresses some of his deepest convictions.

When Stuart decides to go in search of Margalo, he bundles his tooth-brush, his money, his soap, his comb and brush, a clean suit of underwear, his pocket compass, and a strand of his mother's hair in his biggest handker-chief, fastens the bundle to the end of a matchstick, slings it over his shoulder, and "with his gray felt hat cocked jauntily on one side of his head . . . [steals] softly out of the house." He simply leaves home. He doesn't run away from home with a child's desperation or desire to hurt his family. He avoids a useless argument by not telling anyone his plans. In a toy car borrowed from his dentist, Dr. Carey, he drives "through Central Park to One Hundred and Tenth Street, then over to the West Side Highway, then north to the Saw Mill River Parkway," and heads towards New England. On the second day of his journey, he drives into the town of Ames' Crossing, the scene of the last episode in the story. Of all Stuart's experi-ences, it is the most moving and the most meaningful.

White set the stage with unusual concern for the significance of place. "Ames' Crossing" is itself a meaningful name: it signifies an old town, once the site of a ferry landing on a river, and "Ames" is a good old New England name, suggesting New England values. With its country store and its quiet isolation, the town represents a kind of modern American arcadia:

> In the loveliest town of all, where the houses were white and high and the elm trees were green and higher than the houses, where the front yards were wide and pleasant and the back yards were bushy and worth finding out about, where the streets sloped down to the stream and the stream flowed quietly under the bridge, where the lawns ended in orchards and the orchards ended in fields and the fields ended in pastures and the pastures climbed the hill and disappeared over the top toward the wonderful wide sky, in this loveliest of all towns, Stuart stopped to get a drink of sarsaparilla.

The storekeeper tells Stuart that there's someone in this town he ought to meet, a girl named Harriet Ames, who is "just [his] size—maybe a trifle shorter, if anything." Then he tells Stuart enough about her to make her seem to be part of the perfection of Ames' Crossing. She is young, she is pretty, she is well dressed, and she comes from a good family:

"Her people, the Ameses, are rather prominent in this town. One of her ancestors used to be the ferryman here in Revolutionary days. He would carry anybody across the stream—he didn't care whether they were British soldiers or American soldiers, as long as they paid their fare. I guess he did pretty well. Anyway, the Ameses have always had plenty of money. They live in a big house with a lot of servants."

Of course, from some points of view the values implied in this history of the Ames family may seem false or offensive: Yankee shrewdness, prudence, concern for property—all very Protestant, capitalistic, bourgeois. But from the point of view of the son of Mr. and Mrs. Frederick C. Little, of Gramercy Park, New York—or from the point of view of anyone romantically attracted to an old ideal of American gentility or aristocracy—Harriet would seem to be, as far as we know, just about perfect for Stuart.

Stuart first says no thank you to the storekeeper—he must be on his way. But on second thought, at the edge of town, he changes his mind, turns back into town, and writes Miss Ames a letter inviting her to go canoeing with him:

"How about tomorrow afternoon toward sundown, when the petty annoyances of the day are behind us and the river seems to flow more quietly in the long shadows of the willows? These tranquil spring evenings are designed by special architects for the enjoyment of boatmen. I love the water, dear Miss Ames, and my canoe is like an old and trusted friend."

From the storekeeper Stuart buys a little souvenir birch-bark canoe with "Summer Memories" stamped on its side. And here his troubles begin. The canoe lacks paddles, and Stuart is forced to use in their stead cardboard spoons made for eating ice cream from paper cups: "I would hate to meet an American Indian while I had one of *these* things in my hand." It is a compromise that angers Stuart, the perfectionist. When he puts the canoe in the river, he finds that it leaks, and he has to plug the seams with spruce gum. Then he discovers that it is "a cranky little craft" and has to be ballasted with stones. But his dreams of Harriet and of a perfect union between the joys of canoeing and the joys of a perfect girl overcome his acute irritation with the imperfections of the canoe and the humiliating ice cream spoons for paddles. He makes a backrest and a pillow for Harriet and dreams of her trailing her fingers in the water. That evening, with everything set for the next evening's ride, Stuart sat by the river in his "camp."

In imagination he lived every minute of their evening together. They would paddle to a large water-lily pad upstream, and he would invite Harriet to step out on the pad and sit awhile. Stuart planned to wear his swimming trunks under his clothes so that he could dive off the lily pad into the cool stream. He would swim the crawl stroke, up and down and all around the lily pad, while Harriet watched, admiring his ability as a swimmer. (Stuart chewed the spruce gum very rapidly as he thought about this part of the episode.)

Stuart is nervous and anxious. Maybe the letter was not delivered ("it was an unusually small letter, of course"). Next morning the sky looks rainy—and Stuart has a headache. As the day goes on, Stuart's tension mounts. He spends the afternoon "trying on different shirts to see which looked best on him and combing his whiskers." When Harriet appears, her friendly, natural behavior contrasts with his own awkwardness. They walk together to the place on the river bank where Stuart has hidden the canoe. The canoe has disappeared.

> Stuart's heart sank. He felt like crying.
> "The canoe is gone," he groaned.

Stuart has never before expressed such uncontrolled feeling. Having to use ice cream spoons for paddles moved him mightily, but now he loses his self-control: he begins "racing wildly up and down the bank." When he finds the canoe, it is "a mess"; probably some "big boys" had been playing with it. The ballast, the cushion, the backrest are gone; the spruce gum has come out of the seams. What seems to madden Stuart most is that a long piece of coarse string has been tied to the canoe so tight that Stuart cannot get it off. Harriet is for fixing the canoe as well as possible and making the best of their bad luck. But making the best of it is what Stuart is simply not able to do: "It wouldn't be the same." Think of paddling along with that long string trailing in the water: "Did you ever see an Indian paddling along some quiet unspoiled river with a great big piece of rope dragging astern?" Harriet suggests that they pretend they are fishing: " 'I don't *want* to pretend I'm fishing,' cried Stuart, desperately. 'Besides, look at that mud! *Look* at it!' He was screaming now."

Harriet offers Stuart some peppermints she has brought along, but Stuart just shakes his head. It begins to rain. Harriet suggests that they go to her house, and after dinner he can take her to the dance at the Country Club: "It might cheer you up." But Stuart can't dance, and, besides, he plans to be on the road at daybreak. In their brief goodbye Stuart says he is sorry their "evening on the river had to end like this," and Harriet says, "So am I," and leaves Stuart "alone with his broken dreams and his damaged canoe."

Children as well as adults know about the power and treachery of dreams. And children as well as adults can see that Harriet is wiser than Stuart, and more capable of understanding and of love. Stuart is thinking of himself, not Harriet, and he has much to learn. Many young readers are at least vaguely aware of what it will cost Stuart to grow up. The truth of the story is the truth of myth—in various ways we keep living it and we keep reading artistic versions of it. Here, as in other classic children's stories, we may wonder how adult versions of the same story can be truer or more radiant.

Stuart's defeat, his frustration in this attempt to seize perfect beauty and truth, gives meaning to his quest for Margalo, the motif on which the book ends. Next morning, after filling the tank of his car with five drops of gasoline (he had the oil changed the day before), Stuart hits the road: "The sky was growing brighter, and along the river the mists of morning hung in the early light. The village was still asleep. Stuart's car purred along smoothly. Stuart felt refreshed and glad to be on the move again." At a fork in the road, where one road goes west and one north, Stuart stops to decide which to take. There, to his surprise, he discovers a telephone repairman with whom he falls into a conversation that quickly leads to the subject of birds, and to the direct question of whether the repairman has happened to see a bird that looks like Margalo. The repairman pulls out a pad and pencil and makes notes as Stuart describes her: "Brown, with a streak of yellow on her bosom." "She comes," Stuart says, "from fields once tall with wheat, from pastures deep in fern and thistle, she comes from vales of meadowsweet, and she loves to whistle." The repairman promises to keep an eye out for her.

At this point White turns the burden of the conclusion over to the repairman, whose experience gives him the authentic voice of adult sagacity. What he says is consistent with Stuart's intuitive but untested knowledge—or hunch. It is what the author wants to say. It is what makes clear the unity of the book, achieved by the integrity of Stuart's character and of the storyteller's view of the world and human life. It is, finally, what makes the book original and perdurable—fit to stand scrutiny.

"Which direction are you headed?" he asked.

"North," said Stuart.

"North is nice," said the repairman. "I've always enjoyed going north. Of course, south-west is a fine direction, too."

"Yes, I suppose it is," said Stuart, thoughtfully.

"And there's east," continued the repairman. "I once had a interesting experience on an easterly course. Do you want me to tell you about it?"

"No, thanks," said Stuart.

The repairman seemed disappointed, but he kept right on talking. "There's something about north," he said, "something that sets it apart from all other directions. A person who is heading north is not making any mistake, in my opinion."

"That's the way I look at it," said Stuart. "I rather expect that from now on I shall be traveling north until the end of my days."

"Worse things than that could happen to a person," said the repairman.

"Yes, I know," answered Stuart.

"Following a broken telephone line north, I have come upon some wonderful places," continued the repairman. "Swamps where cedars grow and turtles wait on logs but not for anything in particular; fields bordered by crooked fences broken by years of standing still; orchards so old they have forgotten where the farmhouse is. In the north I have eaten my lunch in pastures rank with ferns and junipers, all under fair skies with a wind blowing. My business has taken me into spruce woods on winter nights where the snow lay deep and soft, a perfect place for a carnival of rabbits. I have sat at peace on the freight platforms of railroad junctions in the north, in the warm hours and with the warm smells. I know fresh lakes in the north, undisturbed except by fish and hawk and, of course, by the Telephone Company, which has to follow its nose. I know all these places well. They are a long way from here—don't forget that. And a person who is looking for something doesn't travel very fast."

"That's perfectly true," said Stuart. "Well, I guess I'd better be going. Thank you for your friendly remarks."

"Not at all," said the repairman. "I hope you find that bird."

Stuart rose from the ditch, climbed into his car, and started up the road that led toward the north. The sun was just coming up over the hills on his right. As he peered ahead into the great land that stretched before him, the way seemed long. But the sky was bright, and he somehow felt he was headed in the right direction.

THE END

Hundreds of children have written White to ask what happened to Stuart after he left the repairman, and some adult critics have found the inconclusive ending a flaw. The children's curiosity is understandable; it is not necessarily evidence of dissatisfaction. They know that life simply goes on, that, as White wrote one reader, "life is essentially inconclusive."[13] What happened to Stuart is, after all, pretty much what happens to us all, and the tear we may brush from the corner of our eye as we close the book is a tear for ourselves. What the story leaves us with, however, is not a sense of frustration but a memory of things that give us courage equal to the insults of fate: the contents of the repairman's catalogue—spruce woods on winter nights, freight platforms at railroad junctions, lakes, swamps, odoriferous junipers, turtles on logs, fair skies with a wind blowing—all that and the memory of little Stuart, whose jaunty pluck, passion for independence, and devotion to an ineffable dream make him strong enough to endure.

We know Margalo as an individual less well than we know Stuart, of course; at first she seems to be simply a beautiful heroine, the first romantic object of a boy's love. But by the time White got around to finishing *Stuart Little,* he knew how to make Margalo personify an unattainable ideal, the object of a quest that was its own justification. In *Stuart Little,* as later in *Charlotte's Web,* White described innocent young love by describing the love between animals of different genera: Stuart is male, Margalo is female, and the feelings of each are true to their sex; but sex does not complicate their attraction to one another. Margalo can be, is, purely (or simply) beauty. Her rescue of Stuart is an act of courage and unselfish love; and she can be, is, simply goodness. The truth of Margalo is partly that she is so clearly a manifestation of nature (e.g., she migrates) and partly that she is worth looking for even if the seeker is not sure he will find her. She becomes Stuart's equivalent of the "hound, bay horse, and turtle-dove" that Thoreau said he had lost long ago and was still on the trail of, speaking to many travelers "concerning them, describing their tracks and what calls they answered to," and discovering that some of those he spoke to "seemed as anxious to recover them as if they had lost them themselves."

Some of White's more pragmatic notions about life appear in the episode in which Stuart teaches school for a day. In it he is suddenly, but not unconvincingly, a thoughtful, wise, authoritative young man thoroughly aware of who he is and what he believes. As a teacher he proceeds according to the pedagogical theory he confidently reveals to the Superintendant: "make the work interesting and the discipline will take care of itself." He skips arithmetic and reduces the spelling lesson to a statement that "a misspelled word is an abomination in the sight of every-one," advising his pupils to buy a *Webster's Collegiate Dictionary* and to consult it whenever they are in the slightest doubt. Nor does he choose to conduct a writing lesson: the students, as they agree, already know how to write. As for social studies, Stuart says, "Never heard of them."

With those standard parts of the curriculum out of the way, Stuart suggests that they just talk about a topic chosen by someone in the class. Arthur Greenlaw proposes "the way it feels to hold a snake in your hand," and Lydia Lacey pleads for "sin and vice," but Stuart summarily rejects those topics in favor of one of his own: "the King of the World." In the lively discussion that follows, he develops his ideas of international law and its enforcement. He thinks that the law proposed by Mildred Hoffenstein, "Absolutely no being mean," is a fine law. He agrees that, human nature being what it is, the law might not work, but it is a good law and worth giving a try. He tells Henry Jameson to snatch from Katharine Stableford the little souvenir pillow bearing the legend: "For you I pine, for you I balsam." Then Stuart, in the role of King of the World (or an international police force), leads the students in a prompt, indignant, and threatening move against Henry, who weakens and gives up the pillow. The law, enforced lawfully, has worked pretty well.

The lesson in law was based on a lesson in philosophy. The rules, or laws, have to follow from a common knowledge of the right answers to the question: "What is important?" Henry Rackmeyer knows his catechism: "A shaft of sunlight at the end of a dark afternoon, a note in music, and the way the back of a baby's neck smells if its mother keeps it tidy"; and Mary Bendix remembers one more: "Ice cream with chocolate sauce on it." In his last words before he dismisses the class, Stuart adds one final important thing: Summertime.

So the young man in quest of a grail, or of what Thoreau meant by "a hound, a bay horse, and a turtle-dove," or of what Don Marquis said he had followed all his days but could not name—this hero—is as admirable a humanist as he is a brave and lovable human being.

The contents of the story—the places, things, and people—are, not surprisingly, right out of White's life. Stuart is partly Samuel White: his cane and his attention to dress, as well as his briskness and ingenuity and passion for getting it right are those of White's father. Once, when E. B. White broke his toe and had to use a cane, he wrote his brother Stanley: "Baby, you should have seen me this week—carrying a cane. I not only looked a little like Father, I felt like Father. A cane is what does it, in the end. It gives dignity, direction, restraint, and a general sense of owning whatever you set the point of the cane down on."[14] Stuart's brother, George, may be reminiscent of the character of Stanley. Many of the details in Stuart's life derive from Elwyn's life at 101 Summit Avenue or Andy's life in the Village—and anyone familiar with White's life will recognize at least some of them: the family doctor, colds, bronchitis, and thermometers; the sunny room and the curtains of the house on Eighth Street; the bird, the cat, the small park near Stuart's house—and the tall vine that ran up the side of the house; Ping-Pong, the baby-grand piano; the doorman on Fifth Avenue; the Boston fern like one in the parlor on Summit Avenue; Stuart's love of boats, cars, canoes, skating, and travel; the call of the north and the love of morning and summertime.

It is more instructive for someone wishing to come as close as possible to the psyche of E. B. White to consider the affective aspects of *Stuart Little* or the intellectual and ethical characteristics of Stuart than to speculate about the latent significance of White's preoccupation with mice. (His first published poem was about a mouse; winning a prize and family praise for his achievement gave the boy a sense of power, maturity, size. He may have thought he looked like a mouse; he knew he was the smallest and youngest of his family. As a child he kept as a pet a mouse who was "friendly and without fear," and for whom he "made a home . . . complete with a gymnasium."[15] At Cornell he was, Mrs. Bristow Adams said, "like a mouse." One of his fraternity brothers remembers going down to Andy White's room in the Phi Gam house and finding him alone at an old-fashioned roll-top desk sitting silent and immobile as he looked at a mouse in one of the cubbyholes of the desk: "The mouse was looking at Mr. White. Mr. White was looking at the mouse." The first paragraph White ever wrote for "Notes and Comment" was about buying a mouse trap in Woolworths. And so on.) Stuart came to White in a dream; *Stuart Little* is a work of fiction. In both the dream and the work of art, Stuart is "courageous and questing." In the story, his love of life and his pursuit of the ideal preclude fear.

A few weeks after White turned in the finished manuscript of *Stuart Little* he received a letter from Anne Carroll Moore, children's librarian emerita of the New York Public Library:

Her letter was long, friendly, urgent, and thoroughly surprising. She said she had read proofs of my forthcoming book called *Stuart Little* and she strongly advised me to withdraw it. She said, as I recall the letter, that the book was non-affirmative, inconclusive, unfit for children, and would harm its author if published. These were strong words, and I was grateful to Miss Moore for having taken the trouble to write them. I thought the matter over, however, and decided that as long as the book satisfied me, I wasn't going to let an expert talk me out of it. It is unnerving to be told you're bad for children; but I detected in Miss Moore's letter an assumption that there are rules governing the writing of juvenile literature—rules as inflexible as the rules for lawn tennis. And this I was not sure of. I had followed my instincts in writing about Stuart, and following one's instincts seemed to be the way a writer should operate. I was shook up by the letter but was not deflected.

Stuart was published in October, and other surprises were in store for me. Miss Moore's successor at the Library had some misgivings of her own about the book, and Stuart met with a cool reception. He got into the shelves of the Library all right, but I think he had to gnaw his way in. The press, to my astonishment, treated the book almost as though it were adult fiction. The daily *Times* gave it a full-scale review by Charles Poore, who praised it. Malcolm Cowley, in the Sunday *Times,* said it was a good book but disappointing—

should have been better. This exactly expressed my own feelings about it.

A couple of days after the book appeared, Harold Ross, my boss at *The New Yorker,* stopped in at my office. His briefcase was slung over his shoulder on a walking stick and he looked unhappy. "Saw your book, White," he growled. "You made one serious mistake."

"What was that?" I asked.

"Why the mouse," he shouted. "You said he was born. God damn it, White, you should have had him adopted." The word "adopted" boomed forth loud enough to be heard all down the corridor. I had great respect for Ross's ability to spot trouble in a piece of writing, and I began to feel uneasy. After he left the room I sat for a long while wondering whether Miss Moore had not been right after all. Finally I remembered that Harold Ross was not at home in the world of make-believe, he was strictly for the world of 43rd Street, and this cheered me and revived my spirits.

My next encounter was with Edmund Wilson, who stopped me in the hall. "Hello, hello," he said, in his wonderfully high and thrilling voice that sounds like a coaching horn. "I read that book of yours. I found the first page quite amusing, about the mouse, you know. But I was disappointed that you didn't develop the theme more in the manner of Kafka."

I thanked Edmund and wandered back to my room to chuckle at the infinite variety of *The New Yorker:* the editor who could spot a dubious verb at forty paces, the critic who was saddened because my innocent tale of the quest for beauty failed to carry the overtones of monstrosity. What a magazine. There's never been anything like it.

Despite the rough time the author was having, Stuart himself seemed to be doing all right. The book drew generally favorable reviews, and by October 24th Harper had sold 42,000 copies. . . .

The real returns came when letters began arriving. Some were from children. Some were from teachers. They expressed pleasure, along with a fairly steady stream of abuse about the book's ending, which fails to tell whether Stuart found the bird. The letters have not stopped coming. Of the many thousands I've received, only two, I believe, questioned the odd fact of Stuart's arrival in this world and the propriety of an American family's having a boy that looked like a mouse. After twenty years, I am beginning to relax.

I learned two things from the experience of writing *Stuart Little:* that a writer's own nose is his best guide, and that children can sail easily over the fence that separates reality from make-believe. They go over it like little springboks. A fence that can throw a librarian is as nothing to a child.[16]

The seventy-year-old Miss Moore told a friend that she "was never so disappointed in a book" in her life; she wrote Ursula Nordstrom, editor of children's books at Harper's, that the book "mustn't be published";[17] and she wrote Katharine a fourteen-page letter explaining why she thought White should be persuaded to withdraw it. Katharine wrote a characteristically tactful reply:

I'm of course very sorry that you do not like *Stuart Little* and thank you for writing that letter which I realize must have been very hard for you to do. My husband and I both appreciate the interest which made you write it. I can only hope that you are mistaken of course. Andy likes Stuart and so do I, and his publishers have never before been so enthusiastic over any of his other books as they are over *Stuart Little*. . . .

You are right, of course, that Stuart gets out of hand and it's true, too, that the story follows none of the conventional patterns for fantasy. But I can't help feeling that the unpredictable quality of both Stuart, the character, and *Stuart*, the book, is one of the book's merits. Didn't you think it even *funny?* I can still laugh, reading the proofs, and Ed Aswell of Harper's reported that he and his eight-year-old son laughed out loud all the way when he read it aloud, though not necessarily always at the same places. So what I hope is that children of all ages *may* happen to like *Stuart* for its humor while their elders read it for its satirical and philosophical overtones. Actually, I myself have never known whether this book was a juvenile or a novel. It's a *dream*—quite literally—just as *Alice* is supposed to have been. Just recently the notes Andy made after he had that dream (more than twelve years ago) turned up, and I was surprised to find how clearly the story had followed them. . . . I am honestly not at all afraid of its hurting E.B.W. to have it published, or Harper's either, whether or not it is a financial or literary success.[18]

Harper and Brothers proposed a contract like the contracts for his other Harper books, by which White would be paid royalties of 12 1/2 percent on the first five thousand copies and 15 percent thereafter. The list price of the book was two dollars. Two weeks after the publication date Harper sent White a check for $12,200.50 (prepublication royalties less $500 paid as an advance) and announced that a second printing was in press. By the end of 1946 Harper had printed 105,000 copies, and by January 1977 total sales (exclusive of translations) had exceeded two and a half million. *Stuart Little* has been translated into about twenty languages. In 1956 Pathways of Sound published a recording of the complete text read by Julie Harris, whom Katharine had suggested. And in the same year the National Broadcasting Company presented an hour-long television version in which Johnny Carson was the narrator. The Harriet Ames episode was omitted, and White was dissatisfied with the production for that and other reasons.

In December 1945 Andy and Katharine went to Maine for a family Christmas celebration. Nancy's husband, Louis Stableford, and Roger Angell were both still in the Air Force and could not make it, but everyone else was there: Nancy with her two-year-old daughter, Katharine, and her infant son, Jonathan; Roger's wife, Evelyn; and Joe—home for vacation from boarding school. This year Andy could enjoy his favorite holiday near a real stable, in the presence of a real infant. And there were other reasons for rejoicing. *Stuart Little*, clearly an "original work," was a best-seller, and a long poem, "Song of the Queen Bee," which *The New Yorker* had published early in December, was so popular that the magazine could not meet the demand for copies. In "Song" White ridiculed in high spirits man's presumption of superior human wisdom and his officious interference with the ways of nature. Here is the way it begins:

SONG OF THE QUEEN BEE

"The breeding of the bee," says a United States Department of Agriculture bulletin on artificial insemination, "has always been handicapped by the fact that the queen mates in the air with whatever drone she encounters."

When the air is wine and the wind is free
And the morning sits on the lovely lea
And sunlight ripples on every tree,
Then love-in-air is the thing for me—
   I'm a bee,
   I'm a ravishing, rollicking, young queen bee,
   That's me.

I wish to state that I think it's great,
Oh, it's simply rare in the upper air,
   It's the place to pair
   With a bee.
Let old geneticists plot and plan,
They're stuffy people, to a man;
Let gossips whisper behind their fan.
   (Oh, she *does?*
   Buzz, buzz, buzz!)
My nuptial flight is sheer delight;
I'm a giddy girl who likes to swirl,
   To fly and soar
   And fly some more,
   I'm a bee.
And I wish to state that I'll *always* mate
With whatever drone I encounter.[19]

For its one hundred lines the poem sings a song of sheer delight—delight in asserting a spirit of freedom that, like Ariel, mocks man "the meddler." It also implies that the right pronoun for Nature is "she"—that life and beauty and grounds for hope or courage are found in creatures like Margalo and Charlotte.

CHAPTER XIV

"The Second Tree
from the Corner"

1 9 4 6 — 1 9 4 9

"Suddenly his sickness seemed health,
his dizziness stability."

ORN LUCKY AND SCARED, AND LACKING
nothing but confidence, White was still lucky, scared, and lacking
confidence in 1946. In fact, his anxieties—together with their effect
on his body, as they aggravated his troublesome "gut" and his "jerky
head"—seemed to be taking the fun out of almost anything good luck had
thrown his way. His lack of confidence in himself was compounded by
his lack of confidence in mankind's ability to save itself from destruction
—and by his misgivings about his recent efforts to promote a form of
government that might prevent war. For in promoting a "cause" by
writing *The Wild Flag* he had disregarded, he believed, "the deepest
instincts of a creative person." He sank into a painful depression.

The ending of the war, the solid success of *Stuart Little,* and the bright
flare of popularity of "Song of the Queen Bee" should have been effective
palliatives for his depression, but apparently they were not. During 1946
White produced only half as much copy for *The New Yorker* as he had
the year before, and little of it was very good. In the course of a winter
of "virtually unrelieved trouble and corruption," as he later described it
in a letter to his brother, the only thing he wrote that he ever chose to
reprint was "Window Ledge in the Atom Age," a poem that opens on a
happy note:

> I have a bowl of paper whites,
> Of paper-white narcissus;

> Their fragrance my whole soul delights,
> They smell delissus.
> (They grow in pebbles in the sun
> And each is like a star.) . . .[1]

In the spring he reluctantly agreed to sign a six-year lease for an apartment in Manhattan, the third one on Forty-eighth Street that he and Katharine were to inhabit. But summer in Maine seems to have restored his health and somewhat lifted his spirits. The Whites had fewer guests that year than usual, but the quiet life on the farm was pleasantly enlivened by the presence of fifteen-year-old Joe, who wanted the Plymouth convertible every night and, when he got it, kept his father awake worrying till he came home. As usual the family went to the Blue Hill Fair, where this year Joe took a thirteen-year-old girl for a ride on the Ferris wheel—an episode that later found its way into *Charlotte's Web*.

Once back in New York, White wrote little, and worried about the wisdom of agreeing to the publication of *The Wild Flag*, which was to appear in October. In November he and Katharine went to Ithaca for the Cornell-Dartmouth game, but in a poem called "Under a Steamer Rug" White expressed only melancholy feelings about this "sweet sad day."[2] The news in December that sales of *Stuart Little* had reached 100,000 copies was reassuring evidence of one kind of personal luck, but it might have been more welcome in a world that did not seem bent on destroying itself. For the last issue of *The New Yorker* in 1946 he wrote the following sober paragraph:

> The year ends on a note of pure experimentation. Dr. Fritz Zwicky last week tried to hurl some metal slugs out into space, free of the earth's gravitational pull. Dr. Zwicky stood in New Mexico and tossed from there. He was well equipped: he had a rocket that took the slugs for the first forty-mile leg of the journey and then discharged them at high velocity to continue on their own. The desire to toss something in a new way, or to toss it a greater distance, is fairly steady in men and boys. Boys stand on high bridges, chucking chips down wind, or they stand on the shore of a pond, tossing rocks endlessly at a floating bottle, or at a dead cat, observing closely every detail of their experiment, trying to make every stone sail free of the pull of past experience. Then the boys grow older, stand in the desert, still chucking, observing, wondering. They have almost exhausted the earth's possibilities and are going on into the empyrean to throw at the stars, leaving the earth's people frightened and joyless, and leaving some fellow scientists switching over from science to politics and hoping they have made the switch in time.[3]

The "Age of the Atom" was only seventeen months old, but White, as well as "a few scientists," was more than "concerned"—he was deeply frightened by what it implied.

Early in 1947, after years of trying, White succeeded in persuading Ross to let him conduct his own signed column in *The New Yorker.* It was to be called "Turtle Bay Diary," a title doubly significant because Turtle Bay was the name of the area on the east side of Manhattan where both White and the United Nations were housed—the latter in its splendid new headquarters a few blocks from the Whites' apartment—and it was the goings-on in these quarters that White planned to report in his column. But after two installments in February he had to give the project up "because of sickness." In April he wrote a correspondent that he was on a "non-writing jag," having been advised by his doctor that he would be "all right if he quit writing."[4]

The doctor who gave that advice may have been Carl Binger, the distinguished psychiatrist whom White had first consulted when he had a nervous breakdown in the spring of 1943 and whom he had returned to for help now in the spring of 1947. All we know about his experience as a patient of Binger's must be deduced from one of White's parables, called "The Second Tree from the Corner." It is an account of how a patient named Trexler, in the course of a therapy that is getting nowhere, suddenly makes a discovery that leads him, though not to a permanent cure, to a restorative epiphany.

In White's story Trexler, on his fifth visit to the psychiatrist, is suddenly asked, "What do you want?" and when he says he doesn't know and adds, "I guess nobody knows the answer to that one," the doctor replies, "Sure they do." So Trexler asks the doctor what it is he wants. The doctor wants a wing on the small house he owns in Westport, and more money, and more leisure. After Trexler leaves the office and emerges into the street, he turns west off Park Avenue and starts walking toward Madison, meditating on "what he wanted":

"What do you want?" he heard again. Trexler knew what he wanted, and what, in general, all men wanted; and he was glad, in a way, that it was both inexpressible and unattainable, and that it wasn't a wing. He was satisfied to remember that it was deep, formless, enduring, and impossible of fulfillment, and that it made men sick, and that when you sauntered along Third Avenue and looked through the doorways into the dim saloons, you could sometimes pick out from the unregenerate ranks the ones who had not forgotten, gazing steadily into the bottoms of their glasses on the long chance that they could get another little peek at it. Trexler found himself renewed by the remembrance that what he wanted was at once great and microscopic, and that although it borrowed from the nature of large deeds and of youthful love and of old songs and early intimations, it was not any one of these things, and that it had not been isolated or pinned down, and that a man who attempted to define it in the privacy of a doctor's office would fall flat on his face.

Trexler felt invigorated. Suddenly his sickness seemed health, his dizziness stability. A small tree, rising between him and the light, stood there saturated with the evening, each gilt-edged leaf perfectly drunk with excellence and delicacy. Trexler's spine registered an ever so slight tremor as it picked up this natural disturbance in the lovely scene. "I want the second tree from the corner, just as it stands," he said, answering an imaginary question from an imaginary physician. And he felt a slow pride in realizing that what he wanted none could bestow, and that what he had none could take away. He felt content to be sick, unembarrassed at being afraid; and in the jungle of his fear he glimpsed (as he had so often glimpsed them before) the flashy tail feathers of the bird courage.[5]

The second tree from the corner is, like Margalo, a manifestation of the ineffable and unattainable ideal.

In July Andy wrote his brother Stanley: "I find Not Writing very soothing, but I haven't figured out yet what I will use for money."[6] In late September, however, in response to an invitation to contribute something to the ninetieth-anniversary number of the *Atlantic Monthly,* he wrote "Death of a Pig." Like "The Second Tree from the Corner," this piece of autobiography is an account of an episode in which a sick man is temporarily relieved of his anxiety.

The opening sentence of "Death of a Pig" suggests that both the event it describes and the writing of the account had had a healing effect on the author: "I spent several days and nights in mid-September with an ailing pig and I feel driven to account for this stretch of time, more particularly since the pig died at last, and I lived, and things might easily have gone the other way round and none left to do the accounting." Not that he experienced a miraculous cure. He was still unwell at the end of the story, for he could not remember whether the pig died on the third or fourth night of his illness: "This uncertainty," he says, "afflicts me with a sense of personal deterioration; if I were in decent health I would know how many nights I had sat up with a pig." What physically ailed White at the moment he does not say in the essay, but an undated note he seems to have written about that time in the fall of 1947 suggests that it might have been his stomach. The note says:

K:
    I am going to see [Dr. Dana] Atchley at 3 P.M. The second tree from the

corner would appear to be a barium tree. (And I was waiting for figs and plums.)

A.

If White had not himself been sick at the time the pig fell ill, there would have been no story. The pig's illness, however, aggravated his own. The animal had become precious to him for having "suffered in a suffering world," and as he watched it die he experienced first the same terror, then the same healing purgation that is evoked in an audience watching the performance of a classic tragedy.

Before he had begun to fear for the pig's life, White had been upset simply by the loss of the support he had received until then from the "lustiness of a healthy pig." When that period came "to an end and the food [lay] stale and untouched . . . the pig's imbalance [became] the man's vicariously, and life [seemed] insecure, displaced, transitory." When the pig's ailment was diagnosed as erysipelas, a streptococcus infection that human beings can contract from swine, the man, the antihero in the piece, was further weakened by his hypochondriacal fear that he might have caught the disease himself: "My throat felt dry and I went to the cupboard and got a bottle of whiskey." The realization—when it finally came—that the pig might actually die was a shock to his confidence in a "proud scheme" of life—a scheme that included assumptions about the "essential health of pigs. What could be true of my pig could be true also of the rest of my tidy world." To be sure, the pig's story ended, White said, with a comic, moving scene, about which "everything seemed overwritten." The veterinarian performed the postmortem handily and swiftly at the edge of the grave, "so that the inwards that had caused the pig's death preceded him into the ground and he lay at last resting squarely on the cause of his own undoing." But the writer's recognition of this comic irony testifies to the same basic strength, humor, and intelligence in him that before had saved Trexler.[7]

White's success with this story may have had something to do with the vigorous tone of a letter he wrote to the editor of the *New York Herald Tribune* on Thanksgiving Day, 1947. The paper had defended editorially the right of Hollywood movie producers to fire ten screenwriters for refusing to tell the House Un-American Activities Committee whether they were members of the Communist Party. The editorial maintained that the movie industry, "an industry of mass communication," could not by democratic principles be denied the right to protect itself against the "facts" of Communist infiltration.[8]

The *Herald Tribune* printed White's letter on its editorial page, on the Tuesday following Thanksgiving. It read:

To the New York Herald Tribune:

I am a member of a party of one, and I live in an age of fear. Nothing lately has unsettled my party and raised my fears so much as your editorial, on Thanksgiving Day, suggesting that employees should be required to state their beliefs in order to hold their jobs. The idea is inconsistent with our Constitutional theory and has been stubbornly opposed by watchful men since the early days of the Republic. It's hard for me to believe that the Herald Tribune is backing away from the fight, and I can only assume that your editorial writer, in a hurry to get home for Thanksgiving, tripped over the First Amendment and thought it was the office cat. . . .

I hold that it would be improper for any committee or any employer to examine any conscience. They wouldn't know how to get into it, they wouldn't know what to do when they got in there, and I wouldn't let them in anyway. Like other Americans, my acts and my words are open to inspection—not my thoughts or my political affiliation. (As I pointed out, I am a member of a party of one.) Your editorialist said he hoped the companies in checking for loyalty would use their powers sparingly and wisely. That is a wistful idea. One need only watch totalitarians at work to see that once men gain power over other men's minds, that power is never used sparingly and wisely, but lavishly and brutally and with unspeakable results. If I must declare today that I am not a Communist, tomorrow I shall have to testify that I am not a Unitarian. And the day after, that I never belonged to a dahlia club.

It is not a crime to believe anything at all in America. To date it has not been declared illegal to belong to the Communist party. Yet ten men have been convicted not of wrongdoing but of wrong believing. That is news in this country, and if I have not misread history, it is bad news.[9]

In its defense the *Herald Tribune* said that it might have been "misguided" in its attempts to deal with the problem of how America could defend itself against Communism, but that Mr. White had "failed to deal with it at all."[10] White's published letter elicited many personal letters of praise, and of condemnation. Supreme Court Justice Felix Frankfurter lauded White, saying, "If angels can write, they do not wield a better pen than you do."[11]

At the beginning of 1948 Andy wrote his brother Stanley that his "head" felt "rather better than it did a year ago."[12] Back on a writing jag of sorts, he contributed editorials for all but nine issues of *The New Yorker* that year. Joe, who had graduated from Exeter the previous spring and was taking a year's leave of absence from school before entering college, was working for a construction company in New York, and was living at home for the first winter in four years. His presence must have helped make life more interesting. In April Katharine underwent a spinal fusion operation that kept her in the hospital for six weeks and in a brace for most of the rest of the year. In the face of Katharine's invalidism Andy simply had to cope. As a friend once said, one of the Whites seemed always to be well enough to take care of the other.

In June, perhaps in preparation to attend commencement at the University of Maine, at Yale, and at Dartmouth, the three institutions that were awarding him honorary degrees, White bought a pair of new shoes, and with the excuse of having to break them in, he went one day to the Bronx Zoo. The expedition resulted in a six-hundred-word report, published in "Notes and Comment," that was as good as any "paragraph" he ever wrote. When he republished it, he called it "Twins." Half a dozen sentences from it will illustrate White's skill in conveying his feeling while recording his observations, and perhaps will suggest the cause for the large response from readers that it elicited:

The path there is not much travelled. As we approached the corner where the brook trickles under the wire fence, we noticed a red deer getting to her feet. Beside her, on legs that were just learning their business, was a spotted fawn, as small and perfect as a trinket seen through a reducing glass. They stood there, mother and child, under a gray beech whose trunk was engraved with dozens of hearts and initials. Stretched on the ground was another fawn, and we realized that the doe had just finished twinning. The second fawn was still wet, still unrisen. Here was a scene of rare sylvan splendor, in one of our five favorite boroughs, and we couldn't have asked for more. Even our new shoes seemed to be working out all right and weren't hurting much.[13]

Later that month, when Katharine was still unable to leave New York because of her bad back, Andy sent her a long and amusing letter describing his experience at Dartmouth. After dinner the night before the commencement exercises, he wrote, he "filled up immediately with gas and apprehension," and was too sick to go to the president's reception for honored guests. After some hesitation he finally took a "knock-out capsule" and fell asleep. Still sick the next morning, he nevertheless went through with the ceremony and was amused to hear President Dickey cite him for the "literary bravery" of his writings on world government when all Andy could think of at the moment was his unheroic (and comic) gastritis: "Nobody who has never suffered my peculiar kind of disability can understand the sheer hell of such moments."[14]

In August, after Katharine had come to Maine, Andy spent a week in New York, in a room at the Algonquin Hotel, "half way down an air shaft," writing a seven-thousand-word essay for *Holiday* magazine, called "Here Is New York." In it he describes the glories of the city and speaks of the marks that history and the presence of the great and famous have left on it, and of the needs and aspirations by which men and women are still drawn to it. He speaks of his own nostalgia for the New York of his youth, the New York of the twenties and thirties, with its elevated railways, its half-dozen great newspapers, its Greenwich Village area, which then was still open and airy, and unoppressed by tall buildings. While such memories lead him to compare the then with the now, and he regrets some of the changes that have occurred, it is not until the very end of the essay that he names the one thing which ultimately concerns him most deeply about the New York City of now: it is a "thing people don't speak much about." It is the fact that New York is now "destructible," that it can be quickly annihilated by an atomic attack—and that it will be unless the United Nations, that "struggling Parliament of Men," succeeds in what it is trying to do.

White's hymn to New York thus ends on a solemn note. In his concluding words the city he praises is a city partly gone and partly doomed— one whose survival seems linked to the survival of an old willow tree standing in Turtle Bay Gardens on East Forty-eighth Street.

> A block or two west of the new City of Man in Turtle Bay there is an old willow tree that presides over an interior garden. It is a battered tree, long suffering and much climbed, held together by strands of wire but beloved of those who know it. In a way it symbolizes the city: life under difficulties, growth against odds, saprise in the midst of concrete, and the steady reaching for the sun. Whenever I look at it nowadays, and feel the cold shadow of the planes, I think: "This must be saved, this particular thing, this very tree." If it were to go, all would go—this city, this mischievous and marvelous monument which not to look upon would be like death.[15]

In White's memory and imagination New York had come to be inseparable from *The New Yorker,* with whose rise and continued success his own had been so closely linked. Now Harold Ross was sick, and within a short time he would have to turn over the day-to-day operation of the magazine to someone else. If "Here Is New York" was in part White's expression of gratitude to the city that had nourished him, the editorial he wrote to, for, and about Ross, in December 1948, was a tribute to the man to whom his career owed much—and a man who in various ways had often acknowledged his debt to White.

Neither Ross nor White found it easy to give direct expression to their affection for each other, but Ross had in recent years sent Andy memos of praise unguarded by humor or other masks. One such was a postscript scrawled at the bottom of a letter Ross had received from Fleischmann about recent financial successes of *The New Yorker*. In his note to Andy, Ross alluded to a remark made by Clifton Fadiman in a long, laudatory article about White in the latest *New York Times Book Review:* "Mr. White is not a practical man."[16] Referring to the content of Fleischmann's letter, Ross wrote: "Don't give it a 2nd thought. You are not a practical man. I didn't have to follow you through 8 pages of the Times Book Review to learn that, either. Thanks for carrying me along with you, on your shoulders."[17]

Now, in "Notes and Comment" for the Christmas issue of 1948, partly perhaps out of a sudden realization that Ross, too, was destructible, White wrote a wry greeting to him that Ross as well as all who knew the two men would understand. It took the form of a preposterous Christmas parable in which White expressed admiration for a man whose devotion to the gospel according to Fowler's *Modern English Usage* was a pure, passionate, and saving grace, able to transfigure him:

We had a Scrooge in our office a few minutes ago, a tall, parched man, beefing about Christmas and threatening to disembowel anyone who mentioned the word. He said his work had suffered and his life been made unbearable by the demands and conventions of the season. He said he hated wise men, whether from the East or from the West, hated red ribbon, dripping candles, distant and near relatives, fir balsam, silent nights, boy sopranos, shopping lists with check marks against some of the items, and the whole yuletide strategem, not to mention the low-lying cloud of unwritten thank-you letters hanging just above the horizon. He was in a savage state. Before he left the office, though, we saw him transfigured, just as Scrooge was transfigured. The difference was that whereas Scrooge was softened by visions, our visitor was softened by the sight of a small book standing on our desk—a copy of Fowler's "Modern English Usage."

"Greatest collection of essays and opinions ever assembled between covers," he shouted, "including a truly masterful study of *that* and *which.*"

He seized the book and began thumbing through it for favorite passages, slowly stuffing a couple of small giftwrapped parcels into the pocket of his greatcoat.

"Listen to this," he said in a triumphant voice. "Avoidance of the obvious is very well, provided that it is not itself obvious; but, if it is, all is spoilt.' Isn't that beautiful?"

We agreed that it was a sound and valuable sentiment, perfectly expressed. He then began a sermon on *that* and *which,* taking as his text certain paragraphs from Fowler, and warming rapidly to his theme.

"Listen to this: 'If writers would agree to regard *that* as the defining relative pronoun, and *which* as the non–defining, there would be much gain both in lucidity and in ease. Some there are who follow this principle now; but it would be idle to pretend that it is the practice either of most or of the best writers.' "

"It was the practice of St. Matthew," we put in hastily. "Or at any rate he practiced it in one of the most moving sentences ever constructed: 'And, lo, the star, which they saw in the east, went before them, till it came and stood over where the young child was.' You've got to admit that the *which* in that sentence is where it ought to be, as well as every other word. Did you ever read a more satisfactory sentence than that in your life?"

"It's good," said our friend, cheerfully. "It's good because there isn't a ten–dollar word in the whole thing. And Fowler has it pegged, too. Wait a minute. Here. 'What is to be deprecated is the notion that one can improve one's style by using stylish words.' See what I mean about Fowler? But let's get back to *that* and *which*. That's the business that really fascinates me. Fowler devotes eight pages to it. I got so excited once I had the pages photostatted. Listen to this: 'We find in fact that the antecedent of *that* is often personal.' Now, that's very instructive."

"Very," we said. "And if you want an example, take Matthew 2:1: ' . . . there came wise men from the east to Jerusalem, saying, Where is he that is born King of the Jews?' Imagine how that simple clause could get loused up if someone wanted to change *that* to *who!*"

"Exactly," he said. "That's what I mean about Fowler. What was the sentence again about the star? Say it again."

We repeated, "And, lo, the star, which they saw in the east, went before them, till it came and stood over where the young child was."

"You see?" he said, happily. "This is the greatest damn book ever written." And he left our office transfigured, a man in excellent spirits. Seeing him go off merry as a grig, we realized that Christmas is where the heart is. For some it is in a roll of red ribbon, for some in the eyes of a young child. For our visitor, we saw clearly, Christmas was a relative pronoun. Wherever it is, it is quite a day.[18]

In "The Second Tree from the Corner," "Death of a Pig," "Here Is New York," and such "Notes and Comment" as the above, White wrote at the top of his form. While "keeping the minutes of his own meeting" he had recovered his confidence in his gift and his luck, and he could once again begin to think about writing a *magnum opus.*

By late fall of 1948 Katharine no longer needed the support of a brace, and on New Year's Eve she and Andy gave a party for over a hundred guests, many of whom stayed late and helped make the celebration both joyous and exhausting. On New Year's Day, however, Fred, the red, short-haired dachshund who had lived with the Whites for over fourteen years, died in Maine, "after a drink of brandy, which he enjoyed." Fred had played a comic part in "Death of a Pig," and in a few short paragraphs his character had been more completely realized than that of anyone else in the story. He had also appeared in one of White's last "One Man's Meat" columns:

Next to myself [Fred] is the greatest worrier and schemer on the premises and always has too many things on his mind. He not only handles all his own matters but he has a follow-up system by which he checks on all of mine to see that everything is taken care of. His interest in every phase of farming remains undiminished, as does mine, but his passion for details is a kind of obsession and seems to me unhealthy. He wants to be present in a managerial capacity at every event, no matter how trifling or routine; it makes no difference whether I am dipping a sheep or simply taking a bath myself. He is a fire buff whose blaze is anything at all. In damp weather his arthritis makes stair-climbing a tortuous and painful accomplishment, yet he groans his way down cellar with me to pack eggs and to investigate for the thousandth time the changeless crypt where the egg crates live. Here he awaits the fall of an egg to the floor and the sensual delight of licking it up—which he does with lips drawn slightly back as though in distaste at the strange consistency of the white. His hopes run always to accidents and misfortunes: the broken egg, the spilt milk, the wounded goose, the fallen lamb, the fallen cake.... His activities and his character constitute an almost uninterrupted annoyance to me, yet he is such an engaging old fool that I am quite attached to him, in a half-regretful way. Life without him would be heaven, but I'm afraid it is not what I want.[19]

During the many years that Fred had been his close companion, White had attributed to him a rich and real personality. Fred was "vile," gluttonous, and lascivious, possessing a "heavy charge of original sin."[20] He was incapable of human love or loyalty, and he tended to deflate rather than to build up his master's ego. But White admired him because he was "intensely loyal to himself, as every strong individualist must be,"[21] and because he loved life, and was driven by curiosity. In Fred's individualism, in his loyalty to himself, and in his love of life and curiosity about it, White saw much of White, and for complex reasons, therefore, Fred's death—as well as his behavior in life—may have indirectly played a part in the creation of *Charlotte's Web*. For White's long experience with Fred, his sense of knowing and understanding Fred as well as he did, or thought he did, may have encouraged him to create other animal characters— characters to whom he could ascribe human traits without suggesting that human beings were generally superior to all other creatures. This, of course, is what he did in *Charlotte's Web*.

White's drawing of the farm, showing Allen Cove in the background.

The farmhouse from the northwest. The road in the foreground goes down to the boathouse.

Katharine White on board
Astrid, *about 1935.*

White in Maine,
in the forties.

Joel White at Exeter, *about 1945.*

Katharine White at her desk at The
New Yorker, *in the forties.*

An unusual portrait of White
by Irving Penn,
published in Vogue *in 1948.*

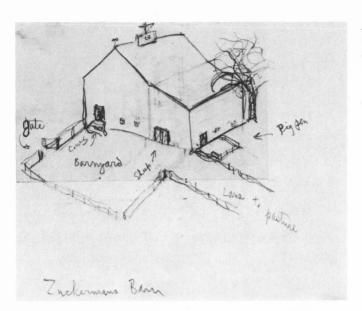

A drawing of Zucherman's barn that White made to guide him as he wrote Charlotte's Web.

Zuckermans Barn

Dearest K. This is a writer trying to look like a writer when he knows full well he is being photographed. Anyway, he loves you. A.

The window of the 10' × 15' boathouse, where White wrote Charlotte's Web *(and much else), looks out over Allen Cove to Harriman Point. With only a mouse and a squirrel for company, White found that the sparsely furnished boathouse "sheltered him better than the large house where his bed was." Here he was a "wilder" and "healthier man." Note White's tender inscription to Katharine. Photograph by Jill Krementz.*

Chapter I. The Barn

CHARLOTTE

A barn can have a horse in it, and a barn can have a cow in it, and a barn can have hens scratching in the chaff and swallows flying in and out through the door — but if a barn hasn't got a pig in it, it is hardly worth talking about. I am very glad to say that Mr. Zuckerman's barn had a pig in it, and therefore I feel free to talk about it as much as I want to. The pig's

~~Do things to have when it at~~
~~Zuckerman's barn as that it was built in the~~
~~top of a hill~~   ~~as possible~~

name was Wilbur. He was small and white, except when he was dirty ~~when them dirty~~ he was small and brown. Wilbur did not get dirty on purpose, but he lived in the a lower part of the barn ~~underneath the where the cows were~~ ~~it~~ where

One of the earliest versions of the first page of Charlotte's Web. "I had about as much difficulty getting off the ground as did the Wright brothers."

and plenty of tricks up her sleeve.

I.

She was about the size of a gumdrop, and she had eight legs, ~~which is enough for any body~~

Charlotte was a ~~big~~ grey spider who lived in the doorway of a barn. But there is no use talking about Charlotte until we have looked into the matter of the barn. This barn was large. It was old. It was white. *painted.* It smelled of hay and it smelled of manure—. It was pleasantly warm in winter, pleasantly cool in summer; it had stalls for horses, tie-ups for the ~~milk~~ cows, an ~~scaffolds~~ *the work* enormous loft above for the hay ~~then chilled~~ *underneath* ~~could jump and roll and~~ *Pen below* a place down ~~below~~ for sheep a ~~place~~ for a pig, a grain bin, a rat trap, a lot of sunlight coming in through the big doors, *on sunny days, and rain beating against the* ~~east windows on~~ rainy days. ~~and the stable (formerly)~~ was owned by a fellow named Zuckerman. ~~If~~ ~~Zuckerman was fond of his barn. He was always~~ *barn of Zuckerman's* ~~All~~

Of all the barns I ever saw, *Charlotte, the spider, must have thought so, too, or* *there was* the most agreeable. ~~There was always~~ something going on she never would have built her web in the *the* doorway, ~~& she picked an awfully quiet doorway,~~ *very carefully* ~~though the the which the net was~~ When I say doorway I don't mean the *big* main doorway where the horses ~~went~~ went in and out, and I don't mean the

A later version before White decided to restructure the story. Some of the detail of the barn survives in Chapter III of the final version.

① *table for breakfast.*

"Where's Papa going with that ax?" said Fern to
her mother ~~as they were having breakfast~~ as ~~the kitchen having breakfast.~~ They were ~~in sitting~~ setting the in

"Out to the hoghouse," replied Mrs. Arable. "Some
pigs were born last night."

"I don't see why he needs an ax," continued Fern,
who was only eight. ~~xxxxxxxx~~

"Well," said her mother, ~~xxxxxxxxxxxxxxx~~ "eleven
~~pigs were born, and~~ one of ~~them~~ the pig is a runt. ~~just a little bit of a~~ It's very small, and
~~thing.~~ doesn't amount to much. Your father will have to do away with it. It's no good."

"Do away with it?" shrieked Fern, "You mean kill
it? Just because it's smaller than the others?"

Mrs. Arable ~~xxxxxxxxxxxxxx~~ put her spoon down
on her plate. "Don't yell, Fern!" she said. "Your father is
~~doing what is~~ right. The pig would probably die anyway."
                              down

Fern slid out of her chair, and ran outdoors ~~to the~~
~~xxxxxxxxxxxxxxxxxxxxxxxx~~ The grass was wet and the earth smelled
~~xxxxxxxxxxxxxxxxxxxxxxxxx~~ of springtime.
~~xxxxxxxxxxxxxxx father.~~ ~~The grass was wet with dew and her~~
                              ~~wxxxx~~ by the time
Fern's sneakers were ~~xxxx sopping wet before~~ she caught up with ~~him.~~ her father.

"Please don't kill it!" she sobbed. "It's unfair.'"

Mr. Arable stopped walking.
                    he
"Fern," said ~~her father~~, gently, "you will have to
learn to control yourself."

"Control myself?" yelled Fern. "This is a matter

*Very close to the final version of the first page, written after White had
decided to "start the narration with the birth of the pig on the Arable farm
and give the little girl a more important place in the story."*

White at age sixty-two. Photograph by Stanton A. Waterman.

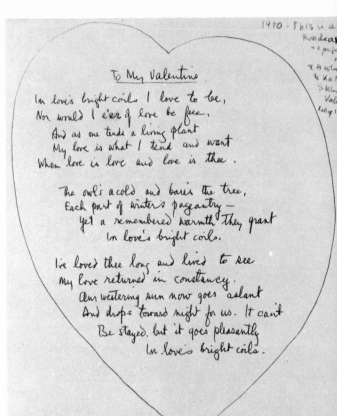

1970 · This is a Rondeau—a perfect one. E B White to K S White Valen Feb 19

To My Valentine

In love's bright coils I love to be,
Nor would I e'er of love be free,
And as one tends a living plant
My love is what I tend and want
When love is love and love is thee.

The owl's a cold and bares the tree,
Each part of winter's pageantry—
Yet a remembered warmth they grant
In love's bright coils.

I've loved thee long and lived to see
My love returned in constancy.
Our westering sun now goes aslant
And drops toward night for us. It can't
Be stayed, but it goes pleasantly
In love's bright coils.

One of White's many unpublished poems to Katharine, written on Valentine's Days, birthdays, and anniversaries. The note in the corner, in Katharine's hand, reads: "1970— This is a rondeau and a perfect one. KSW. E. B. White to Katharine S. White Valentine's Feb. 1970."

Joel White in Brooklin, Maine, about 1976. Photograph by Jill Krementz.

White in the seventies. In the background are the glassed-in porch and the terrace that the Whites added to the house. Some of Katharine's plants are in the window. From here, looking over Blue Hill Bay one can see Cadillac Mountain on Mount Desert Island.

E. B. White walking the track, in the James River valley in Virginia, April 1982. Photograph by Corona Machemer.

Corona Machemer at work on Poems and Sketches of E. B. White, 1980.

*White with garrulous geese, 1973. "Geese are friends with no one, they
badmouth everybody and everything. But they are companionable once you
get used to their ingratitude and their false accusations." Photograph
by Jill Krementz.*

CHAPTER XV

Charlotte's Web

1 9 4 9 – 1 9 5 2

*"The whole problem is to establish communication
with one's self."*

I N JANUARY 1949 WHITE WROTE HIS BROTHER
Stanley that he was in a "somewhat relaxed and benign condition
as the result of a decision to give up the responsibility of *The New
Yorker's* editorial page." From now on, he said, he intended to
"work patiently instead of rapidly, and to improve the nick of time."
Stanley would have recognized Thoreau's phrase "to improve the nick of
time," and would have understood that Andy wished once more to try to
live free from the servitude endured by the mass of men, unable "to stand
on the meeting of two eternities, the past and future, which is precisely
the present moment." He would work when he pleased. He may have
known then that he would write another book for children. During the
first eight months of his new freedom he may have written the preliminary
sketches of what was to become *Charlotte's Web,* for in September he told
his editor at Harper that his next book was in sight: "I look at it every
day. I keep it in a carton, as you would a kitten."[1]

While we do not know exactly when White began to write *Charlotte's
Web*, or when the outlines of its story started to take shape in his mind,
we do know the particular circumstances that led him to its theme. White
once described them as follows:

I like animals, and it would be odd if I failed to write about them. Animals
are a weakness with me, and when I got a place in the country I was quite
sure animals would appear, and they did.

A farm is a peculiar problem for a man who likes animals, because the fate of most livestock is that they are murdered by their benefactors. The creatures may live serenely but they end violently, and the odor of doom hangs about them always. I have kept several pigs, starting them in spring as weanlings and carrying trays to them all through the summer and fall. The relationship bothered me. Day by day I became better acquainted with my pig, and he with me, and the fact that the whole adventure pointed toward an eventual piece of double-dealing on my part lent an eerie quality to the thing. I do not like to betray a person or a creature, and I tend to agree with Mr. E. M. Forster that in these times the duty of a man, above all else, is to be reliable. It used to be clear to me, slopping a pig, that as far as the pig was concerned I could not be counted on, and this, as I say, troubled me. Anyway, the theme of *Charlotte's Web* is that a pig shall be saved, and I have an idea that somewhere deep inside me there was a wish to that effect.[2]

As it turned out, White's wish came true in the story of a pig named Wilbur who is saved by a spider named Charlotte. They live in the same barn and first become acquainted when Charlotte overhears Wilbur lamenting his loneliness and offers to be his friend. Wilbur thinks she is beautiful and, as he gets to know her, finds her fascinating. When he hears that his owner, Mr. Zuckerman, plans to butcher him at Christmastime, Charlotte calms his fears by promising to save him. A loyal (and talented) friend, she is as good as her word. She makes Mr. Zuckerman believe that Wilbur is an exceptional pig by writing words into the webs she weaves in the corner of the doorway to Wilbur's home in the cellar of the barn. The Zuckerman family and all their neighbors are amazed when they read Charlotte's legend SOME PIG, and take it for a miracle—a mysterious sign. And the wonder grows (as does Wilbur's reputation) when she extends her campaign with other legends: TERRIFIC and, later, RADIANT.

When Mr. Zuckerman takes Wilbur to the County Fair, Charlotte goes along in Wilbur's crate, hoping to help him win a prize and believing that if he does Mr. Zuckerman will not kill him. During the night before the prizes are awarded she weaves one more word—this time above Wilbur's exhibition pen, where all can see it. She chooses HUMBLE for her ultimate praise, a word she thinks appropriate because its dictionary definitions, "not proud" and "near the ground,"[3] fit Wilbur, who has remained modest in spite of his fame. The board of governors of the Fair give Wilbur a special award at a ceremony in front of the grandstand, and Mr. Zuckerman's delight assures Wilbur of a long life.

At the Fair, as soon as she has finished writing HUMBLE, Charlotte turns all her energies to making an egg sac and laying five hundred and fourteen eggs, after which achievement, she knows, she will languish and die. The news of her impending death crushes Wilbur, but when Charlotte says she doesn't even have the strength to get to the crate in which he will be returned to Zuckerman's barn, Wilbur has the wit to persuade his friend Templeton, the rat, to detach Charlotte's egg sac carefully from its place high up on the wall of his pen and bring it to him. Wilbur then carries it safely back home, where, in a scooped-out place in his warm manure pile, the eggs will be safe during the long winter.

When Charlotte's children begin to hatch on a warm spring day, Wilbur's heart pounds and he trembles with joy. When they are all hatched, his heart brims with happiness. The story ends:

> Wilbur never forgot Charlotte. Although he loved her children and grandchildren dearly, none of the new spiders ever quite took her place in his heart. She was in a class by herself. It is not often that someone comes along who is a true friend and a good writer. Charlotte was both.

A BIOGRAPHER COULD cite many events in White's life that found their way into *Charlotte's Web,* but none would add so much to its significance as an event that occurred in 1949, just about the time he began to write the book. In August of that year, in a letter to his friend John McNulty, White reported that the only writing he had done that summer was an introduction to a new edition of the late Don Marquis's masterpiece *archy and mehitabel.* He had, he said, "lost the knack of earning money by putting one word after another." The introduction would "just about put a new sole" on his sneakers.[4] It is hard to believe he was seriously worried about income. He had his small salary from *The New Yorker* for doing newsbreaks; he had income from investments; he had royalties from *Stuart Little;* and "Here Is New York," for which *Holiday* had paid him three thousand dollars, was such a success that Harper had decided to republish it as a little book in time for the Christmas trade. (By the end of the year, twenty-eight thousand copies had been printed, and the Book-of-the-Month Club had selected it as part of a dual selection for January.) Moreover, White could scarcely have felt financially pressed at the same time he and Katharine were planning to go to Europe on the *Queen Elizabeth* and he was planning to have a sloop built in a Danish boatyard. In any case, the five hundred dollars he was paid for his introduction to *archy and mehitabel* would have been inconsequential in comparision with the value of certain ideas he may have been reminded of as he read and wrote about Marquis's book—ideas that are important to the story and to the meaning of *Charlotte's Web.*

White had admired Marquis since youth, and now, as he was about to pay tribute to him, he was aware that he resembled Marquis in some ways:

[Marquis] was the sort of poet who does not create easily; he was left unsatisfied and gloomy by what he had produced; day and night he felt the juices squeezed out of him by the merciless demands of daily newspaper work; he was never quite certified by intellectuals and serious critics of belles lettres.[5]

White had not suffered that much, but he knew something about journalism's "merciless demands," and now, in 1949, he felt, in spite of honorary degrees and other recognition, that "serious critics" had never quite certified him. When White described Marquis as "a parodist, historian, poet, clown, fable writer, satirist, reporter, and teller of tales," he also described himself.[6] He also shared Marquis's views of human glory and human folly.

What White wrote about two of the fictional characters in *archy and mehitabel* has an especially interesting bearing on *Charlotte's Web*. Mehitabel, he reminded his readers, was "always the lady, *toujours gai.*" Some years later, describing Charlotte to someone who wanted to make a movie of the book, White said, "She is, if anything, more the Mehitabel type— *toujours gai.*" Charlotte is like Mehitabel in other significant ways—in her independence and self-confidence, in her wit and competence, in her tough-minded generosity, and especially in her loyalty to herself.

About Warty Bliggens, the toad, White said: "[Marquis] was at his best in a piece like 'warty bliggens,' which has the jewel-like perfection of poetry and contains cosmic reverberations along with high comedy. Beautiful to read, beautiful to think about." The cosmic reverberations are produced by Archy, the cockroach, who describes Warty Bliggens as a toad who "considers himself to be the center of the universe":

> the earth exists
> to grow toadstools for him
> to sit under
> the sun to give him light
> by day and the moon
> and wheeling constellations
> to make beautiful
> the night for the sake of
> warty bliggens. . . .
> if i were a
> human being i would
> not laugh

                    too complacently
                    at poor warty bliggens
                    for similar
                    absurdities
                    have only too often
                    lodged in the crinkles
                    of the human cerebrum[7]

White was tuned to the cosmic reverberations of that comment on man's disposition to assume that the whole universe was created to serve him, and *Charlotte's Web* would suggest the absurdity of that assumption. Once, in discussing *Charlotte's Web,* White was more explicit; he distinguished a spider from a human being by saying: "One has eight legs and has been around for an unbelievably long time on this earth; the other has two legs and has been around just long enough to raise a lot of hell, drain the swamps, and bring the planet to the verge of extinction."[8] There is no misanthropy in *Charlotte's Web,* but the heroic spider is both more noble and more adorable than any other creature in the story; and though White's purpose was not to preach a sermon, his fable about a heroic spider did contain cosmic reverberations of the same kind as those contained in Archy's wry comment about human beings who resemble the foolish toad.

The manuscript and notes of *Charlotte's Web* do not reveal much about the stages of its composition. The earliest extant draft is written in pencil on yellow sheets, some of them apparently substituted for earlier, discarded sheets, and a few of them apparently added as afterthoughts. All contain stylistic revisions made at the time of first writing as well as later. What White has labeled "First Draft," at any rate, is substantially the story as it finally appeared, except for the four chapters added in the final draft. There is no evidence that White made any essential changes in the original conception of the plot or its characters.

Apparently, most of the first draft was written in 1950, much of it between April 1 and October 15, in Maine. During this period he contributed nothing to "Notes and Comment," and he cancelled his reservations for the trip to England shortly after having made them. He wrote his editor at Harper that "maybe in the fall," instead of a collection of *New Yorker* pieces, he would "have another sort of book ready." "I guess it depends," he added, "on how many rainy mornings we get between now and fall, rain being about the only thing that brings me and a typewriter together."[9]

When White first met Charlotte A. Cavatica in person, he had called her Charlotte Epeira, because he thought she was a Grey Cross spider, the

Aranea sericata, which in old books on spiders was called *Epeira sclopetaria.*
She looked very much like one of the species of "House Araneas," de-
scribed as "exceedingly abundant on buildings that are near the water."[10]
Shortly after he met her White thought of making her the hero of his story:

> The idea . . . came to me one day when I was on my way down through
> the orchard carrying a pail of slops to my pig. I had made up my mind to
> write a children's book about animals, and I needed a way to save a pig's life,
> and I had been watching a large spider in the backhouse, and what with one
> thing and another, the idea came to me.[11]

A month later he made an observation that led him to the discovery that
she came from a different family than he had first thought. At the same
time he discovered how to end her story:

> One cold October evening I was lucky enough to see Aranea Cavatica spin
> her egg sac and deposit her eggs. (I did not know her name at the time, but
> I admired her, and later Mr. Willis J. Gertsch of the American Museum of
> Natural History told me her name.) When I saw that she was fixing to become
> a mother, I got a stepladder and an extension light and had an excellent view
> of the whole business. A few days later, when it was time to return to New
> York, not wishing to part with my spider, I took a razor blade, cut the sac
> adrift from the underside of the shed roof, put spider and sac in a candy box,
> and carried them to town. I tossed the box on my dresser. Some weeks later
> I was surprised and pleased to find that Charlotte's daughters were emerging
> from the air holes in the cover of the box. They strung tiny lines from my
> comb to my brush, from my brush to my mirror, and from my mirror to my
> nail scissors. They were very busy and almost invisible, they were so small.
> We all lived together happily for a couple of weeks, and then somebody whose
> duty it was to dust my dresser balked, and I broke up the show.[12]

Before he consulted Gertsch, he had discovered in John Henry Comstock's *Spider Book* a spider called *Aranea cavatica,* which "lives in great
numbers about houses and barns in northern New England" and sometimes
builds very large webs. From Comstock he learned that the genus *Aranea*
was for some time known by the name *Epeira,* that spiders had been known
to destroy "small vertebrate animals, including . . . a fish" (a fact upon
which White based one of the stories Charlotte tells Wilbur), and that the
"males of some species at least, dance before the females"[13] (a fact upon
which White based Charlotte's Mehitabel-like boast, in a passage later
deleted, that her husband was "some dancer.")[14] And he could have discovered, if he did not already know it, that if Charlotte's children had not

been confined to his bedroom in Turtle Bay Gardens, they would not have covered his comb and brush with their gossamer, for "very young spiders . . . in warm and comparatively still autumn days . . . climb to the top of some object . . . lift up their abdomens, and spin out threads, and if there is a mild upward current of air, are carried away by them."[15] When he went to see Gertsch, he carried a list of carefully prepared questions, the answers to some of which he used in the final chapter of the book. Later, when Garth Williams agreed to illustrate *Charlotte's Web,* White sent him a copy of Gertsch's *American Spiders.* White was proud of the scholarly accuracy of his text and Williams's drawings.

Near the end of October, White wrote the editor of *Holiday* that he was "engaged in finishing a work of fiction. (I guess that's what it is.)" He finished the first draft on January 19, 1951, and on March 1 he wrote Ursula Nordstrom at Harper that he had finished another children's book but had "put it away for a while to ripen (let the body heat out of it)."[16]

Before he completed his first draft, White had begun to think about a better way to open the story. He had opened it with a description of Wilbur and the barn he lived in (which later became Chapter III). He had not introduced the story's principal human characters, Fern Arable, her brother, Avery, and their parents, until considerably later, at a point after which they played increasingly significant parts in the story. By the time White neared the end of the first draft, Fern's interest in Henry Fussy had become an important element in a complex theme. Though the story ended in the animal world of Wilbur, and with our attention on Charlotte, White decided it would be better to introduce the story from the point of view of a human being, rather than from Wilbur's, and that that human being should be the little girl whose character he had already created. The *Charlotte's Web* manuscripts suggest that he made a good many attempts at a new opening before he found the right one. For some time he tried to let the story begin at midnight, when Fern's father goes out to the hoghouse and by lantern-light finds that his sow has littered eleven pigs, one more than she has teats to feed them with. The trouble with all the variations on that opening was that they lacked dramatic action and failed to introduce the girl whose perception and sensibility would gradually lead the reader into the world of the barn. White did not succeed in shifting the emphasis until he hit upon the lead of the final version: " 'Where's Papa going with that ax?' said Fern to her mother as they were setting the table for breakfast."

In the opening chapters of the revised version White tells how Fern saves Wilbur, the runt, from her father's ax, and delights in feeding and caring for him till he is five weeks old, at which time he has become too big for her to handle and she lets herself be persuaded to sell him to her uncle for six dollars. Chapter I of the first draft became Chapter III, and the rest of the text required only a few revisions to accomodate Fern's presence up to the point where she had originally made her first appearance. As he increased her presence in the story White saw in her some of the characteristics he remembered in himself as a boy. In his notes, White wrote: "She loved being out of bed before the others. She loved early morning because it was quiet and fresh and smelled good and she loved animals. . . . She was small for her age. . . . She was thoughtful, and a great many things bothered her"[17]—in short, she is a lot like Sam, the boy in *The Trumpet of the Swan,* and she is a lot like White.

DURING 1951 White increased his contributions to *The New Yorker* substantially. They included editorial paragraphs for thirty-five issues, and a piece called "Two Letters: Both Open," almost the only funny essay he had written in nearly seven years.[18]

In mid-June, in obvious high spirits, he wrote a long letter to James Thurber,[19] and in August, at the suggestion of *Holiday* magazine, he set out on a coast-to-coast automobile tour. He would write accounts of his travels, reminiscing, perhaps, on the tour he had made thirty years before in his lovely Model T. When he got to Galesburg, Pennsylvania, however, he decided that modern cars and modern traffic made tourists drive too fast to see the country they were passing through, and he turned north to Ithaca, and thence back to Maine.

During that summer Harold Ross became so ill that he had to give up most of his work at *The New Yorker;* and in December he died in a Boston hospital during an operation for lung cancer. *The New Yorker*'s obituary notice, on the opening page of the magazine, was written by White. It was a fine piece, praising Ross in the classical mode of elegy, which leaves its hearers purged of grief and encouraged to go on. White thought Ross would have found it less than perfect, would have "tagged it right away as writer conscious"—an adjective White said he believed Ross invented. But it was White's personal reminiscence of Ross that gave force to White's praise, and it was White's personal philosophy that made the eulogy transcend its purpose of rendering tribute to one man. In its loving memory of the bygone he found reason for hope in the future. It concluded with these paragraphs:

> He left a note on our desk one day apropos of something that had pleased him in the magazine. The note simply said, "I am encouraged to go on." That is about the way we feel today, because of his contribution. We are encouraged to go on.

When you took leave of Ross after a calm or stormy meeting, he always ended with the phrase that has become as much a part of the office as the paint on the walls. He would wave his limp hand, gesturing you away. "All right," he would say. "God bless you." Considering Ross's temperament and habits, this was a rather odd expression. He usually took God's name in vain if he took it at all. But when he sent you away with this benediction, which he uttered briskly and affectionately, and in which he and God seemed all scrambled together, it carried a warmth and sincerity that never failed to carry over. The words are so familiar to his helpers and friends here that they provide the only possible way to conclude this hasty notice and to take our leave. We cannot convey his manner. But with much love in our heart, we say, for everybody, "All right, Ross. God bless you!"[20]

In February 1952 Andy and Katharine gave a party for a hundred and forty guests to celebrate the appointment of William Shawn as Ross's successor. It lasted till after four in the morning, and towards the end Shawn played jazz on the piano. White wrote Thurber, who had been out of town, that "it had a couple of hours of early morning enchantment— the kind of goings on that made you feel that the door would presently open and in would walk Scott and Zelda."[21]

In March 1952 the contract for *Charlotte's Web* was signed. In it Harper agreed to pay White no more than seventy-five hundred dollars in any one year of the royalties earned by the book. In those days the Internal Revenue Service permitted authors to spread out their earnings in this way over the years following the publication of a book. *Charlotte's Web*, however, turned out to be a better trapper than anyone had foreseen: in 1979, when White finally was able, with the permission of the I.R.S., to withdraw the balance of royalties due him, the sum was over half a million dollars— of which, of course, a large part went to pay taxes.

In May the Whites moved to Maine for the summer; in June Andy had the worst hay fever he'd had in many years; and in July Katharine, in the early stages of hepatitis, had to go to the hospital in Bangor. In August, after some effort, Andy located and purchased two Suffolk ewes for $125 each. In short, during the waiting period between the completion of the manuscript and its publication the life of the Whites was normal: they wrote, they edited, they were ill, and they farmed. In "Notes and Comment" for September 13 (a month before *Charlotte's Web* appeared), White described a recurrence of his "head" trouble:

Mid-September, the cricket's festival, is the hardest time of year for a friend of ours who suffers from a ringing in the ears. He tells us that at this season it is almost impossible, walking or riding in the country, to distinguish between the poetry of earth and the racket inside his own head. The sound of insects has become, for him, completely identified with personal deterioration. He doesn't know, and hasn't been able to learn from his doctor, what cricket-in-the-ear signifies, if anything, but he recalls that the Hemingway hero in "Across the River and into the Trees" was afflicted the same way and only lasted two days—died in the back seat of an automobile after closing the door carefully and well. Our friend can't disabuse himself of the fear that he is just a day or two from dead, and it is really pitiful to see him shut a door, the care he takes.[22]

If the ringing in his ears came from anxiety about Charlotte's debut, White could soon slam doors carelessly. From the first, everyone at Harper was sure the book would be a hit. His editor, Ursula Nordstrom, did not let her admiration impede her usefulness. She persuaded White to change the title of the last chapter from "Death of Charlotte" to "Last Day," and she worked well with Garth Williams, whose pictures had truly, and charmingly, illustrated *Stuart Little*. Through her, Andy had tactfully communicated his notions and his concern about the drawings: Charlotte must be "beguiling," and she must be represented as accurately as possible; in *American Spiders* there was no illustration of *Aranea cavatica,* but there was one of *Neoscona* "that looks like Charlotte, pretty much"; "Smooth legs and smooth abdomen are correct. (Actually, Charlotte's legs are equipped with fine hairs, and these are mentioned in the book, but the overall effect is of smooth, silk-stocking legs.)"[23] It was going to be a good-looking book. It was also going out into a world where only seven years ago *Stuart Little* had sold a hundred thousand copies in its first year. Harper ordered a first printing of fifty thousand copies of *Charlotte's Web* and started an intensive advertising campaign a month before the publication date, October 15.

In the pre-Christmas season the book outsold every other title on the Harper list and had to be reprinted. The reviews were good, and the response from friends and acquaintances was reassuring. David McCord said that he had seen the Grand Canyon once and had never been able to talk about it—"It is the same with *Charlotte's Web*." Bennett Cerf guessed that "if there's only one book of the current season still in circulation fifty years hence, it will be *Charlotte's Web*." And Jean Stafford, recovering from a nervous breakdown, wrote:

> Dear Andy,
>   Charlotte's Web is the most beautiful and strengthening book I have read in I don't know when, and I think I will commit the entire of it to memory. I give you fully as much credit as I do my good doctors for relieving my terrors. Thank you for this and for everything else you have written and will write.
>   Yours, Jean[24]

Orville Prescott, in the *Times,* and Lewis Gannett, in the *Herald Tribune,* reviewed the book briefly but favorably. In the *Los Angeles Sunday News* Richard Armour said, "If the story doesn't quite come up to that of *Stuart Little,* it is still better than most children's books." August Derleth, in the Madison, Wisconsin, *Capital Times,* called it "one of those rare stories for young people which bid fair to last longer than their author—a minor classic beyond question."[25]

It did not make the front page of the *Sunday New York Times Book Review,* as most of White's other books have done, but Eudora Welty's review in the special children's-book supplement was an excellent piece of criticism. "The book has," she said, "grace and humor and praise of life, and the good backbone of succinctness that only the most highly imaginative stories seem to grow." Her conclusion that it is "an adorable book," was preceded by a summary, an interpretation (it is "about life and death, trust and treachery, pleasure and pain, and the passing of time"), and a judgment ("As a piece of work it is just about perfect"). On the front page of the *Sunday Herald Tribune Book Review,* Pamela Travers, author of the Mary Poppins books, said that the "tangible magic" of *Charlotte's Web* is "the proper element of childhood, and any grown-up who can still dip into it—even with only so much as a toe—is certain at last of dying young even if he lives to ninety." Pamela Travers also reviewed the book in London (where it had been simultaneously published, by Hamish Hamilton) in *The New Statesman and Nation.* The London *Times Literary Supplement* praised the book, noting that "Mr. White's language is fresh and exciting."[26]

Since that first printing of fifty thousand copies there have been (nearly) innumerable printings, in several editions. By now over six million copies have been sold. In its more than twenty translations there is no telling how many copies have been printed. In 1960 *Charlotte's Web* was the "overwhelming" winner in an informal poll conducted by *Publishers Weekly* to discover "the best children's book written between 1930 and 1960." During the eleven years between 1963 and 1973, when *The New York Times* compiled an annual best-seller list for children's books based on bookstore sales, *Charlotte's Web* was always among the top ten; and from 1967 to 1972, it was always first or second. In 1971 it was second only to *The Trumpet of the Swan.* In 1976, when *Publishers Weekly* polled "teachers, librarians, authors, and publishers," asking them to name the ten best children's books written in America since 1776, *Charlotte's Web* was number one, followed by *Where the Wild Things Are, Tom Sawyer, Little Women, The Adventures of Huckleberry Finn, The Little House in the Big Woods, Johnny Tremain, The Wizard of Oz, The Little House on the Prairie,* and *The Island of the Blue Dolphins.* For the past twenty years in America, *Charlotte's Web* has outsold *Winnie the Pooh,* any single Mary Poppins book, *The Wind in the Willows, The Little Prince,* and *Alice in Wonderland.* [27]

Charlotte's Web is a fabric of memories, many reaching back much further in time than White's life on his farm. It is a pastoral fiction written when, more than ever before, White's vision was retrospective and his sense of life was sharpened by his having seen many things come to an end. *The New Yorker* of Harold Ross, Katharine White, E. B. White, James Thurber, and Wolcott Gibbs had become middle-aged—was no longer so carefree as it had been twenty-five years before. New York itself was not the same city that had drawn the young *New Yorker* writers to it. Joel, White's only son, was no longer a child. White was fifty, slightly beyond middle age. And in the nineteen-fifties the civilized world itself seemed to be past middle age and failing fast. But for White, the most important things that had passed were the sensations and images of infancy, childhood, and youth; and if he could remember them clearly, he could remember the self that had experienced them. If he could evoke that self and keep in touch with it, he could imagine a fiction, write a story, create a world that children would believe in and love.

White was especially pleased with Pamela Travers's review of *Charlotte's Web* in *The New Statesman and Nation* because in it she had confirmed White's own theory of communication. She had said that "anyone who writes for children successfully is probably writing for one child—namely, "the child that is himself."[28]

Perhaps White was especially able to write for the child that was himself because he had never stopped communicating with it. He had in fact, never stopped trying to win the approval of the self he once referred to as "a boy I knew." The integrity of White's view of the world owed much to the boy he kept in touch with despite his own loss of innocence. And the clarity and grace of his writing derived in part from the clarity of his vision of that ideal young self:

> I think there is only one frequency and that the whole problem is to establish communication with one's self, and, that being done, everyone else is tuned in. In other words, if a writer succeeds in communicating with a reader, I think it is simply because he has been trying (with some success) to get in touch with himself—to clarify the reception. . . .[29]

About what he discovered when he got in touch with himself, we should take White at his word. To a reader of *Charlotte's Web* he wrote: "All that I hope to say in books, all that I ever hope to say, is that I love the world.

I guess you can find that in there, if you dig around." And though White does not think much of "diggers," admirers of *Charlotte's Web* need not feel guilty about discussing what and how the story means.

Most of what White loved in the world is represented in *Charlotte's Web*. Essentially it consists of the natural world of creatures living in a habitat filled with objects, animate and inanimate, that White enjoyed seeing, hearing, feeling, smelling, and tasting. The most lyrical passages in the story are celebrations of what's out there—things and actions. Remember, for example, the opening of Chapter III:

> The barn was very large. It was very old. It smelled of hay and it smelled of manure. It smelled of the perspiration of tired horses and the wonderful sweet breath of patient cows. It often had a sort of peaceful smell—as though nothing bad could happen ever again in the world. It smelled of grain and of harness dressing and of axle grease and of rubber boots and of new rope.

The strong organic smells of manure, perspiration of horses, and the breath of patient cows are as reassuring as the smell of hay. Process and plenitude are at the heart of the satisfactory world of the barn, which is a kind of paradise regained where it seems "as though nothing bad could happen ever again in the world." But, better than any ideal world, the real world of the barn was so full of such a variety of things that no one living there should ever be bored:

> It was full of all sorts of things that you find in barns: ladders, grindstones, pitch forks, monkey wrenches, scythes, lawn mowers, snow shovels, ax handles, milk pails, water buckets, empty grain sacks, and rusty rat traps.

Outside the barn there were other accumulations of things, such as the dump, where even refuse was interesting:

> Here, in a small clearing hidden by young alders and wild raspberry bushes, was an astonishing pile of old bottles and empty tin cans and dirty rags and bits of metal and broken bottles and broken hinges and broken springs and dead batteries and last month's magazines and old discarded dishmops and tattered overalls and rusty spikes and leaky pails and forgotten stoppers and useless junk of all kinds, including a wrong-size crank for a broken ice-cream freezer.

Wilbur's slops were plentiful and various. For breakfast he might have:

> Skim milk, crusts, middlings, bits of doughnuts, wheat cakes with drops of maple syrup sticking to them, potato skins, leftover custard pudding with raisins, and bits of Shredded Wheat.

Even in the rain that Wilbur (like his creator) hated, there were variety and plenitude:

> Rain fell on the roof of the barn and dripped steadily from the eaves. Rain fell in the barnyard and ran in crooked courses down into the lane where thistles and pigweed grew. Rain spattered against Mrs. Zuckerman's kitchen windows and came gushing out of the downspouts. Rain fell on the backs of the sheep as they grazed in the meadow.

There were the variety of seasons and the new and plentiful phenomena characteristic of each season:

> The early summer days on a farm are the happiest and fairest days of the year. Lilacs bloom and make the air sweet, and then fade. Apple blossoms come with the lilacs, and the bees visit around among the apple trees. . . .
> Early summer days are a jubilee time for birds. In the fields, around the house, in the barn, in the woods, in the swamp—everywhere love and songs and nests and eggs. . . . The song sparrow, who knows how brief and lovely life is, says, "Sweet, sweet, sweet interlude; sweet, sweet, sweet interlude." If you enter the barn, the swallows swoop down from their nests and scold. "Cheeky, cheeky!" they say. . . .
> Everywhere you look is life; even the little ball of spit on the weed stalk, if you poke it apart, has a green worm inside it.

After Charlotte dies, Wilbur understands that life is a sweet interlude, and the knowledge that he cannot live forever only intensifies his love for life in his world:

> Life in the barn was very good—night and day, winter and summer, spring and fall, dull days and bright days. It was the best place to be, thought Wilbur, this warm delicious cellar, with the garrulous geese, the changing seasons, the heat of the sun, the passage of swallows, the nearness of rats, the sameness of sheep, the love of spiders, the smell of manure, and the glory of everything.[30]

But that is how he felt after Charlotte had taught him that the smell of manure, the love of spiders, and the glory of everything were three parts of a kind of natural divinity.

In all White's writings the smell of manure (or of such other rich organic matter as leaf mold) is always exciting, promising, or reassuring: it "always suggests that life can be cyclic and chemically perfect and aromatic and continuous."[31] In *Charlotte's Web* it is a part of the glory of everything, and in the lullaby that Charlotte sings to Wilbur it is part of the comforting mystery of life:

> "Sleep, sleep, my love, my only,
> Deep, deep, in the dung and the dark;
> Be not afraid and be not lonely!
> This is the hour when frogs and thrushes
> Praise the world from the woods and the rushes.
> Rest from care, my one and only,
> Deep in the dung and the dark!"

But the book makes clear that the world White loves is more than a collection of things, natural and man-made, or a fascinating organization of reassuring cyclical, ongoing processes: it is a world in which the motive for creating, nurturing, teaching, encouraging, singing, and celebrating is love. Charlotte sang away Wilbur's loneliness and his fear of death by persuading him that his world was cuddling him in the warmth and protection of its dung and its darkness. But her power to convince him of this benevolence came from her love for him, whom she called her "one and only." It was the love implied in "Sleep, my love" that cured Wilbur's depression and anxiety, that saved his life, and that taught him how to live out the rest of his life.

White discovered Charlotte, to be sure, when he was looking for a way to save Wilbur, but in making her the savior he served more than the needs of his plot. By making her an admirable creature, he helped readers free themselves from prejudices against spiders. He wanted to write a children's story that was true to the facts of nature and that, by reflecting his own love and understanding of the natural world, might help others to lift up their lives a little. His story turned out to be more than an idyll. It is a fable that subtly questions the assumption that homo sapiens was created to have dominion over every other living thing upon the earth. It also affirms that heroism is not a sexually determined characteristic, nor is it identical with self-sacrifice. Charlotte does not save Wilbur by dying; she saves him by following her instincts, by using her intelligence, and by being true to her individual self without being false to her general nature. Heroes, Charlotte reminds us, have from ancient times been people in a class by themselves because they used their unusual gifts to protect others.

Wilbur's education in the grim facts of life, including fear and death, begins with learning how to accept such facts as Charlotte's nature, her "miserable inheritance," which includes the instinct to live by killing other creatures. She says it's "the way she's made"; she "just naturally" builds webs and traps flies. "Way back for thousands and thousands of years," Charlotte explains, "we spiders have been laying for flies and bugs." But that fact does not explain what caused such behavior in the first place. She doesn't know

> how the first spider in the early days of the world happened to think up this fancy idea of spinning a web, but she did, and it was clever of her, too. And since then, all of us spiders have had to work the same trick. It's not a bad pitch, on the whole.

Charlotte does not know the origin of evil, though perhaps she recognizes its existence when she calls her instinct to kill a "miserable inheritance" and when she says, "A spider's life can't help being something of a mess." Her ethical views resemble those of White's father, who used the word *mistake* for what others called "sins," and those of White himself, who prefers the nonjudgmental word *mess* for what others describe in moral terms.

When Charlotte explains to Wilbur why she saved his life, she gives two reasons: she likes him, and "perhaps [she] was trying to lift up [her] life a little." Here, as the skeptical White comes close to the problem of moral imperatives, he is cautious. *Perhaps,* he says, she was trying to lift up her life a little—to transcend her genetic inheritance, or be a little better than she had to be; and when she adds, "Heaven knows anyone's life can stand a little of that," she carefully, as well as humorously, warns that a little concern for moral improvement goes a long way. Unlike Justa the female canary, wife of Baby, Charlotte does *not* "enjoy the nobility of self-sacrifice."

Charlotte's charity has its limits. When Wilbur asks her what she's doing as she begins to weave her egg sac, she answers, "Oh, making something, making something as usual." Wilbur asks, "Is it for me?" "No," says Charlotte, "It's something for *me,* for a change." She pretends, perhaps, to be harder-headed than she is, but she is nonetheless governed by splendid self-interest and self-respect (or perhaps, of course, by selfish genes).

Charlotte lives and dies a free creature, intellectually as well as instinctively accepting her biologically determined fate. In laying her five hundred and fourteen eggs in her beautifully made sac she is not carrying out the wishes of spider society any more than she is doing it to please her mate. She's pretty sure why she creates her *magnum opus,* in the full knowledge that when it is finished she will die.

Earlier, when she tells Wilbur that she thinks she will not go with him to the Fair because she will have to stay home and lay eggs, and Wilbur suggests that she can lay her eggs at the Fair, Charlotte says: "You don't know the first thing about egg laying, Wilbur. I can't arrange my family duties to suit the management of the County Fair. When I get ready to lay eggs, I have to lay eggs, Fair or no Fair." White does not make Charlotte a victim of anything—even fate. She obeys sensibly the imperatives of being a female spider, knowing that she "has to," and she sounds, in fact, as if she were proud of her part in the great natural scheme, proud of the "versatility" of someone who can write and can also produce five hundred and fourteen eggs—save a friend's life as well as create new lives.

Children's books in the past had seldom faced up so squarely as did *Charlotte's Web* to such truths of the human condition as fear of death, and death itself; and they had not implied the courageous agnosticism that disclaimed any understanding of why life and the world are the way they are. In 1952 few children's books had made so clear as *Charlotte's Web* that the natural world of the barn does not exist to serve the world of the farmers who think they own it. And few children's books have so clearly embodied a love that can cure fear, make death seem a part of life, and be strong without being possessive. Charlotte was "in a class by herself." She was braver and more capable of friendship than Wilbur because she was older and more experienced, and probably because she was a superior individual—that is, a hero. Among heroes, of course, she was *sui generis*.

All of which is to suggest that *Charlotte's Web* was and probably will continue to be a modern book based on the integrity of a humble and skeptical view of the natural world and of the human beings in it. It gives no support to prejudice in favor of the superiority of human beings, or of one sex over another. It does celebrate a child's generous view of the world and a child's love of that world.

Charlotte's Web is a kind of fable, of course; but it is also a pastoral—an eclogue that takes its readers back to an early vision of an arcadia. It is itself a pastoral game, a form of play, and its effects are partly, perhaps heavily, nostalgic. If adults still possessed the world of the barn, they would not be so moved by a description of it. They love its memory because they have lost the original. They also love it because in loving it they are persuaded of its truth and perhaps of its perpetuity. *Charlotte's Web* can be "explained" in Wordsworthian, Blakean, or Proustian ways. As we grow older we lose the vision, but not beyond recall; in the vision of innocence is contained the wisdom of experience; the act of remembrance of things past affirms their value, affirms our value, and creates a sense of man freed from the clutches of time. Readers of *Charlotte's Web* momentarily enjoy this freedom because White succeeded in getting in touch with himself, with "the child that is himself."

CHAPTER XVI

From Turtle Bay
to Allen Cove

1 9 5 3 – 1 9 5 7

". . . torn all his days between two awful pulls—the gnawing desire to change life, and the equally troublesome desire to live it."

DURING THE FIRST THREE WINTERS AFTER THEIR return to full-time work for *The New Yorker*, in 1943, Andy and Katharine had lived in New York in furnished apartments, but in 1946 they had leased an unfurnished one at 229 East Forty-eighth Street, into which they moved their own possessions, and this pleasant duplex looking out on Turtle Bay Gardens was to remain their winter home for the next eleven years.

What mainly had persuaded Andy to move back to New York was his awareness of Katharine's pleasure in living in the city and working at *The New Yorker* as an editor in the Fiction Department. Having discovered how hard on Katharine the move to Maine in 1938 had been, he had decided to stay on in New York until Katharine retired at the age of sixty-five, in 1957. He also had recognized that as long as he had to earn his living by writing "Notes and Comment," New York was the best place for him to live for most of the year. After the financial success of *Charlotte's Web*, however, many of the things Andy did, or that happened to him, seemed to point towards his and Katharine's moving back to year-round life in Maine.

It was not only the financial success of *Charlotte's Web* that had a bearing on the question of how much longer he would have to write his weekly sermon for *The New Yorker*. The critical success of the book must have made White feel that as the author of it and of *One Man's Meat* he had become, at the very least, a distinguished minor writer and that, with such an achievement, he might with a clear conscience anticipate an early release from the obligation to meet deadlines—or to live near the shop.

In the spring of 1953 White returned to some business left unfinished when he decided, in 1949, to concentrate on the writing of *Charlotte's Web*. That business was the preparation for publication of what he called a "clip book," a selection of his pieces first published in *The New Yorker*. It had been fifteen years since he put together his last collection of *New Yorker* pieces, and during that time he had written much that his editor at Harper thought should be collected and published. So, by July Andy and Katharine were selecting and editing the material for *The Second Tree from the Corner*.[1] Before he thought of making the title of one of its pieces the title of the book, Andy wrote Thurber that he was considering "The E. B. White Papers" as a title, suggesting, perhaps, that White was thinking of the book as a collection of his literary remains—fugitive pieces deserving to be preserved in a volume. Even if Andy's joke was only a pun on "white paper"—meaning an official report—there is little doubt, judging from his Foreword to the book, that in White's mind *The Second Tree from the Corner* marked the end of something—goodbye to all that—not his life, but a substantial and definite period of his life. In the Foreword he said:

A man who is over fifty, as am I, is sure that he has only about twenty minutes to live, and it is natural, I suppose, that he should feel disposed to put his affairs in order, such as they are, to harvest what fruit he has not already picked up and stored away against the winter, and to tie his love for the world into a convenient bundle, accessible to all.

If White had died in the fall of 1953, the American literary heritage would have been the poorer by what he was still to produce in the years to come: a dozen or more fine essays, a valuable handbook for writers, and one more children's story; but with the publication of *The Second Tree from the Corner* White did round out an achievement that would have insured him a place in literary history. Of all his books it is still the favorite of some readers because, better than any other single work, it reveals many facets of his character and many aspects of his style. It is, as he said, "a book of revelations: essays, poems, stories, opinions, reports, drawn from the past, the present, the future, the city, and the country."[2]

It contains his "Remarks on Humor" and his essay on Don Marquis. Among its poems are "Song of the Queen Bee" and "Village Revisited." His veiled autobiographical pieces "Hotel of the Total Stranger," "The

Second Tree from the Corner," and "Zoo Revisited" are included, as are "Farewell, My Lovely!" and "Death of a Pig." In it are about fifty paragraphs from "Notes and Comment": some on the terrors of the atom age; others, like his account of the birth of twin fawns in the Bronx Zoo, on the reassurances offered by the forces of life in the natural world; and others on writing, such as "English Usage," which ends, "English usage is sometimes more than mere taste, judgment, and education—sometimes it's sheer luck, like getting across a street."

One of the three "Preposterous Parables" in the book, "The Morning of the Day They Did It," is the strongest satire White ever wrote. It is a story told by a human being who survived the end of the world by landing on another planet after he had observed the holocaust from an airborne television studio. The United States had developed a space plat-form to carry a weapon that made the H-bomb obsolete; and the army officers who manned the platform found that when they were out where they could no longer feel the pull of gravity or "dames" ("when you don't weigh anything you don't *want* anything"), they also could not feel the pull of conscience. In a fit of insolent pique at their commanding officer on earth, but mainly just for the sheer hell of it, they fired on the earth with their New Weapon until the earth disintegrated.

In the course of telling the story White satirized most of the aspects of his culture that made him melancholy: the increasingly foolish complexity of daily life that prevented people from living "deliberately," as Thoreau had urged his fellow men to do; the growing obsession with speed and travel; the atrophy of individual powers of direct observation; the debase-ment of taste and intellectual life; the loss of integrity and the disposition to let the state take care of your conscience as well as your physical and economic welfare.

White himself was among the objects of this satire, but he was also the narrator who, speaking from another planet, concluded his story as follows:

> In many respects I like the planet I'm on. The people here have no urgencies, no capacity for sustained endeavor, but merely tackle things by fits and starts, leaving undone whatever fails to hold their interest, and so, by witlessness and improvidence, escape many of the errors of accomplishment. I like the apples here better than those on earth. They are often wormy, but with a most wonderful flavor. There is a saying here: "Even a very lazy man can eat around a worm."
>
> But I would be lying if I said I didn't miss that other life, I loved it so.

Back in 1938, when he had taken an equally depressing view of the world he was living in, it had prompted him to move to Maine, an act that he had called "in a sense an abdication." Now, in 1953, the fact that he chose to include in "The E. B. White Papers" this alarming, recently written parable suggests that he was once again disspirited and considering a "removal from the city," a second retreat to his beloved farm.

The Second Tree from the Corner was published in January 1954. White had refused to delay its publication long enough for the Book-of-the-Month Club to find another book with which to bracket it in a "dual selection." The BOM, he observed, seemed unable to find his books suitable for an outright selection. Though the guaranteed twenty thousand dollars he spurned by rejecting the offer was a considerable sum, he thought the book would do all right without the club's sponsorship. It was reviewed with strong praise on the front page of the *Sunday Herald Tribune Book Review* by Robert Sherwood, and on the front page of the *Sunday New York Times Book Review* by Irwin Edman. Published by Hamish Hamilton in London, it was favorably reviewed there in the *Times* and in the *Times Literary Supplement*. Within the first month Harper shipped forty thousand copies; by the end of the year it had sold sixty-six thousand.

In December 1953 Andy and Katharine became grandparents. Joel had transferred at the end of his sophomore year from Cornell to MIT in order to study naval architecture, and in his junior year he had married Allene Messer. Their first child, Steven, was born just before Christmas, and Andy shared his pleasure in the event with the readers of "Notes and Comment":

Instead of following a star, we simply followed directions given us by the child's parents; took the ten-o'clock train, and found the infant in Boston, where it lay behind glass in a hospital. No shepherds were abiding there, but there was a nurse in a mask attending and the glory of the Lord shone round about—a child seen through a glass clearly.[3]

After Joel graduated from MIT in 1954, he was drafted into the army, and soon after their second child, Martha, was born, in December 1954, he and his family were shipped to Germany, where he was stationed.

During 1954 White spent six months in Maine, from April to October, but he wrote as much that year as he had written in any year in the recent past, and more than he would ever write in any future year. It was a hectic time. Right after Christmas Katharine came down with intestinal flu; then Andy caught it and immediately built it into cancer of the colon. He went into the hospital for tests, after which he suffered the usual "frightening waves of disappointment" set in motion by the news that the results were all negative. At the end of January Katharine's sister Rosamond died suddenly in Sarasota. Because Andy felt too sick to make the trip south, Katharine had to ask her daughter, Nancy, to go with her to help arrange temporary housing for ninety-two-year-old Aunt Crully, who had been living with Rosamond. While Katharine was away, Andy wrote a review of Elmer Davis's *But We Were Born Free*. White did not like to review books, but he admired Elmer Davis, and he wanted to encourage people to read a book that said so many of the things he himself believed needed saying at the time—especially about current threats to civil liberties. But writing the review gave White a lot of trouble, and he came down with shingles.[4]

When Katharine returned, she had the mumps, and in its wake a severe reaction to penicillin that kept her in bed for a month. On the day Andy learned that sales of *Charlotte's Web* had reached one hundred thousand, he was worrying about whether he would catch the mumps from Katharine. But in mid-March he and she were able to go to Sarasota to bring Aunt Crully north to live with them. As soon as she was settled into the Whites' apartment in New York, Andy drove to Maine to supervise the building of a new terrace on the north side of the farmhouse. He stayed till October.[5]

Andy enjoyed, as always, being on the farm in early spring and coping with the crises of daily life. A late frost froze the pipes, and a barn owl killed two young lambs. During this time, as during the whole year, White kept up his regular contributions to "Notes and Comment."

E v e r since he had given up "One Man's Meat," in 1943, and taken on the chief responsibility for the editorials in *The New Yorker,* White had been slowly changing "Notes and Comment" from a column consisting of five or six brief, self-contained notes or comments on various topics to one in which occasionally the topics were thematically related in a loosely constructed essay, and in which tightly argued essays of a thousand words or more were not uncommon. These were often sober expositions of opinion—on the war, the peace, and the organization of the United Nations. Then, as time went on, he addressed other large and urgent problems, such as the dangers of contaminating the atmosphere of the whole world by testing atomic weapons. When, for example, President Truman sounded a warning against such testing in his last State of the Nation address, in January 1953, White called attention to Truman's warning and added his own:

> The hydrogen bomb releases Carbon 14, which has a half life of 5,600 years. When the planet has enough Carbon 14 kicking around, the so-called higher forms of life find that their reproductive powers either vanish or take odd turns, and at this point the planet becomes habitable only for the so-called

lower forms, such as the cockroach, who can make a nice meal out of Carbon 14 laced with desk paste. This news is beginning to get around, via the grapevine.[7]

William Steig wrote White a note about this editorial: "Your statement, in this week's *New Yorker,* about the nuclear energy contamination of the world's atmosphere is the first editorial comment on that subject that I have seen in any newspaper or magazine."[8] Two years later White would be bolder and more direct. At the end of a thousand-word editorial on the subject he said, "We don't think the problem of contamination-by-experimentation, of extinction-through-curiosity, has yet been presented to the world in anything like the vivid, detailed, and compelling way that it merits." The stockpile of atom bombs is not so threatening as "the peacetime bomb that goes off, from time to time killing fish, killing men, gradually building up the level of radioactivity."[9]

When Senator Joseph McCarthy made his first bid for attention in 1950 by claiming to have a list of names of over one hundred State Department employees whom he alleged to be pro-Communist and therefore security risks, most people, including White, considered him to be more an embarrassment to the Senate (and the nation) than a serious threat to justice. When he went on to question the loyalty of Secretary of State Dean Acheson and of General George Marshall, White still thought it would be a mistake to aggrandize this demagogue by discussing him seriously in print. Even when, near the end of the presidential election campaigns of 1952, McCarthy made his last-minute, nationwide television attack on Stevenson ("Alger—I mean, Adlai . . ."), White refrained from paying editorial attention to him. Not until 1953, when McCarthy became chairman of the Senate Permanent Subcommittee on Investigations, did White give McCarthy any space in "Notes and Comment." At that time he said:

> [A] very great majority of loyal Americans are deeply worried, not because they have a skeleton in their closet or because they disapprove of fact-finding in Congress, but because they see and feel in their daily lives the subtle change that has already been worked by a runaway loyalty-checking system in the hands of a few men who, to say it in a whisper, are not ideally equipped to handle the most delicate and dangerous job in the nation, that is the questioning of values of one's fellow-citizens. A couple of these committeemen don't know a fact from a bag of popcorn anyway.[10]

In late spring of 1954, when McCarthy was on nationwide television chairing his committee's investigation of disloyalty in the army, White finally wrote a long, sober editorial that called for McCarthy's removal from the chairmanship of the committee. The junior senator from Wisconsin, White said, had "succeeded only in making the country less secure," and in keeping America "in an uproar just when it should have a firm grasp on itself." The hearings were not a " 'squabble' (as it is often called) between the army and McCarthy," but a "showdown on the country's top problem in security." In his final paragraph he listed the enormities of McCarthy's mad career as "investigator":

> The twenty-years-of-treason junket, the use of the word "guilt" in hearing rooms where nobody is on trial and where no judge sits, the Zwicker inquisition, the willingness to shatter an army to locate a dentist, the sly substitution of the name "Alger" for the name "Adlai," the labelling of the majority of the press as "extreme Left Wing," the distortion of facts and figures, the challenge of the power of the White House, the use of the grand elision in the phrase "Fifth Amendment Communist," the queer notion that he, and he alone, is entitled to receive raw information that it is illegal for others to have in their possession, the steady attack on national confidence and national faith, as though confidence were evil and suspicion were good—the score is familiar and need not be recited in its long detail. Whatever else can be said for and against the Senator, it has become obvious that he dislikes a great many things about our form of government. To disapprove of these well-loved principles and rules is not a crime, but neither is it a help in performing the duties of a committee chairman in the United States Senate.[11]

Not since his review of Anne Morrow Lindbergh's *Wave of the Future,* in 1940, had White argued so forcefully.

IN JUNE 1954 White received honorary degrees from Harvard University and Colby College (he had regretfully declined offers from Brown University and Kenyon College because of conflicts in dates). Another and perhaps more welcome recognition from the academic world was an invitation from the *Yale Review* to write an essay commemorating the one hundredth anniversary of the publication of *Walden.* White accepted and in July wrote what he later entitled "A Slight Sound at Evening."

Thoreau is the only writer whose influence on White is obvious. White has referred to him more often than to any other writer, written about him more often, and echoed him in thought and style more often. On the occasion of Eisenhower's inauguration, for example, when White imagined how he himself would spend his first day as president in the Oval Office, he thought of Thoreau:

When they tried to catch us at a desk, we would shake our head and issue a statement: "Sorry, got to go out today. Got to call on a bayberry bush, got to see a pond about a man; got to find spruce gum, look under a rock, test rain for wetness and fertility; got to look for Life Everlasting."[12]

A few months later, when White ridiculed McCarthy in a parable called "Visitors to the Pond," he described his relationship to Thoreau:

"Walden" is the only book I own, although there are some others unclaimed on my shelves. Every man, I think, reads one book in his life, and this one is mine. It is not the best book I ever encountered, perhaps, but it is for me the handiest, and I keep it about me in much the same way one carries a handkerchief—for relief in moments of defluxion or despair.[13]

In Thoreau White had found a kindred spirit when he first read *Walden* at Cornell. After he graduated, when he was trying to avoid a life of what Thoreau called "self-imposed bondage," he was sustained by the example as well as the doctrine of Thoreau. Andy had known, almost from childhood, that the mass of men live lives of quiet desperation, and he believed that like Thoreau he could avoid such a fate by boldly taking the time needed to "observe and feel" the world around him. "What seemed so wrong to Thoreau," White once wrote, "was man's puny spirit and man's strained relationship with nature."

In 1927, when he was at loose ends, he bought a copy of the handy little blue-covered Oxford World's Classics edition of *Walden*, which became his "one book." The following year, when he and Rosanne parted, he gave her a copy of *Walden,* as if to offer her an explanation of his need for independence. Then, in December 1928, when he was thinking of leaving New York and *The New Yorker,* he gave Katharine a handsome new edition of *Walden* for Christmas.

He was, of course, aware that he could not himself be fully satisfied by Thoreau's "existence without material adornment." He had only to remember his need for Old Town canoes, and Model T Fords, and twenty-foot catboats—to say nothing of his need for a wife and a family and a saltwater farm. But the contrast between the utopia described in Thoreau's "tale of individual simplicity" and the world that the son of Samuel White had been born into did not weaken for him the attraction (or usefulness) of Thoreau's philosophy.

He found Walden "a document of increasing pertinence" in a technological world that was inextricably tangling itself in its own complexity. "We may all be transcendental yet, whether we like it or not," he wrote in his best-known piece on Thoreau—in the form of a report to Thoreau on his visit to Walden Pond in 1939.[14] But *Walden*'s chief attraction for White was the character of Thoreau the individual, an egocentric, wide-awake, optimistic man who had used as the epigraph for *Walden* a passage from it that read: "I do not propose to write an ode to dejection, but to brag as lustily as a chanticleer in the morning, standing on his roost, if only to wake up his neighbors." Thoreau, White said, was "a writer trying not to act like a writer," and White approved of that. And, on another occasion, White called Thoreau "the subtlest humorist of the nineteenth century." White once paid tribute to Thoreau in a little essay in "Notes and Comment" that opened as follows:

> May 6th is the saddest day in the year for us, as it is the day of Thoreau's death—a grief from which we have not recovered. Henry Thoreau has probably been more wildly misconstrued than any other person of comparable literary stature. He got a reputation for being a naturalist, and he was not much of a naturalist. He got a reputation for being a hermit, and he was no hermit. He was a writer, is what he was. Many regarded him as a poseur. He was a poseur, all right, but the pose was struck not for other people to study but for *him* to study—a brave and ingenious device for a creative person to adopt. He posed for himself and was both artist and model, examining his own position in relation to nature and society with the most patient and appreciative care.[15]

White recognized himself in Thoreau in a variety of ways. Thoreau "was torn all his days between two awful pulls—the gnawing desire to change life, and the equally troublesome desire to live it." "Most of the time," White added, "Thoreau didn't want to do anything about anything." Thoreau's religion suited White, who liked to remember that when the dying Thoreau was asked whether he had made his peace with God, he replied, "I was not aware we had quarrelled." White considered that the "purest religious thought he had ever heard."

The point is not so much that *Walden* influenced White as that, in White's words, it served him well "in moments of defluxion and despair." The spring and summer of 1954 were full of such moments for many Americans who felt helpless in the period of the cold war and in what came to be called the McCarthy era.

"A Slight Sound at Evening" is an intricately constructed interpretation of *Walden* and a celebration of it. White begins by saying that he thinks of the book not as a sermon or an attempt to rearrange society, but as "the best youth's companion yet written in America." It is, he says "like an invitation to life's dance, assuring the troubled recipient that no matter what befalls him in the way of success or failure he will always be welcome at the party—that the music is played for him, too, if he will but listen and move his feet." It "advances a good argument for travelling light and trying new adventures . . . it contains religious feeling without religious images, and it steadfastly refuses to record bad news."

To White, at the age of fifty-five, it still seemed a good companion even for people no longer young, living in an age when many Americans wondered whether their country would have the intelligence, will, and luck to conduct itself generously and prudently in an immensely perilous world. Older readers must listen carefully to hear *Walden*'s message or its music—its slight sound—just as anyone must listen carefully to be able to hear "the uninterrupted poem of creation, the morning wind that forever blows." "In the brooding atmosphere of war and the gathering radioactive storm," White wrote, "the innocence and serenity of [Thoreau's] summer afternoons are enough to burst the remembering heart, and one gazes back upon that pleasing interlude [at Walden Pond]—its confidence, its purity, its deliberateness—with awe and wonder, as one would look upon the face of a child asleep." But, he concluded, he still reread "with undiminished excitement" Thoreau's "famous invitation," which

> will beckon as long as this remarkable book stays in print—which will be as long as there are August afternoons in the intervals of a gentle rainstorm, as long as there are ears to catch the faint sounds of the orchestra. I find it agreeable to sit here this morning . . . and hear across a century of time his flute, his frogs, and his seductive summons to the wildest revels of them all.[16]

Not long before he wrote "A Slight Sound at Evening," Adrienne Rich had written Katharine that she thought, "without detracting an inch from H.D.T., that it must be a good deal more difficult to be E. B. White in the 20th century than Henry Thoreau in the 19th." Still, it would have been harder for White to be himself had not Thoreau, as he said, "served as [his] conscience through the long stretches of [his] trivial days." And we may assume that Thoreau's words were at that very moment encouraging White once more to simplify his life, at least to the extent of getting out of New York and finding a less demanding way to earn a living than writing "Notes and Comment."[17]

Six weeks after he finished his essay on *Walden*, he wrote an account of his experiences in Maine during thirty-six hours of waiting for a hurricane to strike. This thirty-five-hundred-word personal essay in the style of "One Man's Meat" appeared shortly afterwards under the title

"Our Windswept Correspondents/The Eye of Edna," and over the signature of E. B. White. In retrospect it looks like a milestone in White's journey towards retirement from his work as an urban staff writer and the resumption of his career as a rusticated essayist. A whole year elapsed before he wrote another such essay, but within nine months he stopped writing "Notes and Comment."

WHEN AUNT CRULLY died suddenly in the late spring of 1955, Andy and Katharine decided that the time had come to take the trip to England that Katharine had looked forward to for several years. Before they sailed, about the first of June, Andy wrote a paragraph for "Notes and Comment" that was both generally and specifically valedictory, for it was one of his last paragraphs as a regular contributor:

> The two moments when New York seems most desirable, when the splendor falls all round about and the city looks like a girl with leaves in her hair, are just as you are leaving and must say goodbye, and just as you return and can say hello. We had one such moment of infatuation not long ago on a warm, airless evening in town, before taking leave of these shores to try another city and another country for a while. There seemed to be a green tree overhanging our head as we sat in exhaustion. All day the fans had sung in offices, the air-conditioners had blown their clammy breath into the rooms, and the brutal sounds of demolition had stung the ear—from buildings that were being knocked down by the destroyers who have no sense of the past. Above our tree, dimly visible in squares of light, the city rose in air. From an open window above us, a whiff of perfume or bath powder drifted down startlingly in the heavy night, somebody having taken a tub to escape the heat. On the tips of some of the branches, a few semiprecious stars settled themselves to rest. There was nothing about the occasion that distinguished it from many another city evening, nothing in particular that we can point to to corroborate our emotion. Yet we somehow tasted New York on our tongue in a great, overpowering draught, and felt that to sail away from so intoxicating a place would be unbearable, even for a brief spell.[18]

The trip was a disappointment. When they landed at Southampton, there was a rail strike; when they got to the Connaught Hotel in London, Andy was made uncomfortable by its snobbery. When they decided to make some excursions by car, Andy was afraid he would not remember to drive on the left-hand side of the road and chose to engage the services of a liveried driver; when they visited Exeter Cathedral, Andy "complained all the time about how the place smelled"; when they reached

Devon—where Andy was interested in the sheep—he began to worry about news of a strike by the stewards on the Cunard Line, on which they were to travel home, and he instantly changed their return booking to the *America* and to an earlier date than had been originally arranged. Three weeks after the Whites arrived in England they sailed back to the U.S.— much sooner than planned, and without having gone on to visit Joel and his family at his army post in Germany, as Katharine had hoped they would do. They landed in New York on the Sunday of a long July fourth weekend. The city was empty and hot. Katharine and Andy never again went abroad—never went anywhere, except to New York to visit dentists and doctors, and to Florida for the sun. Andy thought (with Thoreau) that people traveled too much.[19]

In the fall of 1955 Andy stopped contributing to "Notes and Comment," and Katharine informed William Shawn that she had decided to stop working full-time for the magazine after February 1956. Poor health may have been one of her reasons for deciding to retire a year earlier than she had planned; Andy's desire to move back to Maine may have been another; a third may have been that the job simply wasn't as much fun as it once was when she had been head of the Fiction Department and working with Ross. Even after she had given up her full-time job in 1937 and was succeeded by Gus Lobrano as head of the Fiction Department, she enjoyed the knowledge that she was working for Ross even though hers was a non-resident and part-time job. When Ross died in 1951, Lobrano had hoped (unrealistically, some thought) to succeed him as editor-in-chief. When Shawn was chosen instead, Lobrano, in White's words, "never forgave Shawn or anybody else." Katharine found it easy to work with Shawn, whom she admired; still, she did not enjoy the same easy relationship with him that she had with Ross. And it may have been that, though Gus was Andy's best friend, Katharine and he did not get on well together.[20]

An essay that appeared in *The New Yorker* for December 24, 1955, made clear where Andy thought "home" was. He had driven to Maine before Thanksgiving and had spent at least a couple of weeks there, during which time he had written another piece reminiscent of his "One Man's Meat" essays, this one consisting of five loosely connected parts, all related to the topic that was its title, "Homecoming." It opened, "On the day before Thanksgiving, towards the end of the afternoon, having motored all day, I arrived home, and lit a fire in the living room."

In a letter to Shawn accompanying the manuscript of this piece White suggested that it be titled "Letter from the East." He was looking for a heading to cover the essays he planned to contribute in the future. "Seems to me," he wrote, "that if I can latch on to the four points of the compass, I can manage anything. A letter from Nome or from 110th Street would be Letter from the North. A letter from Third Avenue would be from the East." "Homecoming" was the first of about fifteen "Letters" he would write for *The New Yorker* during the next six years.[21]

It may have been the nervous strain produced by arriving at the decision to pull up stakes that gave Andy stomach trouble in January 1956, so severe that he was sent to the hospital for X rays. These revealed, he later wrote, that in him "the small exit called the 'pylorus' leading from the stomach" closed up tight "at the slightest hint of trouble ahead."[22] Or it may have been a premonition that in fact he and Katharine would not, after all, make the move to Maine in 1956. Gus Lobrano, who had been in poor health for over a year, was now obviously dying. When he died, would Shawn need Katharine's help, at least for a short while longer? Just before he and Katharine left for Sarasota in February, Andy visited Lobrano in his home in Chappaqua, and as soon as he and Katharine arrived in Florida, they learned that Gus was dead.

What made Andy and Gus so congenial and accounted for their long friendship does not emerge very clearly from the few bits of correspondence between them that have survived, but there may be a clue in the following anecdote White told Frank Sullivan at the time of Gus's death:

> Did I ever tell you about the day when I walked Gus through Boston to show him a few sights—this was a few years ago. We started up Beacon Hill and turned into Louisburg Square. "This," I announced, "is Louisburg Square." Gus gazed quietly at the cozy scene. "Is it all right to smoke?" he asked.[23]

When Lobrano died, Shawn at once asked Katharine to take on her old job as head of the Fiction Department and to stay on for two more years, or as long as necessary to reorganize the department. She must have been pleased to accept the offer, but the return to Maine had to be postponed. Allene White wrote from Germany that she and Joel "were both happy over the outcome of it all, because it sounded like something Mother could do so well and enjoy it too."[24]

The month in Sarasota, sunning and swimming on the shore of Fiddler Bayou, was good for Andy, and before he and Katharine headed north he wrote a "Letter from the South" which he later entitled "The Ring of Time." It is one of the finest of White's "Letter" essays.

On his fifty-seventh birthday, July 11, 1956, at 8:00 A.M., he and Katharine were at dockside when the transport carrying Joel and Allene and their children arrived at a pier in Brooklyn. Within a week of their return Andy went to Maine to see them. His report to Katharine in New York was full of his pleasure in the company of two-and-a-half-year-old Steven White.

Back in New York at the end of the month, Andy learned of the death of his good friend John McNulty, whom he had known since the thirties, when Thurber brought McNulty to *The New Yorker.* White had loved McNulty and was going to miss his company. Four years before McNulty died, White had written a short piece about him for "Notes and Comment" that showed his affection for this wonderfully funny man:

> One of our best friends is a horseplayer. Every year we live through, with him, the agonies of a trackless winter. Nobody who hasn't been through this sterile period year after year can know what it's like. With the first of April only a few days off, with what Mr. Joe H. Palmer terms "the wild clear call of Jamaica" in the secret ear, our friend is reborn; he bursts into bloom as violently as a booth at the Flower Show. Unable longer to apply himself to his profession, he gives up all pretense of earning a living and settles into the climacteric—a gaudy fever of idleness, a muted carnival of unreleased activity. One thing that happens at this point is that he spends more and more time on his appearance; the greater part of every forenoon is devoted to getting decently turned out, as though he really had someplace to go that day. Always a dresser, he goes into the final days of March with smashing effect. Another thing that happens is that his taste in food becomes greatly refined. He is so whetted, so ready for the impending pleasures of the mind, that his system requires some immediate gratification, some readily accessible delight, and this takes the form of high living. Only yesterday, he walked us clear up to Sixty-first Street (he never rides, always walks; it consumes more time to walk, and afoot one meets other horseplayers)—clear up to the men's bar of the Carlton House, where we sat with him over a dish of whitebait and a cold bottle. He finds conversation at this period superfluous. In company with a non-racing man like ourself, he prefers to wait out the last hours in the purity of silence rather than in irrelevant discourse. He marks each tick of the clock, devours the remaining moments one by one, dreamily, as you would finish up a bag of salted nuts.[25]

Before the year was out, White had made three more trips to Maine. During the fall Joel and Allene moved into their own house not far from the farm. On one trip Andy stopped in Boston to see the launching of *Fern,* his new twenty-foot double-ender sloop, built for him in Denmark —a much smaller boat than *Astrid,* the boat he had bought before he retreated to Maine nearly twenty years before. When he got to Brooklin, he went shopping for two steer calves. All this fun, added to his satisfaction in having his son working in the Brooklin Boatyard and his grandchildren living nearby, though it did not keep him in good physical health, helped to keep his courage up and his muse active. Before the end of the year he had written three more "Letters."

Katharine and Andy went to Maine for Christmas, "partly," he wrote his brother Stanley, "because Joel and his family now live there, and it made a nice chance to get out of town for the holidays. Maine was particularly beautiful, as there had been some snow and the woods were white and the weather was wintry without being rough. Only the grandchildren were rough. . . . They went through the pile of presents like a couple of half backs. It was very gay."

Back in New York Katharine had to go to work, but Andy had time to suffer "throat trouble of some sort." One doctor, White wrote Stanley, "says my Adam's Apple is tangled up with my psyche."[26] He went to the hospital for a bronchoscopy in January and, as he had done several times in the past, wrote an account of his experience that helped defray the cost of the examination. Some readers of "Notes and Comment" must have recognized an old friend in a piece that ended with the following paragraph:

> The curative value of a hospital, for us, is that it keeps us busy. In our normal life in the outside world, we seldom have anything to do from morning till night and we simply wander about, a writer who rarely writes, lonely and at peace, getting through the day cunningly, the way an alcoholic works his way along from drink to drink, cleverly spaced. But once we're in a hospital, the nights and days are crowded with events and accomplishment. Supper is at six, breakfast at nine, which means that for about fifteen hours we subsist in a semistarved condition, like a man in a lifeboat; and when our stomach is empty our mind and heart are full, and we are up and about, doing housework, catching up on correspondence, outwitting the air-conditioning system, taking sleeping pills, reading names on nurses' badges, arranging flowers, picking up after the last tenant, fighting the roller shade that has lost its spring, making plans for death, inventing dodges to circumvent therapy, attaching a string to the bed table to render it accessible to the immobilized patient, flushing undesirable medication down the toilet, prying into the private affairs of the floor nurse, gazing out at the wheeling planets and the lovely arabesques of the Jersey shore. Dawn comes, and an early nurse, to test with her little fingers whether our heart still beats. And then we shave and practice counting to fifteen, so that when they jab us with Sodium Pentothal and ask us to count, we can race them to the knockout. Busyness is really the solution to a man's life, in this cold sunless clime. And a hospital is the place.[27]

He wrote Bristow Adams that under the influence of sodium pentothal ("said to be the truth drug") he had begun writing and had been writing ever since. He did, in fact, write all of "Notes and Comment" for a month;

and John Updike wrote to Katharine: "It is wonderful that your husband is doing comment again. My, what a difference!" Katharine passed on the remark to Andy in a letter sent to Maine, where he had gone for a few days to "admire the winter scene and visit with his son and grandchildren." But the compliment did not influence him to return to "Notes and Comment," as perhaps Katharine had hoped it might. As White told Adams at the time, he didn't know which made him more miserable—writing, or being unable to write: "Both are bad."[28]

When he started writing his epistolary essays, White may have thought that turning out a long piece every other month would be easier than (and about as lucrative as) writing *New Yorker* "Comment" every other week, but in 1957 four months went by before he produced an essay. When it finally appeared, it did so under his old departmental heading of "Answers to Hard Questions," and took off from a series of questions about pigeons asked by a feature writer for a hotel house-organ called *Promenade:* Has anyone ever seen a baby pigeon in New York? Where do pigeons nest? Why do they live in cities? White's essay, later published under the title "The Rock Dove," was as good a casual as he had ever written, very funny and very serious, expressing as well as anything he ever wrote his love for the world, his holistic conception of it, and his anxiety that human beings as blind as Warty Bliggens might destroy it. At the end of his careful survey (illustrated by his own drawings) of the various kinds of nesting places pigeons choose in Manhattan, he said:

> Because of the trend toward plainer façades, the city of the future may hold no charm for pigeons. Lever House offers little inducement to a nesting pair. As far as that goes, unless men cultivate the dove more successfully than they appear to be doing in this century, the city of the future may be inhospitable to men and doves alike. (The pigeon, strange to say, is closely related to the dodo.) But there are still doves among us. While they endure we must note their locations, elevate our gaze above the level of our immediate concerns, imbibe the sweet air and perfect promise: the egg miraculous upon the ledge, the bird compact upon the egg, its generous warmth, its enviable patience, its natural fortitude and grace.[29]

By May 1957 Katharine had decided to give up her job at *The New Yorker,* and she and Andy had begun to plan to move to Maine in the fall. When she resigned as head of the Fiction Department, Shawn did not appoint a successor to her but took upon himself the supervision of the department, which had some fine editors. One of the most gifted and experienced of them was William Maxwell, whom Katharine had hired over twenty years before.

The Whites postponed giving notice to their landlord till September, in case, as Katharine said, anything happened to change their plans. They were both worried about their health, and perhaps they hesitated to leave New York doctors and hospitals. But during October and November they moved out of Turtle Bay Gardens, which had been their winter home for fifteen years. In spite of Katharine's deteriorating health, they were to enjoy twenty more years together, on the farm on Allen Cove.[30]

In December Andy sent his and Katharine's Christmas greeting to all the editorial staff of *The New Yorker* in couplets like those of Frank Sullivan's annual *New Yorker* Christmas greeting. *The New Yorker* set the Whites' greeting in type, and proof-sheets of it were posted on bulletin boards in the office. It opened with these lines:

> Unlike Mr. Sullivan, whose friends are scattered,
> We focus our thoughts on the halls that have mattered,
> And at Christmas we particularly desire to greet
> The wonderful cast of the personnel sheet:
> Never mind Doris Duke, Talullah Bankhead, David Dubinsky,
> We say hello to Duncan Longcope, John Flagler, Beverly Krupinski. . . .

And 137 lines and 160 names later, it ended with these:

> The hour grows late, the owl's a-cold,
> Our Christmas tale is almost told;
> A clatter arises from out on our lawn
> As we finish our greetings with love to Bill Shawn.
> May his writers be rolling, his spirits ne'er flag,
> As he edits the world's most lovable mag.
> So from Katharine S. and from Andy White
> Merry Christmas to all and to all a good night!
>
> North Brooklin, Maine[31]

CHAPTER XVII

The Points of
My Compass

1957 — 1961

*". . . living itself, a task of such immediacy, variety, beauty, and
excitement that one is powerless to resist its wild embrace."*

F OR ANDY, MOVING TO MAINE IN 1957 MEANT
coming home; and it meant, not retirement, but increased activity—
more time for the business of living. Now the days would never be
long enough; they would be unlike the days in New York, where
with nothing to do after breakfast he so often felt the "terrible loneliness of
midmorning." Now there were interesting chores, farm work to be supervised, and a natural world on land and sea to be observed and felt. Owning
livestock would now be more practical and less like a hobby than it had
been during the years when he spent most of his time in New York. He
would soon buy two white-faced Hereford heifers, some steers, and some
sheep. He would, of course, continue to raise chickens and geese. From
morning till night, and from season to season, his life would be regulated
by such natural phenomena as sunrise and sunset, the tides, and the weather;
yet his schedule would be flexible enough to accommodate a wide variety
of projects and errands that were more like play than work: replanking an
old scow, building a cow-trap or a wheelbarrow, shopping in Blue Hill, or
making an emergency trip to Bangor or Ellsworth for a new blower-
motor for the brooder. He would continue to write for a living, but he
would no longer be tyrannized by deadlines.

On some mornings White wrote in the boathouse down on the shore.
The same size as Thoreau's house on Walden Pond (10' × 15'), it was
furnished with only a chair, a bench, a table, a nail keg for a wastebasket,

and a wood stove for cool mornings in spring and fall. It had a window looking out on the cove. On other mornings he sometimes wrote in the house, in his tidy study, where he also answered his mail. Even the chore of correspondence was not as onerous as it might have been, for in her less tidy study, across the front hall from Andy's, Katharine often took care of a good part of it for him.

Katharine continued her editorial work for *The New Yorker* from her headquarters in Maine, though on a reduced, one-third-time basis. And as the volume of her professional work decreased, the volume of her personal correspondence increased. Letter-writing had always been important to her, and now more than ever it helped satisfy her need for lively conversation with interesting people, and for opportunities to help others in various ways. "She had her lines out in all directions and to an unbelievably mixed (and mixed-up) bunch of people," White wrote to S. J. Perelman, after Katharine's death:

> Her correspondents came in all shapes, colors, sizes, and depths of sadness and heights of joy. She had the insane notion that if she persevered she could right all wrongs, fix up all the injustice, correct all error, and bind every wound. She worked at it in a rather sneaky way, not wishing to bother me in my pursuit of the literary life, which she felt had nobility and deserved priority.[1]

In the winter of 1957–58, after Katharine and Andy were well settled into their new routines, Andy wrote a "Letter from the East" dated from Allen Cove. It told his readers what he was up to and how he felt about it:

> Margaret Mitchell once made a remark I have treasured. Someone asked her what she was "doing," and she replied, "Doing? It's a full-time job to be the author of 'Gone with the Wind.' " I remembered this cheerful statement this morning as I lay in bed, before daylight, marshalling in my head the problems and projects and arrangements of the day and wondering when I would again get a chance to "do" something—like sit at a typewriter. I felt a kinship with Miss Mitchell and comforted myself with the pleasing thought that just to live in New England in winter is a full-time job; you don't have to "do" anything. The idle pursuit of making-a-living is pushed to one side, where it belongs, in favor of living itself, a task of such immediacy, variety, beauty, and excitement that one is powerless to resist its wild embrace.
>
> Right this minute I am making a brief show of resistance; I have resolved to keep the wolf from the door. But what I'm really trying to keep from my door is the fox—a very different proposition. A loaded gun is at my side, and my typewriter is placed strategically at a window that commands a view of

the strip of woods from which the fox usually emerges. He has been thrice in our dooryard within the week.[2]

White had never intended to stop writing altogether, of course; he had merely looked forward to a time when he would no longer feel pressed to write for a living. For the time being, however, he could not pretend that the wolf was dead. In spite of what may have been a good income from royalties, investments, and the "special payments" from *The New Yorker* that Ross had instituted long ago—and in spite of Katharine's additional income—White could not ignore the possibility that in the future he or Katharine, or both, might become financially drained by the expenses of long illnesses or infirmities, or simply by longevity. In anticipation of future needs, he continued to work for a living for twenty more years. As things turned out, he made a good deal of money during that time from a relatively small amount of writing.

In the spring of 1957 he became involved in a project which ultimately proved to be a far more effective way of keeping the wolf from the door than White or anyone else could have forseen at the time: the revision of *The Elements of Style*—a forty-three-page handbook for students of writing, containing "rules" of English grammar, rhetoric, and usage, written in 1918 by his old Cornell professor, the late William Strunk, Jr. This lucky venture began when a friend at Cornell sent him a rare copy of the first edition of the little book. White was so delighted to be reminded of Strunk that he was moved to write an affectionate piece for *The New Yorker* about his old professor and friend. In his essay he called Strunk's book a "summation of the case for clearness, accuracy, and brevity in the use of English," and he ended his essay with an endorsement that would please any publisher:

> I think . . . that if I suddenly found myself in the, to me, unthinkable position of facing a class in English usage and style, I would [in imitation of Strunk] simply lean far out over the desk, clutch my lapels, blink my eyes, and say, "Get the *little* book! Get the *little* book! Get the *little* book!"[3]

The day after the essay appeared, an editor at Macmillan, Jack Case, asked White whether he would allow it to be used as an introduction if Macmillan should decide to reissue the book. White replied that he might, but that in that case he would like to revise the essay for its new audience, saying more in it on the subject of rhetoric. The editor responded by proposing that White revise Strunk's entire text and that Macmillan publish "a new edition by William Strunk, Jr. and E. B. White."

White became interested in the project, and in the fall, soon after moving to Maine, he began to work on the revision. The job that he thought would take no more than a month took about a year. He soon felt uneasy "posing as an expert on rhetoric" when the truth was that he did his own writing "by ear . . . and seldom with any exact notion of what [was] taking place under the hood."[5] Ten months passed before White formally agreed to Macmillan's proposal, and another five before he signed a contract with the publisher. Though Strunk's copyright on the book had run out, White insisted that Macmillan ask Strunk's heirs for approval to publish a new edition and that he share its royalties equally with Strunk's estate.

Never a collaborator, he claimed from the beginning the right to revise Strunk's text to suit himself. When he explained to Case that he had seldom needed the help of editors, he was not boasting; he was only warning his publisher that neither textbook salesmen nor English teachers, who knew the market, would keep him from his old way of writing "to an audience of one." He did not think that Strunk would have objected to what he was about to do to his little book; on the other hand, he would not try to please the ghost of Strunk.

Since White would probably never have considered writing a handbook on style from scratch, it was lucky for everybody (Strunk's heirs, White, Macmillan, and students of writing) that he had Strunk's book as an armature, though it had its weaknesses—in organization and scope, as well as in style. In his *New Yorker* essay White had called the book "clear, brief, bold," but when he got down to the work of revising the sections on composition he found some of them "narrow and bewildering."[6] Strunk was sometimes too brief to be perfectly clear, and his instructions were too dogmatic and pedantic to encourage young writers to deviate from them occasionally and to trust their ear the way most good writers do. White transformed the book. He gave it a new voice, by introducing it with his *New Yorker* essay on Strunk, by adding to it a twenty-page essay he called "An Approach to Style", and by revising a few passages in Strunk's original version. The revisions illustrate some distinct differences between White's practice and Strunk's theory of the elements of style.

Strunk illustrated the operation of a rule by presenting a faulty sentence side-by-side with a version improved by observing the prescribed rule. For instance, his rule reading "The relative pronoun should come immediately after its antecedent" was followed by these before-and-after examples:

He wrote three articles about his adventures in Spain, which were published in *Harper's Magazine*.

He published in *Harper's Magazine* three articles about his adventures in Spain.[7]

Ignoring the fact that in his revision Strunk had eliminated the relative clause altogether, White chose to improve Strunk's awkward separation of the verb *(published)* from its object *(three articles)*—a separation that interrupts the flow of natural English syntax: subject, verb, object. To White's ear, Strunk's unrevised version may have seemed better than the revision, for White's own sentences derive their power and grace from his habit of keeping subject, verb, and object close together in a tightly bonded, dynamic nucleus. White's revision of Strunk's revision reads simply, " *'He published three articles in 'Harper's Magazine' about his adventures in Spain.'*"[8]

In a comment on the misuse of the word *while*, Strunk had said that many writers use *while* as a substitute for *and* or *but* "*either from a mere desire to vary the connective, or from uncertainty which of the two connectives is the more appropriate.*" White changed the wording of Strunk's comment. He threw out the parallel syntax *"from desire . . . or from uncertainty"* and made the sentence read: *"either from a mere desire to vary the connective, or because they are not sure which of the two connectives is the more appropriate.*"[9] Strunk's version is correct, clear, and briefer than White's, but it lacks one of the chief sources of the "vigor," "pith," and "boldness" of White's own style—strong predication. What White did to Strunk's *"uncertainty"* was to transform it into a statement: *"they are not sure."* He did so because *"from uncertainty"* is not so bold as—does not so fully commit the writer as— *"because they are unsure."*

White's preference for the boldness of predication, for a noun followed by a finite verb, produced another instructive revision. Under the rubric of his Rule 12, "Use definite, specific, concrete language," Strunk had written these leaden sentences:

> *If those who have studied the art of writing are in accord on any one point, it is on this, that the surest method of arousing and holding the attention of the reader is by being specific, definite, and concrete. Critics have pointed out how much of the effectiveness of the greatest writers, Homer, Dante, Shakespeare, results from their constant definiteness and concreteness.*[10]

White's revision reads:

> *If those who have studied the art of writing are in accord on any one point, it is on this: the surest way to arouse and hold the attention of the reader is by being specific, definite, and concrete. The greatest writers—Homer, Dante, Shakespeare—are effective largely because they deal in particulars and report the details that matter.*[11]

"The surest way to arouse and hold" is preferable to *"the surest method of arousing and holding"* because the infinitive *"to arouse"* is more dynamic than

the participle *"of arousing,"* which is more like a noun than a verb. White disliked Strunk's *"effectiveness . . . results from definiteness and concreteness,"* not just because the nouns are abstract, but because the intransitive verb *"results from"* is in itself weak. In his revision White managed to make four predications and to sharpen as well as animate the ideas: writers *"are effective"*: writers *"deal"*; writers *"report"*; details *"matter."*

In the section on punctuation of parenthetic expressions, Strunk wrote:

> *Similar in principle to the enclosing of parenthetic expressions between commas is the setting off by commas of phrases or dependent clauses preceding or following the main clause of a sentence.* [12]

White improved this by eliminating or changing the form of four verbals: *enclosing, setting, preceding,* and *following:*

> *When the main clause of a sentence is preceded by, or followed by, a phrase or a dependent clause, use commas to set off these elements.* [13]

More than anything else, however, it was the thirty-five-hundred-word essay "An Approach to Style," which White added to his old teacher's original text, that gave Strunk's *Elements* White's style. Casual and loose in structure, informal and plain in diction, simple and practical in message, and bold and humorous in rhetoric, the essay rewards the careful reader and gives hope as well as aid to the amateur writer. Its subject was "not style in the sense of what is correct but style in the sense of what is distinguished and distinguishing." White aimed, he wrote to Jack Case, his editor at Macmillan, to "give the little book an extra dimension" by saying "a word or two about attitudes in writing: the why, the how, the beartraps, the power, and the glory." He set up guidelines (e.g., "Place yourself in the background"; "Write with nouns and verbs"; "Avoid fancy words") and explained each briefly. Though definite and demanding, these guidelines are never dogmatic or doctrinaire. White refers to them as "my own prejudices, my notions of error, my articles of faith"; they were, he said in other places, "cautionary remarks" or "subtly dangerous hints." His explanations seem never to ignore the limitations of our verbal aptitude or the recalcitrance of our language that make the rules hard to follow. His humorous tone narrows the distance between himself (the professional) and his readers (the amateurs), and it allows White the writer to sound bolder and yet more modest than Strunk the pedagogue.[14]

It was like White to call his essay an "Approach," since he always felt best not when he thought he had solved a problem or achieved an end, but when he was on a journey, in pursuit of something, "headed in the right direction." Once, in a letter to a reader, he said, "Unlike you, I have no faith, only a suitcaseful of beliefs that sustain me."[15] The skeptic with no doctrinal philosophy of life had no doctrine of style, only a suitcaseful of opinions that he was willing to put into Strunk's funny imperative mode, confident that his readers would not think that he thought he knew the Truth about style.

The essay is deceptively plain. Many students, and teachers, fail to understand it till they have lived with it for a while, reading it slowly, and returning to it often. Only after labor, and with luck, do they discover that White implies some advice that few textbooks or teachers ever give: write to please yourself; do *not* think about whether your reader will like or approve of what you say; try to discover your own mind; do *not* begin your apprenticeship by trying to change the mind of someone else; make sure you have done all you can to help your reader understand what you wanted to say; good writing comes from writers who can be true to themselves (and to the facts as they see them) at the same time that they are being considerate of their readers; be modest; do not offer your opinions "gratuitously" (to do so is "to imply that the demand for them is brisk, which may not be the case"); by politely restraining your ego you will facilitate the revelation of your own individuality, which will inform everything you write. Humor is not one of White's recommended approaches to style (humor, he once said, is only a "sly and almost imperceptible ingredient that sometimes gets into writing").[16]

In talking about the relationship between the character of the writer and his style, White implies that if style is the man, you may change your character to some extent by changing your style. For in the process of trying to say clearly what you mean, or know, or think you know, you learn; and as you learn, you shape your character, for you are what you have learned. Trying to write clearly is an exercise that affects the whole writer ("The practice and habit of writing not only drain the mind but supply it, too.")[17] Instead of trying to improve your character in order to write well, try writing well in order to improve your character. Concluding his remarks about style as the sign of the author's identity, White wrote:

> The beginner should approach style warily, realizing that it is himself he is approaching, no other; and he should begin by turning resolutely away from all devices that are popularly believed to indicate style—all mannerisms, tricks, adornments. The approach to style is by way of plainness, simplicity, orderliness, sincerity.[18]

Ultimately one's style is the result of choices that are as much moral as they are aesthetic.

White was determined, as he told Case, to make *The Elements of Style* into a textbook that would differ from most others "in its being somewhat relaxed and even tinged with levity." He could not, he said, "don the robes of solemnity at this late date."[19] His informality and sincerity made possible the good humor heard on every page.

Here, as elsewhere, White's humor was rooted in his skepticism, as this piece of advice shows: "When you say something, make sure you have said it. The chances of your having said it are only fair." His skepticism made his advice persuasive because it seemed to come from a modest man who did not pretend to great wisdom. In fact, in the conclusion of the essay he attributes the excellence of some lines in a poem by Robert Louis Stevenson to Stevenson's choice of a plain style—and to his having written them in "a moment of felicity." That's how White ends—without telling his readers how to make such happy moments happen. Once asked to give his advice to young writers, he answered, "Be lucky."[20]

But White's parting explanation, that good writing occurs in moments of felicity, does not undercut his instruction in the art of writing well. It only reminds the reader that though an approach to style can be taught, the achievement of memorable writing is a miracle. To be sincere he had to say so.

Several bouts of illness delayed White's completion of the book, but he delivered the finished manuscript in November 1958, the day before Thanksgiving—his deadline. Before he sent it off he did what he seldom did: he asked Katharine for her professional advice. The book would have, he told Case, "the inestimable advantage of coming under her editorial eye. She is a better grammarian, organizer, teacher, editor, and mother than I am, and has saved an untold number of lives."[21]

Prior to publishing the manuscript, Macmillan sent copies of it to several teachers of English composition for criticism and suggestions. In their replies, the teachers' chief criticism was that Strunk and White supported "lost causes" by being too prescriptive about certain rules of English usage. They recommended that White bring the manuscript more into tune with modern educational theory—a theory which stresses the fact that language is constantly changing, and hence opposes the imposition of highly restrictive rules for its usage and considers any usage correct, or acceptable, as long as it conforms to current taste and practice. In relaying these letters to White, Case indicated that he thought White ought to follow the teachers' advice and delete some of his rules of usage. Would he make the book a little more responsive to the demands of the market? White replied in high spirits:

I was saddened by your letter—the flagging spirit, the moistened finger in the wind, the examination of entrails, and the fear of little men. I don't know whether Macmillan is running scared or not, but I do know that this book is the work of a dead precisionist and a half-dead disciple of his, and that it has got to stay that way. I have been sympathetic all along with your qualms about "The Elements of Style," but I know that I cannot, and will-shall not, attempt to adjust the unadjustable Mr. Strunk to the modern liberal of the English Department, the anything-goes fellow. Your letter expresses contempt for this fellow, but on the other hand you seem to want his vote. I am against him, temperamentally and because I have seen the work of *his* disciples, and I say the hell with him. If the White-Strunk opus has any virtue, any hope of circulation, it lies in our keeping its edges sharp and clear, not in rounding them off cleverly. . . . My single purpose is to be faithful to Strunk as of 1958, reliable, holding the line, and maybe even selling some copies to English Departments that collect oddities and curios. To me no cause is lost, no level the right level, no smooth ride as valuable as a rough ride, no *like* interchangeable with *as,* and no ball game anything but chaotic if it lacks a mound, a box, bases, and foul lines. That's what Strunk was about, that's what I am about, and that (I hope) is what the book is about. Any attempt to tamper with this prickly design will get nobody nowhere fast.[22]

When Case and his colleague, Harry Cloudman, read White's letter together, Case reported, they "looked up from it with broad grins." Case said: "All right. He won't go on the defensive. Maybe we ought to let him take the offensive and whale the hell out of 'em." And in his report to White he added, "We both knew that 'let' was the wrong verb." But Case persuaded White, in several instances, "out of fairness to [his] old teacher," not to let Strunk "dwell on things that are of no consequence to anybody now." And in one instance he asked White to change one of his own illustrations because it might embarrass some teachers and students. The illustration concerned the use of the subordinating conjunction *that.* It sometimes can be omitted, but sometimes its omission will produce an ambiguity. Using as an example the sentence "He felt that the girl had not played fair," White had said that if the writer had omitted *that,* his reader might have momentarily understood "He felt the girl." White was in favor of leaving that example in because it "illustrated the embarrassment of prose." But Case in this instance stood his ground, offering as a substitute "Queen Elizabeth felt the head of her hangman's ax was. . . ." White settled for "He felt his big nose was. . . ."[23]

Having had Jack Case as his editor on this book was another instance of White's good luck. Not only was Case experienced in his profession and possessed of taste and tact, but he greatly admired White's writing and had a good sense of humor himself. He and White eventually became good friends.

The Elements of Style was the Book-of-the-Month Club selection for May 1959. In its trade edition it made the best-seller list and remained there for some time. In its college edition it sold two hundred thousand copies in its first year, and only slightly fewer in each of the following two years. By 1972, when a second edition was published, the book had sold over two million copies. By 1982, three years after publication of a third edition, total sales had exceeded five and a half million, and it was "required reading" in several thousand college English courses in America.

D u r i n g the first three or four years after they had moved permanently to Maine, Andy and Katharine occasionally suffered from short spells of various illnesses, but by and large these were reasonably healthy years for both of them. They seem also to have been happy years. Materially Andy could have hardly asked for more. He lived in a handsome white clapboard house that was a monument to early New England taste, and in a part of the world that he had preferred to any other ever since boyhood. He owned pastures and a woodlot, a barn and livestock, a boathouse on a cove, a dock and a boat.

Life inside the house was busy from the very early morning hour when Andy got up, till evening, when he closed the chicken house against predators. During the day he and Katharine usually went their own ways and did their own work till late afternoon, when, the housekeeper having left, the cook having prepared dinner, and the serving girl having arrived to serve it, the two of them had cocktails before sitting down to dinner. After dinner Andy sometimes worked on newsbreaks for *The New Yorker,* the "salaried" job he had now held for more than thirty years.

Over the years the Whites had acquired many friends in Maine. But they were, now as before, sufficient to themselves, and led only a moderately active social life, except in July and August, when their children and grandchildren, as well as other guests, came to visit. Katharine's two children, Nancy and Roger, with their spouses and children, had been coming to North Brooklin for summer visits ever since the early fifties. Eventually Katharine and Andy together had nine grandchildren, and all of them knew Andy well.

In 1959, the year Joel and Allene's third child was born, Joel acquired a half-interest in the boatyard where he had worked since 1956, and three years later he became its sole owner. He and Allene were active in the life of the community, and whereas Andy and Katharine would always be thought of by their neighbors and other native Mainers as "from away,"

the five young Whites up the road were treated by them as native sons
and daughters. Within a few years people were referring to Andy as "Joel
White's father." The two White families were bound together by strong
affection but respected each other's privacy and independence.

Andy wrote in 1958 about the pleasures of being a grandfather:

> I have only three grandchildren, and one of them can't walk in the woods,
> because he was only born on June 24th last and hasn't managed to get onto
> his feet yet. But he has been making some good tries, and when he does walk,
> the woods are what he will head for if he is anything like his brother Steven
> and his sister Martha and, of course, me. . . . We walk in them at every
> opportunity, stumbling along happily, tripping over windfalls, sniffing
> valerian, and annoying the jay. We note where the deer has lain under the wild
> apple, and we watch the red squirrel shucking spruce buds.[24]

One consequence of being the creator of Charlotte and Wilbur was the
occasional arrival of unannounced visitors who came to see him and the
celebrated barn. In a facetious tone White once compared himself to
Khrushchev, who, according to a newspaper story that appeared while he
was in the U.S., always "found time to meet Americans and converse with
them frankly on contemporary world problems":

> I have never been so busy that I wouldn't meet Americans, or they me. Hell,
> they drive right into my driveway, stop the car, get out, and start talking about
> contemporary problems even though I've never laid eyes on them before. I
> don't have the protection Khrushchev has. My dog welcomes any American,
> day or night, and who am I to let a dog outdo me in simple courtesy?[25]

One "contemporary problem" that concerned White much of his life
is environmental pollution. In his first year as editorial writer for *The New
Yorker,* he had called attention to violations of a city ordinance making
it illegal to operate furnaces that "belched black, soft-coal smoke" into the
urban atmosphere of 1927. Before World War II, one of the jokes about
The New Yorker's "editorial policy" was that it consisted chiefly of opposition to the use of poisonous spray on fruit.

Just as, in 1940, White had warned his readers of the dangers of Anne
Morrow Lindbergh's isolationism, and, in 1953, had been one of the first to
editorialize against testing hydrogen bombs, now, in 1959, in the pages of
The New Yorker, he publicized a concern that would soon become popular.
During 1959 and 1960 White edited seventeen columns on environmental
pollution that *The New Yorker* published anonymously under the heading
"These Precious Days." A headnote for the first column read as follows:

Because the slaughter of the innocents continues, here and abroad, and the contamination of air, sea, and soil proceeds apace, *The New Yorker* will undertake to assemble bulletins tracing Man's progress in making the planet uninhabitable. This is Bulletin No. 1.

The first notes in the first bulletin were these:

American citizens are now permitted two-tenths of a microcurie of strontium 90 by the National Committee on Radiation Protection and Measurements—a gain of one-tenth of a microcurie, or double the former recommended dose.

St. Louis led other U.S. cities during 1958 in the amount of strontium 90 in milk. The milk supplies of five large cities were tested by the Public Health Service. Standings (in micro-microcuries):

St. Louis	14.1
Cincinnati	9.1
New York	6.6
Sacramento	5.0
Salt Lake City	4.4

During January, 1959, the St. Louis strontium level rose from 14.1 to 18.6.[26]

Later columns were introduced by this rubric: "The New Yorker's fever chart of the planet Earth, showing Man's ups and downs in contaminating the air, the sea, and the soil."[27] In addition to strontium 90, White noticed other dangers: detergents, increases in atmospheric carbon dioxide, radium, soot, smog, automobile exhaust gases, insecticides, fungicides, herbicides, hormonal fattening agents, and cigarette smoke. The notes were factual, the tone neutral, the effect often ironic, as, for example, in these:

The United States Department of Agriculture believes that it is possible to remove ninety per cent of the existing contamination of agricultural land by scraping off the surface soil (sometimes called "topsoil").

A Turkish towel folded once and held over the mouth will help greatly in the event of air-spread radioactivity. This finding was reported in the *Archives of Industrial Health,* a publication of the American Medical Association.[28]

ON JANUARY 1, 1961, Katharine retired from *The New Yorker*. It was not easy to give up a job into which for thirty-five years she had put so much of herself. Within a few months she began to have headaches so severe that she cut short a Florida vacation to return to New York for neurological tests. She suspected a brain disorder. The results of the tests were inconclusive, and she was told to return for more tests in the fall. In the meantime she had an appendectomy at Blue Hill Hospital. When Thurber learned that Katharine was in the hospital, he telegraphed flowers from himself and Helen, and wrote a warm note to Katharine and Andy: "You do seem," he said, "to have more troubles than should be piled on one woman or one man or one couple." And in a P.S. he said, "This will be sent on Andy's birthday, if my memory serves, and so Happy Birthday, Andy."[29] Andy wrote a thank-you letter—dated a week after the death of Ernest Hemingway. It was Andy's last letter to Jim, who was by then already in poor shape, physically and mentally. After a page about Katharine's troubles and his anxieties about her, Andy wrote: "I am morose to think that when you die, and when I die, there won't be any bullfighter in Spain to kill two bulls in our honor. The hell with Spain." And he closed: "Yrs with love and many thanks for the flowers."[30] Thurber's reply, his last letter to Andy, began, "Dear old Andy," and ended, "Once again, our love and best wishes to Katharine and you. As ever, Jim."[31] Thurber died in November.

Andy's sadness about his loss must have been sharpened by regretful memories of the trying incidents that had once threatened their friendship, just as it must have been sweetened by memories of the affection that had nonetheless endured to the end. After Andy and Katharine had married in 1929 and Jim and Althea had separated, the Whites and Thurber began to grow apart. The thirties brought Thurber fame and fortune, and he and his second wife, Helen, lived a hectic life, as different from Andy's and Katharine's as Manhattan was from North Brooklin. But even after he and Helen had moved to Connecticut in 1934, and Jim had stopped coming to the *New Yorker* office, he and Andy had kept in touch by phone and by mail, and their friendship continued to be firm and rewarding.

In 1940, however, when Thurber seemed to be losing most of the vision in his good eye, he had a nervous breakdown aggravated by heavy drinking, and shortly thereafter underwent a series of eye operations that led to an even more severe breakdown. It was after this dreadful ordeal that Thurber's behavior became increasingly erratic and he developed a deep resentment toward Katharine, partly because, rightly or wrongly, he held her responsible for *The New Yorker*'s rejection of some of his pieces.[32] Whatever he thought about Katharine, however, he continued to write Andy with his old warmth and wit. If over the years he had become increasingly self-important and occasionally condescending, if he bragged about the size of his income tax, that was not unbearable to a friend who had known him in happier times. Some of Thurber's best letters between 1941 and 1945 were written to Andy.

On the day after Ross died, in December 1951, Thurber was among the mourners "in various stages of repair" who wandered into White's office. "Andy wrote the obituary," he told a friend, "while I stood by, that long and awful day." Wishing to contribute in some way to the magazine's statement, Thurber made a small drawing of a Thurber dog lying at the foot of a grave and staring at the headstone. It was a fine drawing, and according to Thurber, White was "all for using it as the illustration for the obituary, but the conservative boys turned it down." "Now," Thurber added in this letter to a friend, "Andy and I have made a pledge to use [my drawing] for the obituary of whichever one of us dies first."[33] The "conservative boys," among whom, presumably, he included Katharine White, chose as the "illustration" for Ross's obituary, in place of Thurber's drawing, a small reproduction of Ross's *R,* in Ross's well-known script —a signature that everyone at the *New Yorker* knew well.

In spite of such tensions, however, Andy and Katharine attended the wedding of Thurber's daughter, Rosemary, in Philadelphia in 1953; and it was not until 1955, when the Thurbers and the Whites were both in London, that in a drunken state Thurber played a practical joke on Andy and Katharine that revealed his suppressed hostility to Katharine. It was intended to be shocking, and by its nature seemed to suggest that Thurber wished to express contempt for some members of *The New Yorker*'s editorial staff, who, "afraid of warmth," were "sometimes more cold than detached, and more bloodless than sophisticated."[34]

In 1957, when the editor of the *Atlantic Monthly* offered White a thousand dollars for an essay on Ross, and White declined the offer, the *Atlantic* approached Thurber, who at the time was already thinking about writing a book about Ross. Thurber proposed that the *Atlantic* publish his book in installments, and the *Atlantic* agreed. The first chapter appeared in the November issue. Thurber's "The Years with Ross," as it appeared serially in the *Atlantic,* was a popular success, and in book form it enjoyed large sales and a good critical reception except in England, where Malcolm Muggeridge and Rebecca West, in their reviews, concluded that for all his marvelously funny anecdotes Thurber had failed to do justice to Ross's genius and achievement. From the very first installment the Whites thought Thurber was not getting the man or the story quite right. In particular they disliked Thurber's discussion of Ross's private life, and his implication that Ross did not pay writers as much as he could afford. After the last installment appeared, White wrote Thurber frankly what he and Katharine thought of "The Years with Ross," and Thurber replied in a long letter, addressed only to Andy, that showed how hard he was trying to conceal his hurt. It opened: "Some of your letter is you, and perfect, and some of it isn't you at all, but you have been through more with a non-real me than I have ever been with the other you. I do not lose great friendships for reasons of weather, mundane or mental."[35] Thurber avoided saying outright that the part of the letter that was not Andy was Katharine, but he told a friend that Andy's letter was "not, however and alas, unsub-committee."[36]

After *The Years with Ross* was published as a book, White summarized *The New Yorker*'s reaction to it, as well as his own and Katharine's, in a letter to Howard Cushman:

> The book has been the cause of much sorrow and pain around the shop. The first couple chapters are pretty good—Jim could always reproduce Ross's mannerisms and general demeanor, and vividly. But most of the book seems to me, and to K, a sly exercise in denigration, beautifully concealed in words of sweetness and love. As soon as Jim got famous and successful—which was very soon—he began brooding about the low pay he had received for his early casuals. And then he remembered that some of his pieces had been rejected, and this was an insult to genius.[37]

Fifteen years later White wrote Burton Bernstein, Thurber's biographer, as follows:

> After the *Atlantic* series we were all up in arms, but now *The Years with Ross* just seems distasteful, not awful. I objected to the distortions in the book, the sex—just Jim showing off—and the payments for the writers. Also, Jim exaggerated his own administrative duties. He never, as far as I know, sched-uled the magazine or attended art meetings regularly. When the book came out, I didn't write Jim about it, and it was the only book of his he never inscribed to us.[38]

When, a short time before Thurber died, Andy and Katharine learned that he had a brain tumor, they ascribed much of his odd and offensive behavior in later years to it, and there was a "small reconciliation" between the Whites and Thurber. Andy felt "very bad about [what happened to Jim], very sad. When he was well and sober, there was never a kinder, nicer friend."[39]

William Shawn wrote the first part of *The New Yorker*'s obituary for Thurber. After describing Thurber's extraordinary contribution to the magazine, he said that Thurber's colleagues agreed that E. B. White should speak for them all, "so the words that follow are his." White wrote the conclusion of the obituary (which appeared without the drawing Thurber had made for Ross):

> He was both a practitioner of humor and a defender of it. The day he died, I came on a letter from him, dictated to a secretary and signed in pencil with his sightless and enormous "Jim." "Every time is a time for humor," he wrote. "I write humor the way a surgeon operates, because it is a livelihood, because I have a great urge to do it, because many interesting challenges are set up, and because I have the hope it may do some good." Once, I remember, he heard someone say that humor is a shield, not a sword, and it made him mad. He wasn't going to have anyone beating his sword into a shield. That "surgeon," incidentally, is pure Mitty. During his happiest years, Thurber did not write the way a surgeon operates, he wrote the way a child skips rope, the way a mouse waltzes.
>
> Although he is best known for "Walter Mitty" and "The Male Animal," the book of his I like best is "The Last Flower." In it you will find his faith in the renewal of life, his feeling for the beauty and fragility of life on earth. Like all good writers, he fashioned his own best obituary notice. Nobody else can add to the record, much as he might like to. And of all the flowers, real and figurative, that will find their way to Thurber's last resting place, the one that will remain fresh and wiltproof is the little flower he himself drew, on the last page of that lovely book.[40]

A MONTH before Thurber's death Katharine was told that her right carotid artery was blocked, and she was advised to have an operation performed by a specialist at Strong Memorial Hospital, in Rochester, New York. Her daughter, Nancy, met her and Andy in Rochester and was a great comfort to Andy during the long operation, when he was sick with anxiety. The surgery was a success, but thereafter Katharine's health never ceased to be a cause for concern. In fact, from 1957 until her death in 1977, her illnesses and invalidism colored almost all aspects of the Whites' life together.

CHAPTER XVIII

"What Do Our Hearts Treasure?"

1 9 6 2 — 1 9 8 3

"When does a man quit the sea? How dizzy, how bumbling must he be? Does he quit while he's ahead, or wait till he makes some major mistake, like falling overboard or being flattened by an accidental jibe?"

I N   T H E   F A L L   O F   1 9 6 2   H A R P E R   A N D   R O W published *The Points of My Compass,* a collection of White's *New Yorker* essays written during the preceding seven years. All but two had originally been entitled "Letters" and were dated from the North, East, South, or West. He opened his Foreword by saying:

> The visitor to the attic knows the risk he runs when he lifts the lid from a box of old letters. Words out of the past have the power to detain. Hours later he may find himself still crouched on the floor, savoring the pains and embarrassments of an early love, and with leg cramps to boot.
> The letters that make up this book, when I dug them out and began rereading them, detained me in much the way I have described, and I have been in some pain. The world that I'm in love with has not resisted my advances with anything like the firmness it is capable of, and I love it as passionately as though I were young, and so it's no wonder I have been heavily involved, no wonder an occasional passage in the letters makes me wince.

He concluded on a different note:

> Since most of my letters were from "the East," I had planned to call this book "Letters from the East, and Other Points." But when my wife got on to this, she said, "You can't do that, it would be misleading." And then, in one of those dazzling shifts of emphasis that are a true adornment of the sex,

339

she added, "The book would be bought only by people interested in the Orient."[1]

The first copy arrived in North Brooklin in September, in time for Katharine's birthday. Of the first printing of twenty-four thousand copies, six thousand were purchased by *The New Yorker* for distribution as gifts by its business office.[2] Another forty thousand copies were printed during the first three months after publication. The reviews were good, both in America and in England.

The success of *The Points of My Compass* would have been more gratifying if Katharine had not been in such poor health. Soon after her operation in Rochester, she began to experience alarming symptoms of circulatory trouble that her New York doctors decided could not be alleviated. To make matters worse, her retirement from *The New Yorker* had left her with too little to do. After a long life as active as hers, after holding an influential position in a demanding profession, she now felt painfully useless. She worried about being a burden to Andy.

Every year since she had moved back to Maine Katharine had written an article on gardening for *The New Yorker,* but in 1963 and 1964, though she wrote letters fluently and frequently to a large number of friends, she was too sick to undertake the hard work of writing for publication. During this period, probably the most difficult in her life and Andy's, he too wrote almost nothing. In a letter to Roger Angell in 1963 he said, "I sometimes think I would give everything I own for one garden piece, one book, and one restored lady."[3]

From time to time Andy himself was sick, and in his depressed periods he worried about whether he would be able to take care of Katharine in the years to come. For one thing, his expenses were heavy, and he may well have wondered how he could continue to maintain the large staff of helpers he and Katharine required: a caretaker, a housekeeper, a cook, secretaries, and nurses. His humor hardly concealed his anxiety when he made such remarks as, "We used to employ one man on the place, but now that K has learned the Latin name of plants it takes three—but it is a nice way to go broke, surrounded by such beauty." His worries seemed only to make it harder to write. He told his publisher some years later that he had been "too busy trying to stay alive and keep his household afloat" to be able to write anything. The Whites' way of life had never been inexpensive. Since childhood, both had lived the life of the well-to-do. But they were not rich, and they had been used to earning what they spent. Now, in their retirement, they faced the possibility of ever-increasing expenses on a more-or-less fixed income.[4]

Their winter vacations by necessity grew longer. Every year since settling in Maine they had spent one month of winter in Sarasota, but now Katharine's doctor advised them to stay there for two or three. Such long vacations were a bore, especially for Andy, who had never liked Florida much during its high season, and who, moreover, did not like to see what once were pleasant interludes in the sun turn now into long periods of exile from Maine and from the fullness of active winter life on the farm. In January 1963, when he and Katharine got off the train in Sarasota, Andy had a stomachache. His doctor discovered a duodenal ulcer which, Andy told his brother, was soon cured with gin. Shortly thereafter he developed an ulcerated tooth, lost his voice, lost his nerve, and had a "total collapse," or "what in happier days we used to call a 'nervous breakdown.' "[5]

In February and March he began to feel better, and after returning to Maine he managed to write a little essay about his love of sailing. "The Sea and the Wind That Blows" describes his life-long attraction to small sailboats and the sea. "I liked to sail alone. The sea was the same as a girl to me—I did not want anyone else along." The essay did not pretend to be a metaphorical expression of his feeling for life, but it did reflect his fears about approaching old age and his characterisitc will to live:

When does a man quit the sea? How dizzy, how bumbling must he be? Does he quit while he's ahead, or wait till he makes some major mistake, like falling overboard or being flattened by an accidental jibe? This past winter I spent hours arguing the question with myself. Finally, deciding that I had come to the end of the road, I wrote a note to the boatyard, putting my boat up for sale. I said I was "coming off the water." But as I typed the sentence, I doubted that I meant a word of it.

If no buyer turns up, I know what will happen: I will instruct the yard to put her in again—"just till somebody comes along." And then there will be the old uneasiness, the old uncertainty, as the mild southeast breeze ruffles the cove, a gentle, steady, morning breeze, bringing the taint of the distant wet world, the smell that takes a man back to the very beginning of time, linking him to all that has gone before. There will lie the sloop, there will blow the wind, once more I will get under way. And as I reach across to the red nun off the Torry Islands, dodging the trap buoys and toggles, the shags gathered on the ledge will note my passage. "There goes the old boy again," they will say. "One more rounding of his little Horn, one more conquest of his Roaring Forties." And with the tiller in my hand, I'll feel again the wind imparting life to a boat, will smell again the old menace, the one that imparts life to me: the cruel beauty of the salt world, the barnacle's tiny knives, the sharp spine of the urchin, the stinger of the sun jelly, the claw of the crab.[6]

On July 1, a few days before his sixty-fourth birthday, the news arrived that White was among those to be awarded the Presidential Medal of

Freedom, whose recipients had been chosen for "meritorious contribution to the security or national interests of the United States, world peace, cultural or other significant public or private endeavor." It came in the form of a long telegram that the Western Union agent in Ellsworth read over the phone to Katharine. White recounted the event to his old friend Cush:

> The President was a bit long-winded, and after K had dutifully scribbled the first thirty or forty words on a scratch pad, she said to the girl, "Is this a practical joke?" (There's a wife for you!) "No," said the girl a little stiffly. "Western Union is not allowed to transmit practical jokes."[7]

When the medals were awarded in Washington in December, about a month after John F. Kennedy's assassination, Katharine's illness gave Andy an excuse for declining the invitation to accept his medal in person. Only a short time before, he had written a part of *The New Yorker*'s obituary for President Kennedy, in which he had said:

> When we think of him, he is without a hat, standing in the wind and the weather. He was impatient of topcoats and hats, preferring to be exposed, and he was young enough and tough enough to confront and to enjoy the cold and the wind of these times, whether the winds of nature or the winds of political circumstance and national danger. He died of exposure, but in a way that he would have settled for—in the line of duty, and with his friends and enemies all around, supporting him and shooting at him. It can be said of him, as of few men in a like position, that he did not fear the weather, and did not trim his sails, but instead challenged the wind itself, to improve its direction and to cause it to blow more softly and more kindly over the world and its people.[8]

In the spring of 1964 Katharine spent two months in the Harkness Pavilion of Columbia-Presbyterian Hospital, in New York, being treated for dermatitis so severe her skin would not tolerate the pressure of clothing. Eventually her doctor was able to prescribe a medicine that alleviated the symptoms but did not cure the disease. During most of this time Andy stayed in New York, at the Algonquin Hotel. At the end of April Katharine was able to leave the hospital, and in spite of Andy's dislike of flying, she and Andy returned to North Brooklin by plane because of Katharine's condition. Back home, Andy wrote a friend that Katharine's courage was "unimpaired."[9]

Andy took courage from her—and hope from his other usual sources, so plentiful in early summer. He described one of them in a letter to Roger Angell:

I'm the father of two robins and this has kept me on the go lately. They were in a nest in a vine on the garage and had been deserted by their parents, and without really thinking what I was doing I casually dropped a couple of marinated worms into their throats as I walked by a week ago Monday. This did it. They took me on with open hearts and open mouths, and my schedule became extremely tight.[10]

In 1964 Andy and Katharine left for Florida in December—earlier than ever before. During their first month there Katharine was not out of the house for more than a total of four hours, but when warm weather returned she began to feel better, and by the time they headed home she was much improved. The following winter, 1965–66, marked a turning point in their luck, although it did not begin very auspiciously. They had rented sight unseen a house in Sarasota which turned out to be made of cinderblock painted pink, and "the principal tree on the place was a tall power pole sprouting transformers; it stood a few feet from the canal and threw a pleasant shade across the drive." It was a dispiriting setting to live in day after day, and having a merry Christmas in it required grim determination for a man who preferred Christmas where "there is a barn attached to the house [that] makes the whole thing a lot more real than when you just see it on television." But a big box from Joe, Allene, and their children, Steve, Martha, and John, arrived in Sarasota in time to supply Andy and Katharine with reminders of their family, as well as with a branch from a balsam fir and a harness-strap of sleigh bells. With that help Andy and Katharine willed themselves a happy holiday. The experience induced White a few days later to write an essay called "What Do Our Hearts Treasure?" It was a good piece, and the very fact that he was writing again was a good omen. Soon after, he was at work on "Annals of Birdwatching," a five-thousand-word *New Yorker* essay about Edward Howe Forbush's *Birds of Massachusetts and Other New England States,* and Katharine began another essay on gardening.[11]

In the winter of 1967 Katharine's health was better than it had been for several years. Now seventy-four years old, she was mentally vigorous—reading, reacting, and judging with the same intelligence, taste, and good humor that had made her an imaginative editor. Her mind was as open as ever to new writing, as she made emphatically clear in her response to Howard Cushman's complaint about "that garbage called Snow White," by which he meant Donald Barthelme's story in *The New Yorker* for February 17. Katharine sent him a page-and-a-half typed reply by return mail:

The New Nonsense or Hysteria School of fiction and satire is not my special cup of tea and I sometimes love Barthelme's writing and sometimes don't, but

I do think he has great gifts. He is an experimentalist and a modern with a sense of satire and humor. This is what *The New Yorker*, if it is to keep up its tradition of innovation, needs and must seek out. In this particular story I think Barthelme has succeeded. It is a wonderful sort of vague satire as a whole, on the mod generation in big cities and their mores, and on modern fiction, and in details it takes off with satire on dozens of ideas, myths, habits, styles of writing, and the new preoccupations, manners, and habits of the young. It's ingenious. . . .[12]

In June Andy's new sloop was launched. She was built in his son's boatyard and named *Martha* after his granddaughter. He described her as follows:

> This sloop was designed by the late S. S. Crocker. She is about 20 feet over all, about 17 feet on the water, has a beam of seven feet seven inches, and draws two feet with the board up. There is a single-cylinder Palmer engine under the self-draining cockpit. That's there so I can pick up my mooring without creating a sensation in the harbor. . . .
> Except for two full-length berths down below, the boat is as bare as a baby. No sink, no icebox, no water tank, no head, no telephone, no depth finder. I plan to find my depth by listening to the sound the centerboard makes as it glides over the ledges.[13]

A year later Andy wrote his brother Stanley:

> I still like to go sailing, and still do, getting all fouled up in the running rigging and having a lovely time of it. The dizzier you are, the more fun it is to sail single-handed. My fingers are now slightly arthritic and refuse to curl strongly around halyards and sheets, grasping them only half-heartedly. And the ringing in my ears is indistinguishable from the sound of bell buoys.

When his doctor sent him to the hospital in the hope of discovering the cause of his dizziness White was tested for glucose tolerance, but to his old friend and physician in New York he wrote that he was "always being tested for the wrong thing." "They ought," he added, "to test me for people tolerance, or events tolerance, or gin tolerance, or human stupidity tolerance. A month later, in a letter to Roger Angell, he offered another diagnosis:

> The weather has looked up lately, and I am waiting for a flush of well-being to overtake me. A clown over in Ellsworth says I am in a Ménière's syndrome. . . . My own suspicion is that I am dizzy for all the old reliable reasons, inability to write being one.[14]

In 1968 White settled down to complete his third children's story, *The Trumpet of the Swan,* which had been half finished for some time. He wrote with the same sense of urgency that twenty-three years earlier had driven him to bring *Stuart Little* to completion—the fear of dying and leaving Katharine inadequately provided for. In February 1969, after weeks of increasing pain, she had to be taken from Sarasota to Columbia-Pres-byterian Hospital, in New York, where she remained for thirteen weeks of treatment for osteoporosis of the spine, a side-effect of the medicine she had been given to control her dermatitis. In March, in a dictated letter to a friend, she alluded to Andy's book: "There is that book—two-thirds written. What a mess I have been!" From that time on Katharine spoke increasingly of being a burden to Andy. Back home in North Brooklin she was installed in a hospital bed, was attended by nurses round the clock, and was able to move about only with difficulty.

While she was still in the hospital, she wrote someone that though Andy's book needed only two more chapters, it would be "years perhaps before he gets a second version that pleases him." But in fact he finished it during the next six months. When he turned in the manuscript just before Thanksgiving in 1969, he and Katharine were in such poor health that he thought one or the other of them might not be around if it was delayed until 1971. In humorous self-pity White said at the time that any friend of his had "to get sick with considerable regularity. He's got to have his days when he can't keep his food down, his bleak mornings, and his midnight agony. Otherwise he doesn't live in my world." He was dis-satisfied with the book, and after he turned it in he wished he had held it a year and then rewritten it, as he had done with his other children's books.[15]

The Trumpet of the Swan tells the story of Louis, a trumpeter swan born without a voice. Being unable to make the "ko-hoh" sound characteristic of his species, he has no means of talking to his fellow swans, or of ever uttering the all-important mating cry. With the help of Sam Beaver, an eleven-year-old boy with whom he becomes friends, he goes to school and learns to read and write, so that with a slate and a piece of chalk he can communicate at least with people—if not with swans. To help him over-come his handicap, Louis's father supplies him ingeniously with an artificial voice by means of a brave, though unlawful, act: he crash-dives through the show-window of a music store and steals a trumpet, on which Louis learns to play. But before he uses this man-made instrument to win the heart of Serena, the young female swan he has fallen in love with, Louis sets out to save the honor of his father by earning enough money to reimburse the music store for the horn and the broken windowpane. His friend Sam gets him a summer job in a boys' camp in Ontario, and at the end of summer Sam suggests that Louis fly to Boston and get a job playing his trumpet for the passengers in the swan boats on the pond of the Public Garden. When that job ends, he accepts the offer of a job playing with a band in a nightclub in Philadelphia. Near the end of the engagement, Serena, "the swan of his desiring," arrives at the bird pond of the local zoo, where Louis has been living temporarily. She has been blown there by a storm that carried her all the way from Montana. She falls in love with Louis, the two fly off happily back to Montana, and Louis's father pays the music store the $4,420.78 Louis has earned.

As White said at the time, he was "not averse to departing from reality" when he wrote for children, but he was "against departing from the truth":

> I feel I must never kid them about anything; I feel I must be on solid ground myself. . . . Before I began the writing of [*The Trumpet of the Swan,*] which is a love story, I read everything I could get hold of about the trumpeter swan, so that, however fantastical the tale, the behavior of the bird is authentic and violates nothing in the natural world of swans.[16]

But White's knowledge of the natural behavior of the trumpeter swan hardly shows in the plot or in his anthropomorphic characterization of Louis. The truth of the tale derives from White's memory of his own experience, as a boy like Sam and as a young man like Louis. He could imagine a swan's nest because forty years earlier he had taken pictures of a loon sitting on a nest in which were a day-old chick and an unhatched egg. He knew the sweetgrass country of Montana from his trip west fifty years earlier. And all of Louis's experiences at Camp Kookooskoos are based on Andy White's memories of Camp Otter. Most important of all, perhaps, was the memory of Elwyn White standing in front of his class in school unable to speak, and of his believing ever afterwards that he could not make speeches in public. He remembered how it felt not to be able to talk to girls. And, finally, there seems to be a connection between the showroom of the Horace Waters Piano Company on Fifth Avenue in New York and the music store in Billings, Montana, and between the character of Samuel White and that of the old cob, though White was unaware when he wrote the book of the possible analogy between Samuel White's deceiving Leeds Waters and the old cob's stealing the horn. The real autobiographical significance of *The Trumpet of the Swan*, however, lies not in such details. The story is as deeply autobiographical as *Stuart Little* and *Charlotte's Web* because it concerns aspects of White's life and character just as true and influential as those that underlie the earlier stories.

The Trumpet of the Swan is less moving than White's preceding children's stories because its humor has fewer serious undertones, its sense of life is less profound, and (most important) its characters are less convincing. White may have weakened the story by dividing his (and his readers') interest between Louis and Sam, who both portray aspects of White's character and enact events based on White's memories. When White wrote the final paragraph of the story he wrote about himself, "who loved the beautiful earth" and who had "solved his problems" by becoming a writer:

> As Louis relaxed and prepared for sleep, all his thoughts were of how lucky he was to inhabit such a beautiful earth, how lucky he had been to solve his problems with music, and how pleasant it was to look forward to another night of sleep and another day tomorrow, and the fresh morning, and the light that returns with the day.

And when, only a few paragraphs earlier, White wrote about Sam Beaver, he wrote about himself:

> Sam chuckled. He had never told his father about the swans in the pond nearby. He kept their secret to himself. When he went to the pond, he always went alone. That's the way he liked it.[17]

White called *The Trumpet of the Swan* a love story, but Louis's love for Serena is not the main subject of the book. It is primarily an adventure story in which the hero's adolescent love is more a preoccupation than it is a motive for his actions. Louis and Sam are both boys in the process of winning the independence of adulthood, an experience that in White's own case left vivid, bittersweet memories, only a part of which concerned romance. We are told that Louis thinks Serena beautiful and "very feminine", and that Serena thinks it "pleasing" to know that she has found "an acceptable mate, a cob [she] can love and respect, a cob that appears to be not only musical but also quite wealthy."[18] Serena does not symbolize for Louis, as Margalo did for Stuart, "a vision of the grail," or an ineffable something he will follow all his days; nor has she Charlotte's greatness.

Though White's description of Louis's feelings of love and triumphant wooing is lyrical, its mode is that of musical comedy. If *The Trumpet of the Swan* is not an interesting love story, however, it is a highly entertaining story about the eventful life of an American boy (or of two "boys") told with White's wise and loving humor. Where evil and pain threaten, readers cannot take the threats seriously, as they do in *Stuart Little* or

Charlotte's Web. Even the musician's agent, the "great of heart" Abe ("Lucky") Lucas, who, White suggests, resembles a racketeer, is only a Damon Runyon character that Louis (like a Horatio Alger hero) is more than equal to.

What is serious, and what helps make the book an extraordinary children's story, is White's treatment of the relationship between father and son. Clearly the most memorable character in the story is the old cob, Louis's father. Though he may be a benign caricature of White's father, he is for most readers not only a recognizable human being, inclined to admire himself, to romanticize his role as husband and father, and to enjoy the sound of his own eloquence—he is also everyone's father, who, because he is of another and different generation, must always seem to his children a little comic in his ways. But the humorous implications of the generation gap between Louis and his father are only half the story; the somber side appears in Sam Beaver's inability to tell his father all he knows and in his uncomfortable feeling about not telling the whole truth. Louis's sense of responsibility for his father's honor, and Sam's love for a father from whom he must distance himself, are the truest and most convincing emotions we meet in *The Trumpet of the Swan*—those and, to a lesser degree, the adolescent affection between Louis and Sam, the delight Sam takes in the natural zoological world, and Louis's desire for Serena.

The Trumpet of the Swan is a remarkable book in several respects, one of which is that it is a young book by an old writer. But, as Thoreau knew, if a writer "is fortunate and keeps alive, he will be forever in love." White said in 1970, in response to an award from the Laura Ingalls Wilder Foundation, "I feel that a writer has an obligation to transmit, as best he can, his love of life, his appreciation for the world."[19] The book speaks to young people who respond to White's concern not just for an endangered species, but for an endangered civilization and an endangered planet. In accepting the National Medal for Literature in 1971, he said:

> Only hope can carry us aloft, can keep us afloat. Only hope, and a certain faith that the incredible structure that has been fashioned by this most strange and ingenious of all the mammals cannot end in ruin and disaster. This faith is a writer's faith, for writing itself is an act of faith, nothing else. And it must be the writer, above all others, who keeps it alive—choked with laughter, or with pain.[20]

When the advisory board for the Pulitzer Prize decided in 1978 to give White not a prize, but a "special citation" for letters, White said to a reporter for the *New York Times*: "I guess they're trying to catch up on things. They think time is running out." During this period White was dogged by his own thoughts of time running out, but his talk about his health and about his hypochondria was infused with self-knowledge and humor: "I have had a frog in my throat for quite some time now, and of course with me this develops almost instantly into cancer of the larynx, because that is the way I'm built." He still suffered, but he still knew how to treat himself. Since the early seventies he had had an irregular heartbeat, a symptom about which he had read, in the *Bangor News,* that it "precedes fatal disturbances." Yet he was able to describe comically the rhythm of his heartbeat by saying that it went "one two three four hello-there-everybody. One two three four." He had worried about his heart for years. In 1957, in *The Elements of Style,* he had illustrated the correct use of quotation marks with this sentence: "I am reminded of the advice of my neighbor, 'Never worry about your heart till it stops beating.' "21

In his seventies White began to notice that he could not write quite as easily as he used to: "The aging mind has a bagful of nasty tricks, one of which is to tuck names and words away in crannies where they are not immediately available. . . . This is extremely annoying to a writer, who wants his words where he can reach them." When he submitted to *The New Yorker* a short, parodic response to Charles Reich's *The Greening of America* in 1970, Shawn's comment on it "sounded so woebegone and melancholy" that White thought that Shawn did not like it and he "tried to persuade [Shawn] to send the thing back." It was published, but a year later *The New Yorker* rejected a parable White had written about the campaign of feminists to abolish the use of the pronoun *his* to mean "his or her." He told Roger Angell that he was "surprised, but not down-hearted, that the piece got sunk. . . . To me, any woman's (or man's) attempt to remove the gender from the language is both funny and futile, and that's what I thought the piece was all about." Roger Angell, anticipating his mother's reaction to *The New Yorker*'s rejection, asked Andy to "discourage KSW from hitting Shawn with a thirty-page demurrer, no matter how right you think she is."22

In 1971 *The Trumpet of the Swan* was number one on the *New York Times* list of best-sellers in children's books, and *Charlotte's Web* was number two; but "1971 was a year of pain, pressure and peril for me," White wrote a friend, "and I'm glad it's over. I've never had such a bad time, never made more money, never done so few things that I wanted to do." Still, in 1971 he wrote two "Letters from the East" that described his continuing pleasure in the routine and in the variety of his daily life on the farm. As he said on turning seventy, old age was a special problem for him because he had never been able to shed the mental image he has of himself—"a lad of about 19."[23] In his seventies many of his pleasures were the same he had enjoyed for fifty years.

Here and there in his letters of this period he gave his correspondent glimpses into some of the ways in which his and Katharine's days rolled along during the last years of their lives together:

> This is one of those sultry Sunday afternoons when we sit around waiting to see whether it's going to rain or snow. Skies are grey, every bone in my body foretells the approaching storm, the thermometer has inched up to forty, Jones [a Norwich terrier] is asleep four feet away on my couch, a small wood blaze snickers in the fireplace, the geese are skating on the pasture pond waiting for the thaw, K has just climbed the stairs to her bedroom for a snooze, and I am marking time until chores, when I will round up the geese, collect the eggs, water the hens, fill the woodbox, empty the garbage, pull the slide in the henpen, load the bird feeder, lay a fire in the living room, feed the dogs, carry the eggs to the arch in the cellar, and lie down for half an hour preparatory to mixing a drink. . . .
>
> K is deep in garden catalogues. The south windows in the living room are already abloom with forced freesias—a triumph. My chick order is in, for April delivery. My revision of "The Elements" is in the works. . . .[24]

But the best of White's accounts of those days occurs in a passage in "A Letter from the East" dated a year earlier, March 27, 1971, from Allen Cove. Here he tells how it was in what has always been the most promising part of the day to him, the early morning, when he is alone:

> Except for winter's causing me to become housebound, I like the cold. I like snow. I like the descent to the dark, cold kitchen at six in the morning, to put a fire in the wood stove and listen to weather from Boston. My movements at that hour are ritualistic—they vary hardly at all from morning to morning. I steal down in my wrapper carrying a pair of corduroy pants under one arm and balancing a small tray (by de Miskey) that holds the empty glasses from the night before. The night nurse has preceded me into the living room and has hooked up the thermostat—too high. I nudge it down. As I enter the kitchen, my left hand shoots out and snaps on the largest burner on the electric stove. Then I set the glasses in the sink, snap on the pantry light, start the cold water in the tap, and fill the kettle with fresh spring water, which I then set atop the now red burner. Then comes the real warmup: with a poker I clear the grate in the big black Home Crawford 8-20, roll up two sheets of yesterday's Bangor *Daily News,* and lay them in the firebox along with a few sticks of cedar kindling and two sticks of stovewood on top of that. (I always put on my glasses before stuffing the *News* in, to see who is dead and to find out what's been going on in the world, because I seldom have time in these

twilight years to read newspapers—too many other things to tend to. I always check on "Dear Abby" at this dawn hour, finding it a comfort to read about people whose problems are even greater than mine, like the man yesterday who sought Abby's advice because his wife would sleep with him only on Thursday nights, which was all right until his bowling club changed *its* night to Thursday, and by the time the man got home his wife was far gone in shut-eye). I drop the match, open the flue to "Kindle," open the bottom draft, and wait a few seconds to catch the first reassuring sound of snap-and-crackle. (That's the phrase around here for a wood fire—always "snap-and-crackle.") As the first light of day filters into the kitchen, I set out the juicer, set out the coffeepot and coffee, set out the pitchers for milk and cream, and, if it's a Tuesday or a Thursday or a Saturday, solemnly mark the milk order blank and tuck it in the milk box in the entryway while the subzero draft creeps in around my ankles. A good beginning for the day. Then I pull my trousers on over my pajama bottoms, pull on my barn boots, drape myself in a wool shirt and a down jacket, and pay a call in the barn, where the geese give me a tumultuous reception, one of them imitating Bert Lahr's vibrato gargle.

The guard changes here at seven: the night nurse goes off (if her car will start) and the housekeeper comes on (if her brother-in-law's truck has started). I observe all this from an upstairs window. It is less splendid than the change at Buckingham Palace but somehow more impressive, the palace guard never having been dependent on the vagaries of the internal-combustion engine in a subzero wintertime.[25]

In 1972 Andy and Katharine began to help Dorothy Lobrano Guth, Andy's goddaughter, to gather, select, and edit the material that would constitute the *Letters of E. B. White.* The proposal for publishing a collection of White's letters had come from Harper and Row, and Andy agreed to it with misgivings that persisted throughout the four years it took to finish the job. At one point he wanted to "drop the whole business," because he did not like the work of supplying the editor with information for headnotes and footnotes, and of deciding what letters or passages should be excluded lest they violate the privacy of his correspondents. In the end, he wrote or rewrote most of the notes himself. What kept him at this uncongenial task was the belief that he might need the income that his publisher predicted the book would produce. He did not take an advance on future royalties but, as he wrote his publisher on another occasion, decided just "to pocket the money as it pours in."[26]

When the book finally appeared, in November 1976, it was an instant success. By Christmas fifty-five thousand copies had been printed. Clearly, the royalties would soon begin to pour in. But White was especially pleased by the hundreds of letters he received from his readers. Many of his old admirers were still alive, it seemed, and the first generation of readers (or hearers) of *Charlotte's Web* were now entering their thirties: "The book generated the most gratifying mail I have ever had—a great outpouring of backed-up feelings, most of it going way back in time to earlier books."[27] In most of those earlier books his best writing had had the virtues of a good personal letter: a sense of pleasure in reporting the news, a preference for good news, informality and directness, a sense of humor, a lively love of the world—and brevity.

K A T H A R I N E had four heart seizures during her last years, but none of them kept her spirits down for very long. Even with her failing vision, she kept right on with her correspondence, dictating long, lively letters to her friends and short, forceful ones to her congressmen. In the spring of her last year she suffered the greatest to her of all deprivations: her eyesight deteriorated so badly that she became unable to read for pleasure. Only then did she grow bitter about her decline. Towards the very end she was barely able to see her way around a room. On the day of her death, July 20, 1977, White "sat on a small stool just inside the door of the Intensive Care Unit and watched the heart monitor send its tiny, bright signals of doom."[28]

Katharine had requested that there be no funeral service and had been "quite specific about what she wanted." There was to be a graveside service attended only by her family. All of her children and five of her grandchildren were there. Andy did not attend.[29] He wrote the script for the service, and he included in it, as she had requested, a poem he had written to her forty years before:

L A D Y   B E F O R E   B R E A K F A S T

On the white page of this unwritten day
Serena, waking, sees the imperfect script:
The misspelled word of circumstance, the play
Of error, and places where the pen slipped.
And having thus turned loose her fears to follow
The hapless scrawl of the long day along,
Lets fall an early tear on the warm pillow,
Weeping that no song is the perfect song.

By eight o'clock she has rewritten noon
For faults in style, in taste, in fact, in spelling;
Suspicious of the sleazy phrase so soon,
She's edited the tale before its telling.

Luckily Life's her darling: she'll forgive it.
See how she throws the covers off and starts to live it![30]

At her grave Andy planted an oak tree, and some time later he published, as an introduction to a collection of her essays on gardening, his final tribute to her. It is a portrait of her as a gardener, but in it White captured much of her essential personality. Here is its conclusion:

I seldom saw her *prepare* for gardening, she merely wandered out into the cold and the wet, into the sun and the warmth, wearing whatever she had put on that morning. Once she was drawn into the fray, once involved in transplanting or weeding or thinning or pulling deadheads, she forgot all else; her clothes had to take things as they came. I, who was the animal husbandryman on the place, in blue-jeans and an old shirt, used to marvel at how unhesitatingly she would kneel in the dirt and begin grubbing about, garbed in a spotless cotton dress or a handsome tweed skirt and jacket. She simply refused to dress *down* to a garden: she moved in elegantly and walked among her flowers as she walked among her friends—nicely dressed, perfectly poised. If when she arrived back indoors the Ferragamos were encased in muck, she kicked them off. If the tweed suit was a mess, she sent it to the cleaner's.

The only moment in the year when she actually got herself up for gardening was on the day in fall that she had selected, in advance, for the laying out of the spring bulb garden—a crucial operation, carefully charted and full of witchcraft. The morning often turned out to be raw and overcast, with a searching wind off the water—an easterly that finds its way quickly to your bones. The bad weather did not deter Katharine: the hour had struck, the strategy of spring must be worked out according to plan. . . .

Armed with a diagram and a clipboard, Katharine would get into a shabby old Brooks raincoat much too long for her, put on a little round wool hat, pull on a pair of overshoes, and proceed to the director's chair—a folding canvas thing—that had been placed for her at the edge of the plot. There she would sit, hour after hour, in the wind and the weather, while Henry Allen produced dozens of brown paper packages of new bulbs and a basketful of old ones, ready for the intricate interment. As the years went by and age overtook her, there was something comical yet touching in her bedraggled appearance on this awesome occasion—the small, hunched-over figure, her studied absorption in the implausible notion that there would be yet another spring, oblivious to the ending of her own days, which she knew perfectly well was near at hand, sitting there with her detailed chart under those dark skies in the dying October, calmly plotting the resurrection.[31]

In the months immediately following Katharine's death White was preoccupied by the usual duties of a survivor and executor, and for the first two or three months he worked steadily at the job of answering hundreds of letters of condolence, some of them from strangers who had only recently come to know her as she appeared in the *Letters of E. B. White.* To each he gave a truly personal reply in which he responded to what his correspondent had said; and in many of these characteristically brief letters he expressed in simple, moving sentences various aspects of his sense of loss and his love for his wife. To a man who had been in love with Katharine when she was a young girl he wrote, "She seemed beautiful to me the first time I saw her, and she seemed beautiful when I gave her the small kiss that was goodbye." To someone who had said that he hoped Andy could be consoled by the knowledge that he had enriched her life, he replied, "I'm not sure I 'enriched' her life—I think I gummed it up at one point, when we moved to Maine—but at least we respected each other and that never failed us." To one of their mutual friends on the staff of *The New Yorker* he wrote, "I don't know what I ever did to deserve a wife with Katherine's qualities, but I have always had a lot of luck, and she was the most notable example." To another he wrote, "I have lost the one thing that seemed to make any sense in my life, and I feel like a child lost at Coney Island." Among his many expressions of loneliness, one example will suffice: "I am just a little man in a ten-room house, with nowhere to go but on."[32]

He did go on. For one thing, he had to meet a late-fall deadline for another revised edition of *The Elements of Style.* In composing new sentences to illustrate rules of punctuation and grammar, he unconsciously proved the truth of one of his old observations about style and the man —that no writer can conceal "his mood and temper":

A dash is a mark of separation stronger than a comma, less formal than a colon, and more relaxed than parentheses.

His first thought on getting out of bed—if he had any thought at all —was to get back in again.

The increasing reluctance of the sun to rise, the extra nip in the breeze, the patter of shed leaves dropping—all the evidences of fall drifting into winter—were clearer each day.

Words that intervene between subject and verb do not affect the number of the verb.

The bittersweet flavor of youth—its trials, its joys, its adventures, its challenges—is not soon forgotten.[33]

But White had never found in bittersweet memories of the past a substitute for the bittersweet experience of the present, and no new temptation to go back to bed could overcome his old instinct to get up, start the day, and keep himself active. He no longer felt a desire to write, but he did feel a compulsive need to see the best of his work selected, arranged, and published according to his wishes. As soon as he had seen Katharine's *Onward and Upward in the Garden* through the press, he turned to the unfinished project of a uniform edition of his works.[34]

Though basically in good health, he was learning to live with some of the vexations of advancing age. He could not hear or see as well as he used to, his arthritis had become more painful, his "jerky head" plagued him more often, and occasionally he had scary spells of arrhythmia. And his state of mind, even more than his physical condition, made it hard to keep going. Without Katharine's presence the house seemed empty, and his days were lonely. At times he felt desolate. The circle of his old friends had dwindled over the years. Those it had once included were now dead or dying. Whatever social life Katharine had brought into the house had died with her. Feeling inadequate in the role of a single host, he became reluctant to invite guests for dinner or to small parties as she had done; and he did not encourage those who would have liked to invite themselves. Thus his life became, as he called it, that of an elderly recluse.

The friendship he now so greatly needed he eventually found in the person who was helping him tidy up his literary properties. She was Corona Machemer, his editor at Harper and Row, a young woman whom he had known since 1976, when she came up from New York to assist in the final stages of preparing his *Letters* for publication. She had stayed at that time with the Whites for several days of hard work, during which Andy and Katharine discovered her to be not only a gifted editor but an attractive person, easy to get on with.

After Katharine's death Miss Machemer saw *Essays of E. B. White* through the press. That book had been essentially ready for printing before *Letters* was published, and it presented no problems. But in putting together the next projected volume, *Poems and Sketches of E. B. White,* Andy faced the formidable task of selecting "from hundred of pieces, old and recent," and he needed help.

When, in 1980, he planned his customary spring trip to Sarasota and needed someone to share the driving, he and Miss Machemer decided to drive there together and, for a few days, combine swimming and cycling with choosing pieces that were to go into *Poems and Sketches.* The success of this first brief working vacation led to others like it, both in Florida and in Maine.

To celebrate his eighty-first birthday, on July 11,1980, Andy invited Corona to join him in camp for a few days of swimming and canoeing at Great Pond, the same Belgrade lake where, seventy years before, he had received a green Old Town canoe from his father, a gift for his eleventh birthday. Corona herself had a birthday to celebrate and at the moment was visiting her family in nearby North Belgrade. When she accepted Andy's invitation, he borrowed a canoe from his doctor, lashed it on top of his car, and drove to Great Pond, picking up Corona on his way. The lake was serene, the weather smiled, and the canoe, which leaked only slightly, could have been called "Summer Memories," for both Andy and Corona had spent many childhood days in the Belgrade region and both had a lot to remember.

Soon after returning home, White drove to Old Town, Maine, and bought himself a new, green, fifteen-foot wood-and-canvas canoe in anticipation of returning the following year to the Pond with Miss Machemer, and with his own canoe.

In 1982, in a letter to a friend, White wrote: "For me, the pleasure of Corona's company in these last difficult years has been great. We see each other only a few days in every year, but the visits are something I look forward to, as a child looks forward to an afternoon at the circus."

AT THE AGE of eighty three, in the preface to a new edition of *One Man's Meat,* White suggested that he was not about to change his way of living:

> I keep telling myself that it is time to quit this place, with its eleven rooms and its forty acres, and cut myself down to size. I may still do it. But I can envision what would happen if I did: I would no sooner get comfortably settled in a small house on an acre of land than I would issue instructions to build a small barn and attach it to the house through a woodshed. A bale of hay would appear mysteriously in the barn, and there would soon be a bantam rooster out there, living in the style to which he feels he should be accustomed. I would be right back where I started.

Staying put, he continues to fill his days with the old routines: his chores of farm and home, and his writing. He seldom writes for publication, to be sure, but he continues to maintain a heavy correspondence, typing scores of letters a week, to friends, relatives, and readers—old and new, young and old—who write out of a need to "break through the barriers of silence and distance into companionship." His letters, usually on a single page, continue to sound like *The Letters of E. B. White.*

Such activity keeps him busy, but neither it nor the pleasure of Corona's occasional company may help him to endure the loneliness of these last years as much as does his gift for enriching his life by examining it—by "taking thought" of himself, alive in a world he loves. He once praised Thoreau for believing that "the big thing was not to create a better mouse trap, or a better lead pencil, or even a better book, but a better man," and that "it was possible, by taking thought, to add a cubit to one's stature." Early on he knew, like Thoreau, that contemplation was a form of creativity; and now, with vision and a healthy intellect unimpaired by age, he can still improve the nick of time by taking thought. This he is able to do in what is for him the best possible setting: his saltwater farm, with its house connected by a woodshed to the barn where Wilbur lived out his days happy in his "warm delicious cellar with the garrulous geese, the changing seasons, the heat of the sun, the passage of swallows, the nearness of rats, the sameness of sheep, the love of spiders, the smell of manure, and the glory of everything." And for White that glory extends beyond the limits of Wilbur's world to take in the whole earth, this planet that man must not destroy. Of that earth he is kept mindful by the sea, whose tides wash the shore of Allen Cove, and whose breezes bear the "smell that takes man back to the very beginning of time, linking him to all that has gone before."

E. B. White at Work:
The Creation of a "Paragraph"

DURING WORLD WAR II A PATRIOTIC MEMBER of the advertising department at *The New Yorker* donated all the magazine's manuscripts prior to 1934 to a paper drive. Hence the earliest extant typescript copy of any of White's paragraphs for "Notes and Comment" is one written after he had been on the job for seven years. From 1934 on, however, White's pieces for "Notes and Comment," in the form in which they went to the printer, were preserved, and they are now in the White Collection at Cornell. As White pointed out when he added them to the Collection, all that these manuscripts show is that he was a neat typist, that he spelled most of the words right, and that he got "almost everything into the confines of a single sheet of yellow paper."

Not until after he had ceased to be a regular contributor to "Notes and Comment" did it occur to White to preserve the drafts of pieces he wrote for *The New Yorker,* and so, for a good example of the way he went about writing a paragraph for "Notes and Comment," one must turn to the very end of his career as a paragrapher—to the manuscript of one of the last half-dozen "Comments" he has written, a paragraph on the occasion of the moon-walk of astronauts Neil Armstrong and Edwin Aldrin, Jr., on July 20, 1969.

White watched the moon-walk on television at his home in Maine on Sunday night from about 11 P.M. till 1 A.M. Since press time at *The New Yorker* was Monday noon, he wrote under some pressure. On Monday morning, when he had typed what he thought was his final draft (No. 3 of the series here reproduced), he sent it by telegraph to *The New Yorker.* Shortly afterwards, he decided that he did not like what he had written, and he composed a new version (No. 4), revised it (No. 5), made a fair copy of the revision (No. 6), and then sent Shawn a telegram (No. 7). When Shawn phoned and, having heard the new version, agreed that it was better than the first, White dictated it to Shawn, who sent it at once to the printer. The paragraph was published on Thursday, in the issue dated Saturday, July 26.

According to Thurber, "The art of paragraphing is to make something that was ground out sound as if it were dashed off." These drafts illustrate the art, as well as its practice, which White described as follows: "I always write a thing first and think about it afterward, which is not a bad procedure, because the easiest way to have consequential thoughts is to start putting them down." After that came the "grinding" and, with luck, a finished piece that sounded as if it had been dashed off.

white

comment

[handwritten top margin: estimate would never have reached their goal. But they sent along something that might better have been left behind—]

Planning a trip to the moon, ~~isxwxxxttxliyxxx~~

~~differ~~ differs in no ~~esstial~~ esstial respect from planning a trip
                                                        along,
to the beach. You have to decide what to take, what to leave

behind. Should the thermos jug go? The child's rubber horse?
The dill pickles?
These are sometimes fateful decisions, on which the success or
failure   outing
~~txxixxppixxxx~~ of the whole ~~expxxitixx~~ turns. Something goes

along that spoils everything because it is always in the way.

Somethihg gets left behind that spoils everything because it is
                                          for   ~~were saddled with the~~
desperately needed for comfort or, safety. The men who had to
                                            send
decide what to ~~take~~ along to the moon must have pondered long and
           [handwritten: Should the vacuum cleaner go? The fever A-tiller?]   *[handwritten: fully]*
hard, drawn up many a list. ~~We're not~~ sure they planned well, *[hw]*
        when they included the
~~foxvixxyxxixxtxxtxxxxtakxxxxixxg~~ the little telescoped flagpole and
        artificially stiffened
the ~~stiffxxxx~~ American flag, ~~artifixxxxlyxxxiffxxx~~d so that it
would fly to the breeze that didn't blow.
flew to the breeze that didn't blow. The Stars and Stripes on

the moon undoubtedly gave untold satisfaction to millions of
                         [hw: But]
~~Whx~~ As we watched the Stars and Stripes planted on the surface of

the moon, we experienced the same sensations of pride ~~and~~ that

must have filled the hearts of millions of Americans. But it
                                        [hw: stone in my stomach]
the emotion soon turned to
    [hw: Here a]   *[hw: to do something new and unparalleled in all ...]*
~~This~~ was ~~our~~ great chance, and we muffed it. The ~~mxxx~~ men who
                                               were
stepped out onto the surface of the moon are in a class by
                              [hw: to ... age of the]   *[hw: of men and women everywhere who]*
themselves---pioneers of what is universal. They saw the
                                                  [hw: dark sky]
earth whole---ju~~s~~t as it is, a round ball in a   But they *[hw: followed]*
[hw: instruction]
colored the moon red, white, and blue0--~~good colors all---but~~
     [hw: the moon that is out of the realm of nationality by its very position]
~~out of place in that setting~~. The moon still ~~influences~~ the
                        [hw: still]
tides, and the tides lap on every shore, right around the globe.

1

still holds the key to madness

Kiss in every land

The moon stil belongs to lovers, and lovers are everywhere--not

just in America. What a pity we couldn't have planted some
        precisely   this unique, this incredible
emblem that ~~exactly~~ expressed the occasion, even if it were

nothing more than a white banner, with the legend: ~~xxxxxxxxxx~~-y."

that simply said:

"At last!"

handkerchief, symbol of the common...
which, like the moon, belongs to all
mankind

white

comment

Planning a trip to the moon differs in no essential respect from planning a trip to the beach. You have to decide what to take along, what to leave behind. Should the thermos jug go? The child's rubber horse? The dill pickles? These are sometimes fateful decisions on which the success or failure of the whole outing turns. Something goes along that spoils everything because it is always in the way. Something gets left behind that is desperately needed for comfort or for safety. The men who drew up the moon list for the astronauts, planned long and hard and well. (Should the vacuum cleaner go? to suck up moondust and save the world?) Among the items they sent along, of course, was the little jointed flagpole and the flag that could be stiffened to the breeze that didn't blow. (It is traditional among explorers to plant the flag.) Yet the two men who stepped out on the surface of the moon were in a class by themselves: they were of the new race of men, those who had seen the earth whole. When, following instructions, they colored the moon red, white, and blue, they were stepping out of character---or so it seemed to us who watched, trembling with awe and admiration and pride. This was the last scene in the long book of nationalism, and they followed the book. But the moon still holds the key to madness, which is universal, still controls the tides, that lap on every shore everywhere, and blesses lovers that kiss in every land, under no particular banner. What a pity we couldn't have played the scene as it should been played, planting, perhaps, a simple white handkerchief, symbol of the common cold, that belongs to mankind invariably and knows no borders

2

white

comment

Planning a trip to the moon differs in no essential respect from planning a trip to the beach. You have to decide what to take along, what to leave behind. Should the thermos jug go? The **child's rubber horse?** The **dill pickles?** These are sometimes fateful decisions on which the success or failure of the whole outing turns. Something goes along that spoils everything because it is always in the way; something gets left behind that is desperately needed for comfort or for safety. The men who drew up the moon list for the astronauts planned long and hard and well. (Should the vacuum cleaner go, to suck up moondust?) Among the *inevitable* items they sent along, of course, was the little jointed flagpole and the flag that could be stiffened to the breeze that did not blow. (It is traditional among explorers to plant the flag.) Yet the two men who stepped out on the surface of the moon were in a class by themselves and should have been equipped accordingly: they were of the new breed of men, those who had seen the earth whole. When, following instructions, they colored the moon red, white, and blue, they were fumbling with the past---or so it seemed to us, who watched, trembling with awe and admiration and pride. This moon plant was the last *chapter* scene in the long book of nationalism, one that could well have been omitted. The moon still holds the key to madness, which is universal, still controls the tides that lap on shores everywhere, still guards lovers that kiss in every land under no banner but the sky. What a pity we couldn't have forsworn our little Iwo Jima scene and planted instead a banner acceptable to all---a simple white handkerchief, perhaps, symbol of the common cold, which, like the moon, affects us all.

3

that

it turn out;

The moon is a great place for men, and when

did they do

Armstrong and Aldrin danced from sheer exuberance, it was

a poor place for

a sight to see. But the moon is ~~no place for banners~~ flags.

a flag

for the breeze doesn't blow   a flag is out

~~They~~ cannot float on the breeze, and ~~they don't~~ belong there

of place on the moon anyway.

anyway. Like every great river, every great sea, the moon

no one

belongs to ~~no one~~ and belongs to all. What a pity we

couldn't have forsworn our little Iwo Jima flag-lanting

scene and planted instead a universal banner acceptable

to all---a limp white handkerchief, perhaps, symbol of the

common cold, which, like the moon, affects us all.

Of course, it is traditional that explorers plant the flag,

and it was inevitable that our astronauts should follow thw

as we watched

custom. But the act was the last chapter in the long book

of nationalism, one that could well have been omitted---or

~~so it seemed to us.~~ The moon still holds the key to madness,

still controls the tides that lap on shores everywhere, still

guards the lovers that kiss in every land under no banner but th

the sky. What a pity ~~that is that~~ that, in our triumph, we

instead

couldn't have forsworn the little Iwo Jima scene and planted

simple

a banner acceptable to all---a ~~simple~~ white handkerchief,

perhaps, symbol of the common cold, whcih, like the moon, affects

us all.

4

white   like two happy children

comment

The moon, it turns out, is a great place for
men. One-sixth gravity must be a lot of fun, and when Armstrong and Aldrin went into their little dance, it was a
moment not only of triumph but of gaiety. The moon, on the
other hand, is a poor place for flags. Ours looked stiff
and dopey, trying to float on the breeze that does not blow.
(There must be a lesson here somewhere.) It is traditional,
of course, for explorers to plant the flag, but it struck
us, as we watched with awe and admiration and pride, that our
two men were universal men, not national men, and should
have been equipped accordingly. The moon,
like every great river, every great sea,
belongs to none and belongs to all;
It still holds
the key to madness, still controls the tides that lap on
shores everywhere, still guards the lovers
that kiss in every land under no banner but the sky. What a
pity that, in our moment of triumph, we
couldn't have forsworn the
Iwo Jima scene and planted instead a device acceptable to all:
a limp white handkerchief, perhaps, symbol of the common cold,
which, like the moon, affects us all, unites us all.

white

comment

          The moon, it turns out, is a great place for
men. One-sixth gravity must be a lot of fun, and when Armstrong and Aldrin went into their bouncy little dance, like
two happy children, it was a moment not only of triumph but of
gaiety. The moon, on the other hand, is a poor place for flags.
Ours looked stiff and awkward, trying to float on the breeze
that does not blow. (There must be a lesson here somewhere.)
It is traditional, of course, for explorers to plant the flag,
but it struck us, as we watched with awe and admiration and
pride, that our two fellows were universal men, not national
men, and should have been equipped accordingly. Like every
great river *and* every great sea, the moon belongs to none and
belongs to all. It still holds the key to madness, still controls the tides that lap on shores everywhere, still guards the
lovers that ~~kiss~~ kiss in every land under no banner but the sky.
What a pity that in our moment of triumph we did not forswear
the familiar Iwo Jima scene and plant instead a device acceptable
to all: a limp white handkerchief, perhaps, symbol of the
common cold, which, like the moon, affects us all, unites us
all.

6

Mr. William Shawn

The New Yorker Magazine

25 West 43 Street

New York, N.Y.

My comment is no good as is. I have written a shorter

one on the same theme ~~whichxmaycheckxtitx~~ but different

in tone. If you want to hear it, I'll read it to you.

                                   Andy

ERW

359-8341

NOTES

In the Notes and in the Index, the following abbreviations are used:

Charlotte	*Charlotte's Web*
Elements	*The Elements of Style,* 3rd ed. (1979)
Essays	*Essays of E. B. White*
Everyday	*Everyday Is Saturday*
Fox	*The Fox of Peapack*
Ho Hum	*Ho Hum: Newsbreaks from "The New Yorker"*
Letters	*Letters of E. B. White*
New York	*Here Is New York*
OMM	*One Man's Meat: A New and Enlarged Edition* (1943)
P&S	*Poems and Sketches of E. B. White*
Points	*The Points of My Compass*
Quo Vad.	*Quo Vadimus?*
Second Tree	*The Second Tree From the Corner*
Stuart	*Stuart Little*
Subtreasury	*A Subtreasury of American Humor*
Trumpet	*The Trumpet of the Swan*
WF	*The Wild Flag*
EBW	E. B. White
KSW	Katharine Sergeant White
N&C	"Notes and Comment," in *The New Yorker*
NYer	*The New Yorker*
SE	Scott Elledge
Talk	"Talk of the Town," in *The New Yorker*
White Collection	The E. B. White Collection, in the Department of Rare Books, Cornell University

CHAPTER I: Summit Avenue

1. *Letters*, p. 384; dust jacket of *Quo Vad.*
2. Interview with Clara White Wyvell, 23 December 1968; EBW to SE, 17 February 1970.
3. Samuel White to EBW, 11 July 1911.
4. Interview with Stanley White, 9 October 1968.
5. Interview with Clara White Wyvell, 23 December 1968.
6. *Waters* v. *Horace Waters & Co.*, 130 AD 678, 115 N.Y.S. 432 (1909), affirmed by 201 NY 184, 94 NE 602 (1911).
7. *Letters*, p. 3.
8. *Trumpet*, pp. 77, 80.
9. *Trumpet*, pp. 30–31.
10. EBW to SE, 8 August 1968.
11. Albert White to EBW, 3 October 1936.
12. Interview with Stanley White, 9 October 1968.
13. EBW to SE, 25 May 1982.
14. *OMM*, p. 51.
15. *Letters*, p. 3.
16. Samuel White to Albert White, 26 January 1909.
17. *Letters*, pp. 388–89.
18. Interview with Lillian White Illian, November 1968.
19. *Letters*, p. 514.
20. Jessie White to EBW, 29 April 1920.
21. Jessie White to EBW, 2 April 1920.
22. Henry T. Tuckerman, *Book of the*

Artists: American Artist Life (New York: G. P. Putnam and Son, 1867), p. 550.
23. *Letters*, p. 4.
24. White Collection.
25. An undated clipping from a newspaper called *The Register.*
26. N&C, 22 December 1951.
27. *Quo Vad*, p. 169; dust jacket for *Quo Vad.*
28. N&C, 23 December 1933; N&C, 16 February 1929; *Letters*, pp. 393, 512.
29. *Letters*, pp. 2–3.
30. N&C, 22 December 1928.
31. Jessie White to EBW, 22 December 1935.
32. *Letters*, pp. 2, 388; N&C, 16 March 1935; *OMM*, pp. 201–2.
33. *OMM*, pp. 168–69.
34. *Charlotte*, p. 104; N&C, 31 January 1953.
35. "Was Lifted by Ears as Boy, No Harm Done," *NYer*, 9 May 1964.
36. EBW to SE, 17 February 1970.
37. EBW to SE, 17 February 1970; N&C, 2 April 1927; EBW to Henry Christman, 1 March 1951.
38. N&C, 9 February 1929.
39. *Letters*, p. 298.
40. N&C, 8 February 1936.
41. Flora B. Hackett to EBW, February 1953(?); N&C, 13 October 1928.
42. *Letters*, p. 8.

CHAPTER II: Belgrade Lake and Siwanoy Pond

1. George A. Plimpton and Frank H. Crowther, "The Art of the Essay, I: E. B. White," *The Paris Review*, no. 48 (Fall 1969), pp. 67–68.
2. "A Boy I Knew," *The Reader's Digest*, vol. 36, no. 218 (June 1940), pp. 33–36.
3. White Collection.
4. *Second Tree*, p. 26 (and *P&S*, p. 113).
5. James Thurber and E. B. White, *Is Sex Necessary? Or Why You Feel the Way You Do*, 3rd ed. (New York: Dell, 1963), p. 130.
6. *Mount Vernon Daily Argus*, 23 January 1963.
7. *Letters*, pp. 8, 384; *Charlotte*, p. 176.

8. *OMM*, p. 250; *Points*, p. 162 (and *Essays*, p. 213); *Letters*, p. 9.
9. White Collection.
10. *Letters*, pp. 9–10.
11. *Letters*, pp. 136–37.
12. *Letters*, pp. 6–7.
13. *Letters*, p. 281.
14. EBW to Albert H. White, 21 October 1908; also some parts in *Letters*, pp. 10–11.
15. "A Winter Walk," *St. Nicholas Magazine*, vol. 38, no. 8 (June 1911), p. 757.
16. "The St. Nicholas League," *NYer*, 8 December 1934 (and *Essays*, p. 228).

17. "A True Dog Story," *St. Nicholas Magazine*, vol. 41, no. 11 (September 1914), p. 1045.
18. *Trumpet*, pp. 2, 3, 6, 24, 34.
19. "A Stratagem for Retirement," *Holiday*, vol. 19, no. 3 (March 1956), pp. 84–87.
20. *Second Tree*, p. 98.
21. *Mount Vernon Daily Argus*, 23 January 1963.
22. N&C, 11 December 1954.
23. Walter K. Towers to EBW, 8

November 1916.
24. *Second Tree*, pp. 17–18 (and *Essays*, pp. 157–58).
25. *Letters*, p. 10.
26. *OMM*, p. 109.
27. *OMM*, p. 115.
28. *Second Tree*, p. 29 (and *P&S*, p. 116); White Collection; *OMM*, p. 39.
29. *OMM*, p. 111.
30. *OMM*, p. 111.

CHAPTER III: Cornell

1. "Naïveté," *The Cornell Era*, vol. 57, no. 2 (January 1946).
2. EBW to E. D. Hirsch, 24 February 1953.
3. *New York*, p. 9 (and *Essays*, p. 118).
4. "I'd Send My Son to Cornell," *University*, vol. 1, no. 5 (1933), pp. 36, 40, 90.
5. "Class History/The Class of 1921," *The 1921 Cornellian*.
6. *OMM*, pp. 111, 112.
7. White Collection.
8. Harry Lyford to EBW 16 August 1941.
9. *OMM*, p. 114.
10. Interview with Alpheus Smith, 17 March 1969.
11. "Letter from the East," *NYer*, 27 July 1957; *Elements*, pp. xii–xvi (and *Essays*, pp. 258–61).
12. "The Manuscript Club," *The Cornell Era*, vol. 53, no. 15 (11 June 1921).
13. Interview with Morris Bishop; review of Walter Pater, *Appreciations*, in Oscar Wilde, *Complete Works* (Garden City, N.Y.: Doubleday, Page, 1923), vol. XII, p. 471.
14. *New York Times*, 11 July 1969.

15. *Letters*, pp. 445–46.
16. Quoted by Arthur Mizener in *The Far Side of Paradise* (Boston: Houghton Mifflin, 1957), p. 35, from Wilson's essay "Thoughts on Being Bibliographed," in *Princeton University Library Chronicle*, February 1944, p. 54.
17. Memorial Day Speech, May 1940, White Collection.
18. "Business and Education," *Cornell Daily Sun*, 11 February 1921.
19. "Activity," *Cornell Daily Sun*, 14 March 1921.
20. "It's Coming On," *Cornell Daily Sun*, 15 March 1921.
21. White Collection.
22. "O Oculi," *Cornell Daily Sun*, 14 April 1921.
23. "I Stood Within a Trolley Car—(and It May Be Added It's a Wonder It Didn't Jump Off the Track)," *Cornell Daily Sun*, 12 October 1920.
24. *Cornell Daily Sun*, 28 May 1920; EBW to SE, 8 August 1968.
25. *Trumpet*, pp. 93–94, 112.
26. Burchfield to EBW, 3 September 1921.

CHAPTER IV: From Sea to Shining Sea

1. EBW to Mrs Bristow Adams, 8 September 1921.
2. J. W. Brown to Bruce Bliven, 10 September 1921.
3. *Second Tree*, p. 217 (and *P&S*, p. 7).
4. EBW to Burchfield, 26 November 1921.
5. Burchfield to EBW, December 1921.

6. EBW to Burchfield, 31 December 1921, and 22 January 1922.
7. *Letters*, pp. 30, 31.
8. "Child's," "The Bowling Green," *The New York Evening Post*, 21 January 1922, p. 8; Adams to EBW, 23 December 1921.
9. *Stuart*, p. 73.

10. Cushman to EBW, 23 August 1935.
11. Samuel White to EBW, 22 July 1922.
12. Samuel White to EBW, 4 August 1921.
13. *Letters*, p. 32.
14. EBW to Jessie White, 26 April 1922; EBW to SE.
15. *Letters*, p. 34.
16. *Letters*, p. 33.
17. "Promise," "Berry Patch," *Cornell Daily Sun*, 14 March 1922.
18. *Letters*, pp. 35–36.
19. Alice Burchfield Sumner to SE, 17 June 1982; *Letters*, pp. 36–37.
20. EBW to SE, 25 May 1982.
21. *Letters*, p. 37.
22. EBW to Burchfield, 20 April 1922.
23. "From Sea to Shining Sea," *Ford Times*, vol. 45, no. 7 (July 1953), pp. 8–12.
24. Cushman to EBW, 1959.

25. "The Life Triumphant," *NYer*, 17 July 1943.
26. EBW to Burchfield, 10 June 1922.
27. EBW to Burchfield, 10 June 1922.
28. Cushman to EBW, 26 June 1953.
29. "From Sea to Shining Sea."
30. *Letters*, pp. 53, 55.
31. Cushman to EBW, 26 June 1953; *Trumpet*, p. 3; *Letters*, p. 55; Nan Hart to EBW, 1950; Nan Hart to EBW, 1937.
32. EBW to Mrs. Bristow Adams, 5 August 1922.
33. Samuel White to EBW, 22 July 1922.
34. EBW to Burchfield, 25 August 1922.
35. *Second Tree*, p. 39 (and *Essays*, p. 167).
36. EBW to Burchfield, 25 August 1922.
37. Samuel White to EBW, 22 July 1922.
38. "From Sea to Shining Sea."
39. EBW to Burchfield, 21 September 1922.

CHAPTER V: From Seattle to Siberia

1. *Second Tree*, p. 10; N&C, 20 December 1930; *Letters*, pp. 275, 61.
2. *Second Tree*, p. 12.
3. *Points*, p. 208 (and *Essays*, p. 171).
4. EBW to Woollcott, 25 February [1927?].
5. *New York Times*, 11 July 1969, p. 31.
6. *Second Tree*, p. 11.
7. EBW to Burchfield, 21 September 1922; 31 December 1922; 26 January 1923; 27 April 1923.
8. Katherine Romans Hall, comp., *E. B. White: A Bibliographic Catalogue of Printed Materials in the Department of Rare Books, Cornell University Library* (New York: Garland, 1979), pp. 222–23.
9. EBW to Burchfield, 26 March 1923.
10. EBW to Burchfield, 21 April 1923.
11. EBW to Burchfield, 30 May 1923.
12. "Personal Column," *The Seattle Times*, 27 March 1923.
13. *Second Tree*, p. 91.
14. "Personal Column," *The Seattle Times*, 13 April 1923.
15. Helen Thurber and Edward Weeks, eds. *Selected Letters of James Thurber* (Boston: Little, Brown, 1980), p. 187.

16. "Personal Column," *The Seattle Times*, 20 June 1923.
17. Helen Louise Cohen, *Lyric Forms from France: Their History and Their Use* (New York: Harcourt, Brace, 1922).
18. "Personal Column," *The Seattle Times*, 31 March 1923.
19. "Personal Column," *The Seattle Times*, 8 May 1923.
20. EBW to Burchfield, 30 May 1923.
21. *Points*, pp. 206 and 207 (and *Essays*, p. 170).
22. "Wander Song," "Personal Column," *Seattle Times*, 9 June 1923.
23. *Points*, pp. 209, 208, 216 (and *Essays*, pp. 172, 171, 177).
24. *Points*, pp. 217–18, 223 (and *Essays*, pp. 178, 182).
25. *Points*, pp. 224, 225 (and *Essays*, pp. 183–84).
26. *Points*, pp. 239–40 (and *Essays* p. 195).
27. *Lady*, p. 80.
28. Philip Schuyler to EBW, 11 January 1923.
29. *Letters*, pp. 68–69, 70.
30. Samuel White to EBW, 22 July 1922.
31. EBW to SE, 17 February 1970.

CHAPTER VI: New York and *The New Yorker*

1. "Bantam and I," "The Bowling Green," *New York Evening Post,* 17 November 1923, p. 10; "The Life Triumphant," *NYer* 17 July 1943; Morley to EBW, 22 April 1936.
2. *New York World,* 11 and 14 February 1924.
3. "Noontime of an Advertising Man," *NYer,* 25 June 1949.
4. "In Re Gladness," "The Conning Tower," *New York World,* 7 July 1924, and as "In Re Life," *Lady,* p. 3.
5. N&C, 2 April 1960.
6. *New York,* pp. 31–32 (and *Essays,* pp. 125–26).
7. Interview with Frank Sullivan, 12 September 1968; EBW to SE, 8 August 1968; *Second Tree,* pp. 217–18 (and *P&S,* p. 7).
8. "Announcing a New Weekly Magazine, *The New Yorker,*" typescript, undated, in the library of *The New Yorker.*
9. Jane Grant, *Ross, "The New Yorker" and Me* (New York: Reynal, 1968), p. 232.
10. N&C, 20 February 1954; "A Step Forward," *NYer,* 18 April 1925; "Defense of the Bronx River," *NYer,* 9 May 1925.
11. Ralph Ingersoll, "The New Yorker," *Fortune,* August 1934, pp. 82, 92.
12. Russell Maloney, "Tilley the Toiler," *Saturday Review of Literature,* 30 August 1947, p. 8.
13. Ralph Ingersoll, *Point of Departure* (New York: Harcourt, Brace and World, 1961), p. 194; Plimpton and Crowther, "E. B. White," p. 84.
14. KSW to SE, 10 September 1970; *Letters,* p. 324–25.
15. *New York,* p. 9; *Letters,* p. 71; dust jacket of *Quo Vad.*
16. N&C, 22 December 1951; N&C, 10 June 1933.
17. Burke Dowling Adams to SE, 21 March 1969.
18. *Second Tree,* p. 216 (and *P&S,* p. 6).
19. EBW to SE, 17 February 1970.
20. "Definitions/Critic," *NYer,* 17 October 1925 (and *Lady,* p. 51, and *P&S,* p. 142).
21. Ellin Mackay, "Why We Go to Cabarets: A Post-Debutante Explains," *NYer,* 28 November 1925; Ralph Ingersoll, "The New Yorker," p. 82; Grant, *Ross,* pp. 229–32.
22. Dale Kramer, *Ross and "The New Yorker"* (Garden City, N.Y.: Doubleday, 1952), p. 152.
23. *Letters,* p. 324; *Second Tree,* p. 214 (and *P&S,* pp. 4–5).
24. "Why I Like New York," *NYer,* 10 October 1925.
25. Plimpton and Crowther, "E. B. White," p. 74; *Letters,* p. 322.
26. *P&S,* p. xiii.
27. "Always," *NYer,* 8 May 1926; "Lower Level," *NYer,* 22 May 1926; EBW, "Harold W. Ross," in *Encyclopaedia Britannica,* 1964 ed.
28. Updike, "Remarks on the Occasion of E. B. White Receiving the 1971 National Medal for Literature, 12/2/71." White Collection. Published with slight revisions in *Picked-Up Pieces* (New York: Knopf, 1975), p. 436.
29. Brendan Gill, *Here at "The New Yorker"* (New York: Random House, 1975), p. 294.
30. Mrs. Phillip Stimson to EBW, 23 July 1977.
31. Katharine S. Angell, "Home and Office," *The Survey,* 1 December 1926, p. 318. Near the end of this article Katharine answered the question "Where does a wife who works fail her husband?" as follows:

Certainly she has not enough time free to perform small personal services for him. She must entrust to a mere servant this matter of holes in socks (and such a husband has to put up with the annoyance of finding a button neglected occasionally). With us, on the evenings we do not go out to dinner or have guests, I often must work on manuscripts in order to have the free daytime hours I have described as stolen from the office for the children. But my husband also often brings work home and neither of us finds that working side by side is any less companionable than reading our separate novels, or even than playing bridge together.

Of course, for the husband of a wife with a gainful occupation there are the pulls of custom, the habits of his class, to overcome. He must of necessity compare himself to the man who has a woman to back him up, to hold up his hands at every turn; to the man whose wife is free to grease every wheel and organize his life so that he has the greatest possible number of hours free from domestic care of any sort in which to devote himself to the achievement of a successful career. It may be that famous careers are often so made, but they are more apt to be careers than lives. Such a man, we think in our family, does not necessarily have the largest or more rewarding life. . . .

In the psychology of all marriages the subtle balance of values and emphasis is of the utmost importance and women, who plunge emotionally so deeply into all their activities, open themselves to the danger of being too much

wedded to their work. A certain masculine detachment is a virtue much to be sought. Tied up with this weighing of values, is also the question of earnings. I cannot myself understand the feminine point of view that assumes that money earned by a wife is hers exclusively. The acceptance of economic equality, to my mind, requires that a husband's and wife's earnings be pooled for the good of the family.
32. *Letters*, p. 72.
33. EBW to SE, 8 August 1968.
34. *Letters*, p. 76.
35. Plimpton and Crowther, "E. B. White," p. 68.
36. "Life Cycle of a Literary Genius," *NYer*, 16 October 1926.
37. *Letters*, p. 72.

CHAPTER VII: "We"

1. Ross to EBW, 7 May 1943.
2. Ingersoll, *"The New Yorker,"* p. 86; Grant, *Ross*, p. 255.
3. Grant, *Ross*, p. 254.
4. Grant, *Ross*, pp. 36–37.
5. Grant, *Ross*, pp. 9, 10, 11, 15.
6. Gill, *Here at "The New Yorker,"* p. 392; N&C, 15 December 1951; Burton Bernstein, *Thurber* (New York: Ballantine Books, 1975), p. 637.
7. KSW to SE, 10 September 1970.
8. *Letters*, p. 74.
9. *Letters*, pp. 324–25; Grant, *Ross*, p. 259.
10. Ross to EBW, [July 1945,] "Friday."
11. Grant, *Ross*, p. 255.
12. "H. W. Ross," *NYer*, 15 December 1951; *Encyclopaedia Britannica*, 1964 ed., s.v. "Harold W. Ross."
13. Kramer, *Ross and "The New Yorker,"* p. 14.
14. Gill, *Here at "The New Yorker,"* pp. 390–93; "Ross," *NYer*, 15 December 1951; *Encyclopaedia Britannica*, 1964 ed., s.v. "Harold W. Ross."
15. *Elements*, p. 85.
16. Typescript note to a collection labeled "The *New Yorker* Book," in the White Collection. The collection consists of notes and letters from Harold Ross, James Thurber, Wolcott Gibbs, et al. that White "extracted from [his] files as

background material" for a book about *The New Yorker* that he and Katharine once thought about writing but never undertook.
17. *Ho Hum*. For White's brief account of his long career as editor of newsbreaks, see Hall, *E. B. White*, pp. 24–25.
18. *Ho Hum*.
19. *Nyer*, 27 July 1963.
20. *NYer*, 13 April 1940.
21. Ingersoll, *Point*, p. 193.
22. EBW, "Harold W. Ross," in *Encyclopaedia Britannica*, 1964 ed.; James Thurber, *The Years with Ross* (New York: Atlantic–Little, Brown, 1959), p. 92.
23. White used the phrase "merry, wise, and subtle" with reference to the aims of *New Yorker* cartoonists, in his Preface to *The "New Yorker" Album* (Garden City, N.Y.: Doubleday, Doran, 1928).
24. N&C, 29 October 1927.
25. N&C, 23 July and 9 July 1927.
26. N&C, 4 March 1944.
27. *The New Republic*, vol. 51 (1 June 1927), p. 29.
28. N&C, 28 May 1927.
29. Talk, 2 July 1927.
30. N&C, 5 October 1946. Margaret McPhedran, the reader who sent the

passage to White, said she hoped it would serve in some measure to thank him for the pleasure and reassurance that she had found in "One Man's Meat" and his *New Yorker* pieces. White Collection.

31. Quoted from Mann's "Freud and the Future," in Benjamin DeMott, "Technicians and Troubadours: How We Lost the Sex-Lab War," *New American Review,* no. 7 (1969), pp. 185–86.

32. N&C, 20 December 1930 (and *Everyday,* pp. 63–64).

33. *NYer,* 2 July 1927; *OMM,* p. 291.

34. Quoted and paraphrased from pp. 577–80 of *A History of Philosophy* (New York: Henry Holt, 1914), by Frank Thilly, in whose "Philosophy 6. Moral Ideas and Practice" White made a grade of C. A fraternity brother later remembered "spending all of one Sunday" discussing Bergson with White. Peter Vischer to EBW, 22 August 1920.

35. Thoreau, *Journals,* entries for 6 May 1864 and 23 June 1840.

36. "One Man's Meat," *Harper's Magazine,* September 1939, p. 440.

37. Updike, *Picked-Up Pieces*.

38. "James Thurber," *NYer,* 11 November 1961; *Letters,* p. 72.

39. For the following account of Thurber I am most indebted to the authorized biography, *Thurber,* by Burton Bernstein.

40. Charles S. Holmes, *The Clocks of Columbus* (New York: Atheneum, 1972), p. 33.

41. Bernstein, *Thurber,* pp. 255, 290; *Letters,* p. 82; interview with Helen Thurber, February 1969.

42. "James Thurber," *NYer,* 11 November 1961.

43. Bernstein, *Thurber,* pp. 248, 226; Holmes, *Clocks,* p. 111.

44. Bernstein, *Thurber,* p. 227.

45. Hall, *E. B. White,* p. 4.

46. *NYer,* 16 April 1927.

47. *NYer,* 18 June 1927.

48. Bernstein, *Thurber,* p. 350.

CHAPTER VIII: Katharine

1. "Coldly, to the Bronze Bust of Holley in Washington Square," "The Conning Tower," *New York World,* 12 March 1926, p. 13 (and *Lady,* p. 34).

2. "Belated Christmas Card," *NYer,* 7 January 1928.

3. "Portrait," *Lady,* p. 75 (and *P&S,* p. 143).

4. "Notes from a Desk Calendar," *NYer,* 14 January 1928 (and *Lady,* pp. 39–40).

5. Ingersoll, *Point,* p. 216.

6. "Rubbing Elbows," *NYer,* 11 June 1927.

7. Interview with Rosanne Magdol McVay; EBW to SE, 16 June 1982; "Gramercy Park," *NYer,* 3 March 1928 (and *Lady,* p. 16); "Mammy India," *NYer,* 3 March 1928.

8. "Bye Low Baby," *NYer,* 17 March 1928.

9. *Lady,* pp. 27 and 72; *NYer,* 5 May 1928 and 2 June 1928 (and *Fox,* p. 125; *Lady,* p. 85).

10. "Potter's Field," *NYer,* 5 May 1928.

11. "The Plan," in "The Conning Tower," *New York World,* 11 May 1928 (and as "Spring Planning," in *Lady,* p. 72).

12. KSW to SE, 10 August 1970.

13. EBW to SE, 17 February 1970; EBW to J. G. Gude, 21 February 1968.

14. "Intimations—Not of Immortality," "The Conning Tower," *New York World,* 9 August 1928, p. 11 (and *Lady,* pp. 70–71).

15. "Of Things That Are," "The Conning Tower," *New York World,* 7 November 1928, p. 11 (and *Lady,* p. 89).

16. "Soliloquy at Times Square," "The Conning Tower," *New York World,* 20 August 1928, p. 11 (and *Lady,* pp. 23–24).

17. "This Is a Prayer Before I Sleep," "The Conning Tower," *New York World,* 4 December 1928, p. 15 (and *Lady,* pp. 87–88).

18. *Letters,* p. 82

19. "Rhyme for a Reasonable Lady," "The Conning Tower," *New York World*, 4 January 1929, p. 15 (and *Lady*, p. 93).
20. EBW to SE, 17 February 1970.
21. EBW to SE, 16 June 1982.
22. KSW to SE, 10 August 1970.
23. *New York World*, 23 June 1929.
24. EBW to SE, 16 June 1982. For humorous accounts of the memorable plane ride see N&C, 26 September 1931 and 18 July 1953.
25. See, for example, N&C, 7 April 1945.
26. KSW to EBW, 31 May 1929.
27. KSW to EBW, [June] 1929.
28. KSW to EBW, 21 June 1929.
29. KSW to EBW, [June] 1929.
30. KSW to EBW, 11 July 1929.
31. KSW to EBW, 29 July 1929.
32. *Letters*, pp. 86–87.

33. *Letters*, pp. 85–86.
34. *Letters*, p. 88.
35. KSW to EBW, 29 July 1929.
36. N&C, 11 May 1929.
37. *Is Sex Necessary?*, p. xix.
38. *Is Sex Necessary?*, p. xiii.
39. *Is Sex Necessary?*, p. xiv.
40. *Is Sex Necessary?*, pp. 189–90.
41. EBW to SE, 9 August 1970.
42. KSW to SE, 10 August 1970.
43. *New York Daily Mirror*, 16 November 1929.
44. *Letters*, p. 82.
45. *Letters*, pp. 88–89.
46. *Letters*, p. 90.
47. *Letters*, pp. 90–91 (and *P&S*, p. 72).
48. N&C, 4 January 1930.
49. Ann Honeycutt to EBW, August 1977.

CHAPTER IX: "Quo Vadimus?"

1. "Memoirs of a Master," *NYer*, 23 December 1939 (and *P&S*, pp. 80–81).
2. *Letters*, pp. 91–92.
3. *Letters*, p. 94.
4. *Letters*, p. 95.
5. "Danbury Fair," *NYer*, 18 October 1930.
6. "Call Me Ishmael," Bryn Mawr *Alumnae Bulletin*, Summer, 1956 (and *P&S*, pp. 88–90).
7. EBW to SE, 16 June 1982.
8. EBW to Joel White, 31 December 1930.
9. "Department of Correction, Amplification, and Abuse," *NYer*, 6 March 1937.
10. "Apostrophe to a Pram Rider," "The Conning Tower," *New York World*, 11 February 1931 (and *Fox*, pp. 99–100).
11. "Quo Vadimus?," *NYer*, 24 May 1930 (and *Quo Vad.*, pp. 23–24).
12. "Obituary," *NYer*, 12 March 1932 (and *Quo Vad.*, pp. 181–83).
13. "After the Ball," *NYer*, 23 January 1932.
14. Plimpton and Crowther, "E. B. White," p. 83; KSW to SE, 9 May 1977.
15. *Letters*, p. 474.
16. Ingersoll, *"The New Yorker,"* p. 88.

17. Dale Kramer and George R. Clark, "Harold Ross and *The New Yorker*," *Harper's Magazine*, April, 1943, p. 519.
18. EBW to SE, 25 May 1982.
19. P. T. Moore to EBW, 26 December 1933.
20. N&C, 25 November 1933 (and *Everyday*, pp. 197–98).
21. "Swing Low, Sweet Upswing," *NYer*, 7 January 1933 (and *Quo Vad.*, p. 118).
22. "Alice Through the Cellophane," "I. Down the Rabbit Hole," *NYer*, 6 May 1933; "II. The Pool of Tears," *NYer*, 13 May 1933; "III. Advice from a Caterpillar," *NYer*, 20 May 1933.
23. "Alice Through the Cellophane," "III. Advice from a Caterpillar," *NYer*, 20 May 1933.
24. *Letters*, p. 114.
25. EBW to KSW, March 1934, Sunday morning.
26. *Letters*, pp. 117–19.
27. Untermeyer to EBW, 6 September 1941.
28. "Dusk in Fierce Pajamas," *NYer*, 27 January 1934 (and *Quo Vad.*, pp. 62–65; *P&S*, pp. 123–24).
29. N&C, 17 February 1934.
30. Ingersoll, *"The New Yorker,"* pp. 85–86.
31. Ingersoll, *"The New Yorker,"* pp. 97, 152.

32. N&C, 5 May 1934 (and partially reprinted in *Everyday*, pp. 229–30).
33. Ingersoll, *"The New Yorker,"* p. 152.
34. The only response *The New Yorker* made to Ingersoll's article was one sentence, written by White, in "Notes and Comment" for 18 August 1934: *"Gossip Note:* The editor of *Fortune Magazine* makes thirty dollars a week and carfare." What Ross and Katharine most objected to was Ingersoll's public

guessing about financial facts, including salaries and ownership of stock.
35. *Cornell Alumni News,* 15 November 1934; *New York American,* 10 October 1934.
36. Ross to White, 4 September 1935.
37. KSW to EBW, September 1935.
38. *Letters*, p. 121.
39. Ross to EBW, 7 May 1935.
40. N&C, 10 October 1936.
41. Jessie White to EBW, 27 June 1935.

CHAPTER X: Mr. Tilley's Departure

1. "My Physical Handicap, Ha Ha," *NYer,* 12 June 1937.
2. N&C, 24 April 1937.
3. Stanley White to EBW, 15 March 1937.
4. N&C, 13 March 1937
5. *Time,* 22 March 1937.
6. Manfred Gottfried to EBW, 13 January 1937.
7. Ingersoll to EBW, 17 March 1937.
8. Ingersoll to EBW, 30 March 1937.
9. *Letters,* pp. 154–56.
10. *Time,* 16 August 1937.
11. *Second Tree,* pp. 24–25 (and *P&S,* pp. 112–13).
12. *Letters,* pp. 135–36. The attributed date in *Letters* is probably incorrect.
13. KSW to EBW, September 1937, 19 September 1937, and October 1937.
14. Gibbs to EBW, September 1937.
15. EBW to Thurber, 25 September 1937.
16. Thurber and Weeks, *Letters of Thurber,* pp. 11–14.
17. Thurber to White, 14 November 1937.
18. *Letters,* pp. 166–67.
19. Thurber to EBW, 22 December 1937.
20. EBW to Thurber, 8 January 1938; parts of it appear in *Letters,* pp. 170–72.
21. Thurber to EBW, 20 January 1938; an abridgment of this letter appears in *Letters of Thurber,* pp. 15–21.
22. Robert van Gelder, "An Interview with

Mr. E. B. White, Essayist," *Sunday New York Times Book Review,* 2 August 1942.
23. *Harper's Magazine,* October 1938, p. 555.
24. *Harper's Magazine,* October 1938, p. 555. In the Introduction to a new edition of *One Man's Meat,* in 1982, White said: "I don't recall being disenchanted with New York. If I was disenchanted at all, I was probably disenchanted with *me."* He was not writing quite the way he wanted to write, was oppressed by weekly deadlines, and was uncomfortable in the role of the editorial "we." Moreover, he "never felt really at home" in the house they were renting: "The rooms were always too hot and dry; I fell asleep every night after dinner" (p. xii). Time may have helped him forget how New York seemed to magnify the weaknesses in American culture that he disliked and feared the consequences of.
25. EBW to KSW, 30 December 1937.
26. EBW to KSW, 1 January 1938.
27. KSW to EBW, 30 December 1937.
28. EBW to Stanley White, 1 March 1938.
29. Gill, *Here at "The New Yorker,"* p. 119.
30. EBW to KSW, 3 May 1938.
31. N&C, 5 December 1953.
32. EBW to Stanley White, 13 June 1936.

CHAPTER XI: "One Man's Meat"

1. *OMM,* p. 257; Jessie White to EBW, 22 December 1935.
2. *OMM,* pp. 127–28.

3. *Letters,* p. 516.
4. *Letters,* p. 211.
5. *OMM,* p. 4.

6. Hartman to EBW, 4 August 1938; *OMM*, p. 2.
7. *Letters*, p. 181.
8. *Harper's Magazine*, May 1939, pp. 665–67.
9. "A Slight Sound at Evening," *Points*, p. 20; EBW to Stanley White, [January 1929].
10. OMM, pp. 88–89.
11. *New York Herald Tribune*, 14 June 1942.
12. *OMM*, p. 292; interview with Bruce Lee, *Newsweek*, 22 February 1960, p. 72; *OMM*, pp. 258–65, 66.
13. *OMM*, p. 212.
14. *OMM*, pp. 238–45.
15. "Walden," *OMM*, pp. 80–87; "On a Florida Key," *OMM*, pp. 217–23 (and *Essays*, pp. 137–41); "Once More to the Lake," *OMM*, pp. 246–53 (and *Essays*, pp. 197–204); "Children's Books," *OMM*, pp. 23–29.
16. *OMM*, p. 20–21.
17. *OMM*, p. 105.
18. *OMM*, p. 102.
19. Saxton to EBW, 5 April 1940.
20. EBW to Saxton, 5 July 1940.
21. Ross to E. B. White, 16 September 1940.
22. *OMM*, pp. 168, 169, 171.
23. *OMM*, pp. 203, 207.
24. *Harper's Magazine*, April 1941, pp. 553–56.
25. *Subtreasury*, pp. xviii–xix.
26. *Subtreasury*, pp. xvi, 517.
27. *Subtreasury*, p. 147.
28. Foreword, *OMM*, 1st ed., 1942.
29. *New York Herald Tribune*, 14 June 1942.
30. *The Nation*, 8 August 1942.

CHAPTER XII: "The Wild Flag"

1. Raoul Fleischmann to EBW, 13 June 1938.
2. Ross to EBW, [October, 1938], [May, 1939]; EBW to Ross, 15 June 1939 (*Letters*, pp. 196–98).
3. Ross to EBW, 31 May 1940.
4. N&C, 22 June 1940.
5. Ross to EBW [May, 1941] and June 24 [1941].
6. *Letters*, p. 212, 213.
7. Richard L. Strout, *The New Republic*, vol. 178, no. 17 (29 April 1978), p. 2.
8. *Letters*, p. 218; John R. Fleming to EBW, 5 January 1942 and 10 January 1942.
9. Fleming to EBW, 10 January 1942.
10. *Letters*, pp. 221–23.
11. *Letters*, p. 226.
12. *Letters*, pp. 224–26.
13. N&C, 14 March 1942.
14. Ross to EBW, 19 June 1942.
15. *Letters*, p. 211–12 (this letter was written in 1942, I believe, though the editor of *Letters* assigned it to 1941).
16. Ross to EBW, [September 1942].
17. EBW to KSW, 2 July 1941; KSW to EBW, 9 February 1941, and 17 February 1942.
18. N&C, 17 October 1942.
19. N&C, 27 February 1943.
20. *Letters*, p. 238.
21. *Harper's Magazine*, May 1943, pp. 596–98.
22. Ross to EBW, [April 1943].
23. Ross to EBW, 9 April 1943.
24. Ross to EBW, 10 April 1943.
25. Ross to EBW, [April 1943].
26. Ross to EBW, 22 April [1943].
27. Ross to EBW, Wednesday, [April 1943].
28. *OMM*, p. 276.
29. *OMM*, pp. 276–77. In later editions White substituted "supranationalism" for his original "internationalism."
30. N&C, 4 September 1943 (and *WF*, p. 17).
31. N&C, 25 December 1943 (and *WF*, pp. 20–23).
32. N&C, 24 February 1945 (and *WF*, pp. 62–63).
33. N&C, 21 April 1945 (and *WF*, p. 76–77).
34. "The Eve of Saint Francis," *NYer*, 5 May 1945.
35. "Beautiful upon a Hill," *NYer*, 12 May 1945.
36. N&C, 2 March 1946 (and *WF*, p. 158).
37. *Letters*, p. 277.

38. Hall, *E. B. White*, p. 94.
39. Ross to EBW, 7 May [1943].
40. Ross to EBW, [October 1944].
41. *WF*, pp. vii–viii, xiv.
42. *The Nation*, 28 December 1946.
43. N&C, 17 February 1945.

44. Acceptance Speech, Gold Medal, AAAL, 25 May 1960, White Collection.
45. Plimpton and Crowther, "E. B. White," p. 85.
46. *Letters*, p. 80.

CHAPTER XIII: Stuart Little

1. *Letters*, pp. 246–47.
2. "Home Song," *NYer*, 5 February 1944. White made this shortened version for the inside of a Christmas card, on the front of which appeared a picture of his and Katharine's house in Maine. He has designed his own Christmas cards for many years.
3. *Letters*, p. 250; EBW to Stanley White, 10 April 1944; *Letters*, p. 261.
4. *Letters*, p. 259.
5. *Letters*, p. 259.
6. "Vermin," *NYer*, 7 October 1944.
7. *Second Tree*, p. 213 (and *P&S*, p. 4).
8. *Second Tree*, p. 196 (and *P&S*, p. 15).
9. *Second Tree*, p. 216 (and *P&S*, p. 6).

10. *New York Times*, 6 March 1966.
11. *Letters*, p. 193; Day to KSW, 22 February 1935.
12. *OMM*, p. 25; Moore to EBW, 16 January 1939; Saxton to EBW, March 1939; EBW to Thurber, 16 April 1939.
13. EBW to Philip E. Burnham, Jr., 12 December 1947.
14. *Letters*, p. 388.
15. *Letters*, p. 512.
16. *New York Times*, 6 March 1966.
17. *Letters*, p. 267.
18. *Letters*, p. 267.
19. "Song of the Queen Bee," *NYer*, 15 December 1945 (and *Second Tree*, pp. 204–5; *P&S*, pp. 192–94).

CHAPTER XIV: "The Second Tree from the Corner"

1. *Second Tree*, pp. 198–99 (and *P&S*, p. 190).
2. "Under a Steamer Rug," *NYer*, 30 November 1946 (and *Second Tree*, p. 201).
3. *Second Tree*, pp. 126–27.
4. EBW to M. K. Barnett, April 1947.
5. *Second Tree*, pp. 102–03.
6. *Letters*, p. 284.
7. "Death of a Pig," *Second Tree*, pp. 243–53 (and *Essays*, pp. 17–24).
8. *New York Herald Tribune*, 27 November 1947.
9. *Letters*, p. 285–86.
10. *Letters*, p. 287.
11. Frankfurter to EBW, 9 December 1947.

12. *Letters*, p. 290.
13. *Second Tree*, p. 228.
14. *Letters*, pp. 293–96.
15. *New York*, pp. 53–54 (and *Essays*, p. 133).
16. *Sunday New York Times Book Review*, 10 June 1945, p. 16.
17. Ross memo to EBW, appended to letter from Raoul Fleischmann to Ross, 8 June 1945.
18. N&C, 25 December 1948.
19. *OMM*, pp. 330–31.
20. *Letters*, p. 440.
21. *Points*, p. 44.

CHAPTER XV: Charlotte's Web

1. *Letters*, pp. 304–5, 314.
2. "Pigs, and Spiders," *McClurg's Book News*, January 1953, p. 49.
3. *Charlotte*, p. 140.
4. *Letters*, p. 312.

5. *Second Tree*, p. 182 (and *Essays*, p. 250).
6. *Second Tree*, p. 188 (and *Essays*, p. 254).
7. *Second Tree*, pp. 187–188 (and *Essays*, p. 254); *Letters*, p. 613; Don Marquis, *archy*

& mehitabel: With an Introduction by E. B. White (Garden City, N.Y.: Doubleday, 1950), pp. 47–48.

8. *Letters,* p. 615.
9. EBW to Cass Canfield, 19 May 1950.
10. John Henry Comstock, *Spider Book,* revised and edited by W. J. Gertsch (Ithaca, N.Y.: Comstock, 1948).
11. *Letters,* p. 375.
12. "Pigs & Spiders," *McClurg's,* p. 49.
13. Comstock, *Spider Book,* p. 208.
14. First draft of *Charlotte's Web,* White Collection.
15. Comstock, *Spider Book,* p. 215.
16. EBW to Ted Patrick, 27 October 1950; *Letters,* p. 331.
17. Notes for *Charlotte's Web,* White Collection.
18. "Two Letters: Both Open," *NYer,* 21 April 1951 (and *P&S,* pp. 195–98).
19. *Letters,* pp. 336–338.
20. "Ross," *NYer,* 15 December 1951.
21. *Letters,* p. 355.

22. N&C, 13 September 1952.
23. *Letters,* pp. 361, 354, 362.
24. McCord to EBW, 1 November 1955; *The Saturday Review,* vol. 36, no. 1 (3 January 1953) p. 6; Stafford to EBW, fall 1952.
25. *Los Angeles News,* 16 November 1952; *Madison Capital Times,* 20 December 1952.
26. *Sunday New York Times Book Review,* 19 October 1952; *Sunday Herald Tribune Book Review,* 16 November 1952; *New Statesman and Nation,* 29 November 1952, p. 60; *Times Literary Supplement,* 28 November 1952, p. 200.
27. *Publisher's Weekly,* 14 November 1960 and 23 February 1976.
28. *Letters,* p. 368.
29. *Letters,* p. 417.
30. *Charlotte's Web,* pp. 13–14, 25, 42–43, 183.
31. *OMM,* p. 212.

CHAPTER XVI: From Turtle Bay to Allen Cove

1 *Letters,* pp. 379, 380.
2. *Second Tree,* p. xi.
3. N&C, 26 December 1953.
4. *Letters,* pp. 389, 395; *NYer,* 20 February 1954.
5. *Letters,* 389, 396.
6. N&C, 24 April 1954.
7. N&C, 17 January 1953. Don Marquis's Archie ate desk paste.
8. Story to EBW, 24 January 1953.
9. N&C, 15 January 1955.
10. N&C, 7 March 1953.
11. N&C, 12 June 1954
12. N&C, 24 January 1953.
13. *NYer,* 23 May 1953.
14. *OMM,* pp. 80–87.
15. N&C, 7 May 1949.
16. *Points,* pp. 15–25 (and *Essays,* pp. 234–242).
17. Rich to KSW, 12 April 1954. *Points,* p. 25.
18. N&C, 11 June 1955.
19. KSW to Cushman, 19 December 1965; *Letters,* p. 410. White doubts that he ever thought people traveled too much.

"I *envied* people who were good travelers—people like Morris Bishop, who had the intellectual equipment for travel, who was a historian and a linguist." EBW to SE.
20. EBW to SE, 25 August 1982. *Letters,* p. 395.
21. *Letters,* p. 410.
22. *Letters,* p. 415.
23. *Letters,* p. 416.
24. KSW to SE, 10 September 1970. Allene White to EBW and KSW, 29 March 1956.
25. N&C, 29 March 1952.
26. EBW to Stanley White, 20 January 1957.
27. *Letters,* p. 433. N & C, 16 February 1957.
28. John Updike to KSW, 15 February 1957. *Letters,* pp. 432, 433.
29. *Points,* pp. 108–9.
30. EBW to Stanley White, 18 May 1957.
31. Hall, *E. B. White,* p. 133.

CHAPTER XVII: *The Points of My Compass*

1. EBW to Perelman, 10 August 1977.
2. "A Letter from the East," *NYer*, 22 February 1958 (and *Points*, p. 131; *Essays*, p. 46).
3. "A Letter from the East," *NYer*, 27 July 1957 (and *Points*, pp. 117, 121–22; and *Elements*, p. xi; *Essays*, pp. 258–61).
4. Case to EBW, 27 July 1957.
5. *Points*, p. 122 (and *Essays*, p. 256).
6. *Letters*, p. 453.
7. William Strunk, *The Elements of Style* (New York: Harcourt, Brace, 1920), p. 28.
8. *Elements*, pp. 29–30.
9. Strunk, *Elements*, p. 46; *Elements*, 1st ed., p. 49. In later editions White restored the parallel, but for Strunk's "uncertainty which" he wrote "doubt about which."
10. Strunk, *Elements*, p. 22.
11. *Elements*, p. 21.
12. Strunk, *Elements*, p. 9.
13. *Elements*, 1st ed., p. 4. In later editions White omitted "or followed by."
14. *Letters*, p. 454; *Elements*, pp. 70, 71, 76, xii, 66.
15. *Letters*, p. 583.
16. *Elements*, p. 80; Plimpton & Crowther, "E. B. White," pp. 80–81.
17. *Elements*, p. 70.
18. *Elements*, p. 69.
19. EBW to Case [December 1958]

20. *Elements*, p. 80; *New York Times*, 11 July 1969, p. 31.
21. *Letters*, p. 454.
22. *Letters*, pp. 454–55.
23. Case to EBW, 22 December 1958; *Letters*, p. 456; *Elements*, p. 78.
24. "Khrushchev and I (A Study in Similarities)," *NYer*, 26 September 1959.
25. "Khrushchev," *NYer*, 26 September 1959.
26. "These Precious Days," *NYer*, 16 May 1959.
27. "These Precious Days," *NYer*, 6 June 1959.
28. "These Precious Days," *NYer*, 22 August 1959, 3 October 1959.
29. Thurber to EBW, 11 July 1961.
30. EBW to Thurber, 8 July 1961.
31. Thurber and Weeks, *Letters of Thurber*, pp. 262–63.
32. Bernstein, *Thurber*, p. 564.
33. Thurber and Weeks, *Letters of Thurber*, pp. 137–38.
34. Bernstein, *Thurber*, p. 565.
35. Bernstein, *Thurber*, p. 634.
36. Bernstein, *Thurber*, p. 637.
37. *Letters*, p. 465.
38. Bernstein, *Thurber*, p. 637.
39. Bernstein, *Thurber*, p. 638.
40. "James Thurber," *NYer*, 11 November 1961.

CHAPTER XVIII: "What Do Our Hearts Treasure?"

1. *Points*, pp. xi, xiii–xiv.
2. Hall, *E. B. White*, p. 144.
3. *Letters*, p. 499.
4. *Letters*, pp. 470, 650.
5. *Letters*, pp. 495, 498.
6. *Ford Times*, vol. 56, no. 6 (June 1963), pp. 2–6 (and *Essays*, p. 207).
7. *Letters*, p. 503.
8. N&C, 30 November 1963.
9. *Letters*, p. 520.
10. *Letters*, p. 521.
11. *NYer*, 15 January 1966 and 26 February 1966; *Essays*, pp. 150–53, 262–77.
12. KSW to Cushman, 25 February 1967.
13. "Dedicatory Address Delivered at the

Brooklin Boat Yard," *Ellsworth Maine Times*, 14 June 1967.
14. *Letters*, pp. 560, 564.
15. KSW to SE, 17 October 1967; 13 March 1969; 31 March 1969; 24 July 1970; EBW to Gude, 28 January 1969.
16. *The Horn Book*, vol. 46, no. 4 (August 1970), pp. 350–51.
17. *Trumpet*, pp. 209, 210.
18. *Trumpet*, p. 163.
19. *The Horn Book*, vol. 46, no. 4 (August 1970), p. 350.
20. "The Faith of a Writer," *Publishers Weekly*, vol. 200, no. 23 (December 6, 1971), p. 29.

21. *New York Times,* 18 April 1978; *Letters,*
    pp. 639, 640, 655; *Elements,* p. 36.
22. *Letters,* pp. 629, 607; EBW to Angell,
    16 September 1971; Angell to EBW, 22
    September 1971.
23. *Letters,* p. 637; *New York Times,* 11 July
    1969, p. 43.
24. *Letters,* pp. 635–37.
25. *Essays,* pp. 55–56.
26. *Letters,* p. 651.
27. EBW to Ted Weeks, July 1977.
28. EBW to S. J. Perelman, August 1977.
29. EBW to Jill Krementz, 10 August 1977.
30. *American Mercury,* vol. 35 (July 1935),

p. 285 (and *Fox,* p. 127; *P&S,* p. 70).
31. Katharine S. White, *Onward and
    Upward in the Garden,* (New York:
    Farrar, Straus, Giroux, 1979) pp.
    xvii–xix.
32. Letters quoted in the paragraph, all
    written in August 1977, were to Stuart
    Chase, Scott Elledge, Louise Bechtel,
    and Lillian Ross.
33. *Elements,* p. 9.
34. The source for what follows is two
    letters from EBW to SE, 25 August
    and 23 September 1982.

BIBLIOGRAPHY

The definitive bibliography of the works of E. B. White is *E. B. White: A Bibliographic Catalogue of Printed Materials in the Department of Rare Books, Cornell University Library*, compiled by Katherine Romans Hall. New York: Garland Publishing, 1979. The following is a selection of titles from that work.

BOOKS AND PAMPHLETS BY E. B. WHITE

Less than Nothing—or the Life and Times of Sterling Finny. [New York], 1927.

The Lady Is Cold: Poems by E. B. W. New York and London: Harper & Brothers, 1929.

Is Sex Necessary? Or Why You Feel the Way You Do. By James Thurber and E. B. White. New York and London: Harper & Brothers, 1929.

Ho Hum: Newsbreaks From "The New Yorker." New York: Farrar & Rinehart, Inc., [1931].

Another Ho Hum: More Newsbreaks from "The New Yorker." New York: Farrar & Rinehart, [1932].

Alice Through the Cellophane. New York: The John Day Company, 1933.

Every Day Is Saturday. New York and London: Harper & Brothers, 1934.

Farewell to Model T. By Lee Strout White [pseudonym for Richard Lee Strout and EBW]. New York: G. P. Putnam's Sons, 1936.

The Fox of Peapack and Other Poems. New York and London: Harper & Brothers, 1938.

Quo Vadimus? Or the Case for the Bicycle. New York and London: Harper & Brothers, 1939.

One Man's Meat. New York and London: Harper & Brothers, 1942.

One Man's Meat: A New and Enlarged Edition. New York and London: Harper & Brothers, 1944.

Stuart Little. New York and London: Harper & Brothers, 1945.

The Wild Flag. Boston: Houghton Mifflin, 1946.

Here Is New York. New York: Harper & Brothers, 1949.

Charlotte's Web. New York: Harper & Brothers, 1952.

The Second Tree from the Corner. New York: Harper & Brothers, 1954.

The Elements of Style. By William Strunk, Jr. With Revisions, an Introduction, and a New Chapter on Writing by E. B. White. New York: Macmillan, 1959.

The Points of My Compass. New York and Evanston, Ill.: Harper & Row, 1962.

An E. B. White Reader. Edited by William W. Watt and Robert W. Bradford. New York: Harper & Row, 1966.

The Trumpet of the Swan. New York: Harper & Row, 1970.

Letters of E. B. White. New York: Harper & Row, 1970.

Essays of E. B. White. New York: Harper & Row, 1977.

Poems and Sketches of E. B. White. New York: Harper & Row, 1981.

One Man's Meat [with a new introduction]. New York: Harper & Row. 1982.

BOOKS AND PAMPHLETS EDITED, OR WITH CONTRIBUTIONS, BY E. B. WHITE

The "New Yorker" Album. Garden City, N.Y.: Doubleday, Doran, 1928. "Foreword" by EBW.

The Third "New Yorker" Album. Garden City, N.Y.: Doubleday, Doran, 1930. "Foreword" by EBW.

James Thurber. *The Owl in the Attic.* New York: Harper & Brothers, 1931. "Introduction," pp. xi–xvi, by EBW.

A Subtreasury of American Humor. Edited by E. B. White and Katharine S. White. New York: Coward-McCann, 1941.

Four Freedoms. Washington, D.C.: Office of War Information, 1942.

Roy E. Jones. *A Basic Chicken Guide for the Small Flock Owner.* New York: William Morrow & Company, 1944. "Introduction," pp. v–viii, by EBW.

Don Marquis. *The lives and times of archy & mehitabel.* Garden City, N.Y.: Doubleday, 1951. "Introduction," pp. xvii–xxiv, by EBW.

Eugene Kinkead. *Spider, Egg, and Microcosm.* New York: Alfred A. Knopf, 1955. "Introduction," pp. v–vii, by EBW.

Henry David Thoreau. *Walden.* Boston: Houghton Mifflin, 1964. "Walden—A Young Man in Search of Himself," "Concerning Henry Thoreau: 1817–1862," pp. xiv–xvi, by EBW.

E. B. White. "Ross, Harold Wallace." *Encyclopaedia Britannica.* 1964 ed.

Morris Ernst, ed. *The Teacher.* Englewood Cliffs, N.J.: Prentice-Hall, 1967. "A Teaching Trinity," pp. 103–105, by EBW.

Katherine S. White, *Onward and Upward in the Garden.* New York: Farrar, Straus & Giroux, 1979. "Introduction," pp. vii–xix, by EBW.

E. B. White: A Bibliographic Catalogue of Printed Materials in the Department of Rare Books, Cornell University Library, compiled by Katharine Romans Hall. New York: Garland Publishing, 1979. "Preface," pp. ix–x, by EBW.

PUBLISHED INTERVIEWS WITH E. B. WHITE

Robert Van Gelder. "An Interview with Mr. E. B. White, Essayist." *New York Times Book Review,* 2 August 1942, p. 2. Reprinted in Van Gelder's *Writers and Writing.* New York: Charles Scribner's Sons, 1946.

Harvey Breit. "Visit," in "In and Out of Books." *New York Times Book Review,* 17 January 1954, p. 8.

[Bruce Lee.] "Typewriter Man." *Newsweek,* 22 February 1960, p. 72.

Roderick Norell. "The Writer as a Private Man." *Christian Science Monitor,* 31 October 1962, p. 9.

Susan Frank. "E. B. White Recalls Cornell Years." *Cornell Daily Sun,* 9 October 1964, pp. S2, S8.

Israel Shenker. "E. B. White: Notes and Comment by Author." *New York Times,* 11 July 1969, pp. 31, 43.

George A. Plimpton and Frank H. Crowther. "The Art of the Essay, I: E. B. White." *Paris Review,* 48 (Fall 1969), pp. 65–88.

Israel Shenker. "E. B. White Rehones His Verbal Razor." *New York Times,* 3 May 1972, pp. 41, 76.

Henry Mitchell. "E. B. White . . . Living in a Peacable Storm," *Boston Evening Globe,* 20 October 1976, p. 2.

Herbert Mitgang. "Down East with E. B. White." *New York Times,* 17 November 1976, p. C19.

Articles about E. B. White

There is only one book on White: Edward C. Sampson. *E. B. White.* New York: Twayne Publishers, 1974.

In it White is presented "as a commentator on the American scene and as a literary artist." It is a survey and appraisal of White's achievement.

Among the following critical essays I consider Warren Beck's the best. I am not sure that any critic has said anything as significant as some of the remarks of book reviewers whom I have quoted in this biography. One remark of one reviewer I did not quote may be the most perceptive observation about White's style thus far made. It is in a review of *Essays of E. B. White,* by Benjamin De Mott: "What is beyond criticism in a White essay is the music. The man knows all the tunes, all the limited lovely music that a plain English sentence can play—the affordable balances ('It took an upheaval of the elements and a job at the lowest level to give me the relief I craved'), the affordable vowel songs ('the tonic smell of coon'), everything. On nearly every page, there are subtleties of rhythm and pace, interweavings of the sonorous and racy rare in most contemporary writing." (*Saturday Review,* 20 August 1977, p. 63.) But an equally valuable and more comprehensive critical appreciation of White's essays is that of Eudora Welty, listed below.

One of the several graduate students who have written theses on White sent him a copy of his study of "Prose Styles in the Essays of E. B. White." In that copy, now in the White Collection, White penciled a marginal comment beside the following sentence: "The gradual increase in punctuation marks from earlier to later works suggests that White's style, especially in ["Notes and Comment"], has grown slightly more deliberate, more involute." White's comment: "No, the NYer hired Eleanor Gould," referring to Eleanor Gould Packard, a copy editor.

[Ralph Ingersoll.] *"The New Yorker."* *Fortune,* 10 (August 1934), pp. 85, 86, 97.

James Thurber. "E.B.W." *Saturday Review of Literature,* 18 (15 October 1938), pp. 8–9.

Clifton Fadiman. "In Praise of E. B. White." *New York Times Book Review,* 10 June 1945, p. 1.

Warren Beck. "E. B. White." *College*

English, 7 (April 1946), pp. 367–73.

Ralph Ingersoll. "White Is the World's Best Writer on the World's Most Vital Issue." *PM,* November 1946. A review of *The Wild Flag.*

Robert Warshow. "Melancholy to the End." *Partisan Review,* 14 (January–February 1947), p. 86. A negative review of *The Wild Flag.*

Wolcott Gibbs. "E. B. White." *Book-of-the-Month Club News,* December 1949, pp. 9–10.

Morris Bishop. Introduction to the Harper's Modern Classics edition of *One Man's Meat.* New York: Harper & Brothers, 1950, pp. v–xii.

William R. Steinhoff. " 'The Door' . . . Jersey." *College English,* 23 (December 1961), pp. 229–32.

Webster Schott. "E. B. White Forever." *New Republic,* 24 November 1962, pp. 23–24. A negative review of *The Points of My Compass.*

W. T. Weatherby. "A Modern Man of Walden." *Manchester Guardian Weekly,* 14 February 1963, p. 14. Reprinted in *San Francisco Sunday Chronicle,* 3 March 1963.

Scott Elledge. "Modern Classics Revisited: *One Man's Meat.*" *Carleton Miscellany,* 4 (Fall 1963), pp. 83–87.

Walter Blair. Introduction to the Torchbook edition of *One Man's Meat.* New York:

Harper and Row, 1967, pp. vii–xxi.

Louis Halsey. "The Talk of the Town and the Country: E. B. White." *Connecticut Review,* 5 (October 1971), pp. 37–45.

John Updike. "Remarks on the Occasion of E. B. White Receiving the 1971 National Medal for Literature, 12/2/71." *Picked-Up Pieces.* New York: Alfred A. Knopf, 1975, pp. 434–47.

Eudora Welty. "Dateless Virtues." *New York Times Book Review,* 25 September 1977, pp. 7, 43.

Roger Sale. *Fairy Tales and After: From Snow White to E. B. White.* Cambridge, Mass.: Harvard University Press, 1978, pp. 258–67. On *Charlotte's Web.*

Helene Solheim. "Magic in the Web." *South Atlantic Quarterly,* 80 (Autumn 1981), pp. 391ff.

Peter F. Neumeyer. "The Creation of *Charlotte's Web:* From Drafts to Book." *Horn Book,* 58 (October and December 1982), pp. 489–97, 617–25.

ARTICLES AND BOOKS ON HAROLD ROSS, JAMES THURBER, AND *The New Yorker*
(a selective list).

[Ralph Ingersoll.] *"The New Yorker." Fortune,* 10 (August 1934), pp. 72–86, 90, 92, 97, 150, 152.

Dwight Macdonald. "Laugh and Lie Down." *Partisan Review,* 4 (December, 1937), pp. 44–53.

Stanley Edgar Hyman. "The Urban New Yorker." *New Republic,* 20 July 1942, pp. 90–92.

"The New Yorker: An Outline of Its History." A booklet prepared and published by the business office of *The New Yorker,* 1946.

Russell Maloney. "Tilley the Toiler." *Saturday Review of Literature,* 30 August 1947, pp. 7–10, 29–32.

"Go Climb a More Meaningful Tree." *Commonweal,* 10 March 1950, p. 573. An editorial on the twenty-fifth anniversary of *The New Yorker* (and on White's essay "The

Morning of the Day They Did It") asserting the meaninglessness of secular satire.

Dale Kramer. *Ross and "The New Yorker."* New York: Doubleday, 1951.

Joseph Wood Krutch. "The Profession of a New Yorker." *Saturday Review of Literature,* 20 January 1954, pp. 15–16. A criticism of *The New Yorker's* taste and influence, apropos White's *Second Tree from the Corner.*

James Thurber. *The Years with Ross.* Boston: Little, Brown, 1959.

Ralph Ingersoll. *Point of Departure.* New York: Harcourt, Brace and World, 1961, passim.

Charles W. Morton. "A Try for *The New Yorker*" and "Brief Interlude at *The New Yorker.*" *Atlantic Monthly,* April and May, 1963, pp. 45–49 and 81–85.

Jane Grant. *Ross, "The New Yorker" and Me.*

New York: Reynal, in association with William Morrow, 1968. "Introduction: The Unique Ross," by Janet Flanner, pp. 7–16.

Charles S. Holmes. *The Clocks of Columbus: The Literary Career of James Thurber.* New York: Atheneum, 1972.

Brendan Gill. *Here at "The New Yorker."* New York: Random House, 1975. "[William] Shawn on Ross," pp. 388–95.

Burton Bernstein. *Thurber.* New York: Dodd, Mead, [1975].

A C K N O W L E D G M E N T S

S O M E O F T H O S E who helped me most in my research for this book are no longer alive, and I regret that now I can do no more than make the gesture of remembering them here, at the head of my acknowledgements. First there was Professor George Harris Healey, Director of the Division of Rare Books of the Cornell University Library, who helped to establish The E. B. White Collection at Cornell, and who vouched for me when I first asked Mr. White's permission to make use of it. And next, there was Katharine S. White, who encouraged me to believe that I was up to the job, and who never failed to respond to my requests for biographical data. I was lucky to have known her and to have discovered for myself some of her remarkable virtues. Then there were Andy's siblings, Clara White (Mrs. Manton) Wyvell, Stanley White, and Lillian White (Mrs. Arthur) Illian, who invited me to visit them and ask them questions about their youngest brother. Each was remarkably different from the others, but all were outgoing, interesting, optimistic, and loving; and from them I learned something of what it meant to grow up in the family of Samuel and Jessie White. There were others: Luella (Mrs. Bristow) Adams, who showered me with vivid memories of Andy White during a long interview, held in the very room in which fifty years earlier, as a Cornell undergraduate, he had spent many a lively Monday evening in the warmth of her and her husband's hospitality; Howard Cushman, who at his club in Philadelphia entertained my wife and me with recollections of his and Andy's transcontinental tour in Hotspur; Robert Coates, in whose office in *The New Yorker* I heard reminiscences of the days of Andy's life in the Village and of his friendship with James Thurber; Frank Sullivan, who in his home in Saratoga

Springs told tales that expressed his love for Katharine and Andy. I consider myself lucky to have met these people and to have had their help and good will.

Among those of the living whose cooperation I gratefully acknowledge are: Alice Burchfield (Mrs. James) Sumner, who in several charming letters described the Cornell senior who fell in love with her; Rosanne Magdol McVay, who in a lively interview described the humorous but intense young *New Yorker* staff writer who for a short while was passionately attracted to her; Nancy Angell (Mrs. Louis) Stableford, Roger Angell, and Joel White, who allowed me to ask them about Andy as stepfather, father, and grandfather. Nancy and her husband were especially generous to invite my wife and me to visit them in their home in Easton, Pennsylvania. There are, further: Helen (Mrs. James) Thurber who, in the course of an interview that began in the lobby of the Algonquin Hotel, adjourned to Tim Costello's bar (then) on Third Avenue, and ended in a midtown Manhattan restaurant, recalled anecdotes about the Whites and described her late husband's feelings toward Andy and Katharine, and told me what she knew about the way others felt about the Whites; William Shawn, who gave me his impressions of the relationship between White and Ross; Milton Greenstein, Vice President of The New Yorker Magazine, Inc., and an old friend of White's, who granted me access to the E. B. White scrapbooks and other records in *The New Yorker*'s library, and introduced me to Ebba Jonsson and Helen Stark, librarians whose help was valuable in the early stages of my bibliographical work. Without Mr. Greenstein's cooperation I could hardly have written this book, and I am happy to thank him for his friendly support.

Stanley White, Katharine White, Alice Burchfield Sumner, Mr. and Mrs. Everett Adams, John Fleming, John Detmold, Professor and Mrs. Morris Bishop, Helen Thurber, and Faith McNulty Martin made available to me their collections of E. B. White letters (or copies thereof) some time before they were added to the E. B. White Collection at Cornell, and long before any of them appeared in Dorothy Guth Lobrano's edition of *Letters of E. B. White*. Because the first draft of my manuscript depended heavily upon these biographically most valuable documents, I became much indebted to their owners. I am also indebted to Mr. Greenstein for sending me copies of White-to-Ross memos and letters whose originals are in the files of *The New Yorker*.

My use of material contained in The E. B. White Collection has been authorized by E. B. White and by the Library Board of Cornell University Library. My indebtedness to Cornell, where I opened an account many years ago, is altogether too large and too personal to examine here and now.

Then there are the friends of mine without whose active support I might never have finished this book: Professor Donald D. Eddy, the Librarian of the Department of Rare Books of the Cornell University Library, for whose many kind favors and inspired suggestions I am especially indebted; Katherine Romans Hall, Joan Winterkorn, and Susan Lovenburg, gifted and devoted curators of the E. B. White Collection; Professor William Rea Keast, who suggested that I write the book that he had once thought of writing himself, who read with great acumen and care an early and a late draft of my manuscript, and whose enthusiasm for the writings of E. B. White has enriched our long friendship; Knox Burger, another old friend, who as a professional editor gave me useful advice and as a literary agent is still looking after my interests.

I am much obliged to other friends, who read all or parts of the manuscript at various stages and helped me to improve it: Mary Boynton, Eva Kathryn and John Shepard, Charles E. Shain, M. H. Abrams, O. B. Davis, Gerry Howard, Lynda Bogel, and Elsie Myers Stainton. I thank them; and I thank Laurie Langbauer and Kathleen O'Neil, who skillfully and goodnaturedly checked references, found lost citations, and normalized the footnotes—and Berniece Roske, Jane Soloman, Janet How, and Catherine Cusick, who typed and typed and typed. I wish especially to thank Emily Garlin for copyediting my manuscript. Finally, to my editor at W. W. Norton, Mary Cunnane, a wise friend and a real pro, I gladly give credit for the miracle of turning my manuscript into a book.

My wife, Liane, counseled me so conscientiously and effectively during the writing of this book that I now think of it as ours. By nature a perfectionist, by inclination an artist, by training a lawyer, and by fate my best friend and severest critic, she did all she could to make me write good sense with clarity and grace. I thank God and her for her devotion to me and for her dedication to the book.

INDEX

400   Index

White (*continued*)
  children of, by first husband, 111, 156, 157, 160, 161,
    165, 167, 171–72, 176, 332, 352
  in Corsica, 156–57, 162
  death of, 352
  described, 109–10
  divorce of, 160–65
  as editor, 103–4, 109, 111, 118–19, 167, 171, 182, 189,
    212, 214, 226, 235–36, 307, 317, 318, 330, 343, 352
  education of, 110
  family of, 110, 156, 160, 161, 173, 213, 309–10, 316
  first marriage of, 111–12, 156, 160
  grandchildren of, 309, 318–21, 332–33, 344, 352
  health of, 206, 237, 250, 272–73, 277, 297, 309–10, 317,
    322, 332, 334–35, 338, 340, 342–43, 345, 352
  humor of, 118, 343
  jobs of, 111–12
  letters written by, to White, 162–65, 204, 210–11
  letter-writing as pastime of, 324, 352
  at *New Yorker,* 103–4, 107, 109, 112, 113, 115, 118–19,
    130, 155, 162, 168, 171, 179, 182, 189, 206, 212, 214,
    235–36, 252, 254, 280, 306, 317, 318, 321, 324
  photographs of, 138, 280
  quoted, 117–18, 162–65, 204, 210–11, 264–65, 339–40,
    342, 343–44, 345, 373–74n
  retirement of, 334, 340
  Ross's relationship with, 117–19, 317
  wedding of, 170–71
  White on, 103–4, 112, 118, 182–83, 324, 330, 352–54
  White's collaboration with, 225–28
  White's courtship of, 149–51, 156–67, 170
  White's first meeting with, 109
  White's letters to, 165–66, 172, 175–77, 186–88,
    200–202, 210, 213, 233–34, 273
  as writer, 340, 343, 353, 355, 373–74n
  writers discovered by, 182
White, Lillian (sister), *see* Illian, Lillian White
White, Marion (sister), *see* Brittingham, Marion White
White, Martha (granddaughter), 309, 333, 343, 344
White, Mary Ann Elizabeth Tilly (grandmother), 5
White, Samuel Tilly (father), 3–15, 17, 20, 28, 30, 53,
  91–92, 96–97, 98, 152, 171–72
  career of, 5–9
  character of, 5, 7–12, 32, 71
  death of, 9, 191, 196
  lawsuit against, 6–7, 27

  letters of, 4–5, 9, 10, 71, 81, 97
  photographs of, 40, 43, 44
  quoted, 4–5, 11, 71, 81, 97
  White influenced by, 11–12, 59
  in White's fiction, 7–8, 262, 304, 346, 348
  White's relationship with, 4–5, 23, 71, 92
White, Stanley "Bunny" (brother), 4, 10, 11, 16, 27,
  40, 42, 50
  White's letters to, 11, 28–29, 151, 197, 203, 211,
    214, 245, 262, 270, 272, 289, 320, 344
  White's relationship with, 28–30
White, Steven (grandson), 309, 319, 333, 343
Whitman, Walt, 88
"Why I Like America" (Cummings), 108
"Why I Like New York" (White), 108
"Why We Go to Cabarets," 106
Wilde, Oscar, 56
Wild Flag, The (White), 242, 245–48, 267, 268
Williams, Garth, 16, 295, 298
Williams, William Carlos, 108
Willkie, Wendell, 244
Wills, Helen, 155
Wilson, Edmund, 58, 264
Wilson, Harry Leon, 86
Winchell, Walter, 171, 232
"Window Ledge in the Atom Age" (White), 267–
  68
Winters, Yvor, 108
Woman's Home Companion, 30
"Woods in Winter, The" (White), 114
Woollcott, Alexander, 84, 100, 239
World Government and Peace, 245
World War I, 36, 37, 51, 108, 116, 229
World War II, 220, 221–24, 228, 231
Wylie, Philip, 101
Wyvell, Clara White, 4, 10, 12, 16, 40, 196

Yale Literary Magazine, 135
Yates, James C., 194
"Years of Wonder, The" (White), 93
Years with Ross, The (Thurber), 336–37
Yeats, William Butler, 107

Zimbalist, Efrem, 34
"Zoo Revisited" (White), 25, 36–37, 203–4, 308
Zwicky, Fritz, 268